THINKING ABOUT
WOMEN

THINKING ABOUT
WOMEN

Sociological Perspectives on Sex and Gender

SECOND EDITION

Margaret L. Andersen
University of Delaware, Newark

Macmillan Publishing Company
New York

Collier Macmillan Publishers
London

Earlier edition entitled *Thinking About Women: Sociological
and Feminist Perspectives,* copyright © 1983
by Macmillan Publishing Co., Inc.

Macmillan Publishing Company
866 Third Avenue, New York, New York 10022

Collier Macmillan Canada, Inc.

Library of Congress Cataloging-in-Publication Data

Andersen, Margaret L.
  Thinking about women.

  Bibliography: p.
  Includes index.
  1. Women — United States — Social conditions.
2. Feminism — United States.   3. Social institutions —
United States.   4. Social change. I. Title.
HQ1426.A6825   1988   305.4′2′0973   87-12285
ISBN 0-02-303350-9

Printing: 1 2 3 4 5 6 7   Year: 8 9 0 1 2 3 4

ISBN 0-02-303350-9

For my Grandmother,

Sybil R. Wangberg

Preface to the Second Edition

Since the publication of the first edition of *Thinking About Women*, feminist scholarship in all the disciplines has grown and flourished. There is now extensive research and policy on topics that were barely named when the first edition appeared in 1983. The second edition of *Thinking About Women* incorporates several new topics, including sexual harassment, marital rape, and eating disorders, as well as new research on other topics throughout. There is additional material included on sexuality, a new chapter on women and religion, and more inclusion of material on men. Data are updated throughout the book to include the most current available.

The study of sex and gender remains an interdisciplinary subject; *Thinking About Women* is a comprehensive review of feminist scholarship in the social sciences, although it is grounded in sociological theory and research. The first edition of *Thinking About Women* also attempted to recognize diversity among women by including discussion of race and class throughout the text. Because integrating race and class is an ongoing process in the reconstruction of knowledge, this edition has been updated to reflect the increasing scope of the subject.

Part I introduces the sociological perspective and the emergence of feminist thinking in sociology. Chapter 1 is a discussion of feminist perspectives in sociology, and it outlines the criticisms that new scholarship on women has brought to traditional sociological ways of thinking. Chapter 2 develops the perspective of the sociology of knowledge — one that sees ideas as socially constructed; the chapter introduces students to this framework through examination of women's roles as depicted in the media and education. Chapters 3 and 4 focus on the most immediately experienced part of the sex/gender system relations — human biology and the individual in society. Chapter 3 reviews research on biology, sex, and gender and their relationship to culture and social structure. Chapter 4 examines the process of sex role socialization and the acquisition of gender identities.

Part II studies the significance of gender in contemporary social institutions. Chapter 5 discusses women, work, and the economy. Chapter 6 is an analysis of women and families. Chapter 7 discusses women, reproduction, and health care. Chapter 8, a new addition in the second edition, is a discussion of women and religion, based on the idea that religion is both a liberating and oppressive part of women's experiences. Chapter 9 reviews research on women and crime, women as victims of crime, and women in the criminal justice system.

Part III reviews theoretical perspectives in feminist thought and the origins of the women's movement. These chapters are organized according to the dialogue that has emerged between liberal and radical perspectives in feminist thinking and research; both perspectives are also examined for their implications for social change. Chapter 10 discusses liberal feminism and its origins in liberal social thought and also includes a discussion of liberal strategies for social change. Chapter 11 reviews socialist and radical feminism, both as theoretical viewpoints and as the basis for feminist activism. The development of the women's movement is discussed throughout both of these chapters.

Acknowledgments ────────────────────────────

In addition to those who gave their assistance and support for the first edition, there are many whose support for this work has been invaluable to me. I especially appreciate the comments I have received from students and faculty who have used the book. And, I thank Niki Benokraitis, Bill Chambliss, Anne Fausto-Sterling, Valerie Hans, Gloria Hull, Peggy McIntosh, Gerry Turkel, and Kathy Turkel for their encouragement for this project and the time they have taken to discuss different aspects of this book with me. The following reviewers also provided extensive suggestions that improved the second edition: Susan E. Marshall, University of Texas at Austin; Margaret L. Signorella, Pennsylvania State University; Peter J. Stein, William Patterson College; Martha Thompson, Northeastern Illinois University; and Kersti Yllo, Wheaton College. Helen Gouldner, Dean of the College of Arts and Science at the University of Delaware, and Russell Dynes, Chair of the Department of Sociology, provided funds that facilitated the book's completion. I thank Susan Brytenson, Director of Morris Library, for providing "a room of my own" where I could work uninterrupted and Becky Knight for helping, especially at the last minute, to locate government documents. Although I do not know them all by name, the staff of the Reference Room at Morris Library gave extensive assistance throughout the preparation of this book; I am enormously grateful to them for their skills and patience. I thank Mary Thornton for her enthusiastic support and for using her extraordinary organizational skills to help in preparing the final manuscript. Without the hard work of Carol Anderson, Claire Blessing, Judy Watson, and Anna Wu, this would never have been finished on time. Ken MacLeod and Christine Cardone, editors at Macmillan, both encouraged the publication of a second edition and worked hard to see that it took place. I appreciate their editorial advice and encouragement, as well as Aliza Greenblatt's work as production editor. Most of all, I thank Richard Rosenfeld for his love, support, and patience; he is a sea of calm in what often feels like a gale of work.

M.L.A.

Preface to the First Edition

Thinking About Women introduces students to the contemporary research and theoretical perspectives which observe and explain the sociological character of women's lives in American society. The idea for this book emerged from my dissatisfaction with textbooks on sex roles and gender that take primarily a social-psychological view and that also ignore theoretical issues about gender relations. Since I began teaching courses on the sociology of sex roles in the early 1970s, a rich and intellectually exciting literature has developed among feminist scholars. In the most recent years, this scholarship has not only contributed new research insights, but it has also initiated theoretical discussions that make women's lives central to the basic concepts and perspectives of sociological thinking.

The sociological perspective is one that roots the experience of individuals and social groups in the social organization of the society in which they live. But much of the sociological theory and research has been flawed because it has largely overlooked women's roles in society and the way in which gender influences social organization. Like other major sociological categories — class and race — gender influences who we will become in society, what resources will be available to us, and how we are defined by others. The wealth of research that has emerged from feminist analysis of sociological issues shows how gender shapes our personalities, skills, and self-concepts, organizes the social institutions in which we live, and influences the distribution of wealth, power, and privilege.

This book is intended to sensitize students to the position of women in American society and to give them the intellectual tools with which to comprehend women's experience. The sociological perspective is particularly significant to feminist thought because it ties individual experience to the social organization of society. Although this book is not intended to help students find personal solutions to collective problems, it does show how individual experiences are created and transformed through social, political, and economic institutions. Feminist scholarship helps explain the structure of these institutions and is also a means of dispersing this knowledge to promote liberating social changes for women and for men.

In developing research and theory on gender relations in society, feminist scholars do not mean merely to create another abstract category for sociological analysis. Like race and class, the social organization of gender has specific social, economic, and political consequences for women, as well as for men. Feminist studies in sociology are not intended to construct abstract empirical analyses of gender, nor to develop grand theories that have no relevance to the lives of actual human beings (Mills 1959). While concept-building and observational studies are necessary in constructing accurate feminist accounts of social life, their purpose is the transformation of gender relations and the society in which we live. Thus, complete accounts of social life must explain the experiences of all women. Just as male-centered sociological studies are biased by their omission of women, so are feminist studies flawed when they are based only on the experiences of white, middleclass, and heterosexual women. Throughout this book, the questions must be asked, "Is this true for women of color and lesbian women?" and "How is their experience similar to and different from other women?" Because feminist analysis seeks to understand the commonalities and the differences in women's experiences, sound feminist scholarship must entail an understanding of race, class, and heterosexual relations. Although this book may not stand up completely to the challenge, I hope that it does contribute to feminist scholars' growing analysis.

Acknowledgments

Many people have contributed to the development of this book. Their ideas about women and their encouragement and support for this project have been invaluable to me. Many provided thoughtful reviews of earlier drafts of this book and many worked long hours typing and editing the manuscript. I see it as a measure of the success of the women's movement that this project has been accomplished with the help of such a strong network of women friends and colleagues and the lively and interdisciplinary community of feminist scholars who are working to transform the academic disciplines.

In particular, I thank Peggy Phelan, Valerie Hans, Gloria Hull, Gerry Turkel, Leslie Goldstein, Tricia Farris, Caryn Horwitz, Jan DeAmicis, Patty Klausner, and Marion Palley for discussing numerous parts of this book with me and providing careful reviews of my work. I also thank the members of Sociologists for Women in Society for sharing their criticisms of this book with me and for the many stimulating discussions we have had. Although many of my students remain unnamed here, they have stimulated the creation of much of this book, through both their enthusiasm for the material and their questioning about the issues involved. I appreciate the timely support of a Grant-in-Aid from the Dean of the College of Arts and Science at the University of Delaware.

I thank Gaye Tuchman, Anne Pottieger, and the anonymous reviewers who provided valuable criticisms on earlier drafts of the manuscript. I especially appreciated the assistance of Rachel Kahn-Hut whose excellent editorial work provided careful criticism of the substance of the book, at the same time that she gave excellent advice for the book's style and organization with an emphasis on clarity for readers. Ken Scott, my editor, deserves special thanks because he is a superb editor with great academic integrity and an encouraging attitude. And, without the ongoing support of a group of wonderful, hardworking, and grossly underpaid women, this work would never have been published; I thank Carol Anderson, Marie Gregg, Claire Blessing, Sylvia Knight, Fran Price, and Shirley Anderson for typing this manuscript and for their generous assistance during the two years of writing this book.

Although I have no wife to thank for her constant support, attention to detail, and undying loyalty, I do express my thanks to friends who, in their own ways, helped me complete this book. Time and time again I faced the problem of expressing my ideas with confidence and clarity while retaining the intellectual doubts and questions that are essential to the development of ideas. The very act of writing brings authenticity to what we think and there were many times when maintaining the balance between doubting and knowing would not have been possible without the support of some very special friends. Especially, I want to thank Lewis Killian and Michael Lewis for teaching me the value of sociological thinking and the necessity for creating a humanistic approach to the study of social problems. There is no one who has contributed so enormously to my feminist thinking as Sandra Harding. Her friendship, wisdom, and intellectual challenge have kept me working when it seemed impossible. I thank her deeply for her careful reading of my work, her work as a coteacher, and her persistent passion for feminist theory. Linda Hall and Jane Bennett have shown me the value of women's lives in a way that no academic study could, and I thank them for the support they provided throughout the time I was working on this book. Also, I thank Jane, whose meticulous attention to detail made order of a chaotic bibliography. And, in more ways than I could show in print, I thank Richard Rosenfeld for his patience, humanity, and humility and for keeping the home fires burning.

M.L.A.

Contents

PART II

Gender and Social Institutions

CHAPTER 5   Women, Work, and the Economy   103

CHAPTER 8 Women and Religion 222

CHAPTER 9 Women, Crime, and Deviance 250

PART **III**

Feminist Theory and Social Change

PART I

Women's Lives and the Sociological Perspective

CHAPTER 1

Sociological and Feminist Perspectives

Introduction

In the ordinary course of our daily lives, we are surrounded by evidence of the position of women in American society. In the checkout lane at the grocery store, most of the cashiers are women; the managers and baggers, men. Where children are playing, there is usually a woman nearby. In bars, men touch women more often, more aggressively, and in more different places than happens when women touch men. Also, many current social problems call attention to women's experiences in society. Violence against women is a matter that has drawn increasing public attention, and, recently, changes in American households have resulted in an increasing incidence of households headed by women — many of whom are poor.

Each of these examples reveals patterns of sex and gender relations in contemporary society and, though much of the time these patterns go unnoticed, they are an important part of our experience. Many of these patterns go unnoticed because they are so deeply embedded in the minds of women and men that, unless they become a problem, we are hardly aware of them. Often we take these patterns of everyday life for granted and they become part of the social world that surrounds us and of which we are a part.

This book examines patterns of behavior and social organization in society as they are influenced by sex and gender relations. It is only recently, because of the influence of the feminist movement and the resulting growth of women's studies as an academic area of study, that sociologists have begun to think about sex and gender as sociological issues. As sociologists began to look more carefully at sex and gender in society, they often had to change some of the previous assumptions about the roles of women and men and the ways in which gender relations were organized in society. Consequently, new studies about gender roles and women's status have transformed sociological perspectives on the positions of women and men in society. This book studies how sociological and feminist perspectives inform us about women's lives and reviews some of the recent research and theory that scholars have produced in studying that experience.

Moreover, because of the changes in our thinking that scholarship in women's studies has generated, scholars have had to reconsider some of their basic assumptions about social life. As a result, such scholarship transforms not only our understanding of women's experiences, but also our thinking about the features of social life and the assumptions of the disciplines that study the social world. While this single book cannot discuss all of the potentials for change that scholarship on women generates, it does suggest ways that sociology can be reconceptualized to take full account of women's experience and the fact that sex and gender relations are central to all experience.

This chapter begins by discussing feminism and its influence on sociological thinking. The chapter introduces students to some of the basic premises of sociological perspectives and discusses the development of feminism as a social movement and its pertinence to sociological study. As we will see, the rebirth of feminism in the 1960s has caused us to reconsider much of what we thought we knew about women and men in society. As a result, the influence of feminism on sociological thinking has been considerable; feminist scholars have raised new questions about the social organization of gender relations, the possibilities for social change, and the relationship of social change to academic knowledge. This chapter introduces students to these issues and discusses the emergence of feminist perspectives in sociology and related disciplines.

Feminism and the Sociological Perspective —————————

Personal Life and Sociological Issues

As already noted, patterns in gender relations are found throughout society, although much of the time these patterns remain invisible to us. But at some point, we may start to notice them. Perhaps at school we see that most of the professors are men and that, among students, men are more outspoken in class. Or perhaps at work we notice that women are concentrated in the lowest-level jobs and are sometimes treated as if they were not even there. Or it may occur to us one night as we are walking through city streets that the bright lights shining in the night skyline represent the thousands of women — many of them black, Hispanic, or Asian — who clean the corporate suites and offices for organizations that are dominated by white men.

Recognizing these events as indications of the status of women helps us see inequities in the experience of men and women in society. Once we begin to recognize these patterns, we are often astounded at how pervasive they are. And, as the unequal status of women becomes more apparent, we might feel overwhelmed by the vast extent of a problem we never acknowledged before. What we see might become troubling, and we may find it difficult to imagine ways in which these long-standing inequities can be changed. But once we start to question the position of women in society, we will want to know more and will begin to ask questions such as: What exactly is the status of women in society? How did things become this way? How does learning about women's experience change our thinking about men? How can we change the inequalities that women experience?

Adrienne Rich (1976), a feminist poet, suggests that simply asking "What is life like for women?" will create a new awareness of the situation of women in society and history. This questioning, in part, is what the feminist movement has encouraged in most of the academic disciplines. With whatever question we begin, whether it is "Why are there no great women artists?" (Nochlin 1971) or "Why is it that women clean the offices and men manage them?" by virtue of asking, we are creating new questions and new issues for investigation. These questions, then, form the basis for emerging feminist theory, and it is this process of questioning that gives birth to a sociological and feminist imagination.

The sociological imagination was first described by C. Wright Mills (1916–1962), an eminent sociologist and radical in his time. Mills's radicalism is founded, in part, on his passionate belief that the task of sociology is to understand the relations between individuals and the society in which they live. Furthermore, he argued that sociological understanding must be used in the reconstruction of more just social institutions. Except for the masculine references in his language, his words still provide a compelling argument that sociology must make sense of the experience of women and men as they exist in contemporary society. He writes:

> Nowadays men often feel that their private lives are a series of traps. They sense that within their everyday world, they cannot overcome their troubles, and, in this feeling, they are often quite correct. What ordinary men are directly aware of and what they try to do are bounded by the private orbits in which they live; . . . The sociological imagination enables its possessor to understand the larger historical scene in terms of its meaning for the inner

life and external career of a variety of individuals. . . . This first fruit of this imagination — and the first lesson of the social science that embodies it — is the idea that the individual can understand his experience and gauge his fate only by locating himself within his period, that he can know his chances in life only by becoming aware of those of all individuals in his circumstances. (Mills 1959:3–5)

Mills's ideas are strikingly parallel to the feminist argument that women can see how their private experience is rooted in social conditions by discovering their shared experience with other women. In fact, Mills professes that the central task of sociology is to understand personal biography and social structure and the relations between the two. His argument is best illustrated in the distinction he makes between personal troubles and social issues.

Troubles are those that are located in the personal experience of an individual. They are privately felt, and they involve only those persons and events in an individual's immediate surroundings. Public issues are events that originate beyond one's immediate experience, even though they are still felt there. Public issues involve the structure of social institutions and their historical development. Mills's own example is that of marriage. He says, "Inside a marriage a man and a woman may experience personal troubles, but when the divorce rate during the first four years of marriage is 250 out of every 1,000 attempts, this is an indication of a structural issue having to do with the institutions of marriage and the family and other institutions that bear upon them" (1959:9). Mills's point is that events that are felt as personal troubles often have their origins in the public issues that emerge from specific historical and social conditions.

Another example is that of a woman who is beaten by her husband. She experiences deep personal trouble, and perhaps her situation appears to her as unique or as only a private problem between herself and her husband. But when others in the society have the same experience, then a public issue is found. Common patterns in the experiences of battered wives reveal that wife beating is more than just a private matter. It has its origins in complex social institutions that define women's place as in the home, as subordinate to their husbands, and as dependent upon men. In this sense, wife beating is both a personal trouble and a public issue. As Mills would conclude, it is then a subject for the sociological imagination. For feminists, this junction between personal experience and the social organization of gender roles is also a starting point for analysis.

The relationship between personal troubles and public issues reveals an essential premise of the sociological perspective — that individual life is situated in specific social and historical environments. These environments condition not only what our experience is, but also how we think about it. This premise is also basic to feminist perspectives on society and women's and men's experiences within it. Although, as this book will show, feminism encompasses a variety of perspectives, one basic premise of feminist thought is that women's experience emerges from the social, political, and economic structure of society. Both feminists and sociologists recognize that individuals are caught up in the social institutions of their time. This insight forms the beginning of sociological and feminist perspectives on social life.

Feminist Questions and Perspectives

Feminist perspectives in sociology were formulated only recently when women (and some men) in the profession of sociology began applying the tools of sociological analysis to their understanding of the position of women in society. Many questions that form the crux of the sociological imagination have now been revised by feminist scholars in trying to comprehend women's experience.

For example, C. Wright Mills identified a series of questions that have been consistently asked by sociologists. They include: What is the structure of this particular society as a whole? How does it differ from other varieties of social order? Where does this society stand in human history, and what are the mechanics by which it is changing? What types of men and women now prevail in this society and in this period (1959:6–7)?

Feminist investigations of these questions have revealed that the structure of American society is one of inequality between women and men. Although women constitute over 40 percent of the total labor force, they earn sixty-two cents for every dollar earned by men. And if we include housework in the definition of productive work, these women, in fact, work longer hours every week than full-time employed men (Hartmann 1981). Worldwide, a United Nations study shows that women are one-third of the world labor force and do most of the unpaid work. But women receive only 10 percent of the world's income and own less than 1 percent of the world's property (United Nations Commission on the Status of Women in 1980, cited in Leghorn and Parker 1981:4–5).

Yet the inequality of women is not an inevitable fact; studies of a variety of societies indicate that women's status varies cross-culturally and over time. We learn from cross-cultural and historical research that women's role in society is one of great diversity, even though there are many commonalities from society to society. For instance, not all societies see women as powerless citizens, and in some societies women exercise more control over reproduction and production than in others. These varieties of social organization show us that women's role is not innate and, therefore, is subject to social change. Feminist scholars believe that study of the differences and similarities in women's experiences can lead us to new directions for social change and liberation.

Feminist studies have also revealed the varieties of women and men who exist within our own society. They have done so by rediscovering groups of women who are rendered invisible by studies that concentrate only on the experiences and perspectives of dominant groups. Thus, feminism recognizes the experience of black, Hispanic, Asian, and native American women as unique, founded in the intersection of racism and sexism. Feminist studies also require us to include the experiences of lesbian women in our analysis of how society is organized and how groups within society are socially controlled. Therefore, the feminist perspective brings issues of racism, class, and heterosexist oppression to our analysis of gender relations, and it causes us to consider all of the varieties in women's experience that occur in this society.

Moreover, feminist perspectives also change the way we see men in the world, because traditional studies see men in terms of what they ought to be, not necessarily what they are or even what they want to be. As feminist scholars have studied men's lives, they find that, although men benefit from institutionalized power and privilege, they too are subjected to cultural expectations of masculinity that affect their emotions, identities, and social roles (Pleck and Brannon 1978). Feminist scholars have defined patriarchy as a hierarchical system of social relations among men which creates and maintains the domination of women. Though not all men benefit equally from patriarchal systems, as a system of social organization patriarchy patterns and shapes relations between and among men and women.

In sum, in considering old sociological questions, feminists have discovered new facts about society that emerge from documenting patterns of gender inequality and from studying the experiences of all women within the society. Feminist research in sociology has unmasked the biases in conventional studies and has shown how these studies result in inadequate accounts of the lives of both women and men. And as feminist sociology has developed, scholars have begun to explain the emergence and persistence of gender inequality.

Yet it is important to point out that, just as there is no single sociological interpretation of complex social issues, there is no single feminist perspective. Within feminist thought, different assumptions and observations lead to a rich and varied analysis of the position of women in society. There are some basic premises that feminists share, as we will see, but feminist explanations of women's experience are the subject of scholarly as well as political debate.

Feminism begins with the premise that women's and men's positions in society are the result of social, not natural, factors. The meaning of feminism has been developed and understood in different ways, but it begins with the idea that social institutions and social attitudes are the basis of women's position in society. Furthermore, feminism takes women's interests and perspectives as not inferior to those of men, believing that when women are treated as inferior citizens, liberating social changes on their behalf can and should be made. Thus, feminism is both a way of thinking and a way of acting, and the union of action and thought is central to feminist programs for social change. Although feminists would not necessarily argue that women should be like men, they do believe that women's experiences and perspectives are as valuable as those of men. Moreover, feminism makes women's interests central to all movements for liberating social change.

Some people are uncomfortable with the label *feminist,* thinking that it makes them sound like fanatics or man-haters. Objections to calling oneself a feminist sometimes reflect disagreement with feminist analyses of social and political issues, but often these objections also represent misunderstandings about what feminism is. Stereotypical portrayals of feminists in the media as radical "women's libbers" make calling oneself a feminist seem like a stigma, even though public opinion polls indicate that the majority of American women agree with many feminist issues (Harris Survey 1985). Moreover, a few believe that we live in a postfeminist world where feminism is no longer necessary. This belief rests on the false assumption that sex discrimination has been eliminated and that women now have equality in the workplace — an assumption this book will examine more carefully in subsequent chapters. While not everyone who reads this book will decide she or he is a feminist, they should have a better understanding of what constitutes feminist thinking and should have a more complete understanding of the situation for women in contemporary American society.

Feminist Scholarship and Social Change

The Women's Movement

The reemergence of feminism in the 1960s signaled the beginning of a decade in which social changes in women's roles would extend to every area of life, ranging from the workplace and the courts to religion, the arts, and the private dynamics of family life. Within American society, the feminist movement has made significant changes in the ways men's and women's roles are defined and the ways in which they think of each other. At the individual level, many women, as well as many men, have questioned their traditional social roles and the beliefs about themselves that they have acquired. And in institutions such as the family and work, new practices and policies have transformed male and female behavior. These individual and social changes reveal the impact of feminism upon our daily lives and the structure of our society.

Transformations in men's and women's roles are reflected in public opinion. In 1985, 76 percent of American women and 75 percent of men believed women's roles would continue to change. Only 10 percent of women and 9 percent of men believed women would return to more traditional roles. Women's own goals have also changed. By 1985, 48 percent of women (compared with 64 percent in 1974) said that having a loving husband who was able to take care of them was more important than making it on one's own. And only 37 percent of women in 1985, compared with 50 percent in 1974, thought the most satisfying lifestyle was having a traditional marriage with the husband assuming responsibility for providing for the family and the wife being responsible for the house and taking care of children (Roper organization 1985).

As significant as these changes are, many changes are still needed and we cannot take for granted those changes that have already occurred. To the limited extent that they have occurred, transformation in the roles of men and women has been hard fought for, but these changes can be eroded by changing political and historical conditions. Anti-discriminatory policies, for example, have recently met with increased resistance and, in many cases, have been eroded through changed federal policy. Still, changes in the fabric of American society show that feminism is one of the most significant social movements of modern times. Its impact has been made not only on the individual and collective lives of people, but also on the way we think and on how knowledge about our society is developed and used. The effects of feminism can be found both in the societal changes it has generated and in the transformations in social thought and scholarship it has inspired.

The women's liberation movement began in the late 1960s in a climate of political activism and criticism of traditional societal institutions and policies. The civil rights movement, the anti–Vietnam War movement, and the student movements of the 1960s focused attention on issues of the inequality of economic and social resources, on the need for a realignment of power in the society, on the inhumane character of war and our national policies, and on the need to establish political and civil rights for all social groups.

For women who participated in these movements, a new political consciousness was born as they used the analysis of oppression being created in these movements to comprehend their own experience. Frequently, they observed contradictions between the analysis of equality and liberation developed in these movements and the existence within these movements of the same sexist attitudes and behaviors that were demonstrated in the society at large. These movements generated an analysis by women of their oppression as women (Evans 1979). Moreover, the movements provided black and white women with opportunities to use and develop skills in political organizing and consciousness raising.

At the same time, structural changes in the employment and education of white, middle-class women fostered a sense of contradiction, or relative deprivation, among them. More white, middle-class women were working than ever before. They were also becoming better educated because post-World War II expansion in higher education had created new opportunities for men and women of the white middle class. Yet, in spite of their educational backgrounds, most of these women still found themselves isolated in the family or trapped in sex-segregated jobs where they earned less and had less chance for advancement than their male counterparts. Thus, relative to their training and their aspirations for success, these women were deprived of an equal share of the social and economic resources of society. To the extent that they received such resources, their status remained one of dependence upon men if they were married or poverty if they were not.

For black women, as well as other minority women, the disadvantages imposed by sexism are added to those already incurred by racism. Although the middle-class bias of the white women's movement has alienated many black women, black women clearly see the effects of sexism in their own experiences. Even with the gains resulting from the civil rights movement, black women have remained in sex-segregated jobs, thus fostering feminist perspectives among them (Lewis 1977). Many black women have a stronger tendency to identify with the principles of feminism than do white women even though they perceive the women's liberation movement as being primarily for white women (Hemmons 1980).

Thus, from the start, modern feminism had its origins in the experiences of both well-educated, white, middle-class women and minority women. Moreover, feminism emerged in a political context that drew connections between the experience of women and those of other oppressed groups. Yet, differences between white women and women of color have created both tensions and bonds within the women's movement, and this fact has important implications for the race and class analyses needed in feminist theory and feminist programs for change. The problem of racism within the women's movement remains critical; however, the feminist movement is one of the few movements today that is actively concerned with both racism and sexism and is critical of the public and private institutions in which sexism and racism flourish.

Women's Studies and the Academic Disciplines

The effects of the women's movement have been profoundly felt within American colleges and universities where feminist students and faculty have criticized existing knowledge for excluding women and have begun to reconstruct academic studies to be inclusive of women. During the 1960s, activists within American universities defined the university as representing the interests of powerful elites. Universities were criticized for their complicity in the Vietnam War and were accused of being racist and sexist — both in their treatment of women and minorities and in their presentation of a biased curriculum. Black studies and women's studies were created as new fields of study in this context and were intended as educational programs that would teach students about the contributions of women and minorities to society, history, and culture while also generating the knowledge base on which to make social policies that would meet the needs of oppressed groups.

While women's studies has its origins in the feminist movement, it has become a field of study that is grounded in research and theory while still being informed by political commitments to improve and transform the status of women in society. Feminist scholars see that educational curriculum are nested within the traditional culture and, therefore, reflect the same sexist, racist, cultural, and class biases that are found in the dominant culture. Women's studies originated with the recognition that traditional scholarship was partial, incomplete, and distorted because it excluded women. And women's studies rests on the premise that changing what we know about women will change women's and men's lives; consequently, developing women's studies as an academic field is seen as part of the process of transforming women's situation in society.

Feminist scholars share with other radical scholars the idea that the purpose of knowledge must be social change (Flacks and Turkel 1978). Feminist inquiry takes human emancipation as the goal of social-scientific study and claims that knowledge must be used in the construction of more egalitarian societies — ones in which both women and men are freed from sexist and other forms of oppression. Feminists have different visions of what an egalitarian society would look like, some solutions being more radical than others. But all feminist scholars insist upon a political and academic ethic that sees social change as part of the purpose of academic knowledge.

Not only do feminist scholars believe that academic inquiry must be tied to social change, but their critique of traditional scholarship is focused on problems in the content and method of traditional scholarly work. They assert that what is known by scholarly study must make sense of women's experience. Traditional social thought and scholarship, based largely on the lives of men, have not provided such an account. As a result, feminist scholarship has begun to transform academic knowledge and the theories and research on which it rests.

Since the resurgence of feminism in the 1960s, women's studies has produced a dramatic outpouring of studies and theories about women in society. These studies have questioned the assumptions and biases of existing work in almost every field, including science, the humanities, and the social sciences. Women working in different fields soon discovered that much of what stood for knowledge in their disciplines either was overtly sexist or ignored women altogether. Often, academic women found that they had more in common with each other than they did with the men in their disciplines. As they began to study what their disciplines said about women, they forged new ideas that were critical of the preestablished thinking in traditional disciplines and that fostered interdisciplinary women's studies. Feminist reconstructions of academic scholarship have now touched every discipline and have resulted in major changes in the assumptions, theoretical frameworks, and research data upon which the disciplines rest.

Phases of Curriculum Change

Several scholars have identified transformation of the curriculum through women's studies as occurring in several phases (McIntosh 1983; Schuster and Van Dyne 1985; Tetreault 1985). The first phase is the "womanless curriculum"—the phase in all of the disciplines in which women are excluded. The second phase is an "add-women-and-stir" approach (Smith 1974). This phase recognizes the presence of women in the world and adds them to the curriculum, but only on the same terms in which outstanding men have been included. Those who do appear in this phase are still seen as exceptions and their experiences and contributions are still measured through the standards established by men's experiences. In the field of history, this approach took the form of studying the contributions of notable women to history—labeled the "women worthies" approach by historian Gerda Lerner (1976).

In sociology this phase can take the form of adding a chapter on sex roles to a sociology text without rethinking the implications of women's experience for other material in the book. It is also reflected in studies that add sex as a variable but do not reconceptualize problems and topics in a way that takes gender to be fundamental in the organization of society and social life. This phase also encourages researchers to add sex as a variable in research designs—comparing, for example, men's and women's income or showing differences in the socialization patterns of boys or girls.

The add-and-stir method of studying women was valuable for discovering women's experience and moving women from an invisible to a visible location in social science research. But ultimately, it has proven inadequate as an approach, for it still accepts male-centered models as the proper form of analysis and seeks to find out how many women fit into these perspectives. More often than not, feminist scholars have determined that because women's experience is unlike that of men, traditional models of social life do not reveal women's situations; therefore, more revisions are necessary.

The add-and-stir approach leads to a third phase in the curriculum — one in which women are conceptualized as a subordinate group and their experience is defined as problematic. In this phase, scholars have documented the barriers that women and minorities have experienced in society and history. This phase shows how pervasive and systematic discrimination is in women's experiences, but it also is a phase of scholarship that conceptualizes women primarily as victims. For students, this can be a depressing phase of learning, though it is important to our comprehension of the conditions that women and minorities have faced in society and history.

None of the above phases takes women's experiences as the primary lens through which we see society, culture, and history. In the fourth phase, unlike the previous phases, women are seen in their own terms — not as deviants, exceptions, or problems. Scholarship in this phase values the world of women that has been overlooked and trivialized by studies that take only the dominant-group perspective to be the norm; as a result, scholars working from this perspective have discovered a richness and vitality in women's experiences and cultures (Bernard 1981; Smith-Rosenberg 1975) and they have shown how traditional concepts and theories are revised when centered in the experience of previously excluded groups.

One of the best examples in sociology comes from considering the issue of housework. Although feminists have encouraged us to think of housework as work, it does not fit neatly into the frameworks sociologists use to study work. For example, one's occupation usually provides a good measure of one's social status. But because status is also derived from income and because housework is unpaid labor, the status of housewives is difficult to evaluate. Moreover, sociologists usually distinguish work from leisure, although this distinction is not so clear in the case of housework. Would we, for example, consider mothering a child to be work or leisure? Child care certainly contains many of the features of work, including a schedule, routinization of tasks, and physical exertion, but it also includes elements of leisure, such as reading a story or walking to a park. Moreover, it would be difficult to compare the emotional commitment of a mother with that involved in other forms of labor.

These examples show how asking sociological questions from a woman-centered perspective necessarily transforms traditional models of sociological inquiry. Examples from other disciplines as well show that, when women's experiences are taken seriously, new methods and perspectives must be established. For example, in history, feminist scholars have criticized the "women worthies" approach for recognizing only women who meet the male standards for eminence in history. Although it is important to recognize the contributions of prominent women in history, these women stand out because they are deviant. They do not represent the experience of the majority of women in their time. In their transformations of historical scholarship, feminist historians have shown how even the periods used to define time frameworks in history are based on men's achievements and men's activities (Lerner 1976). The Renaissance, for example, is typically depicted as a progressive age that encouraged humanism and creativity. Yet, for women, the Renaissance was a time of increased domestication of bourgeois wives and intensified persecution of witches — most of whom were single peasant women. To see the Renaissance from a woman-centered perspective is to see that this is a period marked by increased restriction of the powers of women (Kelly-Gadol 1976), not the era of creativity and humanism that male-based studies have defined.

Similarly, in the area of psychological development, feminists are revising models of development that have been on male experience. Gilligan's (1982) work on moral development shows how theories of moral development have taken male experience as the norm and then measured female experience against it. In fact, as Gilligan shows, women's moral development follows a different plan than men's, women's orientation toward morality being more contextual than that of men. In other words, women make moral judgments based on their assessments of conflicting responsibilities in a given situation, whereas men are more likely to make moral decisions based on their judgments of competing rights and abstract principles. Gilligan's point is not only to show that men and women have different conceptions of morality, but also that male experience has been taken by psychologists to be universal standard by which both men and women are evaluated.

A woman-centered phase in the development of scholarship shows how ideas and theories have been derived from the particular experiences of some men and then have been used as the universal standards against which all others have been seen and judged. In any field, when men's experience is the standard, women and other subordinated groups (including many men) can only appear incomplete, inadequate, or invisible. Thus, the add-and-stir method does not fully explore women's experiences because it assumes that such experience has no legitimacy of its own. Seeing women as a problem also loses sight of the structure of women's culture and women's own definitions and experiences of the world. Thus, it has taken the women-centered perspectives of women's studies to revise existing knowledge.

But the ultimate phase of curriculum change is what some have called "relational" scholarship (Tetreault 1985) or "inclusive" scholarship (Schuster and Van Dyne 1985). In this phase women's and men's experiences are seen in relationship to the other, and multiple human groups are included in the concepts, theories, and content of human knowledge. Feminist scholarship revises our understanding of not only women's experiences, but also of men's. Expanding the focus of scholarship to include women has led feminists scholars, including both women and men, to ask new questions of women's lives. But in addition, it has raised new questions about men. In fact, the growth of women's studies has stimulated the formation of another new area — men's studies — studies of men that are informed by feminist perspectives and that explore topics and areas of men's lives that have been misrepresented, neglected, or ignored in traditional studies.

These different phases are important descriptions of the process of transforming the curriculum to include women, not so much because they measure one type of thinking against another, but because they help us identify hidden assumptions in the curriculum. Revealing the hidden assumptions embedded in ideas or knowledge helps us envision the process by which knowledge can become genuinely inclusive and take gender, race, and class together as part of the complexity of human experience.

This book reviews studies that document women's experience and observes patterns found by looking at gender as a category of social experience and interaction. Some of the studies we review use traditional research techniques even when they aim to correct the mistakes and omissions of earlier studies. This research has produced volumes of new research findings that detail patterns of behavior such as gender differences in conversational interaction (West and Zimmerman 1983), patterns of female crime and victimization (Bowker 1981), and earning differentials between men and women (Benokraitis and Feagin 1986). These studies are valuable because they provide the factual basis for understanding gender relations in society. An important part of developing an awareness and analysis of women's and men's situations in the world is to examine such evidence carefully and ask how to interpret this data. But, in addition, scholarship in women's studies brings new questions to light, and, while using some of the preestablished techniques and ideas of social inquiry, feminist scholarship also challenges some of the presuppositions, conceptual frameworks, and conclusions of traditional studies. This ongoing process is forging new questions, new topics, new interpretations, and new directions for studies of women and men in society, culture, and history. In the final section of this chapter we look more explicitly at the nature of these revisions in the field or sociology.

The Feminist Critique of Sociology

Sociology is defined as an empirical discipline, meaning that its method of study is the observation of events in the social world. The sociologist observes social events, discovers their patterns, and formulates concepts and theories that interpret relationships among them. An important point about empirical studies is that, when the theories that explain observed events no longer make sense of what is observed or when one's observations change, then revisions are necessary. A central point in feminist criticism of sociological work is that conventional theories have not always made sense of women's experience and, therefore, must be revised.

Sociology is also a discipline that claims social improvement as part of its goal. The history of sociology as a discipline is related to the search for humanitarian social change, and most sociologists believe that sociology should contribute to the improvement of social life. They differ in how to produce this change — some emphasizing gradual improvement through existing governmental and political channels and others believing that only radical social change can solve contemporary social problems. But regardless of their differences, sociologists believe that the purpose of sociological investigation is to generate improved social policies and, consequently, to generate social change.

In sum, we can say that sociology is a discipline that purports to give accurate accounts of the social world and its social problems with the purpose of suggesting policies and possibilities for humanitarian social change. But feminists have argued that sociology has not made good on its claims because of the masculine perspective it has taken. Consider, for example, an early and classic study in the study of social stratification. In *The American Occupational Structure,* Blau and Duncan (1967) conclude that social mobility in this society is "simply a function of education and social origins and there are no further conditions that affect the mobility chances of the various educational groups" (p. 159). Although their research is based on a "national" sample is 20,000 men, they generalize their conclusions to "the" American occupational structure. Would the same conclusion be reached had they included women?

Blau and Duncan's study is now over twenty years old, but even with increased attention on gender as a sociological variable, social scientists continue to exclude women from their research and generalize their conclusions. In 1979, Christopher Jencks published a book titled *Who Gets Ahead? The Determinants of Economic Success in America;* his national sample includes only men aged 25–65 who were not in schools, armies, prison, or hospitals, or were not unemployed. And studies published in major sociological journals in the 1980s continue to make false generalizations from limited samples. One study purports to identify the determinants of the major channels of social mobility, yet the author omits both blacks and women from his analysis. Why? In the author's words, "In this paper I limit my analysis to non-black men to simplify the model" (Yagamuchi 1983:722). In another example, a study of personality and job placement concludes that "ideational flexibility and a self-directed orientation lead to a more responsible job and a greater latitude for occupational self-direction" (Kohn and Schooler 1982:1257); however, the study is based exclusively on a sample of men. And, in a study of unemployment, the researchers conclude that job tenure is a more important determinant of unemployment than any other factors, but again the data for this study include only men (DiPrete 1981).

Making general conclusions based only on the experience of white men assumes that men's experience is the universal form of social life in this society. This could be true only if we assume that the world of women and of racial and ethnic minorities is either nonexistent, uninteresting, or trivial and dull. Implicitly, sociological research has assumed that the world of women can be subsumed under the world of men. Research showing that women use language differently from men (McConnell-Ginet 1978), that black adolescent girls develop unique definitions of womanhood (Ladner 1971), or that lesbian couples are freer from restrictive roles than heterosexual couples (Tanner 1978) belies such an assumption.

Millman and Kanter (1975) have highlighted six major points on the feminist critique of sociology. They are:

1. Conventional topics studied by sociologists lead us to ignore issues that would further illuminate women's lives.
2. Sociology, by focusing on public roles and behaviors, ignores the areas where women's experience is more likely revealed.
3. Sociology tends to depict society as a single generalizable entity.
4. Gender is seldom considered by sociologists to be a significant factor that influences behavior.
5. Sociology focuses on the status quo, thus giving it a conservative bias.
6. Conventional sociological methodologies are likely to elicit only certain kinds of information, most notably the kind is least likely to reveal new data.

The first point states that sociologists have focused on topics and concepts that implicitly bias the study of women. For example, sociologists tend to see social behavior as rational and goal-oriented — an assumption that, from the outset, takes male behavior as the norm. Throughout sociological work, there is an emphasis on conceptual dichotomies such as community and association, Gemeinschaft and Gesellschaft, or expressive and instrumental action. In these dichotomies, the rationalized forms of interaction (association, Gesellschaft, and instrumental action) are seen as indicative of modern social structures. Other forms of interaction (community, Gemeinschaft, and expressive action) are often considered to be of secondary interest or assumed to be relics of past traditions. Implicitly, the argument is made in sociological analysis that these forms of interaction either disappear in modern society or are restricted to the primary world of the family — assumed to be the world of women. In addition to treating the world of women as unimportant or secondary, this perspective creates a sociological picture of the world as more rational than it is, and it glosses over the emotions that human beings feel in their confrontations with the world (Hochschild 1975). In sum, this perspective in sociology projects the traditionally masculine trait of rationality onto the sociological accounts that men have created of the social world.

The second point made by Millman and Kanter is that sociology has focused on public and official roles and behaviors as the foremost subjects of inquiry. Again, by dividing emotional from intellectual life, conventional sociology tends to ignore the private realms of existence. This fact has particular significance for women's studies because of the fact that women have traditionally been relegated to the private realms of social structure. Even in their public role, women do emotional work, meaning that they provide personal services, negotiate social relations between people, and are often responsible for the kinds of jobs that are oriented toward people. Thus, emotional work is considered to be women's work (Chodorow, 1978; Hochschild 1983), and sociologists who ignore the areas of life where emotional work is most obviously performed also ignore much of the social activity of women. Secretaries, housewives, nurses, and maids all work in ways that bridge public and private life. To restrict the study of women to their contributions to public life is to overlook a major part of women's contributions to society. By rethinking the assumed dichotomy between public and private life, feminists have concluded that conventional sociology has constructed an inaccurate account of the lives, feelings, and thoughts of women and men.

Third, Millman and Kanter argue that sociology tends to depict society as if it were a single entity. They write, "Sociology often assumes a 'single society' with respect to men and women, in which generalizations can be made about all participants, yet men and women may actually inhabit different social worlds, and these must be taken into account" (1975:xiii). Evidence for their assertion recurs in the sociological literature, as study after study makes conclusions about the society based on investigations in which all of the research subjects are male.

Millman and Kanter's fourth point is that, in sociological work, gender is seldom considered to be a factor that influences social behavior. They point out that the sex distribution of social groups is often assumed to be irrelevant to social behavior and, second, that when a group is all-male, then it is assumed to be gender neutral. Feminist studies show the falsehood of such a claim, as in Kanter's (1977) work on formal organizations. Kanter shows that the experience of women in corporations is greatly influenced by the proportion of women in the company. Women, as well as other minorities, become tokens in predominantly white male settings. Those in the majority, in the presence of token members, exaggerate the dominant culture, isolate the token outsiders, and constantly remind tokens of their difference. As proportions by gender shift, so do the social experiences of both sexes.

The fifth point of feminist criticism is that sociology is implicitly a conservative discipline because of its tendency to explain the status quo. From its origin, the central problem of sociological inquiry has been the question, "How is social order possible?" Although much of sociological inquiry has emerged from studying the conflicts and contradictions in social life, there is also a strong interest in the persistence of behavioral patterns and the mechanisms of social stability. The focus on norms, roles, and stability emphasizes the status quo, whereas feminists argue that sociology must provide the foundation for social transformation and the liberation of oppressed groups.

Finally, Millman and Kanter make the point that conventional sociological methodologies are likely to elicit only certain kinds of information. The methods that sociologists use may blind them to certain views of the world. For example, the frequently used questionnaire method provides research subjects with responses that have been preestablished by the researcher. This method tends to impose the researcher's ideas upon the persons being studied. An alternative strategy, and one that Millman and Kanter suggest, is to encourage researchers to let subjects speak for themselves. By hearing subjects speak in their own words, sociologists are more likely to discover new ideas than to reinforce their old ones.

Despite the growth of feminist scholarship in sociology and the far-reaching critique of sociological thought this scholarship generates, there has been resistance to the transformations of sociological thought suggested by feminist theory and research. Stacey and Thorne (1985) have asked why this is so. Comparing sociology to the disciplines of anthropology, literature, and history, they argue that feminist sociologists have been less successful in reconstructing the basic paradigms of the field. A paradigm refers to the assumptions and conceptual frameworks that are basic to any discipline. "Paradigm shifting" is a process that involves "(1) the transformation of existing conceptual frameworks; and (2) the acceptance of those transformations by others in the field" (Stacey and Thorne 1985:302). Feminist studies in sociology, they argue, have been contained in three major ways: "by the limiting assumptions of functionalist conceptualizations of gender; by the inclusion of gender as a variable rather than as a central theoretical concept; and by the ghettoization of feminist insights" (p. 306).

Functionalist theory in sociology directs our attention to concepts like "roles" and "socialization." While we discuss these in further detail in Chapter 4, Stacey and Thorne's point is that this orientation in sociology emphasizes societal consensus, stability, and cohesion and tends to see men and women as complementary. Feminists, on the other hand, tend to see gender relations in terms of power and conflict, not just as individuals inhabiting social roles.

Their second point, that in sociology gender tends to be thought of as a variable, not a theoretical concept, speaks to the scientific orientation of sociology. Other disciplines, without claims to scientific status, tend to use more interpretive methods — methods that reflect upon the circumstances in which knowledge is produced. As we will see in Chapter 2, this understanding of the sociology of knowledge is central to feminist thought and to some forms of sociological thinking, but the positivist bias in sociology — that is to say, the tendency to see social life as measurable in the same ways that scientists measure and describe the physical world — has limited gender to being a variable, rather than a more general theoretical category.

Their last point, about the ghettoization of feminist studies in sociology, speaks to the resistance of many scholars to the insights of feminist thought. When women are not omitted altogether from sociological studies, they are often relegated to specialized areas in sociology — originally, the family, and now, the sociology of sex and gender. This compartmentalization of knowledge about women produces a segregated curriculum in sociology where primary concepts, studies, and ideas remain centered in the lives of men. As a result, many remain unaware of the theoretical, methodological, and substantive contributions that new research in women's studies and the sociology of sex and gender makes in to sociology. As we will see in the chapters that follow, these contributions are substantial and promise to create knowledge that is far more inclusive than that which precedes. As we examine this new scholarship, students should see that feminist perspectives in sociology emerge from the exchange of new data, new ideas, and newly imagined possibilities for social change.

Summary

Feminist perspectives in sociology are critical of frameworks that are derived solely from male experience or that merely recapitulate traditional perspectives on the social relations of the sexes. In revising traditional work, feminist scholars are creating a new sociology, one that intends to better represent the experience of women and men in the world and to make a stronger contribution to policies for social change.

Feminist perspectives in sociology have opened up a new discourse and encouraged scholars to observe social relations of the sexes without the blinders that have been encouraged by earlier work. By providing a new discourse, feminists would argue that we are improving sociological methods because we are more aware of observations and ideas that have hitherto gone unnoticed. Millman and Kanter aptly describe this process through their rewriting of a classic parable:

Everyone knows the story about the Emperor and his fine clothes: although the townspeople persuaded themselves that the Emperor was elegantly costumed, a child, possessing an unspoiled vision, showed the citizenry that the Emperor was really naked. The story instructs us about one of our basic sociological premises: that reality is subjective, or, rather, subject to social definition. The story also reminds us that collective delusions can be undone by introducing fresh perspectives. Movements of social liberation are like the story in this respect: they make it possible for people to see the world in an enlarged perspective because they remove the covers and blinders that obscure knowledge and observation. In the last decade no social movement has had a more startling or consequential impact on the way people see and act in the world than the women's movement. Like the onlookers in the Emperor's parade, we can see and plainly speak about things that have always been there, but that formerly were unacknowledged. Indeed, today it is impossible to escape noticing features of social life that were invisible only ten years ago. (1975:vii)

Seeing without the blinders of earlier perspectives will not reveal ultimate truths about social life any more than will other forms of social thought. And the feminist critique of knowledge does not offer final solutions to the problems experienced by women or men in contemporary society. But it has dramatically shown how little we know and what distorted information we have about at least one-half of the human population, and it casts doubt upon what we know about the other half. Also, the feminist critique emphasizes that what we have known in the past is tied to the perspectives and interests of dominant groups. The insights feminist thought provides and the self-criticism it encourages have created a new challenge for scholars who are committed to new visions of the future.

CHAPTER 2

Sexism and the Social Construction of Knowledge

Introduction

The ad reads, "Some women can never have too much of a good thing" (*New York Times Magazine,* August 3, 1986). What is being sold here? Food? Sex? No, it is shoes, though the shoes and the text of the advertisement pale beside the sexual overtones. In another example, an advertisement widely shown on national television, a sultry woman's voice announces, "Gives you the protection of a man, but lets you feel like a woman." This ad is for underarm deodorant, and it lends the impression, as one commentator has suggested, that femininity is located in a woman's armpits! (Kilbourne 1979).

Other advertisements evoke images of women as beguiling and seductive and as needing protection — as is clearly illustrated in advertising campaigns for menstrual napkins and tampons. Many ads seemed designed to make women fearful — fearful of aging, fearful of being overweight, and fearful of being alone. Some intimidate women with implied threats of danger, as in the sales campaign for shoes that warns, "When you go out for the evening, leave your lights on" — the "lights" referring to spike-heeled, open-toed, strapped sandals!

Advertisements are only one source for the ideas about women that are generated in the mass media and popular culture. Popular music, advice columns, television shows, and other cultural materials all carry explicit and implicit suggestions regarding the appropriate social roles for women and men. A recent analysis of computer trade magazine shows, for example, that men appear in the illustrations twice as often as do women. In the same magazines, women are overrepresented as clerical workers and sex objects, while men are overrepresented as managers, experts, and repair technicians. Men are shown primarily in positions of authority, while only women are shown as rejecting computers (Ware and Stuck 1985).

The sexism found in popular culture, while transformed over time, has not necessarily declined. A recent analysis of the image of women in popular music makes this point well. Cooper (1985) studied images of women in popular music over a forty-year period. She found that while images of women as needing a man were more common in the 1940s and 1950s, images of women as sex objects and possessions of men have remained unchanged. In addition, mention of women's physical characteristics in popular songs rose over time, and images of women as evil increased during the 1970s. Moreover, depictions of women as supernatural increased during the 1960s and 1970s.

The ideas and images presented to us, whether through advertisements or other cultural media, exert a powerful influence over our lives. It is estimated that each of us sees an average of 1,600 advertisements per day and notices 1,200 of them, though we respond, positively or negatively, to 12 (Draper 1986). Advertisements not only sell the products we use, but also convey images of how we are to define ourselves, our relationships, and our needs.

The ideas about women and men that these cultural objects portray greatly influence our thinking about gender roles in society. They convey an impression about the proper roles of women and men, their sexual identities and their self-concepts. The ideas we hold about women and men, whether overtly sexist or more subtle in their expression, create social definitions that we use to understand ourselves and the society we live in. The ideas that people have of one another guide their behavior, even though there is no direct fit between what people believe and say and what they actually do (Deutscher 1973). What is known or believed about women and gender relations, even when it is based on distortions of social realities, influences our mental experiences. These experiences, in turn, become part of the basis for sexist social arrangements.

Ideas, although based in the interpretive realm of thought and subjectivity, direct our behavior and constrain the ways in which we see each other and others see us. Ideas also have a political reality because they affect how society works, who gets rewarded, and how things should and should not be. For example, if we believe that women's proper place is in the home, we are not likely to object to the sexist practices of employer discrimination. However, if we believe that women are as capable as men, we are likely to support policies and changes that would make more opportunities available to them.

This chapter studies the social construction of knowledge about gender, especially as that knowledge is reproduced in the media and academic institutions. Although these institutions are not the exclusive sources of sexist ideas, they exert a powerful influence on the way we define reality and women's role within it. Although it is easy to oversimplify the influence of these institutions, there is little doubt that both of them have a tremendous impact on the ways we define our society and ourselves within it. In fact, it can be argued that in a highly complex technological-industrial society, these systems of communication and knowledge making play an increasingly important part in the generation and transmission of ideas.

Moreover, as the feminist movement has shown, images of women conveyed by the media and in educational materials have been based on distortions and stereotypes that legitimate the status quo at the same time that they falsely represent the actual experience of women in the society. Thus, the ideas we acquire regarding gender relations poorly prepare us for the realities we will face.

Gendered Images in the Media

Even a cursory review of the image of gender roles in the mass media shows that women and men are portrayed in stereotypical ways. Not only are they cast in traditional roles, but both men and women are omitted from roles that portray them in a variety of social contexts. Women tend to be portrayed in roles in which they are trivialized, condemned, or narrowly defined, resulting in the "symbolic annihilation" of women by the media (Tuchman, Daniels, and Benét 1978). Men, on the other hand, are usually depicted in high-status roles in which they dominate women (Lemon 1978).

The research method most often used to study media images is called *content analysis*. This method is a descriptive one whereby researchers analyze the actual content of documents or programs. By counting particular items within a defined category, researchers are able to systematize their observations of the content of the media (Wiseman and Aron 1970).

Some might say that images of women on television and in other media have improved in recent years. To a limited extent this is true, since in some serials, such as "Cagney and Lacey," "The Cosby Show," "Hill Street Blues," and "St. Elsewhere," women do portray strong and intelligent characters. But in most shows, men are still the major characters and women are cast as glamourous objects, scheming villains, or servants. And for every contemporary show that includes more positive images of women, there are numerous others, such as "Hunter," "Miami Vice," and "Scarecrow and Mrs. King," where women are shown as either sidekicks to men, sexual objects, or helpless imbeciles.

Content analyses of television show that, during prime-time hours, men make up a large majority of all the characters shown. Moreover, women prime-time characters are found primarily in comedies and men in dramas, giving the impression that men are to be taken seriously and women are not (Tuchman, Daniels, and Benét 1978). And on soap operas (such as "Dynasty" and "Dallas"), strong, successful women are depicted as villains while "good" women are seen as vulnerable and naive (Benokraitis and Feagin 1986). Content analysis also shows that men on television are more likely depicted in high-status occupations than are women (Lemon 1978), and women are more likely depicted in family roles than work roles (Busby, 1975). In fact, 75 percent of all television ads using women are for products found in the kitchen or the bathroom (Tuchman, Daniels, and Benét 1978).

Images of men and women on television reinforce not only gender stereotypes but those of class and race as well. Studies of dominance in television shows find that both men and women of high occupational status are more likely found in dramas than in comedies. Working-class characters are more frequently depicted in comedies, where they are presented in class stereotypical roles. The impression is created that working-class lives are funny, whereas serious drama occurs elsewhere. *Dominance* is defined as behavior that influences, controls, persuades, prohibits, dictates, leads, directs, restrains, or organizes the behavior of others. Studies find that white men are most dominant on television except in situation comedies, where low-status women tend to be more dominant than low-status men (Lemon 1978).

These patterns are further complicated by race. White men and women far outnumber minority men and women on television. Although estimates are that blacks watch television 10 percent more than whites do, they are a small proportion of the characters seen. Perhaps with the exception of "The Cosby Show," there are limited positive images of blacks on television and they appear in a narrow range of character types — 49 percent of all blacks on television are portrayed as either criminals, servants, entertainers, or athletes; rarely are blacks portrayed as loving, sexual, sensitive people (Douglas 1984). When black women are portrayed, they appear in stereotypical roles, such as the sophisticated mammie image of Nell in "Gimme a Break" (Staples and Jones 1985). Black men fare no better, such as the A-Team's Mr. T, cast as "a black male in the role of a super masculine menial — a brainless eunuch who is no real threat to the white male" (Staples and Jones 1985:14).

Asian-Americans, Hispanics, and native Americans are virtually absent from television programming except as occasional diversions, exotic objects, or marginal and invisible characters. In fact, in 1984, of the 264 speaking roles on television, Hispanics only had 3. Two-thirds of Hispanic characters were cast as criminals (Staples and Jones 1985). Asians were in none of the leading roles. The invisibility of minority groups on television is also noticeable in the "disappearing" roles that blacks, Hispanics, and Asian-Americans often play in television dramas. On popular shows such as "Dallas" and daytime soap operas, minority women and men silently appear in backgrounds to cater to the needs of dominant households or individuals. Also, in popular shows such as "Spenser: For Hire" and "Magnum, P.I." minority persons frequently portray assistants to leading white male actors. In their interactions, the minority character is deferential, respectful, and dutiful to his dominant partner.

In a slightly different vein, black women in situation comedies dominate more than any other characters. In crime dramas, although black and white men are more dominant than either black or white women, black women are shown as more dominant than white women. On all shows, black women are usually portrayed as dominant in all black interactions. Such depictions of black women reproduce racist stereotypes of the mythical black matriarch by casting black women in the role of humorous but dominating characters. In this example, as well as others, television acts as a system of social control, narrowing our understanding of people's experience, discrediting and ridiculing serious subjects such as racism and sexism, and undercutting any resistance that the public might generate against dominant social institutions (Gerbner 1978).

In children's television programming, gender and race stereotypes are probably at their worst—a particularly disturbing fact considering the number of hours children spend watching television. Television acts as a powerful agent of socialization for young children. Ninety-six percent of American homes are equipped with at least one television, and these sets are turned on an average of six hours per day. By the time an American child is 15 years old, he or she will have spent more hours watching television than attending school (Sprafkin and Liebert 1978). A study of sixth through ninth graders finds that 40 percent of the children watch television for five hours or more per day; 25 percent watch for six or more hours per day; and only 10 percent report watching for less than two hours per day (Gross and Jeffries-Fox 1978).

What do children see when they watch television? Children's cartoons include even fewer women than do adult shows, and, as in adult shows, female characters are likely to be seen as comical, as located only in family roles, or as victims of male violence (Gerbner 1978; Liebert, Neale, and Davidson 1973). The influence of gender stereotyping on television can be seen in the fact that children who watch the most television are those with the most stereotypic sex role values (Frueh and McGhee 1975). And a large proportion of elementary school children report that they learn about how blacks look and dress by watching television (Greenburg 1972).

As we increasingly rely on television and other media for information about our society, these restrictive images become especially troublesome. Segregation by race, class, and sex in the real world keeps us distant from each other and gives us little access to the experiences of others. Thus, it is likely that, for many, the media present the only information they know about people with whom they have had no direct experience and the only information about places where they have never been.

The nature of printed and electronic media is such that once an image is represented, it loses the fluid character it would have in reality. Thus, ideas and characters appear fixed, giving a singular impression of reality. Moreover, the mass media carry a certain authority, particularly because they provide a common basis for public interaction. Even the news, where we hope to get factual, objective reporting of world events, is packaged with authoritative commentaries, moral admonitions, comic relief, and sensationalized presentations. Because of the televised or recorded format of the news, all items appear equally serious, resulting in the trivialization and ultimate distortion of world events. Moreover, the gender biases common in fictional media also appear in the news, where women are underrepresented as reporters and commentators, where female reporters are more likely to report on "soft" news or human-interest stories, where news about women is seldom found, and where, when it does appear, it is likely to celebrate traditional sex role values.

Some suggest that television acts as a national religion in contemporary American society because it establishes a common culture and is resistant to cultural change. Gerbner writes,

> [Television] is used by practically all the people and is used practically all the time. It collects the most heterogeneous public of groups, classes, races, and sexes, and nationalities in history into a national audience that has nothing in common except television or shared messages. Television thereby becomes the common basis for social interaction among a very widely dispersed and diverse national community. As such, it can only be compared, in terms of its functions, not to any other medium but to the preindustrial notion of religion.

If television provides for the maintenance of culture, then it must resist social movements that challenge the culture and seek to transform social institutions. The media do not fully resist such changes; rather, they defend the traditional system by coopting new images that social movements generate. Consequently, we now see "liberated" images of women in the media, but ones that still carry stereotypic gender assumptions. For example, women may now be shown as working, but these women are all beautiful, young, rich, and thin. At the same time, because the media cannot ignore the feminist movement, it is portrayed as trivial (as represented in the media phrase *women's lib*), and feminists are shown as extremists or as acceptable only when they are moderate.

Women's magazines have been more responsive to social change than other media, in part because of changes in the experiences of their audience (Tuchman, Daniels, and Benét 1978). Yet these magazines still portray women in sex role stereotypes in which youth and good looks are emphasized and women are still defined by the men in their lives or by their absence (Flora 1971; Tuchman, Daniels, and Benét 1978). Some class differences in images of women also appear in women's magazines; those with middle-class audiences have been more responsive to changes in women's roles. One study comparing magazines with working-class and middle-class readers finds that by 1975 working-class fiction was more likely to portray women in dependent and passive roles than was fiction in middle-class magazines. In 1970 the reverse had been true, indicating that the media have responded more to changes in the lives of middle-class women than to others (Flora 1979).

Content analyses of the media tell us a great deal about the image of women in modern society. But these descriptions alone provide no direct evidence of the character of communication systems, their audiences and producers, and their actual effects. To understand these issues, we require other material to provide theoretical direction to empirical observations about the media and their content, organization, and effects. The following section discusses explanations of women's depiction by the media.

Explaining Women's Depiction by the Media ———————

Understanding women's depiction by the media would not be so important if we did not assume that there is some relationship between media images and social reality. This is not to say that the images are real; we have already seen how they involve distortions and misrepresentations. But there is a relationship between images and reality, either because images reflect social values about women's roles or because images create social ideals upon which people model their behavior and attitudes. Moreover, these images are produced by working people; even if we see them as social myths, they are connected to the social systems in which they are created. Theories of women's depiction by the mass media must explain this relationship between media images and the social worlds in which they are produced and consumed.

Several approaches have been taken by sociologists and communications specialists to explain the depiction of women by the media. These include the reflection hypothesis, role-learning theory, organizational theories of gender inequality, and economic explanations of media organization (Tuchman 1979). Each of these approaches has its own strengths and weaknesses, which are discussed here.

The Reflection Hypothesis

The first and theoretically the most simple explanation is called the *reflection hypothesis* (Tuchman 1979; Tuchman, Daniels, and Benét 1978). This hypothesis assumes that the mass media reflect the values of the general population. Images in the media are seen as representing dominant ideals within the population, particularly because the capitalistic structure of the media is dependent upon appealing to the largest consumer audience. According to Gerbner (1978), the ideals of the population are incorporated into symbolic representations in the media. The reflection hypothesis asserts that, although media images are make-believe, they do symbolize dominant social beliefs and images.

The volumes of data produced by marketing researchers and ratings scales indicate that popular appeal is significant in decisions about programming content. Observations of shows such as soap operas also show that television attempts to incorporate into its programming social issues that reflect, even if in an overblown way, the experiences (or, at least, the wishes) of its viewers. Although viewers may escape into soap operas as a relief from daily life, the fact that they can do so rests upon some form of identification (even if fanciful) with the characters and the situations they are in (Modleski 1980).

But the reflection hypothesis leaves several questions unanswered. To begin with, as content analysis studies have shown, much if not most of what the media depicts is not synchronized with real conditions in people's lives. In part, this phenomenon is explainable by a time lag between cultural changes and changes in the media (Tuchman, Daniels, and Benét 1978). It is also explainable by the fact that the media portray ideals, not truths. Nevertheless, people may not actually believe what they see in the media and, if they do, it may be because the media create their beliefs as much as it emerges from them. Thus, a causal question is asked in theoretical explanations of media images: Do the media reflect or create popular values? The reflection hypothesis makes the first assumption. Other explanations begin with the second one.

Role-Learning Theory

The values and images of women and men in the media represent some of the most conservative views of women and men. Role-learning theory hypothesizes that sexist and racist images in the media (and the absence thereof) encourage role modeling. That is to say, "the media's deleterious role models, when internalized, prevent and impede female accomplishments. They also encourage both women and men to define women in terms of men (as sex objects) or in the context of the family" (Tuchman

1979). The assumption that the media encourage role modeling has been the basis for organized challenges by feminist groups that are opposed to sex role stereotyping in the media. Children's programs especially have been examined for their effect upon children's development (Gross and Jeffries-Fox 1978; Sprafkin and Liebert 1978), and even the more liberated shows such as "Sesame Street" have been criticized for their portrayals of female characters (Cathey-Calvert n.d.).

Feminist opposition to gender stereotypes in the media often assumes that these stereotypes encourage people to model their behavior in stereotypic ways. But the role-modeling argument does involve naive theoretical assumptions that the media should truthfully reproduce social life and that there is some causal connection between the content of the media and its social effects (Tuchman 1979). In other words, the role-modeling argument assumes that media images produce stimuli that, when mediated by social variables (such as age, gender, race, and class), have predictable responses from the public. This portrayal of social reality and human responses to the environment entails a pessimistic view of human beings as totally passive receptacles for whatever media inputs are poured into them. People may, in fact, view media images much more critically or even with cynicism, making it unlikely that they would modify their behavior in accordance with them. However, this possibility does not deny the fact that people, especially children, do learn from the media. Rather, this criticism of role-modeling theory suggests that it is an oversimplified perspective.

Organizational Theories of Gender Inequality

Although both the reflection hypothesis and the role-modeling argument alert us to the fit between images and reality, neither adequately explains the reasons for sexism in the media. Thus, scholars have attempted to explain sexism in media content by studying gender inequality within media organizations. This perspective assumes that the subordinate position of women and minorities in the media influences the ideas produced about them. If women and minorities are absent from the power positions where ideas and images are produced, then their world views and experiences will not be reflected in the images those organizations produce (Smith 1975). Moreover, since those who occupy power positions come to share a common world view, the ideas they produce tend to reflect the values of the ruling elite.

There is little doubt that women and minorities remain in subordinate positions in media organizations, despite recent gains they have made. They work in sex- and race-segregated positions and are a tiny proportion of reporters, writers, announcers, and managers in television and radio stations and on the major networks. And despite a spurt of hiring around 1970, the number of women holding administrative positions in the media has declined (Tuchman 1979).

The situation for minorities is no better. Blacks make up only 8.9 percent of those in the broadcasting industry. Black women in this industry are most likely employed in clerical and service jobs; black men, as operatives, laborers, and in service jobs (Adams 1985). Only 5.6 percent of the staff of daily newspapers in the nation are minorities. In fact, 97 percent of newspaper news executives are white, the vast majority of them men. Sixty percent of the news dailies in the country employ no blacks at all. And in the movie industry, where blacks make up 11.8 percent of actors, they hold only 8.85 percent of the lead roles and only have 5.9 percent of time played (Bowie 1985).

These data provide convincing evidence that more women and minorities need to be hired if they are to have equality in media organizations, but do they explain the images produced by the media? The argument that increasing the presence of women in the media will transform images of women assumes that men and women and whites and blacks hold different values; this belief has not been demonstrated in research. Women and men in the fields of journalism and television production seem to share the same stereotypes of women, and most female journalism students believe that the majority of women prefer traditional content in women's magazines (Orwant and Cantor 1977). Female editors of women's pages also share the preferences of their male counterparts (Merritt and Gross 1978), and women make the same judgments as men regarding the general news (Phillips 1975).

These comparisons make sense if we recognize that persons who work in organizations become socialized to accept the organization's values. Those who do not conform are less likely to build successful careers. Hence, organizational workers more often than not adopt the values of the organizations in which they are employed. Within the media, professional attitudes discourage workers from offending the networks; thus, professionalism encourages workers to conform to the bureaucratic and capitalist values of their organization (Tuchman 1979). This influence affects the way black and white, male and female workers portray gender and racial issues in the media because the organizational culture discourages them from appearing controversial. Values promoting the idea of individualism and upward mobility are so much a part of this culture that even feminism becomes portrayed in the media in terms of individual achievement, consumerism, personal style, and individual rewards (Ehrenreich 1978; Tuchman 1979). That men and women working in the media adopt similar values tells us not so much that men and women think alike, but that all workers' behaviors and attitudes are shaped by the organizations in which they are employed (Kanter 1977).

Capitalism and the Media

A fourth perspective used to explain sexism in the media is an economic approach that attributes sexism to the capitalist structure of media organizations. According to this approach, it is in the interests of sponsors to foster images that are consistent with the products they sell. Many of these products encourage particular values, such as obsessive cleanliness, which is necessary to sell the numerous household cleaning products placed on the market. The depiction in the media of housewives who are pathologically concerned with cleanliness (Kilbourne 1979) reflects the manufacturers' attempts to sell their products.

This perspective also claims that it is in the interests of a capitalist power elite to discourage images of reality that would foster discontent. Thus, not only will sponsors promote any values that will sell, but they will also encourage traditional views that uphold the status quo while discouraging those that challenge it. When they do respond to social criticism, they do so within the limits of existing institutions. For example, following the civil rights movement, when pressure was generated to increase the number of blacks in the media, more blacks appeared in advertisements and on television programs, but they were and continue to be primarily depicted in middle-class settings where they hold middle-class value systems and are not radically critical about American society. Moreover, as noted previously, the feminist movement has been depicted by the media as radical, trivial, and extremist. As the women's movement has gained public support, the media have selected its more moderate programs and leaders for public display.

As economic perspective on the media reminds us that the media are owned and controlled by the major corporations of American society. The popular magazine *Cosmopolitan*, for example is owned by the Hearst Corporation — the same organization that controls several major newspapers, has representatives on the board of regents of the University of California, and owns vast amounts of property and other business organizations. Similar examples are found in other corporate conglomerates that own networks, newspapers, and recording companies. From this perspective, Marx's idea is true that those who control economic production also control the manufacture and dissemination of ideas.

The economic structure of the media explains much about how women are exploited through commercialism. Thus, this perspective has frequently been cited by feminists as the reason that women are portrayed either as sex objects or as household caretakers. These values, they point out, are consistent with capitalist needs to maintain women's services in the home and to make commercial objects out of everything, including sexuality (Mitchell 1971).

But in itself, this explanation encourages a conspiratorial view of media owners and management who, although they are motivated by economic profit, may not have the specific intent of exploiting women. But this perspective, along with the gender-inequality approach, gives us a more complete understanding of sexism in the media. Observing the economic and social organization of the media causes us to ask who produces media images and how these images define legitimate forms of social reality. Images of women are tied to both their economic and social origins.

Feminist sociologist Dorothy Smith suggests that "social forms of thought originate in a practice of ruling — or management, or administration, or other forms of social control. They are located in and originate from definite positions of dominance in the society. They are not merely that floating thing, the 'culture'" (1975:355). Because of this logic, some suggest that the concept of images be discarded by feminists because it connotes a somewhat vacuous and abstract idea and underplays the social production and reproduction of thought (Tuchman 1979).

Alternatively, women's depictions in the media can be seen as social myths by which the meaning of society and women's place within it are established. Anthropologists study social myths to gain an insight into the culture and social organization of a people. Myths provide an interpretation of social truths, beliefs, and relationships that guide a society in its vision of the past, present, and future. Myths establish a "universe of discourse" that integrates and controls its members, gives them a common reality, and creates structures for what is said, done, and believed (Tuchman 1979). By creating a universe of discourse among their audience, the media act as powerful agents of social control. They engage people in passive fantasies, encourage dreams and visions that are consistent with the social structure, and establish a common basis for social interaction. Therefore, in a fundamental way, the depiction of women in the media infiltrates our social consciousness and embeds itself in our imagination. In sum, the media establish popular culture, which in turn establishes our definitions of social reality.

The media are powerful sources for communicating sexist ideas about men and women and their roles in society. What we absorb from the media is learned subtly and informally and in the context of everyday life. But in addition to the influence of the media and the popular culture they represent, sexism is also learned through the formal process of education. In the next section, we look at the social construction of knowledge as it occurs in educational settings.

Women and Educational Thought

The pursuit of knowledge has historically been considered the work of men (Sherman and Beck 1979). In the history of education, women have been outsiders. Either they were excluded by formal admissions policies or they were tracked into sex-typed fields and specialties.

In the early history of higher education in this country, women's education was restricted by ideologies that depicted their minds as directed and limited by their bodies. Especially in the post–Civil War period, when major transformations were occurring in the traditional gender roles, leading educational reformers claimed that women's wombs dominated their mental life and that, therefore, they should not study or work vigorously!

One such reformer, Dr. Edward Clarke, was a member of the Harvard Board of Overseers and a member of its medical faculty. He published several popular books in the late nineteenth century warning of the dangers that education and study posed for women. Clarke wrote, "A girl upon whom Nature, for a limited period and for a definite purpose, imposes so great a physiological task, will not have as much power left for the tasks of school, as the boy of whom Nature requires less at the corresponding epoch" (Clarke 1873:54, cited in Rosenberg 1982:10). Accordingly, he advised young women to study one-third as much as young men and not to study at all during menstruation!

Others also agreed. Professor Charles Meigs had admonished his class at Jefferson Medical College to think of the womb as a "great power and ask your own judgments whether such an organ can be of little influence on the constitution and how much!" (Meigs 1847:18, cited in Rosenberg 1982:6). And the prominent gynecologist Thomas Emmet argued:

> To reach the highest point of physical development the young girl in the between classes of society should pass the year before puberty and some two years afterwards free from all exciting influences. She should be kept as a child as long as possible, and made to associate with children. . . . Her mind should be occupied by a very moderate amount of study, with frequent intervals of a few moments each, passed when possible in the recumbent position, until her system become accustomed to the new order of life. (Emmet 1879:21, cited in Rosenberg 1982:10)

These admonitions reflect class biases of the time and also are consistent with racist arguments that defined blacks as biologically unfit for the same privileges accorded whites. Such biological explanations of inequality, as we can see in the following chapter, are often used to justify oppression by race, class, and gender. Biological explanations of inequality seem to become especially popular during periods of rapid social change in class, race, and gender relations, because such beliefs develop as justifications for maintaining the status quo.

Despite ideological restrictions and formal barriers designed to reserve education for white privileged men, many women and blacks did become highly educated during this period. Still, the power of these beliefs influenced the development of sex-segregated educational institutions.

Although women have now been present in the university system for more than a century, they still have the status of outsiders because they are not yet as numerous as men in the academic professions and, when they are present, they are not as highly placed in the educational system. Women's status as outsiders has important ramifications for the way in which academic knowledge is constructed and the way women are defined within it. Academic knowledge is created within specific institutional structures. Because the production of research and scholarship is tied to the setting in which it develops, the noticeable absence or invisibility of women in these settings has contributed to the invisibility and distortion of women.

Commonsense attitudes about scholarship may make it seem odd to think of it as institutionalized. Popular images of university scholarship tend to see it as produced in "ivory towers" — places with little connection either to common sense or to the events of everyday life. Thus, scholarship is perceived as if it were somehow detached from the events of the world at large. But popular connotations of the word *scholarship* overlook the fact that the institutions in which scholarship is produced share the same characteristics that are found in other institutions.

Institutions are *established* patterns of behavior with a particular and recognized *purpose,* and they include specific *participants* who *share expectations* and act in *specific roles* with *rights and duties* attached to them (Payer 1977). Institutions define reality for us insofar as they exist as objective entities in our experience. They are "experienced as existing over and beyond the individuals who 'happen' to embody them at the moment. In other words, the institutions are experienced as a reality of their own, a reality that confronts the individual as an external and coercive fact" (Berger and Luckmann 1966:58).

A closer look at institutions where scholarship is created reveals that there are unequal distributions of resources within them, power relationships between dominant and subordinate groups, beliefs and attitudes that define the work of some as more legitimate than that of others, and socialization processes by which newcomers are taught the ways of the system. And just as in other institutions, for those who do not conform a variety of sanctions can be applied, ranging from ridicule to exclusion.

Moreover, persons who participate in the life of an institution tend to share its definitions of reality and its definitions of themselves. As the collective knowledge of the institution's members becomes taken for granted, the institution becomes reified. That is to say, it is assumed to have an objective (i.e., real) existence even though its objective existence is subjectively based. The process of reification is complete when the relationship between the institution and its origins (in other words, its social development) is forgotten. Institutions

are not only here-and-now, given, and self-evident, but also arise within particular and historic environments, and in response to certain felt interests and needs; and as these interests are served, and needs are met and continue to be met in certain typical ways, actions are repeated, grow into patterns, and become firmly entrenched in practice and consciousness. It is just at this stage, when practice and habits pass over into highly organized forms, that we begin to speak of "institutions" as opposed to mere custom or habitual activity. (Payer 1977:30)

This perspective on institutions makes it possible to understand that those who are not fully integrated into the institutional structure are the least likely to share the conventional wisdom of the institution as a whole. As outsiders to these institutions, women's status is critical in explaining the gendered character of academic knowledge.

The Status of Women in Academic Institutions

Most women who enter academic life will find themselves alone, or nearly so, in a group of men. Statistically, they constitute a small minority of the persons in all but the most traditionally female disciplines in American universities (Hornig 1980). Women are not only underrepresented as faculty in higher education; they are also less likely to be tenured (see Table 2-1). This situation is partly explained by the fact that women are more concentrated at the lower ranks than men (see Table 2-2). Although women have made slight gains in academic rank in recent years, they still remain predominantly at lower levels and in less prestigious institutions.

Women's token status in academia has several consequences both for the personal experiences of women faculty and for the state of knowledge in general. At the personal level, women may find that their personalities (formed as they are through cultural expectations of femininity) are at odds with the values and behaviors surrounding them. This dilemma is best described by Alice Rossi, who wrote in 1970:

TABLE 2-1   Percent of Faculty with Tenure, 1983

	Percent with Tenure (All Ranks Combined)	
	Male	**Female**
Universities	70.9%	42.9%
Other four-year institutions	67.3	46.4
Two-year institutions	78.9	68.2
All institutions (public and private)	70.4	51.0

Source: Betty M. Vetter and Eleanor L. Babco, *Professional Women and Minorities.* Washington, D.C.: Commission on Professionals in Science and Technology, February 1986.

TABLE 2-2   Faculty by Rank and Sex, All Institutions

	Percent of Male Faculty at This Rank	Percent of Female Faculty at This Rank	Men as Percent of All Faculty at This Rank	Women as Percent of All Faculty at This Rank
Full professor	29.8%	12.1%	89.4%	10.6%
Associate professor	26.0	21.9	78.1	21.9
Assistant professor	24.7	34.1	64.0	36.0
Instructor	7.3	14.6	47.9	52.1
Lecturer	1.7	3.1	52.5	47.5
No rank	10.5	14.2	64.6	35.4
All ranks combined	100%	100%	73.9%	26.1%

Source: Betty M. Vetter and Eleanor L. Babco, *Professional Women and Minorities.* Washington, D.C.: Commission on Professionals in Science and Technology, February 1986.

Women who are intellectually or politically brilliant are more readily accepted by men if they are also properly feminine in their style and deportment with men. This helps to assure that there will be few women of achievement for men to "exempt" from the general category of women, since the traits associated with traditional femininity — softness, compliance, sweetness — are rarely found together with the contradictory qualities of a vigorous and questioning intellect, and a willingness to persist on a problem against conventional assumptions. (p. 36)

The isolation women encounter in academic life (as well as other work organizations) creates a feeling of standing out — if only by reason of their differences (Epstein 1970; Kanter 1977). Moreover, women will probably find that, in their professions, their experience is translated into the concepts and categories that have been used to describe male experience. And as women begin to rethink the character of scholarship in their disciplines, they are frequently charged with being trivial, insignificant, or simply "into that women's stuff"!

For students, the secondary status of women in education can also seriously affect their learning. Sexist attitudes about women students can discourage them from classroom participation or may even steer them away from particular courses and departments. Professors who fill their classes with sexist, racist, or homophobic comments can fill students with such anger that it is impossible for them to learn in that environment. Male students, too, are affected by a sexist environment because such an environment makes it difficult for men to see women as full peers and hampers men's ability to relate to women as equals in the worlds of work and families. And for men with negative views about women, negative attitudes about women and sexist behavior in the classroom reinforce these views because they are confirmed by people with knowledge and high status (Hall 1982).

Women as "Outsiders"

The personal consequences of women's status in academia are troubling and, no doubt, result in the demise of many women's careers. But women's status in the academic disciplines has also influenced what is known about them. Male domination of academic institutions influences the social production of knowledge because the existing schemes of understanding have been created within a particular setting, one in which men have authority over women. In sociology, for example, "how sociology is thought — its methods, conceptual schemes and theories have been based on and built up within the male social universe — even when women have participated in its doing" (Smith 1974:7). Because the male-constituted world stands in authority over women (both inside and outside the academy), sociologists "impose the concepts and terms in which the world of men is thought as the concepts and terms in which women must think about their world" (Smith 1974:7). Women then become outsiders, not only because their status in universities is less than that of men, but also because they are estranged from the dominant world view surrounding them in academic life.

Sociological theory provides insight in understanding how the status of outsiders influences their perspectives. Georg Simmel (1858–1918) describes a stranger as one who is "fixed within a particular spatial group whose boundaries are similar to spatial boundaries. But his [sic] position in this group is determined, essentially, by the fact that he has not belonged to it from the beginning, that he imports qualities into it which do not and cannot stem from the group itself" (1950:402). Thus, the stranger (or the outsider) is both close to and distant from the group and its beliefs. The outsider is both involved with and indifferent to the shared perspectives of the group as a whole. This detachment creates critical distance, so that what is taken for granted by group members may be held in doubt by outsiders. As feminists have put it, "the outsider is denied the filtered vision that allows men to live without too troubling an insight" (Gornick 1971:126).

Feminist criticism of the social sciences also describes the vision that women as outsiders bring to intellectual life. The feminist sociologist Marcia Westkott writes:

> When women realize that we are simultaneously immersed in and estranged from both our own particular discipline and the Western intellectual tradition generally, a personal tension develops that informs the critical dialogue. This tension, rooted in the contradiction of women's belonging and not

belonging, provides the basis for knowing deeply and personally that which we criticize. A personally experienced, culturally-based contradiction means that in some fundamental way we as critics also oppose ourselves, or, at least, that part of us continues to sustain the very basis of our own estrangement. Hence, the personal struggle of being both an insider and outsider is not only a source of knowledge and insight, but also a source of self-criticism. (1979:422)

In the history of sociological thought, marginality and alienation, especially during periods of rapid social change, have produced many valuable insights (Nisbet 1970). Scientific thinking, including sociological thinking, has flourished in periods of uncertainty because doubt and transformation foster the development of personal and collective creative thought. As C. Wright Mills suggests, personal and societal troubles that destroy the façades of conventional wisdom also form the scientific basis of the sociological and feminist imagination.

For outsiders, their paradoxical closeness to and remoteness from social groups may result in new perspectives on knowledge. It is the outsider who suspends belief in the taken-for-granted attitudes of institutions. As a result, the status of women as outsiders in intellectual life results in new methodologies and new perspectives in social and political thought.

Because of the influence of the feminist movement, women who entered the academic world in the 1970s did so while they were self-conscious of their status as women. As these women saw that gender influenced all aspects of their lives, they also began to recognize the gender bias inherent within the scholarship of traditional academic fields. Consequently, work by feminist scholars provides an ongoing critique of the distortions that the exclusion of women has created in academic knowledge.

The Sociology of Knowledge _____

The preceding discussion of ideas about women, as they are shaped by mass media and educational institutions, underscores three essential sociological points: that knowledge in society is socially constructed, that knowledge emerges from the conditions of people's lives, and that knowledge is ideological — that is, it justifies the conditions under which we live. We explore these points in more detail below, but they are essential to understanding how the construction of new knowledge about women and gender is an essential part of the process of transforming society and women's and men's place within it.

In sociology, the study of the social construction of ideas is called the sociology of knowledge. The sociology of knowledge begins with the premise that ideas emerge from particular social and historical settings and that this social structural context shapes, although it does not determine, human consciousness and interpretations of reality. Studies in the sociology of knowledge relate ideas and consciousness to social structure and human culture. Intellectually, this perspective originates primarily in the works of Karl Marx and Karl Mannheim, both of whom, in distinct ways, grappled with the relationship between human knowledge and human existence. It was Mannheim who, in the early twentieth century, labeled the study of the sociology of knowledge and delineated its specific program; but Marx's study of ideology and consciousness is the intellectual precursor of this endeavor. We first consider Marx's ideas about the social construction of knowledge, following it with a discussion of Mannheim.

Marx and the Social Construction of Knowledge

Marx began his study of human ideas with the premise that the existence of living human beings, that is, their actual activities and material conditions, forms the basis for human history and the ideas generated in this history. Although Marx recognizes that human beings live within particular physical settings (including climatic, geographical, and geological conditions), it is the social relationships formed in these settings that make up human society. In other words, human beings transform their environmental conditions through the activities in which they engage. Human society and history emerge as people use their labor to create their social environment. Marx argues that human beings are distinguished from animals by the fact of their consciousness. Although we now know that other animal species have linguistic ability and rudimentary systems of social organization, no other species has the capacity of humans for the elaboration of culture.

Marx's theory of ideas originates with his argument that ideas follow from human behavior. In other words, thinking and the products of thinking are derived from the actual activity in which human beings engage. Marx discards the philosophical view that what humans think, imagine, or conceive precedes their actual life experiences. Thus, within Marx's framework, it is not the consciousness of persons that forms the bonds (and chains) of human society. Rather, specific relationships among people shape human society and, therefore, the ideas of its people.

Marx is not denying that social relations involve an interpretive dimension. He is arguing, however, that ideas emerge from our material reality. This theory has important consequences for social change, for it implies that changes in consciousness alone do not constitute the social changes necessary for the liberation of people. Instead, it is the material conditions of society that must be changed if we are to liberate people from oppression.

Marx goes one step further by arguing that within society, the dominant ideas of any period are the ideas of the ruling class. It is they who have the power to influence the intellectual production and distribution of ideas. Consequently, although persons ordinarily form their ideas within the context of their practical experience, ideas produced within powerful institutions take on an objective form that extends beyond us and acts as a system of social control. In fact, Marx goes on to say that in societies with a complex division of labor, a split develops between mental and material labor. Those who work with their hands are not those who produce the society's dominant ideas. Thus, especially for persons who are not in the ruling class the dominant ideas of a society stand in contradiction to their experience.

A Marxist perspective relates ideas directly to the societal conditions in which they are produced. This view is summed up by Marx's statement that "it is not the consciousness of men that determines their being, but, on the contrary, their social being that determines their consciousness" (Tucker 1972:4). In capitalist societies, those who own the means of production also determine the ruling ideas of the period. As Marx wrote,

> The ideas of the ruling class are in every epoch the ruling ideas: i.e., the class which is the ruling material force of society, is at the same time its ruling intellectual force. The class which has the means of material production at is disposal, has control at the same time over the means of mental production, so that thereby, generally speaking, the ideas of those who lack the means of mental production are subject to it." (*The German Ideology,* in Tucker 1972:136)

From a Marxist perspective, under capitalism consciousness is determined by class relations, for even though persons will normally try to identify what is in their best interest, under capitalism the ruling class controls the production of ideas. Also, even though humans create practical ideas from experience, most of our experience is determined by capitalist relations of production. Thus, the ideas that are disseminated through communications systems, including language, serve to authorize a reality that the ruling class would like us to believe. Furthermore, according to Marx, when subordinate groups accept the world view of dominant groups, they are engaged in "false consciousness."

Marx's ideas have been modifed by feminist scholars who see class relations alone as inadequate in explaining the evolution and persistence of sexism. Feminists add to Marx's perspective on the social construction of ideas that it is men who own the means of production and, therefore, determine the ruling ideas of any given time. Sexist ideas justify the power of men over women and sanction male domination. From a feminist perspective, ideas serve not only capitalist interests, but also men's interests. Moreover, men's ideas stem from their particular relationship to the gender division of labor, as explained by Canadian scholar Dorothy Smith.

According to Smith (1975), in patriarchal societies there is a gender-based division of labor in which men typically do not do the work that meets the physical and emotional needs of society's members. As a result, men's ideas (especially of those who engage primarily in intellectual work) assume a split, or bifurcation, between mind and body, and rational thought is accorded the highest value. But this belief in the bifurcation of mind and body is made possible only because the labor of women provides for men's physical needs, mediates their social relations, and allows them to ignore bodily and emotional experience as an integral dimension of life.

Sexism as Ideology

Karl Mannheim (1893–1947) further developed the sociology of knowledge. Mannheim's sociology of knowledge seeks to discover the historical circumstances of knowledge by relating ideas to the conditions under which they are produced. His work also provides a foundation for feminist scholarship because he develops the thought that ideas grow out of the relationship of knowledge to social structure.

Feminists (as we discussed in Chapter 1 and further elaborate in this chapter) suggest that what has been taken as knowledge reflects the system of male domination in which it is produced. This insight stems from the work of Mannheim, who relates what is known to the social existence of the knower. Mannheim and feminist scholars who have followed him challenge the idea that objectivity is based on the detachment of the knower from the surrounding environment. Instead, Mannheim suggests that the individual does not think alone. Not only do persons participate in what others have thought prior to the individual's existence, but even more fundamentally, all social thought involves a "community of knowing" (1936:31). Ideas expressed by a person are, therefore, a function of the person's experience as well as his or her social and historical milieu.

The task of the sociology of knowledge is to discover the relational character of thought, meaning to study how ideas are embedded in the social experience of their producers and the social-historical milieu within which ideas are formed. Intellectual change must likewise be seen in the context of social change, and all ideas must be evaluated within the context of their social making. This view is true not only for the grand ideas of intellectual history, but also for the consciousness of human beings in their ordinary experience (Berger and Luckmann 1966).

Mannheim suggests that new ideas are most likely generated during periods of rapid social change. He explains this belief by suggesting that as long as group traditions remain stable, then traditional world views remain intact. New ideas appear when old traditions are breaking up, although the persistence of customary ways of thinking is also likely to make new ideas appear to be "curiosities, errors, ambiguities, or heresies" (1936:7).

Mannheim is best known for his study of ideology. *Ideology* refers to a system of beliefs about the world that involve distortions of reality at the same time that they provide justification for the status quo. Following from Marx, Mannheim sees ideology as serving the interests of groups in the society who justify their position by distorting social definitions of reality. Ideologies serve the powerful by presenting us with a definition of reality that is false and yet orders our comprehension of the surrounding world. When ideas emerge from ideology, they operate as a form of social control by defining the status quo to be the proper state of affairs.

From Mannheim's work, we can understand sexism as an ideology that defends the traditional status of women in society. Although, as Mannheim says, no single idea constitutes an ideological belief system, the collective totality of an ideology (such as sexism) permeates our consciousness and our comprehension of the world in which we live. It is here that the sociology of knowledge merges with the political goals of feminism because in debunking sexist ideology, the social-historical origins of sexist thought are found and new definitions of reality can be forged. Although Mannheim is careful to distinguish political argument from academic thought, he recognizes that the unmasking of ideological systems is a function of sociological theory. Thus, politics and theory are interconnected (although not identical) because both recognize the relatedness of ideas to social structure.

For feminists, the sociology of knowledge creates the theoretical framework in which sexism and the generation of ideas about women can be understood. The theoretical perspectives of both Marx and Mannheim underlie the analysis of sexism and knowledge that feminists have offered. Understanding the perspective of the sociology of knowledge helps us make sense of the images of women in the media, the gender bias of academic studies, and the patriarchal structure of popular culture. The perspective of the sociology of knowledge helps us understand how ideas reproduce our definitions of social reality, who produces ideas, under what conditions ideas are made, and the consequences of ideas and beliefs that, in the case of sexism, systematically define women and men in stereotypical and distorted terms.

Summary ———————————————————————————

Images of women in both popular and academic culture have historically rested on distortions and the exclusion of women and their experiences. Though distorted and false, these images deeply influence our understandings of ourselves and the society we live in. Theoretical perspectives on the sociology of knowledge explain how such distorted images emerge in particular social and historical settings and reveal how they shape our intepretations of reality. Feminist scholars also argue that negative images of women are a function of male domination in that they try to legitimate women's status in society.

The development of the women's movement negates these images by teaching us to recognize their distorted content and helping us imagine ways of constructing knowledge about women and men in society and culture that are not bound by sexist assumptions. In subsequent chapters we review research and theory that have reshaped our understandings of gender relations and the status of women in society.

CHAPTER 3

Sex, Biology, and Culture

Introduction

In her book *Myths of Gender,* biologist Anne Fausto-Sterling describes a day when a friend of hers, a math professor, called for her professional advice:

> A few few years ago, a friend phoned me for some advice. His ten-year-old daughter was upset because she had just heard on the radio about the hot new discovery that boys are genetically better at math than are girls. Girls, she had heard, would be less frustrated if they recognized their limits and stopped their fruitless struggle to exceed them. "Daddy," she had said, "I always wanted to be a math professor like you. Does this mean I can't?" My friend wanted to know if I had read the article. "Is it true? What can I tell my daughter?" (1985:53–54)

Fausto-Sterling goes on to describe the events leading up to this phone call. A study published in *Science* magazine claiming that boys had superior math ability to girls had been seized by the national press. *The New York Times, Time,* and *Newsweek* all carried highlights of the study; some magazines even featured the study in their advertising campaigns. The message was clear: New evidence about "male math genes" (*Time* 1980:57, *Newsweek* 1980:73, cited in Fausto-Sterling 1985:54) meant that girls had inferior skills in math and, furthermore, that their genes doomed them not to succeed in math at the same rate as boys. Fausto-Sterling describes one cartoon used by *Time* to illustrate the study's results:

> The cartoon portrayed a girl and a boy standing in front of a blackboard, with a proud, smug-looking adult — presumably a teacher — looking on. The girl frowns in puzzlement as she looks directly at the reader. On the blackboard in front of her stands the multiplication problem 8×7, which she is clearly unable to solve. The boy looks with a toothy smile toward the adult, who gazes back at him. The cause for the satisfaction? The correct answer to the multiplication problem $7,683 \times 632$. (1985:54)

Aside from the embellishments of the media, the results of this study indicate that, based on a sample of seventh and eighth graders who were exceptionally talented at math, girls scored 7 – 15 percent lower than boys on College Board Scholastic Aptitude Tests (SATs) in mathematics. The researchers concluded that this could not be based on differences in the number of math courses taken, since at this age girls and boys have had the same math courses. Furthermore, they claimed that cultural expectations about boys' and girls' performance in math could not explain this sex difference, although they did not directly test this assumption or their other conclusion that there is some endogenous basis for male mathematical ability (Benbow and Stanley 1980; Fausto-Sterling 1985).

This study has been heavily criticized by other scientists working on this same topic. Critics have questioned the validity of using the SATs as the sole measurement of mathematical aptitude and of restricting the meaning of "mathematical ability" only to formal mathematical experience. Furthermore, investigators have also argued that although boys and girls may have had the same math courses, they have not necessarily received the same training. As we can see in the next chapter, a wealth of other research specifically contradicts the conclusions of this study. Then why was this study so popularized?

Scientific studies purporting to have found a genetic basis for differences between the sexes frequently appear in the popular and scientific press. Moreover, "it is a disturbing fact about the public presentation of scientific results that a theory's success in garnering media attention and in influencing popular perceptions may have little to do with the validity of its arguments or evidence" (Fee 1986:9). Citing one new study after another, the media often exclaim to the public that, once again, scientific proof of women's biological inferiority has been found. Like the old belief that anatomy is destiny, these claims continue to insist that there is a biological basis for women's status in society and that psychological and social differences between the sexes can be attributed to biological causes.

Feminists begin with the opposite claim — that women's status in society is socially, not biologically, rooted. Because of this fact, feminists see the status of women as subject to change. On the other hand, conservatives who argue that women's status is based in their biological make-up tend to see women's status as natural and inevitable (Jaggar and Struhl 1978). If this were true, attempts to change women's status would be fruitless. In fact, conservatives who hold such beliefs typically wish to maintain a traditional division of labor between the sexes, with women in the home and men in the workplace.

In the face of such diverse claims, the relationship between biology and culture is central to any discussion of the relations between the sexes. What is the evidence for a biological basis of human sex differences and how can we evaluate claims like those made in the study mentioned above? Is there scientific evidence for sex differences and, if so, what is the nature of the evidence?

Answers to these questions require the careful attention of scientists who approach the study of sex and biology with care and circumspection. But, in addition to biological questions, there are sociological questions to be asked. Why are studies purporting to have found a biological basis for sex differences so often spotlighted by the press, when scientific studies negating such claims are seldom, if ever, given such enthusiastic reception? When differences are found, why are they so typically interpreted as deficits on the part of women? How do the assumptions of researchers filter what they observe in scientific research? And how does the overly masculine composition of science influence scientific study?

This chapter shows that human biology and culture are intricately intertwined. Science itself is produced under sexist conditions, thereby reproducing assumptions and conclusions that can seriously distort scientific descriptions and explanations. We begin in this chapter by looking at the biological formation of sex.

Biology, Sex, and Gender

Sexual Differentiation

Sociologists use the concept of gender to refer to socially learned behaviors and expectations that are associated with members of a biological sex category. Gender is an acquired identity; biological sex usually is not. One's *biological sex* refers to genetic and physical sexual identity. The biological sex of a person is established at the moment of conception and is elaborated during the period of fetal development in the womb. During conception, each parent contributes 23 chromosomes to the fertilized egg, for a total of 46 (or 23 chomosomal pairs). One of these pairs determines the sex of the offspring; these are called the *sex chromosomes*. Under normal conditions, the sex chromosomes consist of an X from the mother's egg and an

X or a Y from the father's sperm. The 23 paternal chromosomes (including the X or Y sex chromosome) are selected randomly when the sperm is formed (Hoyenga and Hoyenga 1979). Genetically, normal girls have a pair of X chromosomes (designated 46, XX) and normal boys have the chromosomal pair XY (designated 46, XY). Because the sex chromosome from the ovum is always an X, the chromosome carried by the father's sperm (either an X or a Y) determines the sex of the child. Despite popular belief, there is no evidence that Y chromosomes are stronger than Xs. In fact, the XY male chromosome pair forms a link that is less viable in genetic coding than is the XX female pair. This fact accounts, in part, for the greater vulnerability of male fetuses in the womb and may contribute to higher prenatal and early childhood mortality rates for males (Harrison 1978).

Following fertilization of the egg, a complex process of fetal sex differentiation begins. Prior to the sixth week of development, the XX and XY embryos are identical; the external genitalia of the embryo remain identical until the eighth week of development. But scientific reports of the process of sexual differentiation of the fetus have been clouded by pervasive images of the passivity of females. Consequently, the process of sexual differentiation has routinely been reported in scientific work as determined primarily by the presence or absence of the Y chromosome, leaving the impression that females develop as incomplete or deficient males.

In fact, during the sixth week of fetal development, the Y chromosome stimulates the production of proteins that assist in the development of fetal gonads (Hoyenga and Hoyenga 1979; Lambert 1978). But sexual differentiation also involves complex genetic messages encoded on the Y chromosome, the X chromosome, and the nonsex chromosomes. Therefore, the Y chromosome, though involved in the process, is not solely responsible for the process of sexual differentiation. Moreover, recent research suggests that the XX gonad may synthesize large amounts of estrogen at about the same time that the XY gonad begins synthesizing testosterone, making it appear that ovarian hormones are just as involved in the development of female genitalia as androgens are involved in the development of male genitalia (Fausto-Sterling 1985).

Ambiguous Sexual Identities

Under normal circumstances, the process of fetal sexual differentiation results in unambiguous sex characteristics. However, cases of chromosomal abnormalities do sometimes occur that result in biologically mixed or incomplete sex characteristics. Studies of such cases reveal the complex relationship between biological sex and the social definition of *masculine* and *feminine*.

Two such conditions, Turner's syndrome and Klinefelter's syndrome, result from sex chromosomal abnormalities. Turner's syndrome is a condition occurring when the fetus has only one X (and no Y) chromosome present. Physically, the child is female in appearance, although she is genetically incomplete. Typically, Turner's syndrome individuals have the physical abnormalities of shortness (four to five feet tall); malformation of the nails, feet, and fingers; and cardiac difficulties. Although Turner's syndrome females are typically infertile, researchers have reported that their social behavior displays exaggerated feminine traits compared with that of other girls matched for age, IQ, race, and socioeconomic background (Money and Ehrhardt 1972). Turner's females show greater interest in feminine dress, have stronger preferences for dolls, and daydream more about marriage and motherhood. The appearance of these socially feminine traits among genetically incomplete females indicates that complete genetic status as a female is not necessary to produce socially feminine results (Hoyenga and Hoyenga 1979).

In another chromosomal abnormality, Klinefelter's syndrome, persons may be born with extra X chromosomes (47, XXY or 48, XXXY). Genetically, they have both the male (XY) and female (XX) chromosomal patterns and thus have ambiguous sex characteristics. Klinefelter's individuals are male in external appearance, although they show low levels of testosterone, the male sex hormone. Typically, they show breast enlargement and have small penises. Although they appear to be men, Klinefelter's individuals are frequently confused about their gender identity. Klinefelter's syndrome has often been associated with mental retardation (Hoyenga and Hoyenga 1979), although patterns of intelligence do vary among these individuals, with some showing very high IQs. Researchers have concluded that it is unclear to what extent the behavioral effects of Klinefelter's syndrome are caused by genetic problems, by abnormalities in brain activity, and by societal reactions to persons exhibiting the physical appearance of the syndrome (Hoyenga and Hoyenga 1979).

Hermaphroditism is "a condition of prenatal origin in which embryonic and/or fetal differentiation of the reproductive system fails to reach completion as either entirely female or entirely male" (Money and Ehrhardt 1972:5). Normally, during fetal development, fetal gonads would produce sex hormones that, in turn, produce the internal and external sex organs (Hoyenga and Hoyenga 1979; Lambert 1978). In cases of hermaphroditism, babies are born with their sexual anatomy improperly differentiated; thus, they may be born with both testes and ovaries or will appear ambiguous or incomplete.

Such cases add an important dimension to discussing the relationship among genetic sex, biological appearance, and sex of rearing. True hermaphrodites typically possess the chromosomal patterns characteristic of normal females or normal males. For example, a genetic female who is prenatally androgenized may be born looking like a boy, that is, with a penis (though sometimes incomplete), and no clitoris. Or a genetic male may be born with the genital appearance of a normal female. Other cases of hermaphroditism may involve mixed genital appearance. Since we typically assign sex according to the appearance of the external genitalia at birth, cases of hermaphroditism allow us to look carefully at the role of biology and culture in the development of gender identity.

Money and Ehrhardt's studies of hermaphroditism and other cases of sex reassignment reveal the complex interaction of genetic, biological, and cultural factors in the development of a social gender identity. In one case a genetic male was born with a tiny penis (one centimeter long) and no urinary canal. At age 17 months, the child was reclassified as a girl. She was given a new name, hairdo, and clothing. Shortly after the sex reassignment, the parents noticed a change in the older brother's treatment of her. Before the sex reassignment, he had treated his "brother" roughly; now he was very protective and gentle toward his new "sister." By age 3, the daughter had developed clearly feminine interests. "For Christmas, she wanted glass slippers, so that she could go to the ball like Cinderella, and a doll. The parents were delighted. The girl continued to receive typically girlish toys from her parents. She continued more and more to show feminine interests, as in helping her mother" (Money and Ehrhardt 1972:125).

And, in a different case not involving hermaphroditism, a normal male identical twin at the age of 7 months had his penis burned off by a too-powerful electrical current during a routine circumcision. The entire tissue of the penis died and sloughed off; the parents were advised to change the sex of their child to female. At age 17 months the sex transformation was begun, and the child was given a new name, hairstyle, and clothing; at 21 months reconstruction of the genitals was surgically initiated, to be followed by vaginoplasty (construction of the vagina) when the body was full-grown. Meanwhile, the child's pubertal growth and feminization were regulated by estrogen therapy. In this case, the genetic sex of the child remained intact (XY = male), even though her physical sex was indistinguishable from that of genetic females. The researchers in this case point out that social transformations in gender identity are a necessary part of the process of sex reassignment. The child's parents were carefully advised on her social development, and the researchers observed their socialization practices. They dressed the child in pink, frilly, feminine clothes, and her mother encouraged her to be tidy.

One incident aptly shows how different the parents' social expectations are for their genetically identical but now differently gendered children. The mother reports of her son, "One time I caught him — he went out and he took a leak in my flower garden in the front yard, you know. He was quite happy with himself. And I just didn't do anything. I just couldn't. I started laughing and told Daddy about it." About the daughter, she said, "I've never had a problem with her. She did once when she was little, she took off her panties and threw them over the fence. And she didn't have no panties on. But I just, I gave her a little swat on the rear, and I told her that nice little girls didn't do that, and she should keep her panties on. . . . And she didn't take them off after that" (Money and Ehrhardt 1972:120). It is little wonder that, as the mother put it, "one thing that really amazes me is that she is so feminine" (Money and Ehrhardt 1972:119).

These studies demonstrate that biological sex alone does not determine gender identity. In fact, one's social gender can be different from one's genetic sex. Although statistically very few individuals are born with these abnormalities, the cases in which they do occur reveal much about the normal evolution of gender identity. Research shows that sex of rearing is the key factor in determining gender identity even though prenatal hormones can have some effect on behavior (Money & Ehrhardt 1972). Money and Ehrhardt's research clearly shows that something as complex as the formation of gender identity cannot be reduced to biological categories alone. Their research reveals the power of social learning, not only in unusual situations of ambiguous biological identity, but also in cases of normal gender development.

Sex Differences: Nature or Nurture?

Controversies about the relative effects of nature versus nurture on human social behavior have been plentiful in the scientific and social-scientific literature for years. Though the nature/nurture debate has been posed as an either/or question, it is reasonable to conclude that individual and group characteristics emerge from the complex interdependence of biological factors and social systems. Indeed, any given behavior — including those seeming to be mostly biological events, like body size and strength, hormone levels, and brain development — can be changed considerably through environmental influences (Lowe 1983). Moreover, all behavior has multiple causes; as a result, searching for a single determinant of behavior is likely to lead to questionable scientific results (Fausto-Sterling 1985; Lowe 1983).

Body size provides a good example. Although men are, on the average, larger than women, body size is known to be influenced by diet and physical activity. These factors in turn may be influenced by culture, as well as by social class, race, and gender. Explanations of sex differences that ignore these factors distort our understanding of the nature of those differences that are observed between the sexes.

Genes, Gender, and Sexual Dimorphism

Beginning with genetic structure, human life involves the interplay of biology and culture. Geneticists distinguish between *single-gene traits* (those controlled by a single gene) and *polygenic traits* (those controlled by multiple genes). Single-gene traits include characteristics such as blood type and albinism; they are known to be discontinuous traits. In other words, single-gene traits vary qualitatively from each other; polygenic traits (such as height, hair color, skin pigment, and sex) show continuous and quantitative variation. Polygenic traits occur along a continuum, and thus vary in degree but not kind. Furthermore, polygenic traits are known to interact with the environment in which they exist.

Consequently, even those traits that might be said to have a genetic basis cannot simply be described as genetically caused. In fact, scientists have pointed out that the exercise of trying to separate the influence of genetic and environmental factors is only conceptual since, in the actual development of human beings, the separation of the two never really occurs (Wittig 1979).

Geneticists use the term *genotype* to refer to inherited genetic characteristics; the *phenotype* is the observed expression of the genes as they interact with each other and with the environment in which they appear. This is no simple process, though popular conceptions of genes imagine them as mechanical things that exert a direct influence on human behavior. The expression of genetic codes is, in fact, a complex process, involving the molecular structure of DNA and protein synthesis (Fausto-Sterling 1985). Even the most simple traits involve complex processes of genetic expression. Explaining these traits requires an elaborate and multidimensional analysis. Simple assertions claiming a direct association between genetic structure and social behavior do not match the intricacy of this process.

Sex differences that do appear between males and females are known as *sexually dimorphic traits*. Sexually dimorphic traits include physical as well as social and cultural differences; they are traits that occur in different frequencies among male and female populations. For example, color blindness is a sexually dimorphic trait that is found more often in men than in women. But most sexually dimorphic traits are distributed widely throughout both male and female populations. They are dimorphic usually because there is a significant difference in their distribution between the two populations, not usually because a sexually dimorphic trait appears only in one sex.

Statistical measures of the variation of a trait within a given population represent the degree to which the population deviates from the typical case. Most sex differences are distributed widely throughout the population, leaving a wide range of variation on any given trait appearing among men or among women. Body weight provides a good example. On the average, men weigh more than women, but weight differences among women and among men far exceed the average weight difference between men and women as populations. Moreover, a sex difference may be found when comparing male and female populations as a whole, but it may not be found when comparing any given male-female pair.

The point is that the variability within gender is usually larger than the mean difference between genders. Sexually dimorphic traits are so labeled because they are found in different frequencies in men and women. For any given trait, there may be a substantial degree of overlap between the two populations. Usually, sexually dimorphic traits represent quantitative, not qualitative, differences between the sexes.

Research has found very few consistent sex differences, although discussions of male-female traits almost always emphasize traits that are different instead of similar in men and women. Simply put, the vast majority of human traits are shared by both men and women. Because knowing a person's biological sex does not even provide a very accurate prediction of his or her physical characteristics, we have to wonder why biological differences are so often claimed as explaining inequality between the sexes (Lambert 1978; Reid 1975).

Biological Reductionism

Although there may be a general biological basis for human societies, human biology sets extremely broad limits for behavior. Most of us vastly underuse our biological capacities, including both motor skills and cognitive ability. Yet differences between the sexes have often been attributed to their biological origins, thereby giving the impression that nature is more significant than nurture in determining our social identities and social positions. An argument that reduces a complex event or process (such as social identity) to a single monolithic cause (such as the form of one's genitals) is called a *reductionist argument*. A related form of argument is known as *determinism*. Determinist arguments are those that assume that a given condition (such as the presence of a penis) inevitably determines a particular event (such as male aggression). Arguments about the biological inferiority of women are usually both reductionist and determinist in that they explain sex differences in the social world as the natural and inevitable consequence of the singular fact of women's biological nature.

Determinist and reductionist arguments are closely related and can be made in any number of forms, including psychological, economic, and cultural contexts. But biological determinism and reductionism have been especially rampant in the discussion of sex differences, and they have been the basis for conservative views about the proper role for women in society. Consider, for example, the following argument taken from Steven Goldberg's book, *The Inevitability of Patriarchy:*

> We are assuming . . . that there are no differences between men and women except in the hormonal system that renders the man more aggressive. This alone would explain patriarchy, male dominance, and male attainment of high-status roles, for the male hormonal system gives an insuperable "head start" toward attaining those roles which any society associates with leadership or high status as long as the roles are not ones which males are biologically incapable of filling. . . . One need merely consider the result of a society's not socializing women away from competitions with men, from its not directing girls toward roles women are more capable of playing than are men. . . . No doubt some women would be aggressive enough to succeed in competitions with men and there would be considerably more women in high-status positions than there are now. But most women would lose in such competitive struggles with men (because men have the aggression advantage) and so most women would be forced to live in adult lives as failures in areas in which the society had wanted them to succeed. (1974:104–107)

Goldberg's book is a good example (although a bad piece of scholarship) of biological reductionism and determinism, and his argument that anatomy is destiny is a familiar one. He makes several assumptions pertinent to a discussion of sex differences, all of which need close examination.

First, his argument is determinist because he sees biological differences alone as explaining the complex systems of patriarchy, male dominance, and male attainment — systems that feminists would say involve a wide array of social, psychological, historical, economic, and political as well as cultural factors. Second, Goldberg seems to assume that patriarchy is compatible with the biological needs of all men, and yet, clearly, not all men are equally aggressive, nor do they participate equally in patriarchal systems of power. His argument leaves him with no explanation of race and class inequality (even among men) except to rely on biological claims alleging the innate inferiority of racial groups and lower social classes. We can see from this example how racism and sexism each rest on faulty biological claims. And, third, Goldberg assumes that aggressive differences between men and women are universal — a fact that simply does not stand up to the cross-cultural evidence (Mead 1949).

But because it is a common argument, let us examine Goldberg's fundamental premise that hormonal differences are the basis for different levels of aggression between men and women. Many biologists have studied the association between the hormone testosterone and aggressive behavior, and their conclusions reveal important issues in the association between biological factors and social behavior.

Hormones and Aggression

To begin with, both males and females have measurable quantities of the three major sex hormones — estrogen, progestin, and testosterone. Hormonal sex differences are caused by differences in the levels of production and concentration of each, not in their presence or absence per se. The greater production of testosterone in males is due to stimulation by the testes, whereas in females the ovaries secrete additional estrogens and progestins. Before puberty, however, there are few or no sex differences in the quantity of sex hormones in each sex; at this time, all of the sex hormones are at very low levels. If high levels of testosterone were needed to produce aggression, then we would expect to see little difference in aggressive behavior between prepubescent boys and girls. However, much research shows that boys are more aggressive at an early age, thereby contradicting the implications of biologically determinist arguments.

Similarly, following menopause, women actually have lower levels of estradol (the major estrogen) and progesterone (the major progestin) than do men of the same age (Hawkins and Oakey 1974; Hoyenga and Hoyenga 1979; Tea et al. 1975). Because there is no empirical evidence that older men are more feminine than older women, we must doubt the conclusion that hormonal differences explain differences in the behavior of the sexes.

Research on human males shows that changes in testosterone levels do not consistently predict changes in aggressive behavior (Hoyenga and Hoyenga 1979). Studies of chemical "castration" show that the procedure is not very effective in reducing violent or aggressive behavior in men; similarly, studies of castrated rhesus monkeys show no straightforward relationship between castration and the lessening of aggression (Fausto-Sterling 1985).

Some studies find small correlations between the level of testosterone and aggressive behavior, but correlations show only association, not cause. Although there may be a slight tendency for aggression and testosterone to vary together, "this does not mean that testosterone caused aggression or dominance; the reverse could just as well be true" (Hoyenga and Hoyenga 1979:139). In fact, much of the research on hormones and aggression shows that experiential factors (such as stress, fatigue, or fear) may have a greater effect on hormonal production than hormones have on behavior (Hoyenga and Hoyenga 1979).

A recent study of testosterone levels found among different occupational groups of women workers provides a case in point. The study found somewhat higher levels of testosterone among students and professional and managerial women than among women clerical and service workers and housewives (Purifoy and Koopmans 1980). While at first glance this may make it seem that "male hormones" encourage women to move into "male" occupations, the researchers found support for a very different conclusion. Because stress is known to lower testosterone levels, the greater stress experienced by clerical and service workers and housewives resulted in a lowering of their testosterone levels compared with other women in the sample (Fausto-Sterling 1985; Purifoy and Koopmans 1980).

In sum, reductionist arguments do not account for the complexities of patterns of human aggression or for the wide variation in patterns of aggression among and between men and women. No single hormonal state is a good predictor of any form of social behavior. Studies of the relationship between hormones and aggression typically confuse biological and social facts anyhow, because measuring and defining aggression is itself a matter of interpretation.

The Interplay of Biology and Culture

Biologically reductionist arguments rest on the assumption that differences between the sexes are "natural;" yet, in fact, it is quite difficult, if not impossible, to distinguish so-called natural and social events. Cultural attitudes influence what we think of as natural, since what is deemed natural is typically only that which we believe is unchangeable. Biology itself is neither fixed nor immutable, since biological processes themselves can be modified through cultural conditions (Lowe 1983).

Because the biological and social worlds so overlap, even events that we think of as physiological processes — such as aging, illness, and reproduction — are heavily influenced by the social–cultural systems in which they occur. This fact has particular significance for feminist studies because it demonstrates the inadequacies of explanations of sex differences that rest upon biological explanations alone.

Aging and Menopause

Consider, for example, the biological process of aging — clearly one that is universal, inevitable, and based on human physiology. Research shows that how long one lives is strongly influenced by one's gender. Life expectancy is shorter for men (71.0 years in 1984) than for women (78.3 years), and males have higher accidental death rates (in both childhood and adulthood) than do females. Men also have higher suicide and homicide rates than do women (Hess and Markson 1980). Some research has shown that men with personalities marked by ambition, single-mindedness, and devotion to work are more prone to heart attacks than others (Friedman and Rosenman 1974). In fact, the risks associated with traditionally masculine roles are so great that one psychologist has called masculinity a "lethal role" (Jourard 1974).

But even the physiological changes associated with aging are greatly affected by the social context in which aging occurs. Nutrition, for example, affects the biological health of aging persons, but social factors such as living alone or in an institution are known to affect dietary habits, as are factors such as income, cultural preferences for food, and exercise. Aging is also aggravated by stress — a condition generated by a variety of social and psychological difficulties.

For women, the aging process has its own strains. In a society in which women are valued for their youth and beauty, aging becomes a difficult social and psychological experience. Birthday cards that joke about women deteriorating after age 29 and commercials for creams that "hide your aging spots" tell American women that they should be ashamed of growing old. It should be no surprise, then, that a biological process such as menopause can become a difficult psychological experience. Research shows that menopause produces more anxiety and more depression in cultures that are less supportive of women as they age (Bart 1979; Clay 1977; Hess and Markson 1980; Reitz 1977).

Cultural beliefs about biological events imbue them with significance and a character different from that produced by the physiology alone. In the case of menopause, the scientific and popular literature is replete with the metaphor of menopause as a disease — a fact that has severely biased both the scientific and popular understanding of menopause.

New research on menopause finds that the social context in which middle-aged women live, including their life histories and family relationships, is a more important predictor of emotional response to menopause than are the actual hormonal changes associated with menopause. In fact, most women do not report menopause as a time of crisis, and there is no research to support the usually assumed association between menopause and serious depression (Fausto-Sterling 1985). Postmenopausal women who do experience psychosis are women who have had a prior history of psychotic episodes (Winokur and Cadoret 1975), a finding that suggests that depression and mental illness among menopausal women are a function of other factors in their experience, not menopause per se.

The most current research on menopausal women, conducted by researchers who do not see menopause as a set of disease symptoms, finds that menopausal women report no greater frequency of physical symptoms or concerns about these symptoms than do pre- or postmenopausal women (Frey 1981). Moreover, these new investigations find that only 28 percent of postmenopausal Caucasian women and 24 percent of postmenopausal Japanese women report experiencing hot flashes and sweats during menopause. Restated, this means that the overwhelming majority of menopausal women reported none of the stereotypical menopausal symptoms (Fausto-Sterling 1985). Remarkably, 16 percent of the nonmenopausal Caucasian women and 10 percent of the nonmenopausal Japanese women in the study also reported these menopausal symptoms (Goodman 1980).

Menstruation

Menstruation also is a universal phenomenon, yet, like menopause, it is one that takes on different meanings in different cultures. In many cultures menstruation is symbolic of the strength of women, and elaborate rituals and rites of passage symbolize that power (Powers 1980). Yet, in other cultures, menstruation is seen as symbolic of defilement, and elaborate practices may be developed in isolate and restrict menstruating women. In the nineteenth century, for example, Southeast Asian women could not be employed in the opium industry, for it was believed that, were a menstruating woman nearby, the opium would turn bitter (Delaney, Lupton, and Toth 1976). And in contemporary American culture, menstruation is depicted as secretive and invisible, as best seen in the advertising industry, which advises menstruating women to keep their "secret" protected, yet to feel confident, secure, and free.

Like menopause, most studies of menstruation define it as a disease. Exaggeration and alarm run throughout discussions of menstruation, probably showing more our culture's fear of women's reproductive processes than a genuine understanding of the menstrual cycle. Consider, for example, the apprehension generated by the so-called dangers of premenstrual syndrome (PMS). According to news tabloids, PMS is responsible for a wide range of deviant behaviors, including insanity, murder, and other criminal acts. When scientists declare that 25–100 percent of women experience PMS, what does that mean? It may simply mean that most women recognize bodily signs of oncoming menstruation, though it is possible that a small proportion of women do find the physical changes associated with menstruation to be incapacitating (Fausto-Sterling 1985). Nevertheless, public alarm about PMS far outweighs its significance, as we have tended to assume that women, but not men, are regulated by bodily changes. Studies of PMS also poorly define and measure premenstrual symptoms (Fausto-Sterling 1985; Parlee 1973).

Self-fulfilling beliefs have a great deal to do with how menstruation is experienced by women. Studies show that most premenstrual girls and boys of the same age believe that menstruation is a physical and emotionally disruptive event. Also, 85 percent of girls believe that it is inappropriate to discuss menstruation with boys (Golub 1983). In fact, menstruation is so imbued with fear and repulsion in this culture that most boys and men probably find it discomforting to discuss or think about.

Work on menstrual moods shows, in another context, the interactive effect of culture and biological events (Rossi and Rossi 1977). The Rossi's research studies college-aged men and women who were asked to rate their daily moods over a forty-day period. Women in the sample also noted their first day of menstruation as it occured during the rating cycle. The Rossis then compared mood ratings as clocked by biological time (measured by phases in the menstrual cycle) and by calendar (or social) time. Surprisingly, the results show that men marked more days per month when they felt "achy," "crampy," and "sick" than did women. But, more to the point, the Rossis's results show that the most significant changes in moods occurred for women according to changes in the calendar week, not their menstrual cycles.

Women were more likely to feel "happy," "loving," and "healthy" on weekends and "depressed," "unhappy," and "sick" on "blue Wednesday." The research also finds no significant elevation of negative moods in the premenstrual phase for women; there was, however, an elevation of positive moods in the ovulatory phase of menstruation and an elevation of negative moods in the luteal phase (days 17–24 in a twenty-eight day menstrual cycle). But, more important than the independent effects of biological and social time, this research finds that moods (especially positive moods) were most strongly affected when biological and social cycles were synchronized (e.g., when ovulation occurred on a weekend).

In another example of the interaction of biology and culture, something once dismissed as an old wives' tale now appears to have scientific validity. It appears that menstrual cycles become synchronized among women who live in close proximity to each other and as close friends (McClintock 1971). Although the explanation for this phenomenon is not yet clear (Comfort 1971), it is likely that *pheromones* — a generic term used to refer to communication by chemical signals — are responsible for synchronization of menstrual cycles.

This suggests that even biochemical responses can be triggered by the social arrangements found in human society. Such a conclusion indicates that human biology cannot in and of itself explain much about the consequences of the social arrangements we create. This is especially clear in discussions of human sexuality.

Human Sexuality

Our sexuality is an essential part of our understanding of ourselves and our relationships to others, and it involves deep emotional feeling, as well as issues of power and vulnerability in relationships (Boston Women's Health Book Collective 1984). Human sexual expression takes a variety of forms, though the expression of sexual behavior can be and has been influenced and constrained more by cultural definitions and prohibitions than by the physical possibilities for sexual arousal. In fact, what distinguishes human sexuality from sexual behavior among animals is that "human sexuality [is] uniquely characterized by its overwhelmingly symbolic, culturally constructed, non-procreative plasticity" (Caulfield 1985:344). Yet much of what we assume about sexuality is distorted by assuming that sexuality is a "natural drive" or an internal state that is acted out or released in sexually exciting situations. But anthropologists have pointed out that "the culturalization of sex, the social production and reproduction of our sexual beings, is precisely that which is 'natural' about human sexuality" (Caulfield 1985:356). In other words, how sexuality is expressed and felt varies according to the cultural context.

Information about sexuality is transmitted across generations and through the institutions of society (Vance 1984). Thorne and Luria's (1986) research among fourth- and fifth-grade children shows, for example, that through gender segregation in play and in classrooms, children learn heterosexist and homophobic meaning systems and behaviors that are the basis for the later sexual scripts of adolescence and adulthood. Some claim that children in our society are also socialized to have negative feelings about their own sexuality because sex is associated with shame and taboo (Richardson 1981). As a result, sexuality is often associated with feelings of inadequacy, a problem that is exacerbated by the narrow definition of "sexy" established by the advertising industry.

In fact, one of the ironies of our society is the fact that it is so sex-conscious, at the same time that it represses sexuality (Johnson 1968). Traditional definitions of sexuality see women as sexually passive and sex for men as performance and action. Cultural proscriptions have also traditionally defined sex primarily in terms of heterosexual monogamy; consequently, our understanding of sexuality has fused sexuality, reproduction, and gender (Freedman and Thorne 1984). More recently, the separation of sexuality from procreation, through the widespread availability of birth control, has revolutionized sexual behavior in contemporary society. But many feminists argue that the "sexual revolution" has not liberated women from oppressive sexual practices, in part because the sexual revolution has simply made sex a new commodity — something to be bought and sold and that uses women as sexual objects in a new, though still demeaning, manner (Mithcell 1971).

In this culture, male and female sexuality have been patterned by cultural definitions of masculinity and femininity. Female sexuality is defined as more passive and inhibited, while male sexuality is defined in terms of performance and achievement. As a result, for men performance anxieties about sexuality are a primary source of sexual impotence. In fact, the use of the word *impotence* to describe the absence of male sexual arousal indicates how our concepts of male sexuality are rooted in the context of male power (Julty 1974). Female sexuality, on the other hand, is seen as something to be contained and controlled, as we see in the traditional dichotomy of labeling women either as virgins or as whores. Such labels depict female sexuality as evil and dangerous if not constrained and imply that "good girls" repress their sexual feelings.

Women's sexuality in this culture has also been defined as male-centered, as female sexual reponse has been seen primarily in relationship to phallic intercourse. This idea is especially revealed by Freud's theory of the double orgasm, a sexual myth that long distorted our understanding of female sexuality. Freud's argument, and one that was widely believed until very recently, was that women have two kinds of orgasm — clitoral and vaginal. Clitoral orgasm, in Freud's view, was less "mature." He maintained that adult women should transfer their center of orgasm to the vagina, where male penetration made their sexual response complete. Freud's theory of the double orgasm has no basis in fact. The center of female sexuality is the clitoris; female orgasm is achieved through stimulation of the clitoris, whether or not accompanied by vaginal penetration (Masters and Johnson 1966). But, for nearly a century, the myth of the double orgasm led women to believe that they were frigid — unable to produce a mature sexual response. During this period, psychiatrists (most of whom were male) reported frigidity as the single most common reason for women to seek clinical therapy (Chesler 1972). In fact, the emphasis on male penetration meant that most women were not sexually satisfied in heterosexual relations because sexual intercourse and the ideology that buttressed it served only male interests. This fact, in turn, supported the attitude that women needed men for sexually mature relationships, even though, as recent research shows, women have higher rates of orgasm when they masturbate, have sex with another woman, or engage in cunnilingus (English 1980). One study, in fact, reports higher rates of orgasm for female virgins (through mutual masturbation and cunnilingus) than for coitally experienced females (Sorenson 1973, cited in Rossi and Rossi 1977).

The belief that women need men to achieve a mature sexual reponse reflects the assumption that women are dependent on men for their sexual, emotional, social, and economic well-being. This assumption not only legitimates "compulsory heterosexuality" as an institution (Rich 1980), but denigrates women's relationships with other women and subjects them to continued domination by men.

Still, we are typically told (implicitly and explicitly) that women's primary sexual orientation is naturally directed toward men. If we are heterosexual, we might never question that claim. But if we view the claim from the perspective of lesbian women's experience, we are likely to think otherwise. The belief that heterosexuality is the only natural form of sexual expression is rooted in a cultural framework that defines heterosexuality as compulsory and homosexuality as deviant or pathological (Rich 1980). Although it may at first seem odd to think of heterosexuality as a compulsory institution, the social sanctions brought against women who do not couple with men show how heterosexuality is maintained through social control. Even if women remain single and couple with no one, they are ridiculed and ostracized. If they love other women, they are seen as deviant or sexually pathological. In addition, lesbian women and gay men are subjected to legal sanctions that deny their basic civil rights, and they are often subjected to overt acts of violence and personal harm.

The U.S. Supreme Court ruled in 1986, *(Bowers* v. *Hardwick)* that the Constitution does not protect rights even for consenting adults to engage in homosexual conduct in the privacy of their own homes. This decision upheld state laws prohibiting homosexual and heterosexual sodomy. *Bowers* v. *Hardwick* originated in Georgia, where state law prohibited sodomy. According to the Georgia law, "A person commits the offence of sodomy when he performs or submits to any sexual act involving the sex organs of one person and the mouth or anus of another" (*New York Times,* July 1, 1986:A18). The police had come to the home of the defendant to serve him a summons for failing to pay a fine for public drunkenness. He was arrested for violation of the sodomy law after he was found in his bedroom engaging in oral sex with a male partner.

This case explicitly shows how cultural restrictions surrounding sexuality also must be seen in relationship to social control by the state. The state can regulate both heterosexual and homosexual practices (Freedman and Thorne 1984), meaning sexuality is subject to institutionalized control. And, since the state is both patriarchal and heterosexist, those who are most likely to be subjected to the social control of sexuality are men and women whose sexual experiences and practices violate patriarchal and heterosexist interests (MacKinnon 1982, 1983).

Across cultures and within our own, human sexual expression includes a wide range of behaviors and attitudes. And, though we tend to think of our sexuality as internally situated, it involves a learned relationship to the world (Bleier 1984). The feminist movement has inspired among us a new openness about women's and men's sexuality and has helped free women's sexual behavior from its traditional constraints (Bleier 1984). Yet the persistent belief that heterosexuality is the only natural way of expressing sexual feeling continues to blind us to other possibilities for human sexual feeling and practice. As we discard the notion that there is some single and unchanging way of expressing sexual feeling, we are much more likely to understand human sexuality in all its variety and forms.

The Sexes in Human Evolution

As we have seen, human society and the character of persons living within it are complex processes that involve both biological and social causes. Explanations that reduce human life simply to nature or nurture are unlikely to reveal the complex dynamics produced by the interdependence of biology and culture. Moreover, the physical and social aspects of the human environment exert profound influences on human life, both socially and biologically. Because human beings are essentially adaptive creatures, they continuously respond and change within their environments. Any argument that reduces the complexity of human life to its biological basis alone makes the fallacious assumption that biology sets an inevitable course for human social and physical development. Vast recorded differences among human cultures demonstrate the inadequacy of such an argument and challenge the assumption that biology somehow sets predetermined limits on the expression of human skill and ability. And in fact, the evolution of human society shows that the adaptation in interaction with the social and physical environment is an essential process in the development of human life and society.

The evolution of human life is said to have begun about 5 million years ago in the forests and savannahs of eastern Africa. Although the earliest hominid (prehuman, bipedal primate mammals) groups vastly differed from *Homo sapiens* today, the transformations that occurred in these early species provide several clues to the role of gender in the evolution of human society.

Because of the lack of fossil records for this early period, evolutionary theorists have constructed their evidence from observations of living chimpanzee populations; these groups represent the kind of population from which human beings have evolved. Studies of primates reveal that humans are closely related in genetic structure and biochemical make-up to some primate species. The genes of humans and chimpanzees are 99 percent identical, and studies on blood proteins and DNA show remarkable commonalities between chimpanzees and humans (Tanner and Zihlman 1976). For this reason, chimpanzee behavior has provided an opportunity to observe some of the rudimentary forms of social organization and behavior from which humans have likely evolved.

Primates engage in a variety of social behaviors, the specifics of which vary from species to species. But chimpanzees hunt, gather, and share food; feed and groom their offspring; make tools; and develop systems of social organization. Male and female chimpanzees develop patterns of sociability and engage in extensive gestural and nonverbal communication. In most primate species, maternal involvement with offspring exceeds paternal care, but in some species the reverse is true. In the South American titi monkey, for example, males carry the infant except when it is nursing.

Studies of the evolution from primates to humans show that changes in behavioral patterns and, eventually, in morphology (structure) occurred as new environments were encountered. As early hominids moved in search of food, they adopted new physical and social forms to cope with the new environments they found.

The transition from ape to human began when ape populations moved from the forests to the more open savannahs of eastern Africa. As these groups moved to different regions, new patterns of food gathering emerged that, over time, influenced the bipedal locomotion of the species and led to the creation of tools, new defense patterns, flexible systems of food sharing, and new patterns of communication and social organization (Tanner and Zihlman 1976). New methods of acquiring food and a reduction in competition with other populations also created an environmental basis for major transformations and adaptations in the species.

The role of females in the evolution of human society is critical. Females were most often responsible for the survival of offspring; they invested more time than males in gathering food and tending the young. Among the earliest ancestors, *Australopithecus,* plant foods gathered by women provided a higher proportion of caloric intake than was obtainable through the hunting of meat (Zihlman 1978). As feminist scholars have reexamined the archaeological record, they have found that the importance of meat in early human diets has been exaggerated, in part because bone matter is more durable than vegetative matter and leaves a more obvious record. But recent research shows that females have an equally important (in fact, central) role in the evolution of innovative skills and social organization, in spite of the fact that Western anthropologists have traditionally cast evolutionary theory and the anthropological record in terms of "man the great hunter" and "woman the silent gatherer."

The transition from *Australopithecus* to *Homo erectus* is believed to have occurred 1.8 to 1.2 million years ago. Fossil records show the transition to involve a slight increase in body size, increased cranial capacity, and an increased ratio of brain to body size. Evidence of stone tools from this period shows signs of human workmanship, marking the introduction of human creativity. The increased mental capacity of humans makes social learning possible, thus introducing a capability to remember larger home terrains. Between 1 million and 500,000 years ago, populations of *Homo erectus* had spread from southern and eastern Africa to northern Asia and Europe. More regular use of cave shelters and constructed huts increased cooperative food sharing because dependent children could remain in the hands of caretakers while mothers assisted in the gathering of food. By the time of the evolution of *Homo sapiens,* between 100,000 and 200,000 years ago, the brain had expanded to nearly its present size. Along with that adaptation, complex communicative, technical, and conceptual skills evolved, forming the basis for what we would now call human culture.

Throughout the evolution of human society, flexibility and cooperation between males and females were essential for human survival. As early hominid groups found new food sources, predators, and environmental hazards, the key to their survival was the invention of new patterns of social cooperation. Females did not merely benefit from the inventions of males; they were central actors in the adaptations leading to human life (Zihlman 1978; Zihlman and Tanner 1976).

As primary caretakers of new members of the population, females developed food-sharing networks and systems of communication to train the young and protect them from environmental hazards. The reproductive and socialization tasks for which the women were responsible did not exclude them from the fabric of society, but instead made their role fundamental to the emergence of human groups. As these early groups developed home bases in caves and huts, it is likely that systems of shared child care emerged. Dependent children could remain with adult caretakers while their mothers gathered food. In fact, it is suggested that "the sharing of child care beyond the immediate kin group may have been a further step toward building networks within a larger community that shared food and defended itself against predators and cooperated for survival in the harsh environment of this colder world" (Zihlman 1978:17).

The evolutionary record reveals three essential points. First, females have an essential and central role in the making of human society. In addition to developing food-sharing systems and networks for child care, women probably invented basketry, weaving, and pottery. And as the feminist writer Dorothy Dinnerstein has suggested, "receptacles in which to store food are by no means a trivial cultural achievement. They extend the time scale on which life can be lived, changing food gathering from a hand-to-mouth activity to one that refers to the future and whose results can be experienced with reference to the past" (1976:22).

Second, it is clear from the evolutionary record that human society emerges from the complex interaction of biological and environmental conditions. Human begins developed as they adapted to environmental conditions. As environmental conditions changed, adaptations in human life were made. As we can see in the final chapters of this book when we examine systems of gender inequality in different societies, human societies have evolved through complex adaptations to their physical environments and their modes of subsistence. The sex/gender systems of different societies show a remarkable degree of flexibility and capacity for change, depending on a complex host of factors that influence the development of human culture and social systems. This point should serve as a reminder not only of the past from which we come, but also of the need for flexible human arrangements that we face in the present and future.

Third, discussions of the evolutionary record have been heavily biased by gender-laden assumptions about the proper roles of males and females. Scientific analyses and anthropological descriptions of human societies often reflect patriarchal values, showing how contemporary culture distorts our view of the past. For example, the evolutionary record has been filled with descriptions of "dominance hierarchies," or "male competition for female sexual favors" — descriptions that tell us more about the values of the observer than the actual conditions of earlier human groups.

Despite the seeming importance of cooperative arrangements in the evolution of human society, most discussions of human evolution have ignored or belittled the role of women in the origins of human society. Projecting their own cultural bias onto the past, evolutionary theories have left the impression that "only men evolved" (Hubbard 1979) and that women played a passive role in the care of offspring and the nurturance of their kin. This problem of the projection of social values onto scientific research has been endemic in discussions of sex, biology, and culture and thus warrants further examination.

Sexism, Science, and Society

Scientific knowledge in our society is seen as a source of great authority. Scientific careers carry much prestige and scientists have a great deal of power to influence the everyday experiences of our lives. Scientific explanations are generally thought to be objective accounts that are uninfluenced by the values and interests of scientific thinkers. Thus, science has the image of being value-neutral and true to the facts. Objectivity in science is depicted as stemming from the calculated distance between the observer and the observed. In the scientific framework, personal characteristics of scientific observers are not expected to influence their results.

Despite the strong claims of neutrality and objectivity by scientists, the fact is that science is closely tied to the centers of power in this society and interwoven with capitalist and patriarchal institutions. This has many implications for understanding the social structure of science as well as for understanding how the social structure of science influences the production of scientific knowledge.

The feminist critique of science involves several questions, including: Why are women excluded from science? How is the exclusion of women from science related to the way science is done and thought? And, what research questions would science ask were science produced in a nonracist and nonsexist society?

Asking how and why women have been excluded from the practice of science is one way to reveal deeply embedded gender, race, and class patterns in the structure of scientific professions and, consequently, in the character of scientific thought. Rossiter's (1982) work on the history of women in science shows that the concept of a woman scientist is a contradiction in terms, since scientists are supposed to be tough, rigorous, rational, impersonal, unemotional, and competitive, while women are not. She and others (Fee 1983; Harding 1986) show that gender identity is at the very heart of the definition of science since to be scientific is to be masculine.

Science bears the imprint of the fact that scientists have been men, as many have documented the small proportion of women in virtually every scientific field (Aldrich 1978). Our understanding of the presence of women in science can change, however, depending on whom we think of as doing scientific work. Women are, in fact, very much present in science; they constitute a large proportion of the technical, clerical, domestic, teaching, and plant maintenance staffs required to do scientific work. Women, and especially women of color, appear as objects and "others" in science; they are exploited as research subjects and their labor in the production of science remains invisible to the scientific elite. The decision makers in science — those who define scientific problems, set scientific agendas, fund scientific projects, and relate science to public policy — are overwhelmingly men (Harding 1986).

Thus, science is produced and applied within a distinctively masculine framework — one that values objective separation from the objects of research and, yet, is nonetheless gendered in the descriptions and explanations it offers of the natural and social worlds. Evelyn Fox Keller calls this a "science/gender" system — a network of associations between our concepts of masculinity and femininity and the construction of science. She argues that to examine the roots, dynamics, and consequences of the science/gender system, we have to understand how ideologies of gender and science inform each other and how this affects our social arrangements between men and women, science and nature (Keller 1985).

Scientific descriptions project masculine cultural values onto the physical and natural world. Ruth Hubbard (1984), for example, explains that kingdoms and orders are not intrinsic to the nature of organisms but have evolved in a patriarchal world that values hierarchy and patrilineage. There are numerous examples showing how patriarchal values have been intrinsic in scientific thought. Note, for example, the description of the experimental scientific method offered by Francis Bacon, one of the sixteenth-century founders of modern scientific thought:

> For you have but to follow and as it were hound nature in her wanderings, and you will be able when you like to lead and drive her afterward to the same place again. . . . Neither ought a man to make scruple of entering and penetrating into those holes and corners, when the inquisition of truth is his whole object. (Cited in Harding 1986:116)

The emergence of modern science is founded upon an image of rational man as conquering the passions of nature, which is depicted as female. Consider Machiavelli's famed quotation regarding fortune:

> Fortune is a woman and it is necessary if you wish to master her to conquer her by force; and it can be seen that she lets herself be overcome by the bold rather than by those who proceed coldly, and therefore like a woman, she is always a friend to the young because they are less cautious, fiercer, and master her with greater audacity. (From *The Prince;* cited in Harding 1986:115)

Such depictions of science and nature might be dismissed as old-fashioned ramblings of patriarchal days gone by, except for the fact that gendered descriptions of biological phenomena continue to appear in scientific texts. One of the best examples comes from Alice Rossi's description of the way in which male fantasies of sexual power have been projected onto descriptions of biological reproduction. Rossi writes:

> A good starting place to observe such fantasy is the initial coming together of sperm and ovum. Ever since Leewenhoek first saw sperm under the microscope, great significance has been attached to the fact that sperm are equipped with motile flagella, and it was assumed that the locomotive ability of the sperm fully explained their journey from the vagina through the cervix and uterus to the oviduct for the encounter with the ovum. . . . Rorvik (1971) describes the seven-inch journey through the birth canal and womb to the waiting egg as equivalent to a 500-mile upstream swim for a salmon and comments with admiration that they often make the hazardous journey in under an hour, "more than earning their title as the most powerful and rapid living creatures on earth." The image is clear: powerful active sperm and a passive ovum awaiting its arrival and penetration, male sexual imagery structuring the very act of conception. (1977:16–17)

In fact, as Rossi points out, uterine contractions, stimulated by the release of the hormone oxytocin, propel the sperm through the female system so that "completely inert substances such as dead sperm and even particles of India ink reach the oviducts as rapidly as live sperm do" (Rossi 1977:17).

Sociologists use the concept of *ideology* to refer to systems of belief that distort reality so as to justify and maintain the status quo (Mannheim 1936). Biological explanations of gender inequality are a case in point. It is interesting to note that biologically determinist arguments tend to flourish in times of political conservatism, when powerful groups are working to maintain their own advantages. In such a setting, claims to scientific truth lend legitimacy and scientific authority to beliefs that otherwise would have a clear political bias.

In the history of social thought, Social Darwinism is a good example. Social Darwinism emerged at the turn of the twentieth century during a time of rapid expansion of capitalist wealth together with extensive exploitation of immigrant and racial minorities (Hofstadter 1959; Rossi 1977; Schwendinger and Schwendinger 1974). Capitalists such as John D. Rockefeller were inspired by Social Darwinism — a doctrine that claimed that only the most fit would survive and rise to the top. Such a belief justified their own accumulation of wealth while fostering the racist belief that those who failed did so out of biological inferiority. Rockefeller declared in a Sunday school address:

> The growth of a large business is merely survival of the fittest. . . . The American Beauty rose can be produced in the splendor and fragrance which bring cheer to its beholder only by sacrificing the early birds which grew up around it. This is not an evil tendency in business. It is merely the working out of a law of nature and a law of God. (Ghent 1902:29)

Social Darwinism justified the emergence of capitalism by claiming it to be the result of natural laws over which man has no control. Clearly, Rockefeller's arguments rested on both racist and class-bound claims. Similarly, analyses that explain gender inequality as naturally arising from differences between the sexes are an ideological defense of patriarchal privilege. They justify the rule of men over women while at the same time distorting women's actual experience, both in a biological and a social sense. When these distortions become part of the scientific record, then science clearly is serving an ideological purpose.

Within scientific studies, bias can enter in the scientists' choice of topic, choice of research subjects, definitions of concepts, method of observation, analysis and interpretation of data, and manner of reporting (Longino and Doell 1983; Messing 1983). Feminist research in science unravels the way that gendered assumptions infiltrate the scientific record and shows how many of the "truths" alleged by scientific studies merely reflect the interests of a male-dominated society. Feminist revisions of science call for a more inclusive and reflective perspective by recognizing the interplay between scientific knowledge and the social systems in which science is produced. And, finally, feminist revisions of science seek a more humanistic science — one in which science is used for human liberation from race, class, and gender oppression.

Summary _____

Scientific studies alleging a genetic or biological basis for gender and race inequality are frequently popularized in the press. Feminists understand the status of women and racial-ethnic groups to be socially, not biologically, rooted. Research in the natural and physical sciences points to the extreme difficulty of separating biological from social influences on human behavior. Human biology is itself influenced by cultural change, and evolutionary studies show that human biological organisms must be flexible enough to allow for environmental change and adaptation.

Social scientists distinguish between sex and gender. *Sex* refers to genetic and physical sexual identity; *gender* refers to socially learned behavior. Studies of biological abnormalities in fetal sex differentiation reveal the importance of sex of rearing in determining gender identity. *Sexual dimorphism* refers to sex differences appearing between populations of males and females. Studies of sexually dimorphic traits reveal a complex interaction between biological and sociological causes, discrediting biologically reductionist claims about the biological basis for differences between the sexes. Biological processes such as menstruation and menopause are much influenced by the cultural contexts in which they occur. Our understanding of female sexuality has been distorted by a male-centered perspective. Human sexuality is also constrained and influenced by cultural arrangements and can be controlled, as in the case of compulsory heterosexuality, by state and other societal institutions.

Scientific knowledge in our society is also linked to the masculine structure of scientific institutions and knowledge. Scientific knowledge projects cultural values onto its description and explanations of the natural, physical, and social worlds. The exclusion of women from science gives scientific knowledge a masculine character and creates bias in the production of scientific work.

In conclusion, the study of human culture shows that there is no fixed correspondence between innate human dispositions (if they exist) and human social forms. Whatever link exists between biology and social life is mediated by the influence of culture. Because culture is symbolic (its meaning is derived from social interaction), it cannot be found in the intrinsic properties of persons or objects. One of the unique characteristics of human societies is their freedom from natural relationships (Sahlins 1977). For example, even though the act of human reproduction is a physical one, its significance lies as much, if not more, in its social meaning. Moreover, what we reproduce is not just a genetic object, but a human being whose life is part of a system of human groups.

This does not mean that the biological basis for human life is irrelevant or unimportant, but it stresses the mutual and interdependent influence of even biological events with human culture. With regard to sex differences, culture exerts a powerful influence on who we are and what we become. In the next chapter we study the process by which culture is learned and the ways in which our gender identities are acquired.

CHAPTER 4

Sex Role Socialization

Introduction

In the village of Uder, located in the rugged hills of northern Nigeria, lives a population of people who call themselves Birom. When a boy is born here, his umbilical cord is cut with an iron knife used to cut acha — the most valued staple grain of the culture. Traditionally, women were forbidden to grow acha; the size of a man's acha crop is taken as a measure of his strength and virility. When a girl is born, her umbilical cord is cut with a blade of grass or a bamboo knife. The afterbirth of a boy is placed in a clay pot and put high on a branch of a cottonwood tree; the girl's afterbirth is buried in the soil, usually during a fertility ritual. In the same society, crying in boy infants is regarded as a sign of strength, virility, and lust for life; crying in girls is regarded as indicative of a fretful and complaining personality (Smedley 1974).

To an outsider, these practices may seem unusual and strange. However, if we as outsiders considered our own cultural practices surrounding birth, they too would seem quite odd. In American culture, baby boys are dressed in blue, girls in pink. Although the origins of this practice are obscure, most parents comply with the cultural habit. Some will dress their daughters in blue as well as pink, but it is a rare parent who dresses a boy in pink. Children's names in our culture are also selected according to the masculinity or femininity that they symbolize. A pamphlet distributed to expectant parents by a baby product company gives advice on the selection of the baby's name:

Choosing a suitable name for your new baby is very important. The name you decide on will be much more than just a term of identification. It will, to a degree, be a reflection of how you picture your baby as a grownup. . . . Even though they're lovely names, be careful of names that, at least soundwise, fit both sexes. Examples are Francis (Frances), Jean (Gene), Kerry (Carrie), and Gail (Gale). These are safer used as a middle name with a first name that is unmistakenly masculine or feminine. . . . In the case of boys, parents should beware of giving names that will forever, have a "little-boy" sound, such as Dickie, Bobby, Jimmy, and Bill. (Mead Johnson and Company 1978:2–3).

In our own culture, we engage in social practices that differentiate boys and girls, and we make assumptions about appropriate masculine and feminine names; names are labels that we carry throughout our lives. Girls' names are supposed to be feminine — soft, pretty, and symbolic of goodness, sweetness, and beauty; boys' names are supposed to be masculine — short, harder in tone, and symbolic of strength, determination, and intellect. More diminutive endings are found on girls' than on boys' names (for example, Debbie, Nanette, Jeannie, Anita), implying the lesser status of women. In fact, research shows that female given names have more sounds and syllables, more frequently vary the position of the stressed syllable, and more often conclude in a vowel or resonant sound than do male given names (Slater and Feinman 1985).

Fear of crossing traditional sex role boundaries also discourages parents from giving names that might fit both sexes. Also, names reveal our cultural fear of homosexuality, especially among boys, as evidenced by the fact that girls' names are sometimes feminized forms of boys' names, but the reverse seldom occurs (Richardson 1981).

Naming is only the beginning of the practices that socialize the young into culturally prescribed gender roles. When parents take a child home from the hospital, they begin a complex, often unintentional, series of practices that slowly but effectively create the gender of their child. In fact, with the advent of technologies that can identify the sex of a child before birth, many parents and grandparents initiate sex role expectations even before the child is born.

These illustrations are only a small part of the cultural practices that shape our gender identity. Every human infant is born into a cultural environment. That environment shapes what persons become, what chances in life are available to them, and how they perceive the world in which they live.

This chapter discusses the process by which persons learn the gender roles that their culture defines as appropriate for them. Sociologists use the term *socialization* to refer to the process by which social roles are learned. Because gender is a significant part of our acquired identity, the learning of gender (or sex roles) through socialization is a primary part of the process of growing up. In this chapter, we will see that socialization goes on throughout life, although it is particularly critical in our early years. We examine different sources of sex role socialization and study the consequences of sex role socialization for our identities, skills, and relationships. Finally, this chapter examines some of the theoretical perspectives that have been developed by sociologists and psychologists to explain the socialization process.

Sex and Gender in Human Culture

Culture as the Basis for Gender

Culture is defined as "the set of definitions of reality held in common by people who share a distinctive way of life" (Kluckhohn 1962:52). Culture is, in essence, a pattern of expectations about what are appropriate behaviors and beliefs for the members of the society. Thus, culture provides prescriptions for social behavior. Culture tells us what we ought to do, what we ought to think, who we ought to be, and what we ought to expect of others.

The concept of culture explains a great deal to us about variation in human life-styles and human societies. Cultural norms (the expectations that culture provides) vary tremendously from one society to another and, within any given society, from one historical setting to another and among different groups in the society. Cross-cultural studies reveal an immense diversity in human social relations, because human creativity and cultural adaptations to different circumstances create a rich and complex mosaic of the different possibilities for human life.

In every known culture, gender is a major category for the organization of cultural and social relations, although specific cultural expectations vary from society to society. One feature of a culture is that its members come to take cultural patterns for granted. Thus, culture provides its members with tacit knowledge; much of what they believe as true or what they perceive as real is learned to the point where it is no longer questioned. Culture provides assumptions that often go unexamined but that, nonetheless, fundamentally guide our behavior and our beliefs.

Gender expectations in a culture are sometimes expressed subtly in social interaction, as, for example, in American culture, where men interrupt women more frequently than women interrupt men (Frieze and Ramsey 1976), where women smile more than do men (Mehrabian 1971), and where men stare at women more than women stare at men (Frieze et al. 1978). At other times, gender expectations are not so subtle, as in the cultural practices of Chinese foot binding, Indian suttee, European witch hunts, and the genital mutilation of women documented in some African countries (Hosken 1979; Jacobson 1974; Stein 1978; Wong 1974). Within American culture, such extreme physical practices are also evidenced in the sadistic treatment of women in pornography and in the common surgical practices of face lifts and silicone implants.

In different ways and for a variety of reasons, all cultures use gender as a primary category of social relations. The differences we observe between men and women can be attributed largely to these cultural patterns. This in itself is strong evidence for the cultural basis of gender roles. Were sex differences determined by biological factors alone, we would not find the vast diversity that exists in gender relations from society to society. Moreover, were sex differences universal in content, masculinity and femininity would not vary in meaning from one culture to another. Masculinity and femininity, although attached to persons usually by virtue of their biological sex, are cultural ideals. They refer to expectations established by society, not categories that are fixed by one's biological status. The discussion of hermaphroditism in the preceding chapter provides an example of the importance of gender rearing in the creation of gender identity.

Distinguishing Sex and Gender

The terms *sex, gender,* and *sex roles* have particular definitions in social science usage. *Sex* refers to the genetic and physical identity of the person and is meant to signify the fact that one is either male or female. One's biological sex usually establishes a pattern of gendered expectations, though one's biological sex is not always the same as one's gender identity. Moreover, the fact that someone is born female or male does not mean that she or he will become stereotypically feminine or masculine. Femininity and masculinity are cultural concepts and, as such, have fluctuating expectations, are learned differently by different members of the culture, and are relative to the historical and social settings in which they emerge.

Gender refers to the socially learned behaviors and expectations that are associated with the two sexes. Thus, whereas "maleness" and "femaleness" are biological facts, masculinity and femininity are culturally constructed attributes. Similar to the social categories established by race and social class, gender patterns what others expect of us and what we expect of ourselves. Gender also establishes, in large measure, our life chances and directs our social relations with others.

Although sex and gender can be easily confused, the distinction between them is important, for it emphasizes that gender is a cultural, not a biological, phenomenon. Moreover, the distinction also demonstrates that one's biological sex need not necessarily correspond with one's gender identity.

Sociologists use the concept of *social roles* to refer to culturally prescribed expectations, duties, and rights that define the relationship between a person in a particular social position and the other people with whom he or she interacts. For example, to be a mother is a specific social role with a definable set of expectations, rights, and duties. We all occupy multiple roles in society, and we can think of roles as linking individuals to society. It is through social roles that cultural norms are patterned and learned.

Sex roles are those expectations for behavior and attitudes that the culture defines as appropriate for men and women. Gender is, however, a broader concept than sex role, as we will see in subsequent chapters. Its use is not restricted to the framework of learned roles, since feminists have conceptualized gender to refer to the complex political, economic, psychological, and social relations between men and women in society. While gender is partially constructed through learned sex roles, gender relations, as we will see in subsequent chapters, encompass much more than learned identities. In this chapter, however, our topic is sex role socialization and the way it is learned by women and men.

Socialization as Social Control

Sanctions and Expectations

Peter Berger (1963) describes social control as something like a series of concentric circles. At the center is the individual, who is surrounded by different levels of control, ranging from the subtle — such as learned roles, peer pressure, and ridicule — to the overt — such as violence, physical threat, and imprisonment. According to Berger, it is usually not necessary for powerful agents in the society to resort to extreme sanctions because what we think and believe about ourselves usually keeps us in line. In this sense, socialization acts as a powerful system of social control.

In the case of sex roles, social control is shown by the pressure we experience to adopt sex-appropriate behaviors. Sex role socialization refers to the process by which sex roles are learned by a society's members. Through sex role socialization, different behaviors and attitudes are encouraged and discouraged in men and women. That is, social expectations about what is properly masculine and feminine are communicated to us through the socialization process. Our family, peers, and teachers, as well as the media, act as agents of the socialization process. Although probably none of us becomes exactly what the cultural ideal prescribes, our roles in social institutions are conditioned by the gender relations we learn in our social development.

Some persons become more perfectly socialized than others, and sociologists have warned against the idea of seeing humans as totally passive, overly socialized creatures (Wrong 1961). To some extent, we probably all resist the expectations society has of us. Our uniqueness as individuals stems in part from this resistance, as well as from variations in the social experience we have. The idea of sex role socialization does not deny individual differences, but it does point to the common experiences shared by girls as they become women and boys as they become men. However much we may believe that we were raised in a gender-neutral environment, research and careful observation show how pervasive and generally effective the process of sex role socialization is. Although some of us conform more than others, socialization acts as a powerful system of social control. The conflicts we encounter when we try to cross or deny the boundaries between the sexes are good evidence of the strength of sex role expectations in our culture, although there is evidence of some change in people's attitudes and behavior. One experimenter asked college women to select a man and, for an hour, to act in accordance with the ideals of the women's liberation movement. One-quarter of the students said that this action required no change in their behavior, and another 10 percent received positive support from their peers for rejecting the traditional feminine role. Still, a majority of the women reported anger, conflict, surprise, and resistance from their male friends (Weitzman 1979).

The pressure to adopt sex-appropriate behavior is evidence that the socialization process controls us in several ways. First, it gives us a definition of ourselves. Second, it defines the external world and our place within it. Third, it provides our definition of others and our relationships with them. And the socialization process encourages and discourages the acquisition of certain skills by gender.

Sex Roles as Hazards to Health

Many have argued that traditional sex roles are hazardous to our health. Conformity to traditional roles takes its toll upon both men and women, and research shows that those who conform most fully to sex role expectations experience a range of negative consequences. Higher male mortality rates can be attributed to the stress in masculine roles (Jourard 1974); among women, those with the most traditionally feminine identities are more likely to be depressed (Tinsley et al. 1984). Also, women who score as very feminine on personality tests tend to be dissatisfied and anxious and to have lower self-esteem than do less traditionally feminine women (Bem 1972). Research also indicates that depression is more frequent and more intense among both men and women who are too tightly integrated into their traditional roles. So, for example, supermothers — those who overly conform to the maternal role — are more depressed than other women (Bart 1979). Housewives are more often depressed than employed women, and when housewives are depressed, they show more impairment in physical and mental functioning than do working women (Weissman and Paykel 1974).

Conversely, men and women with more androgynous sex role orientations — that is to say, those having a balance of masculine and feminine personality characteristics — show signs of greater mental health and more positive self-images. For example, research among middle-aged professional men shows that those who are the most androgynous perceive themselves to be more healthy than do more traditional men of their age and status (Downey, 1984). Personality tests given to male and female college students also show that those who score high on both masculine and feminine traits (and, therefore, are defined as more androgynous) have higher self-esteem than students who score high on one gender type or another (Spence et al. 1975). Finally, current research also shows that, in spite of the strains experienced by women with multiple roles, those with multiple roles report more gratification, status security, and enrichment in their lives (Gerson 1985).

The restrictions of traditional sex roles do not only have consequences for our mental health; they also divide men and women from each other. Tolson (1977) suggests that by shaping persons into masculine and feminine types, we condemn both to a "one-sided existence." Traditional sex roles deny women access to the public world of power, achievement, and independence at the same time that they deny men the nurturant, emotive, and other-oriented world of domestic life. In this sense, traditional sex roles limit the psychological and social possibilities for human beings.

Socialization and Homophobia

Some argue that the pressures of sex role socialization are even more restrictive of boys, at least at the early ages, than they are of girls (Fling and Manosevitz 1972; Hartley 1959). Male roles are more rigidly defined, as witnessed in the more severe social sanctions brought against boys not to be sissies, compared with girls who are thought of as tomboys. For girls, being a tomboy may be a source of mild ridicule, but it appears to be more acceptable (at least until puberty) than being a sissy is for boys.

Some researchers explain this finding as the result of male homophobia — fear of being homosexual (Morin and Garfinkle 1978; Sears 1959). Male homophobia acts as a system of social control because it encourages boys and men to act more masculine, as a way of indicating that they are not homosexual. Male homophobia further separates the cultural roles of masculinity and femininity by discouraging men for showing so-called feminine traits, such as caring, nurturing, emotional expression, and gentleness.

Research supports this point. One study observing boys and girls "playing store" found that boys were more upset than girls by customers who chose sex-inappropriate toys (Ross and Ross 1972). Based on a review of the research on male homophobia, Morin and Garfinkle also conclude that "homophobia thus appears to be functional in the dynamics of maintaining the traditional male role. The fear of being labeled homosexual serves to keep men within the confines of what the culture defines as sex-appropriate behavior, and it interferes with the development of intimacy between men" (1978:41). Men who endorse the norms of traditional male roles are also more homophobic (Thompson et al. 1985).

Race and Socialization

It is important to point out that very few of the studies of sex role differences also consider the issue of race differences in sex role development. Consequently, many of the studies of sex differences are race-biased, and their results should not be generalized to all women or all men. The identity development of black, Hispanic, Asian-American, and native American women is complicated by the particular features of their culture and their devaluation by the dominant culture. Contrary to what many believe, research finds that minority women and men maintain positive images of themselves because they rely on their own group's assessment of the dominant white society (Carrington 1980; Myers 1975; Rosenberg and Simmons 1971). Many of the characteristics associated with the feminine stereotype — dependence on men, weakness, and learned helplessness, for example — simply are not typical of minority women who have to rely on themselves and their community for survival.

Research on black women speaks to this point. Although black women are socialized, like white women, to place primary emphasis on nurturing their loved ones (Carrington 1980), black adolescent girls are also socialized to become self-sufficient, to aspire to an education and occupation, to regard work as part of the normal female role, and to be more independent than white girls (Ladner 1971).

Other researchers have confirmed this point, arguing that "the traditional role, as it is generally understood, probably does not exist for black women" (Gump 1980:353). Current research on black women's sex role attitudes confirms this point. Based on interviews with black urban women, Malson (1983) finds that, when they were growing up, 89 percent thought they would have a job or career; those who thought otherwise attributed this to a lack of educational and job training opportunities. Eighty percent of the same women thought they would be mothers and 95 percent of them had mothers who were employed when they were children. In addition, 80 percent said they preferred employment to being at home.

Likewise, the experiences of Asian and Hispanic women create sex role expectations that are situated in their particular historical experiences. Asian-American women, for example, have a strong degree of gender consciousness, based in part in their socialization in traditional cultures with restricted definitions of sex roles, the maintenance of sex stereotyping, and devalued and subordinated roles for women (Chow 1985). But, like other minority women, their gender consciousness intersects with their consciousness of their racial and class status in American society (Chow 1987). Similarly, in Chicano communities women's roles are adaptations to the conditions of exclusion, marginality, and hostility that have characterized the relations of Chicanas to American society (Baca-Zinn 1982b). Clearly, generalizations about sex role socialization need to be carefully examined in the context of the experience of women of color. This is often difficult to do since authors do not always report the racial composition of groups on which they have based their conclusions. Consequently, as students read the results of studies, including those related here, they should ask themselves if the same conclusions would be reached were the studies based on the experiences of women and men of color.

These cautions are not meant to deny the significance of gender expectations in the experience of women of color. Sex role socialization is an important part of the experience of all women and men in this society. But it also may be true that the further one moves into the social system, such as in joining a corporation or moving into a position of power, the more rigid sex role expectations become. Because success in the dominant world tends to demand conformity, it is likely that those who benefit the most from sexist and racist institutions are those most likely to uphold the attitudes, beliefs, and behaviors upon which such institutions rest.

Socialization Across the Life Course

Socialization begins from the moment one is born, and it continues throughout our adult lives even though our gender roles are established very early. Although much sex role research focuses on childhood socialization, socialization is an ongoing process. When we encounter new roles and new social experiences, we are socialized to adopt these new roles through the expectations other have of us. Socialization patterns can be observed in many individual and group experiences and in the context of all of the institutions of society. This section examines the processes and consequences of sex role socialization as it occurs throughout the life cycle.

Infancy

Beginning in infancy, boys and girls are treated differently. Research on infant socialization shows, in fact, how quickly gender expectations become part of our experience. One innovative study asked first-time parents to describe their baby only twenty-four hours after birth. Although physical examination revealed no objective differences between male and female infants, the parents of girls reported their babies to be softer, smaller, and less attentive than did the parents of boys. This study also shows that fathers are more influenced by the child's gender that are mothers. More than mothers, fathers describe their sons as larger, better coordinated, more alert, and stronger than girls; more than mothers, fathers describe their daughters as delicate, weak, and inattentive (Rubin, Provenzano, and Luria 1974).

Research on child-parent interaction does not, however, reveal consistent patterns of sex differences in social interaction between parents and newborns. There is a tendency for parents to elicit motor behavior more from sons than from daughters, but little difference appears by sex in the amount of affectionate contact between mother and infant (Maccoby and Jacklin 1974). Studies find that there are no consistent sex differences in the incidence of separation anxiety among male and female infants, and research findings are mixed on the question of whether girl infants smile and respond more to human faces than do boy infants (Frieze et al. 1978).

Taken together, research on sex differences in infants shows that parents treat their infants differently according to their sex, but that differences in infants' actual patterns of behavior are extremely small. One frequently cited study shows that, by age thirteen months, girls are more likely than boys to cling to, look at, and talk to their mothers (Goldberg and Lewis 1969), but attempts to replicate this study have failed to confirm these results (Coates, Anderson, and Hartup 1972; Jacklin, Maccoby, and Dick 1973). However, mothers do tend to touch and talk to infant girls more than infant boys (Kagan and Lewis 1965), and fathers are likely to mock-wrestle with baby sons and to play more gently with baby daughters (Komarovsky 1953).

Because sex differences in human infants are negligible and inconsistent, we cannot draw conclusions about the immediate effect of socialization on baby boys and girls. However, even though gender expectations may be subtle and without conscious intent, they are likely to be effective in guiding the later behavior of the child. As the child grows older, gender expectations seem to increase. Long before boys and girls reach the age of puberty (when the effect of biological hormones is at its greatest), differences in the behavior of each sex appear, though research on sex roles now shows that differences between the sexes in cognition and personality are neither as great nor as consistent as has been thought.

Childhood Play and Games

Research in child development emphasizes the importance of play and games in the maturation of children. Through play, children learn the skills of social interaction, develop cognitive and analytical abilities, and are taught the values and attitudes of their culture. The games that children play have great significance for the child's intellectual, moral, personal, and social development.

George Herbert Mead, a social psychologist and major sociological theorist in the early twentieth century, describes three stages in which socialization occurs: imitation, play, and game. In the imitation stage, infants simply copy the behavior of significant persons in their environment. In the play stage, the child begins "taking the role of the other" — seeing himself or herself from the perspective of another person. Mead argues that taking the role of the other is a cognitive process that permits the child to develop a self-concept. Self-concepts emerge through interacting with other people and from learning to perceive how others see us. The other people most emotionally important to the child (who may be parents, siblings, or other primary caretakers) are, in Mead's term, *significant others*. In the play stage, children learn to take the role of significant others, primarily by practicing their social roles — for example, "playing Mommy" or "playing Daddy."

In the game stage, children are able to do more. Rather than seeing themselves from the perspective of only one significant other at a time, they can play games requiring them to understand how several other people (including more than just significant others) view them simultaneously. Playing baseball, to use Mead's example, involves the roles and expectations of many more people than does "playing Mommy." Eventually, children in the game stage learn to orient themselves not just to significant others but to a *generalized other* as well. The generalized other represents the cultural expectations of the whole social community.

Throughout Mead's analysis of the emergence of the self, he emphasizes the importance of interpretive behavior in the way the child relates to others in the social environment. Early activity, especially through play, locates children's experience in a social environment; therefore, meanings communicated through play help the child organize personal experience into an emerging self. Children's play is then a very significant part of the socialization process.

With regard to sex roles, research reveals the pervasiveness of gender stereotyping as it is learned in early childhood play. Researchers have observed that, compared with girls' rooms, boys' rooms contain toys of more different classes (educational, sports, animals, spatial-temporal objects, depots, military equipment, machines, and vehicles) and that boys' toys tend to encourage activities outside of the home. Girls' toys, on the other hand, both are less varied in type and encourage play within the home (Rheingold and Cook 1975). Additionally, Rheingold and Cook find that boys' toys have a greater "competency-eliciting potential" than girls' toys. That is, boys' toys encourage more flexible responses, diverse reactions, and improvisational play.

Socialization controls us by defining the external world and our relationship to it. Girls learn that women's place in the world is in the home, and they therefore learn early to prefer domestic activities and toys (Maccoby and Jacklin 1974). Several studies indicate that children (both girls and boys) differentiate between "inside" and "outside" activities for men and women. Children perceive men as working in the yard and fixing things, and women as staying inside with domestic chores (Fauls and Smith 1956). However, black male adolescents expect to have egalitarian roles in marriage (Rooks and King 1973).

Children's literature is also an important source of their learned images of women's and men's places in the world. Content analyses of children's literature show that females are underrepresented in the titles, pictures, character roles, and plots (Weitzman et al. 1972). Longitudinal studies also show that there has been little significant change in the content of children's literature in recent years. One study comparing nonsexist picture books with conventional children's books did find that females are shown as more independent and nurturing and men as less aggressive in the nonsexist books. However, females in the nonsexist books are also shown as more nurturing, more emotional, and less physically active than they are in the conventional books (Davis 1984). Also, when women are shown in children's books as exhibiting power and leadership, they tend to be mythical figures — either superheroines or fairy godmothers (Weitzman et al. 1972).

Detailed observations of children's play and games reveal the significance that they have for learning gender roles. Lever (1978) observed fifth-grade children (most of whom in her study are white and middle class) and measured the complexity of boys' and girls' activities. Based on observations in school playgrounds and analyses of questionnaires, interviews, and the children's diaries of leisure activities, she measured the complexity of play along six dimensions: role differentiation (how many distinct roles occur in the game), player interdependence (whether the action of one player affects the performance of another), size of the play group, explicitness of goals, number and specificity of rules, and, finally, team formation. She distinguishes play from games by noting that play does not involve explicit goals, whereas games tend to have a recognized goal or end point. Also, games tend to be structured by teams that work together toward a common goal; play, although it involves cooperative interaction, is not structured in team relationships.

Lever's findings reveal several patterns in the sex differences of children's play. Girls tend to play, whereas boys interact through games. Girls' games have fewer rules than boys' games and, for girls, the largest category of activity is play involving a single role. Girls' games focus on a single central person (e.g., tag), whereas boys play in larger groups and with more complex role differentiation. Girls are also more cooperative, whereas boys are more competitive; boys' play and games often include face-to-face competition, whereas girls' competition is more indirect. Girls are more likely to play games involving repeated ritual (such as jumping rope), whereas boys will follow more elaborate rules. According to Lever, ritualistic play does not exercise physical and mental skills to the extent that rules do because it is repetitive and more passive. Finally, when girls play games with rules, they tend to ignore the rules, whereas boys more rigidly adhere to established principles of play.

Lever concludes that through play and games, boys learn involvement with the generalized order; girls, on the other hand, are more involved with "particular others." Such differences are significant because the dimensions of complexity that characterize children's play also describe the organization of modern industrial societies. Complex societies involve an elaborate division of labor and elaborate differentiation of roles; these societies also are heterogeneous and are organized according to rationalized rules and social structures. Lever concludes that boys' games better prepare them for leadership and organizational skills that are useful both in childhood and in adult life. Her implication is that girls' socialization through games leaves them inadequately prepared to succeed in the complex organization of modern society.

Lever's conclusions imply that girls' experience is deficient because they develop different skills and modes of relating than do boys. However, although to function in a male-dominated society girls may need some of the skills that boys develop, we should be careful not to make the normative judgment that the female world is inferior to the male world. Childhood sex role socialization certainly teaches boys and girls different abilities and different identities. But just as girls may not learn to be rational, competitive, and rule-oriented, so boys may not learn to be nurturing and emotionally expressive.

Socialization and the Schools

As the research on childhood play and games shows, socialization takes place not only in the family, but also through other institutions and relationships. Though we tend to think of the family as the primary source for one's social values and identity, peers, teachers, the media, and other significant others are important agents of the socialization process. As parents who attempt to raise children who are not sex-stereotyped will tell you, institutions other than the family can have as great an influence on learning gender roles. Schools, in particular, exercise much influence on the creation of our sex role attitudes and behavior, so much so that some researchers call learning gender the "second curriculum" in the schools (Best 1983). In the schools, curriculum materials, teachers' expectations, educational tracking, and peer relations encourage girls and boys to learn skills and self-concepts that are often differentiated by gender.

Beginning with curriculum material, textbooks convey limited images of females that subtly communicate the idea that women and girls are less important than men and boys. Studies of textbooks show that men and women are portrayed in sex-stereotypic roles. Women are represented in far fewer occupations than men, and boys are more often shown as solving problems, displaying aggression, and being physically active (Women on Words and Images 1972). Compared with boys, girls are shown to be more conforming, more engaged in fantasy, and more involved in verbal rather than physical behavior (Child, Potter, and Levine 1960; Richardson 1981). Moreover, the situation does not seem to be improving. A survey of children's readers in 1972 found a five-to-two ratio of boy-centered to girl-centered stories; in 1977, the ratio had increased to seven-to-two (Tavris and Offir 1977). Researchers also found that test items on standard achievement tests show substantial bias by referring more often to males and the male world (Sario, Jacklin, and Tittle 1973).

Studies of teachers' expectations also find gender patterns in the behavior of teachers toward their students. Teachers respond more often to boys than to girls who misbehave (Serbin and O'Leary 1975), thereby calling more attention to them and perhaps encouraging them even further. Boys in school receive more reprimands and physical restraint (Serbin et al. 1973), but they also receive more praise than girls (Meyer and Thompson 1956). Even in progressive schools where there are deliberate attempts to avoid sex role stereotyping, researchers find that teachers subtly communicate gender expectations by, for example, complimenting girls when they wear dresses but not pants, and seldom commenting on the way boys dress (Joffe 1971).

Sex Differences in Intellectual Skills

The skills and self-concepts that boys and girls learn in school will shape their experiences beyond the school environment. The sex role messages they receive, both subtle and explicit, will guide the direction of their later lives. Research on sex differences in intellectual skills suggests the importance of social influences on the acquisition of skills.

It is generally believed that boys have better mathematical skills than girls and that girls have better verbal skills than boys. What is the evidence for this? Research does show a tendency for girls to have better verbal skills than boys (Fox, Fennema, and Sherman 1977), but the evidence about mathematical skills and cognitive abilities reveals that differences between the sexes are neither as consistent nor as predictable as previously assumed (Linn and Petersen 1985). Reported sex differences in research on verbal ability, quantitative reasoning, and visual-spatial ability are extremely small (Hyde 1981). Moreover, early research on intellectual ability tended to be conceptually underdeveloped, thereby leading to misleading or faulty conclusions.

For example, the claim has been made in the past that boys have better analytical ability than girls, though the exact referent of this term is unclear. Early studies of analytical ability tended to focus primarily on spatial perception — one's ability to perceive an object independently of its background. Conclusions showed that girls were more field dependent — that is, they had more trouble seeing an object independently of its context (Richardson 1981). Yet, this is a narrow reference for the broader concept of analytical ability and it makes implicit value judgments about the preferability of seeing things in isolation. As research on the subject of spatial ability has become more finely tuned, the conclusions reached are different. Defining spatial ability to include its different dimensions (spatial perception, mental rotation, and spatial visualization), research finds sex differences appear in some areas of spatial ability, but not in others (Linn and Petersen 1985). This complicates the analysis of sex differences in intellectual skills and reveals the narrow conceptualization upon which early studies of sex differences sometimes rested. Moreover, differences in spatial ability do not appear among young children (Maccoby and Jacklin 1974), nor have they been found in cross-cultural studies among non-Western or nonindustrialized people (Berry 1971). This lends support to the argument that, when differences appear, they are culturally learned.

Contemporary studies of sex differences in cognitive abilities differ significantly in their findings; moreover, the magnitude of sex differences found on cognitive skills varies significantly from study to study (Rosenthal and Rubin 1982). Studies do show that sex differences in cognitive skills have decreased over time, but researchers conclude either that this reflects increases in educational opportunities for women or, more likely, that the differences found in early studies reflect the design of the research, not actual differences between boys and girls.

There is some systematic support for this latter view. A study systematically examining the reported variability of sex differences on cognitive skills in published research has determined that whether sex differences are found is purely a function of the publication date of the research and how selective its research samples are (Becker and Hedges 1984). This raises the considerable possibility that reports of sex differences in intellectual skills are as much a function of the research design and researchers' preconceptions about the sexes as they are about actual differences between the sexes.

Similarly, sex-related differences in mathematical aptitude and achievement are not consistently shown in the research literature. They are not found among elementary school students (Fox, Tobin, and Brody 1979). The research does show that, where sex differences appear, they are more easily attributable to social reinforcements than to innate differences in male and female ability (Fox, Tobin, and Brody 1979). Males and females do not study mathematics at the same rate since girls take fewer advanced mathematics courses than boys in high school and college. Although studies of mathematical achievement seldom control for differences in the number of courses taken, observed sex differences in mathematics can be largely attributed to the number of courses taken (Fox, Fennema, and Sherman 1977). The fact is that in the early years boys and girls report liking math equally (Ernest 1976). However, math eventually becomes identified as a male preserve (Weitzman 1979), thereby discouraging girls from further coursework.

It seems that the focus of courses is important in conveying the message to girls that they can do well in mathematics. Girls do poorly on word problems that are based on male-typed activities, such as woodworking and guns, but do better when the same logical problems are put in the context of female-typed activities, such as cooking and gardening (Milton 1958). Also, girls' math skills improve when they are examined by other women (Pederson, Shinedling, and Johnson 1968).

It has been suggested that students do well in math depending upon its perceived usefulness to their future careers (Fennema and Sherman 1977; Hilton and Berglund 1974). This finding suggests that sex differences in intellectual skills do not appear in the absence of societal influence. If, for example, girls do better in computation than in abstract reasoning, this may be because of their implicit understanding that computational skills may be more useful to them in their future roles in the family and the workplace.

A wealth of research indicates that cultural norms discourage women from excelling at math (Tobias 1978). Critics contend, though, that the attention given to math anxiety among women may be a self-fulfilling prophecy. No one seems too concerned, for instance, about the extent of language anxiety among men, leading us to wonder if the focus on math anxiety is a reflection of the superior status attached to areas that are identified as male skills.

In summary, sex differences in intellectual skills are not as clearly shown as might be expected. When they appear, research suggests that they can be explained by the different role expectations placed on women and men in this society. Some work shows, for example, that girls, who are expected to be more oriented toward others, do best at skills requiring contextual understanding. If they have more facility with verbal reasoning, perhaps it is because of the expectation that they will be talkers, not thinkers. On the other hand, boys, who are expected to move into scientific and technical professions and to be in a position to manipulate and control their environment, are more likely to learn skills of abstract reasoning and intellectual detachment that allow them to enter such roles. As long as opportunities for success are more limited for women than for men, we can expect girls and boys to learn different skills that are appropriate for the chances that await them.

Sex Roles and Self-Concepts

Socialization helps us establish our definition of ourselves by creating our self-concept (the way we think of ourselves). Although men are usually stereotyped as more self-confident than women, research shows this not to be true. Most personality tests do not reveal sex differences on generalized measures of self-esteem (Frieze et al. 1978; Maccoby and Jacklin 1974). However, some studies of achievement-related competence and expectations for success show that women have more negative evaluations of their own abilities and performance and are less likely than men to believe in their future success (Frieze et al. 1978; Maccoby and Jacklin 1974). Other studies have claimed that successful women are more likely than men to attribute their success to luck, not skill, whereas successful men do just the opposite (Deaux, White, and Farris 1975). Based on these studies, researchers have suggested that women think of themselves as externally controlled, whereas men think of themselves as internally controlled (Tavris and Offir 1977). However, current research does not find much difference in women's and men's attribution of their success (Frieze et al. 1982). Research also fails to link how men and women attribute their successes and failures to their aspirations. This same research finds no support for the popular hypothesis that women do not achieve because they have a learned sense of helplessness. Instead, this research shows a strong link between achievement choices and one's perceived chances for success (Eccles, Adler, and Meece 1984).

Rather than casting women's aspirations as somehow deficient, this research suggests that women (and men) base their aspirations and motivation to achieve on their realistic assessments of their life chances. Perceiving themselves as externally controlled may only be a function of their consciousness of gender inequality; men, on the other hand, might be more likely to attribute their success to individual ability because their privileged status makes patriarchal social organization less visible to them. Other research shows that women and blacks who blame "the system" for what happens to them have higher self-esteem than blacks and women who blame themselves (Tavris and Offir 1977). Such responses seem to be psychologically healthy adaptations to structural inequality.

On other personality characteristics, research is inconclusive. No consistent differences have been found between women and men on measures of dependent behavior (Maccoby and Jacklin 1974); some suggest that the methods used to study sex differences tend to exaggerate the extent to which masculine and feminine traits are polarized (Cicone and Ruble 1978). However, there is strong support in the research evidence that men are more aggressive (Frieze et al. 1978; Maccoby and Jacklin 1974) and women are more emotional, although problems in interpreting what constitutes emotion remain unresolved (Frieze et al. 1978).

Much of the research on sex roles, in fact, fails to find consistent sex differences in abilities, personality, or how boys and girls relate to others (Frieze et al. 1978). Although sex differences do appear in many cases, the failure of research to predict them consistently speaks to the fluidity of men and women in their confrontations with society. The fact that we do not end up equally feminine or equally masculine attests to the incredible human resilience and flexibility that exist even in the face of powerful processes of social control.

Adult Socialization and the Aging Process

As we encounter new experiences throughout our lives, we learn the role expectations associated with our new statuses. Although our gender identity is established relatively early in life, changes in our status in society — for example, graduation, marriage, or a new job — bring new expectations for our behavior and beliefs. In later chapters, we can see that occupational and family roles carry explicit expectations for men and for women. Here we look specifically at the process of aging and the expectations that men and women face as they grow older.

Aging is perhaps the one thing about our lives that is inevitable. Yet, as a social experience, it has different consequences for men and women. Physiologically, the process of aging is similar for both sexes, with the exception of menopause. But social myths surrounding menopause have made it a more difficult process than its physiology alone creates. Physiologically, at menopause the ovaries stop producing 90 percent of their hormones, and following menopause, women become infertile. However, women may be as sexually active as before, and many women report an even more satisfying sex life once they are relieved from the connection between sexuality and childbearing.

Still, social myths portray the menopausal woman as prone to depression and anxiety, lacking sexual interest, and without self-confidence (Hess and Markson 1980). Yet, research indicates that when these problems exist, they stem from the social devaluation of aging women, not from the physiological process of aging itself (Clay 1977; Collins 1976; Livson 1977; Reitz 1977). In fact, Bart (1979) finds cross-cultural evidence showing that aging is less stressful for women in societies where there is a strong tie to family and kin, not just to a husband; where there are extended, not nuclear, family systems; where there is a positive role for mothers-in-law (rather than the degrading status attached to it in our society); and where there are strong mother-child relationships throughout life. Even in our own society, racial and ethnic groups attach more value to older persons, thereby easing the transition to later life. Although the elderly in black and minority communities experience even greater difficulties with poverty and health than do the white elderly (Jones 1985), their valued role in the extended family seems to alleviate some of the stress associated with growing old (Hess and Markson 1980).

Sex differences in the social process of aging can be attributed greatly to the emphasis on youth found in this culture and, in particular, to the association of youth and sexuality in women. Cultural stereotypes portray older men as distinguished, older women as barren. Unlike a man, as a woman ages, she will generally experience a loss of prestige; men gain prestige as they become more established in their careers. The consequences for both are great. Because men draw their self-esteem and their connections to others largely from their jobs, they may find retirement to be an especially stressful period (Bell I. 1979). Sociologists also point out that because men have learned to be task-oriented rather than person-oriented, they may have difficulty establishing new relationships in retirement or widowhood (Hess and Markson 1980).

For women, on the other hand, the disappearance of their mother role at middle age may be particularly stressful. Women who play this role to its fullest can become depressed and anxious when their children leave home and leave her behind (Bart 1979). Many of these women now find themselves reentering the labor force, either to help support their families (Currie, Dunn, and Fogarty 1980) or as the result of being displaced by divorce or widowhood (Jacobs 1979). It is important to point out, however, that for many women their middle-aged years are among the most satisfying.

Friendship patterns among the elderly also show some sex differences in experience. At all ages, men report more friends than do women, but men's friendships are not as intimate as those of women (Lewis 1978). Likewise, among older people, men, have a wider circle of friends, but women have more diverse and intense friendships (Hess 1977; Powers and Bultena 1976). Men at all ages are more likely to describe their spouse as their best friend; for these men, the death of their spouse may be even more troubling than for men with other friends. Some researchers report high risks of mental illness and suicide among these men (Bock and Webber 1972). It is also true that women who were especially devoted to their husbands find the death of a spouse to be an especially difficult adjustment (Lopata 1973).

Once past the empty nest syndrome, women generally report more satisfaction and personal freedom in their later years than they had in their earlier life (Hess and Markson 1980; Neugarten 1975). Although aging is a difficult and stressful time for both men and women (and economic pressures contribute to this stress), it seems that aging also relaxes some of the social pressure experienced as a younger person. One study of college students' expectations of their grandparents found, for instance, that images of grandfathers and grandmothers did not appear to be sex-linked (Hess and Markson 1980). In fact, the adjectives used to describe grandparents *(loving, supportive, teacher, generous, concerned)* moved in the direction of female-type nurturant values for both sexes, as images of grandparents seem to become more gender-neutral.

The influence of sex role socialization is strong throughout our lives because it is so pervasive in our social relations and our social institutions. We turn now to examining the theories used to explain this socialization process.

Theoretical Perspectives on Socialization

Three perspectives are typically used to explain the socialization process. They include identification theory, social learning theory, and cognitive-developmental theory.

Identification Theory

Identification theory sees children as learning gender-appropriate behaviors by identifying with their same-sex parent. This explanation is based on a Freudian psychoanalytic perspective that assumes that children unconsciously model their identities upon the behavior of their parents. Identification theory posits that children learn behaviors, feelings, and attitudes unconsciously; through unconscious learning, children develop motivational systems. The child's identification with the same-sex parent, coupled with the powerful emotion associated with the parent-child relationship, results in an unconscious psychosexual bond that shapes the child's sex role identity.

Empirical evidence to support the perspective of identification theory is, at best, shaky. Because the focus of this theory is on unconscious states of mind, it is impossible to measure directly the internal motivation of the child. Instead, researchers study motives indirectly by examining characteristics of the parents and associating them with behaviors and attitudes of the child. But such associations do not show a causal relationship between the parents' characteristics and the personality tendencies of their child. Because there is no direct way to observe the process of identification, this theory remains largely speculative. Moreover, evidence that children are oriented to same-sex models is inconclusive, casting further doubt upon the validity of identification theory.

More recently, Nancy Chodorow (1978) developed a theory of gender identity that is related to the perspective of identification theory. Chodorow's work is an explanation of how gender identities emerge from the social organization of parents' roles in society. We discuss her work in more detail in Chapter 6 on the family, but her work is also important in understanding the socialization process.

Chodorow argues that modern nuclear families are characterized by an "asymmetrical structure of parenting," meaning that parenting is characterized by a division of labor in which women "mother" and men do not and in which women's work is devalued. This creates a dynamic of identification in which only girls adopt the personality characteristics associated with mothering. In Chodorow's theory, called *object relations theory,* as boys and girls develop their own identities, they must become psychologically separate from their parents. Boys, who gender-identify with their fathers, form personalities that are more detached from others, because family structures in this society are based largely on the father's absence. Girls, who gender-identify with their mothers, become less detached because the mother's role in the family is one of close attachment to others. Girls' personalities, then, are more focused on attachment behaviors and on orientation to others. Boys, on the other hand, have personalities characterized by repression of their emotional needs and their commitments to others.

Chodorow's work maintains some of the orientation of identification theory in its emphasis on unconscious psychic processes. But it is distinguished from traditional psychoanalytic theory by placing gender identity clearly in the context of the division of labor by gender in work and in the family. The importance of Chodorow's work lies in the connection it makes between gender identity and the structure of the family in Western capitalist societies. But it is important to point out that, because this family form is not universal, her theory may be highly specific to families based on a traditional division of labor. Still, it is useful in explaining how gendered personalities are re-created through the social structure of the family. Her theory also suggests that transformation in family structures is a necessary prerequisite toward creating more gender-balanced personalities.

Social Learning Theory

A second theoretical perspective on socialization comes from *social learning theory,* which is highly critical of identification theory and the psychoanalytic perspective. These theorists argue that Freud's work was culture bound and, in particular, that it reflects the bias of Western patriarchal societies. The debate over psychoanalysis, from a feminist point of view, has been long and heated, and it will not be repeated here (see Figes 1970; Mitchell 1974; Weisstein 1971). Whereas identification theory rests on the idea of unconscious learning, social learning theory emphasizes the significance of the environment in explaining sex role socialization. Social learning theory is a behaviorist orientation, meaning that it sees social behavior as explained in terms of human responses to the environment.

According to behaviorists, appropriate social responses are positively rewarded, whereas inappropriate responses are punished. Thus, social learning occurs through an ongoing process of reinforcement from other people (Frieze et al. 1978). Like identification theorists, many social learning theorists believe that children model themselves based on the behaviors and attitudes of same-sex parents. But social learning theorists reject the idea that humans have stable, fixed internal motives (Mischel 1970), suggesting instead that persons "reproduce actions, attitudes or emotional responses exhibited by real-life or symbolic models" (Bandura and Walters 1963:89). From a social learning perspective, behavior is not fixed according to early established patterns; rather, behavior and attitudes change as the situations and expectations in the environment change. Sex role learning, although very significant in childhood, continues throughout life. Thus, one's gender identity is not fixed or permanent except when the social environment continues to reinforce it.

Like identification theory, social learning theory rests on the assumption that children model their behavior according to the roles of same-sex significant others. But social learning theorists posit that emotional identification is not a prerequisite for sex learning, nor are parents the only significant role models. Consequently, observations of a wide array of sex role images and expectations in the culture serve as reinforcement for sex role modeling. Empirical evidence to support social learning theory comes from the vast amount of research on variations in parental expectations for children of different sexes, stereotypic responses from teachers and peers, and the influence of institutional practices that reinforce sex role stereotypes. One implication of social learning theory is the view expressed by some feminists that women need female role models in positions of leadership and authority to compensate for the learned sense of self that they acquire through traditional socialization practices.

Cognitive-Developmental Theory

The third theoretical framework used to explain sex role learning is *cognitive-developmental theory*. This theory is based largely on the work of the Swiss psychologist Jean Piaget and, more recently, the psychologist Lawrence Kohlberg (1966). Piaget suggested that people create *schemata* —mental categories that emerge through one's interactions with the social world. These schemata, in turn, are used in the child's subsequent encounters with his or her environment. Thus, the child accommodates and assimilates new information into this existing stock of knowledge. According to Piaget, all children experience distinct stages of cognitive development, so that the developmental process is marked by alternate states of equilibrium and disequilibrium. In other words, as the developing child discovers new information or experiences in the world, he or she must adjust previously existing schemata to fit these new observations. At various points in cognitive development, the child reaches equilibrium because the child's reasoning ability is limited. Most importantly, cognitive-developmental theory emphasizes that the process of social development is one in which the child interacts with the social world through the mediation and active involvement of his or her cognitive abilities.

Kohlberg uses Piaget's perspective to explain the emergence of children's gender identities. According to Kohlberg, children discover early that people are divided into two sexes. Thus, they come to know their own sex, and they categorize others as either male or female. As their own gender identity stabilizes, they also begin to categorize behaviors and objects in the social world as appropriate for one sex or the other. At this point, gender has become an organizing scheme for the developing child, and the child attributes value to the traits and attitudes associated with his or her own sex. Children also begin to believe that gender is an unchanging category. As a result, they model their own behavior on the behaviors of those of the same sex, and they develop a strong emotional attachment to the same-sex parent.

Comparing Theoretical Perspectives

Although Kohlberg's work on gender concepts is similar, in part, to identification and social learning theories, there are important differences among the three perspectives. Identification theorists assume that imitation of same-sex persons is motivated by fear — the fear of separation from a psychosexual love object. Cognitive-developmental theorists assume a more positive motivational basis for learning, namely, mastery. In the cognitive-developmental framework, children are actively involved in the construction of their social world. In contrast, both social learning and identification theories assume a more passive view of the child's development. That is, "in contrast to both identification and social-learning theories, cognitive developmentalists assume that the initial emergence of gender as an important social category is the result of the child's cognitive system rather than the result of either psychosexual dynamics or the impact of external models and rewards" (Frieze et al. 1978:120).

Both the social learning and cognitive-developmental perspectives emphasize the role of culture in shaping gender identity. But social learning theorists have a more deterministic view, in that they see culture as a model and reinforcer for what the child becomes. In the cognitive-developmental framework, the child does more than simply react to the culture. He or she searches for patterns in the culture and actively seeks to structure and organize the conceptions of the world that the culture provides.

The three theories described in the preceding paragraphs have been primarily developed by psychologists, but the cognitive-developmental perspective is related to the sociological perspective called *symbolic interactionism.* This perspective is based heavily on the work of George Herbert Mead, whose work was described in the section on children's play and games. According to the symbolic interactionist perspective, the process of socialization rests on our ability to take the role of the other. That is, we come to see ourselves as others see us. Through a reflective process of envisioning ourselves from the perspective of others, we form our self-concepts. Thus, the self is established as one becomes an object to oneself. Symbolic interactionism emphasizes the human ability to form and understand symbols, for it is through symbolic interpretation that consciousness and, therefore, the self is possible.

Each of these perspectives on sex role socialization shows us how central gender is to the formation of our gender identity. From the day we are born to the day we die, social expectations about our gender confront us in the everyday world. Through the sex role socialization process, these external social expectations become internalized in our self-concepts, and they become identities through which we experience the social world. Thus, socialization is an essential sociological concept, for it describes the process that relates individuals to society.

Limitations of the Socialization Perspective

Questions about sex differences and socialization as an origin for difference are more than academic matters. A recent legal case indicates their seriousness for matters of public policy about sex discrimination. In 1979 the Equal Employment Opportunities Commission (EEOC) brought a sex discrimination suit against Sears, Roebuck and Company. The EEOC alleged that Sears had engaged in sex discriminatory practices by failing to hire female job applicants for commission sales positions on the same basis as male applicants, failing to promote female noncommission salespersons to commission sales positions on the same basis as males, and paying women in certain management jobs less than similarly placed men. The EEOC presented extensive statistical and qualitative evidence of the disparities at Sears between women and men in commission sales; Sears did not deny these data. Sears's defense, however, was that there were fundamental differences between men's and women's qualifications and prefer-ences for such work. Sears argued that men were more interested in and willing to accept commission sales jobs, in part because they were willing to take more risks. According to Sears, women's underrepresentation in commission sales was not because of discrimination, but because of women's own job preferences. The plaintiff (EEOC) argued that "what appear to be women's choices . . . are, in fact, heavily influenced by the opportunities for work made available to them" (Milkman 1986:376). The case was tried in 1984 and 1985; in 1986, a U.S. District Court ruled in favor of Sears, though the EEOC filed an appeal.

The issue of sex differences figures prominently in the Sears case and raises the question of whether social policies should treat men and women differently or treat them identically. Do women make different choices than men, and, if so, how can we develop policies that will not systemati-cally disadvantage women for the choices they make? If policies are sex-blind, will they inadvertently benefit only women who make choices as men would make them? Sears argued that men and women differ in their expectations regarding work and, therefore, that gender segregation is a matter of women's choice. Some feminist scholars have argued that, since the separate spheres of men's and women's experiences condition them to respond in different ways, if women were treated the same as men, there would not be such difference in their choices. But feminists also contend that women should not have to become like men in order to be accorded the privileges of the male world. Instead, there should be greater recognition for women's values, cultures, and forms of behavior.

The question of separate spheres lies at the heart of our discussion of sex roles. Do differences between the sexes exist and, if so, are they actually learned preferences or do they only reflect institutionalized practices of sex discrimination? The answer, of course, lies in both, although, in the con-text of public policy, there is little room for such analytical nuance. But the complexity of these questions and their seriousness for social policy bring urgency to our discussion of gender relations. Socialization does not occur in a vaccum. It is a process by which human beings adapt to their environ-ment, and in this culture that environment is one structured on gender inequality. Socialization does explain the origins of inequality, but it is also a very effective way of explaining how that inequality is reproduced. But if we limit ourselves to thinking of sex differences as only a matter of learned choice, we would overlook the patterns of institutionalized gender inequal-ity that pervade this society.

Individual experience reflects the larger society in which one lives; reex-amining the events in our lives that socialized us into sex roles is a funda-mental step in recognizing how we came to be who we are and how we can change. Thus, understanding the socialization process and the emergence of sex roles is a critical part of developing a feminist perspective and a sociological analysis of gender relations in society. But there are a number of limitations in seeing gender relations as emerging primarily through socialization.

Although the socialization process shows how individuals become gendered persons, it does not explain the social structural origins of gender inequality. Understanding socialization helps us to see that gender expectations have their origins outside the individual, but socialization theories do not explain the institutional bases of those origins and, therefore, they are not causal theories of women's status in society.

If we limit our understanding of gender relations to a perspective on sex roles, we tend to downplay the significance of gender in the social-institutional framework of society. To illustrate this point, consider how absurd it would be to explain racism in society in terms of a role perspective. No one uses the term *race roles* to describe patterns of inequality between blacks and whites, although surely it is true that, because of racism, blacks and whites establish expectations of each other. Similarly, to assume that roles are the only appropriate framework for studying gender is to assume that consciousness, not structured inequality, is the sole basis for women's subordination (Lopata and Thorne 1978).

Because the sex role perspective neglects the institutional basis for gender inequality, it tends to explain gender relations exclusively in psychological terms. This does not mean that *sex roles* and *socialization* are incorrect concepts, merely that we should not oversimplify our analysis of women's and men's status in society by seeing these only in terms of learned roles. A *social role* is merely an abstract concept used by sociologists to describe and explain patterns of social behavior. If this concept is overused, we run the risk of assuming that simply rejecting our social roles will being social change. Such a perspective underestimates the influence of the institutionalized gender inequality in creating gender roles. Moreover, the role perspective encourages us to think of men and women merely as passive vessels into whom a variety of expectations are poured. This assumption ignores the extent to which people are active agents in their social relations. People are not mere receptacles for social life; rather, they actively participate in and create social change. The sex role perspective may exaggerate the extent to which we become socialized, leading to an oversocialized view of human life.

The focus on sex roles tends to exaggerate the differences between the sexes because, by definition, its emphasis tends to be on differences, not similarities. In sex role research, sex differences are typically built into research designs. The items on questionnaires, for example, or the factors selected for manipulation in experimental studies necessarily reflect the differences that a researcher wants to test. The end result may be that the research literature on sex roles exaggerates and polarizes masculine and feminine differences (Cicone and Ruble 1978).

Additionally, it has been found that the sex of the researcher is a good predictor of whether sex differences will be found in research studies. Men are more likely to find sex differences than women; thus, research conclusions may subtly reflect the gender biases of the researcher (Eagly and Carli 1981). In other words, if a researcher expects to find sex differences, chances are that the research will reveal this finding.

Research on socialization may also exaggerate the extent to which the sexes are different. It is important to remember that not all girls and boys grow up in the sex-stereotyped way that the research literature sometimes suggests. Moreover, research on sex roles to date primarily reflects the experience of white, middle-class persons, those who are most frequently found as research subjects in these studies.

Nevertheless, research on childhood learning underscores the point that sex role socialization is situated within social institutions that do tend to value masculine, not feminine, traits. Were female-oriented values — such as flexibility, orientation toward others, and cooperation — to be incorporated into dominant social institutions, then we might well produce more gender-balanced boys and girls. As it is, the process of socialization throughout life separates men and women and creates gender differences among children and adults.

Summary

Cultural practices shape gender identity through the process of sex role socialization. Sex roles are learned through social interaction in the various institutions of society, including but not limited to families and schools. Socialization operates as a system of social control by encouraging different behaviors and attitudes in men and women. Through these expectations we learn what is properly masculine and feminine, though we do not all conform to these roles in identical ways.

Sex role attitudes and behaviors affect us in a variety of ways and take their toll upon our physical and mental health. Sex roles may also shape our skills, personalities, and relationships with others. Socialization continues throughout our life course and can be observed in infancy, through childhood play and games, in our experiences in schools, and throughout the process of aging. Though sex roles are an important predictor of many behaviors, sex differences in many areas may not be as great as is traditionally believed.

Three theories are used to explain the socialization process: identification theory, social learning theory, and cognitive-development theory. Each has its own strengths and weaknesses in explaining the socialization process. Socialization does not, however, explain the origins of gender inequality. The utility of the sex roles framework is limited because it is inadequate to explain institutionalized gender inequality.

Focusing only on sex differences leads us to ignore the vast similarities between the two sexes. Research on sex roles is often biased because of its selective use of white middle-class subjects in research populations. Still, understanding the process of sex role socialization is an important part of understanding gender relations in society.

Cite Weitzman's 2nd thought.

PART II

Gender and Social Institutions

CHAPTER 5

Women, Work, and the Economy

Introduction

In 1985, the median income for women employed year-round and full-time was $15,422; men employed year-round and full-time earned $24,999. Even after the women's movement drew our attention to the earnings gap between women and men and also following more than a decade of some reforms intended to reduce sex discrimination, employed women still earned only 62 percent of what men earned. Moreover, only 6½ percent of employed women earn more than $25,000 a year, compared with almost 30 percent of employed men. And, in 1985 women with college educations still earned less ($17,235) than men with only high school diplomas ($18.997)! Male college graduates earned $31,946 (U.S. Department of Commerce, Bureau of the Census August 1986).

Women's role in economic life has been obscured by social myths about the work that women do. These myths include the idea that women who work at home as full-time housewives are not working; that women who work for wages work for extra money, not because they must; and that women's work is not as valuable as men's. As a result, women's work has been undervalued both in its objective rewards and in the ideas we have about women and work. Furthermore, because women's work has been seen as less important than men's it has not, until recently, been seriously studied.

Historical Perspectives on Women's Work _____

Studying the history of women's work shows the societal developments that result in women's economic inequality and the devaluation of women's labor both inside and outside the home. As this section shows, the history of gender inequality in the Western world is intertwined with the history of racial subordination. A full analysis of the history of women's work examines the work experience of women of color as an integral part of the history of women's labor; moreover, studying race and gender inequality hand in hand furthers our understanding of contemporary developments in women's work both nationally and internationally.

A complete history of women's labor would also include their roles in preindustrial societies, since these earlier forms of social organization reveal much about the relationship of women's status to their roles in systems of production. But the character of women's labor in the contemporary economy is most significantly influenced by the transformation from domestically based production to industrialized production and a consumer-oriented market system. Historians describe this transformation in terms of three economic periods: the family-based economy, the family-wage economy, and the family-consumer economy (Tilly and Scott 1978).

The Family-Based Economy and Slavery

In western Europe the first period, the *family-based economy*, dates roughly from the seventeenth century to the early eighteenth century; the household was the basic unit of the economy because production occurred primarily in the home. As late as the seventeenth century, there was no sharp distinction between economic and domestic life because household members (including non-blood kin) were responsible for the production of goods. Work in this period was productive activity for household use; all members of the household, including children, contributed directly to household labor (Tilly and Scott 1978). Women in these households would most likely supervise much of the household work, especially the labor of children; they were also engaged in agricultural labor and the production of cloth and food. The typical household unit (in England and France) during this period was largely agricultural, although later, as cities developed, the wives of shopkeepers and artisans would also share in the household's work. In both rural and urban settings in the domestic economy, the work of women and children was interdependent with that of men. Although the tasks done by each might vary, "production and family life were inseparably intertwined and the household was the center around which resources, labor, and consumption were balanced" (Tilly and Scott 1978:12).

In the colonial United States, families were also the center for economic activity though single women (either unwed or widowed) would work in others' households doing traditional women's tasks like spinning, weaving, and sewing or work in fields (Kessler-Harris 1982). As slavery developed as an integral part of the U.S. economy, black women and men labored as slaves, though in many states, black men and women worked as free laborers, doing a variety of jobs, as skilled craft workers, farm laborers, and domestics.

Black women and men were forcibly brought to the United States by the slave trade beginning in the early seventeenth century and persisting at least until 1807, when England and the United States agreed, at least in law, to prohibit the trade (Meier and Rudwick 1966). It is estimated that over 9.5 million Africans were transported to the United States, the Caribbean, and Brazil during this time, not counting the probably 20 million who died in passage (Genovese 1972, Meier and Rudwick 1966).

Black women in slavery did most of the same jobs as men, though in addition, they worked in the masters' home and on behalf of their own families (Jones 1985). The plantation economy functioned somewhat like the domestic economy because the plantation, like a household, functioned as the major unit of production. In the American South, one-quarter of white families held slaves, though half of the slaves lived on farms with fewer than twenty slaves and three-quarters lived on farms with fewer than fifty slaves (Genovese 1972).

Under slavery, slaves provided most, if not all, of the productive labor, while white slave owners had total control and ownership of slave labor and the profits it generated. The plantation economy represents a transition between an agriculturally based society and an industrialized one because the population of slaves worked as a cheap and fully controlled labor force. After the abolition of slavery, black women and men entered the labor market as free laborers, but, even then, the dynamics of racism maintained blacks as an underclass that could not compete equally for the same jobs available to white women and men (Wilson 1978).

The Family-Wage Economy

In the second period of the transformation to advanced capitalism, called the *family-wage economy*, the center of labor moved out of the household and into the factory system. This shift is the result of industrialization that began in England in the mid-eighteenth century, followed in France and the United States somewhat later. In the family-wage economy, workers earned their living outside the home and the household became dependent on wages that the workers brought home. The shift to wage labor and the production of commodities outside the home had several influences on the character of women's work. It led to the development of dual roles for women as paid laborers and as unpaid housewives (McBride 1976).

With industrialization, the household was no longer the primary center of production, although women's work in the home was still socially and economically necessary. Yet, as the focus of work moved beyond the home, the worth of all persons became measured in terms of their earned wage; therefore, the work of women in the home was devalued. And with goods being produced largely outside the home for profit (not just exchange or subsistence), international mercantilism developed that further eroded the position of women (Dobash and Dobash 1979).

In a wage system, producing, distributing, and purchasing goods requires cash. Although women and children worked for wages in the factory system, they received less pay than men and, in fact, were chosen as workers because they were a cheap supply of labor. Male control of the wage labor system, along with the capitalist pursuit of greater profits, weakened women's earning power (Hartmann 1976). And because cash resources were needed to survive in the new economy, women became more financially dependent on men (Tilly and Scott 1978).

Black and immigrant women in the United States during this period worked primarily as domestics or in factory labor. Following slavery, the vast majority of black women were employed as private domestic workers; their wages were notoriously low. At the same time, immigrant women in the Northeast for the most part filled factory jobs in the textiles and garment industries or, on the West Coast, worked in domestic, agricultural, and factory labor.

Throughout the period of the family-wage economy, at least until World War I, most single, working-class, and immigrant women worked as domestic servants. In 1870, one-half of all women wage earners in the United States were domestic workers. However, by 1920, the percentage of women wage earners working as domestics declined to 18.5 percent, reflecting the changes in women's employment as they entered new fields as clerical workers, teachers, and nurses. Still, domestic work remained a major source of employment for Japanese and Chinese women immigrating to the United States in the first half of the twentieth century (Glenn 1986) and it continues to be a major means of employment for contemporary immigrant women.

As production and commerce grew during this period, management also became more complex, leading to vast increases in clerical and administrative occupations. For women workers, the invention of the typewriter created a new concentration of women in the clerical labor force. The typewriter was introduced to the public in 1873 and, because there was a shortage of labor for the new jobs it created, women were recruited for typing jobs based on the ideological appeal that they were naturally more dextrous than men (Benet 1972). In other fields, too, women were recruited when labor shortages necessitated a new work force. As public education was expanded in the late nineteenth century, women were said to be naturally suited for a profession that required patience, nurturing, and the education of children. Similarly, when the middle class organized the public health movement of the early twentieth century to ward off the "contagions" of the poor, female nurses were recruited to serve doctors and to bring "feminine compassion" to the sick (Ehrenreich and English 1973).

The Family-Consumer Economy

The third period of economic change is called the *family-consumer economy*. This period, also characteristic of the present, is really an extension of the family-wage system. In this period, technological change increased productivity, and the mass production of goods created households that specialized in consumption and reproduction (Tilly and Scott 1978). Although, in the family-consumer economy, economic production goes on outside the home, the labor of family members does contribute to their economic standing. As we have already seen, in this period women's work as housewives is often coupled with their participation in paid labor. Thus, in the family-consumer economy, women's economic productivity is even higher than in the past (Tilly and Scott 1978). Although women continue to do the same amount of housework as in earlier periods (Vanek 1978), public institutions (such as schools, welfare systems, and the fast-food industry) also take over activities that were once located in the household. Women, consequently, become defined primarily as consumers even though, in most cases, their wages are still necessary for household support.

In sum, the middle and late nineteenth century in America brought about vast changes in the organization of labor, with enormous consequences for women's work even in the contemporary period. The history of women in the labor force shows that women have served as a reserve supply of labor, meaning that women are kept out of the paid labor force until there is a labor shortage or demand for less expensive labor. When there is a need for additional or cheaper workers, women are brought into the labor force. Corresponding to the fluctuating needs for women workers are changes in the cultural definitions of women's place in the home and in the workplace.

Throughout the twentieth century, women's labor force participation continued to rise. Much has been made about the dramatic influx of women into the paid labor force during World War II. Popular wisdom has it that because of the need for women's labor, women entered the labor force in unprecedented numbers, only to leave it and return to their homes at the end of the war. In fact, women did respond to the appeals for war-time work with enthusiasm, but three-quarters of those who were employed during the war had work for wages before. Historians estimate that a sizable group of new women workers would have entered the labor force anyhow; thus, the influx of women to paid work during the war is not as dramatic as usually assumed. Women saw the emergency as an opportunity to get ahead and black women, professional women, and older women took advantage of the reduction in discrimination to enter well-paying jobs (Kessler-Harris 1982). During the war, women were employed not so much in unprecedented numbers, but in unprecedented jobs — jobs that were well-paid, were industrialized, and that gave a new legitimacy and value to the work that women did (Sacks 1984).

At the conclusion of the war, many women did not leave the paid labor force, but found jobs in other areas — jobs that did not pay as well as those they had left. Women were laid off after the war at a rate double that of men and were shunted into jobs in the clerical and service sectors. Older women, married women, black women, and ethnic women had a hard time finding jobs after the war.

Ideology and the History of Women's Work

In Chapter 2 we defined ideology as a belief system that seeks to explain and justify the status quo. The economic and technological changes that marked the transitions from the domestic economy to the consumer economy were historically accompanied by changes in the ideological definition of womanhood. The "cult of true womanhood" (Kraditor 1968), popularized in the nineteenth century, glorified women's ideal place as the home, where women were seen as having a moral calling to serve their families. The aristocratic lady of leisure became a model to be emulated and set the ideal, although not the reality, for women of the bourgeois class. At the same time, the Protestant ethic, which stressed individualism, success, and competition in the workplace, also encouraged women to submerge their wills to piety, purity, and submissiveness (Kessler-Harris 1976). Thus, at least in bourgeois families, women's destiny became defined as a separate sphere in which home, duty to the family, and religion would prevail.

Despite these ideals, women of the working class and black and immigrant women continued to work both in the public labor force and in the home. The reality of their working lives in the early industrial period stands in contradiction to the myth of true womanhood. Only the most affluent families could maintain an idle woman; most women worked long hours in factories and then at home. While the cult of true womanhood was at its peak, black women were working as slaves, and no ideal of femininity was bestowed upon them. In fact, the myth of the ideal woman could be created only at the expense of other women because black, immigrant, and poor women still performed the necessary household and factory tasks.

For example, around the turn of the twentieth century in the United

States, the woman who stayed at home to do her own housework became a symbol of middle-class prosperity (Davis 1981). Consequently, black and immigrant women who had found employment as domestics were expelled from white middle-class homes and replaced by new technological devices that promised to make women's work easy. In fact, some of the advertising campaigns for new products in this period (such as irons) presented explicit images of these new products purging middle-class homes of the alleged germs and social diseases of black and Chinese women (Cowan 1976). Homes became depicted during this period as bulwarks of defense against the rapid social changes occurring in the industrial workplace. The new ideology of domesticity portrayed women's place in the home as a moral alternative to the effects of the bustling, nervous organization of public labor. And because many of the industrial changes taking place involved the migration of blacks and immigrants to the cities, it can be said that the cult of domesticity was intertwined with the dynamics of racism. White, middle-class women were not only seen as pious and pure, they were also perceived as the moral antithesis of allegedly inferior black, Oriental, and immigrant women.

At the same time, by the early twentieth century, middle-class women were expected to apply the skills of rational professional men to the maintenance of their homes. Inspired by modern models of rational management, housework (under the guise of the domestic science movement) was to be efficient, sanitary, and technologically streamlined. Order, system, and efficiency were the goals of domestic science, and the housewife was to become an engineer who would keep accurate records, color-code her appliances, maintain an efficient schedule, and, in the modern sense of the word, *manage* her home (Andrews and Andrews 1974). Once again, clean houses and efficient management were seen as the antithesis of immigrant lives. Racism in this period depicted blacks and immigrants as slovenly, diseased, and ridden with contagious germs (Higham 1965). Racist fears about the underclass propelled the middle classes to a new sense of themselves as both the moral agents of society and the social engineers of the future.

It is from this period that we have acquired many of our common household practices today. During the 1920s, many of the household designs that are now commonplace were introduced. Kitchens and bathrooms were to be pretty, as indicated in the following editorial:

Time was when kitchens were gloomy and dark, for keeping house was a gloomy business. . . . But now! gay colors are the order of the day. Red pots and pans! Blue gas stoves! . . . It is a rainbow, in which the cook sings at her work and never thinks of household tasks as drudgery. (*Ladies Home Journal*, March 1928, cited in Cowan 1976:150–151)

Old wooden furniture was painted pastel colors; new brides were advised to keep the gray out of their husbands' shirts; and protecting the family from germs became evidence of good maternal instincts (Cowan 1976). Thus, the ideology of domesticity added an emotional dimension to what had previously been the work of servants.

Women's roles in the home were further elaborated by the new importance placed on child care and the psychological life of infants and children. In the early twentieth century, the child became the leading figure in the family, and child psychology experts admonished mothers to turn their attention to their babies' emotional development and security (Ehrenreich and English 1978). In the end, both the concepts of housewife and motherhood emphasized new standards for women's services in the home. So, although technological change created the potential for a reduction in household labor, ideological shifts in the concept of women's roles increased the social requirements for women's work. Whereas housework before had been necessary labor, it now carried ideological significance as well. As contemporary ads imply, cleaning the rings from one's husband's collar is not only doing the laundry, it is supposed to be an expression of love as well. These new standards of housework effectively raise the level of consumption by individual households, leading to the conclusion shared by many social scientists that consumption, not production, is one of the major functions of contemporary household units today.

The preceding discussion shows that an analysis of women's roles in economic production cannot be separated from their roles in family life. Although the family and the economy are usually perceived as separate institutions, they are, both in history and in the present, intertwined through the activities of production and reproduction. Women work both for wages and without wages. Our discussion of women and work must be understood in this context.

Sociological Perspectives on Work and Gender Stratification

There are two ways one can approach the contemporary issues of women and work. One is an individualistic perspective; the other is sociological. From an individual point of view, we might ask such questions as: How can I choose the right job? How can I be successful and earn a good income? How can I find a job that will satisfy my interests? And how can I manage having both a career and a family? Additionally, as women enter the labor force, particularly in traditionally male jobs, they might ask, How can I find support for myself and my abilities in a company that is primarily organized for men?

All of these questions are important, and individuals will no doubt ask them at various points in their working lives. But for sociologists, questions about work have a different focus. Sociologists are concerned with the quality of individual experiences, but they are more likely to ask questions about the social organization of work, gender, and economic relations. From a feminist perspective, the important sociological questions about work are those that examine men's and women's experience within the context of gender stratification and the gender division of labor. Therefore, the questions inspired by a feminist perspective in sociology include: What is women's role in the labor force? How do we explain historical change in women's labor force participation? What is the socioeconomic status of women and the households in which they live? What factors influence the economic mobility of women workers? How are gender issues at work complicated by those of race and social class? These questions form the basis for sociological investigations of the relationships between women's work and the larger economy. Before proceeding, some concepts used by sociologists in discussing work must be defined.

Work

As we have seen in discussing the history of women's work, work itself is a problematic concept when we use it to describe what women do. We tend to think of work as that which people do for pay, and traditional sociological definitions of work have restricted its meaning to activity for the acquisition of financial resources. But as the history of women's work shows, women (and sometimes men) often work without pay. Housewives work, but do not get paid; black women worked as slaves, but did not get paid. Volunteers work and, in fact, many women have full-time careers as volunteers (Daniels — forthcoming). Moreover, problems in the concept of work are not just a question of whether work is paid or unpaid, but are more fundamental to the question of what constitutes work.

One consequence of feminist revisions of sociology has been to question the traditional concept of work and its ability to include the full range of women's and men's productive activities. Feminists have pointed out that mothering is work, though it does not fit the criteria imposed by the traditional definition of work. Moreover, if mothering is work, should fathering be considered work as well? And, in considering the case of housework, feminist sociologists observe that there is an invisible dimension to the work, not only including the fact that it goes unnoticed, but also the fact that part of doing housework is the work of "keeping in mind" various aspects of the tasks that constitute housework (De Vault 1985). Housework involves not only the physical work of doing tasks, but also the mental efforts of noticing and remembering the chores that need doing, mentally arranging the tasks that need doing, and keeping track of the work to be done. None of this work can be actually measured or observed; as a result, it is difficult to share, though it is an essential aspect of the work.

In addition to these added dimensions to the concept of work, Arlie Hochschild (1983) has developed the concept "emotional labor" to refer to the work people do in managing the emotions of others. Emotional labor, she argues, is work that is done for wages and that is meant to achieve a desired emotional effect in others. Emotional labor is done in jobs that require personal contact with the public, wherein creating a given state of mind in the client or user is part or all of the product being sold. Hochschild's research is a study of airline flight attendants, for whom emotional labor is a central part of job training, activity, and evaluation. Hochschild shows that because of the shift from a production-based to a service-based economy and given the fact that women predominate in service-oriented jobs, emotional labor is a growing part of the work that women do. It is monitored by supervisors and is the basis for job rewards and reprimands. She concludes that doing emotional labor often requires putting on a false front; as a result, engaging in emotional labor is a source of workers' stress. Moreover, emotional labor is required in an increasing number of jobs and is, therefore, subject to the rules of mass production. This is resulting in what Hochschild calls "the commercialization of human feeling."

Gender Stratification

Gender stratification refers to the hierarchical distribution by gender of economic and social resources in a society. All societies are organized around a system for the production and distribution of goods. In addition, most societies are marked by a system of social stratification. Sociologists define *stratification* as the process whereby groups or individuals in a society are located in a hierarchical arrangement on the basis of their differential access to social and economic resources. But sociologists also point out that there is nothing inherent in human nature or inevitable in social organization that requires unequal access to social and economic resources. Were inequality an inevitable result of human nature, stratification patterns would not vary in societies to the extent that they do. Moreover, we would not find egalitarian societies in the record of human history.

But because these differences in stratification are found, sociologists are very interested in the conditions that generate social inequality. Many point out that socioeconomic inequality emerges when there is a surplus of goods available in the society (Blumberg 1978; Marx and Engels 1970). Simply put, a surplus of goods creates the possibility that one group of people can appropriate the surplus for themselves. This action forms the initial basis for class systems in which one class controls the resources of other groups in the society.

In most societies, gender is a primary category that stratifies social groups. Women's access to societal rewards is greatly influenced by the degree to which they control the means and forms of social and economic production. In virtually all societies, women's work sustains the economy, although in many societies (such as our own) women's work is either invisible or devalued (Leghorn and Parker 1981). Cross-cultural research shows us that women tend to have the most egalitarian status in societies in which they directly contribute to the production of goods (Blumberg 1978; Leacock 1978). In hunting and gathering societies, for example, women produce most of the food supply. Their status in these societies is relatively equal to that of men, even though a gender division of labor still exists. In agricultural societies, although women continue to be primary producers, their status deteriorates because land, economic surplus, and, subsequently, political power are concentrated in the hands of male rulers (O'Kelly and Carney 1986).

In preindustrialized societies, women's labor in the home is a vital part of the productive system because it is in the home that goods are produced. Moreover, in these societies, women also have visible roles outside the home, as they distribute their goods in markets or even operate small businesses. As industrialization advances, though, economic production is shifted from the home to the factory, and although working-class and immigrant women hold factory jobs, women's domestic labor becomes both invisible and devalued. In American history, the devaluation of household labor not only resulted in a loss of status for middle-class women who worked at home but also created a class of the most severely underpaid and socially devalued laborers — black domestic workers (Davis 1981).

Class and Status

Sociologists use the concepts of *class* and *status* to refer to the different place of workers in the economic system and the different value they are perceived as having. As we will see, both of these concepts raise particular conceptual difficulties when we use them to refer to women's role in the economy.

Two different definitions of *class* form two schools of thought among sociologists. Weber defines class in terms of one's access to social and economic resources. Typically, sociologists who think of class this way see stratification as involving a class hierarchy, with the upper class having the greatest access to resources and the middle and lower classes having proportionately less. In this definition, class is most typically measured in terms of one's income or the relative status of one's occupation. *Status* (also called *prestige*) is a related concept, defined as the social value attached to one's position in the stratification system (Gerth and Mills 1958). Typically, status or prestige is associated with one's occupation.

Therefore, sociologists who study stratification often measure social class by a combination of variables such as income and occupation.

From a different perspective, one informed by the work of Karl Marx (1818–1883), class is defined in terms of the relationship of groups to the system of production. Marx's theory is concerned with the class system of capitalism and is particular to that economic system. He defines the *capitalist class* as those who own the means of production (i.e., the factories where goods are produced); the *bourgeois class* include those who identify with capitalists and are functionally dependent on them, but who do not own the means of production (e.g., business managers). The *working class*, or *proletariat*, includes those who sell their labor to the capitalists in return for wages, (i.e., laborers). The *lumpenproletariat* are those who have been permanently discarded by the system and, thus, no longer have an economic role (including the permanently unemployed, the mentally ill, and the aged). Marx's concept of class is a dynamic one in that, unlike the more simple hierarchical definition previously described, it assumes an active relationship between the formation of classes and developments in the economic system of capitalism.

Although each of these perspectives has contributed much to sociological research and theory, both have problems when they are applied to women's experience. The two concluding chapters of this book discuss theoretical perspectives on women's experience in more detail, but for now, it is important to see that both concepts of class are inadequate in understanding women's economic role.

In the case of the first definition, we can see that many women workers (housewives, in particular) have no income. Thus, a measure of their class standing is impossible to derive. Moreover, housework has not been defined as an occupation and, thus, has no clear occupational status. Traditionally, a woman's status and class have been seen as derived from her husband's. There is a certain degree of truth in this belief, because many of us probably think of all members of a family as being of the same class. But there are numerous problems with this assumption as well. How, for instance, would we describe the class position of single women or women who head families with no husband present? Or, in another example, how do we describe the class standing of a women divorced from a middle-class man? Although she may have been considered middle-class while married, following her divorce she may have lost her house, access to her husband's income, her car, and even her own definition of her class position. And how do we define the class position of lesbian women who, although they may earn middle-class incomes, may legally not have the right to own property or maintain custody of their children?

Similarly, in the Marxist concept of class, women also seem to have no place. Although many women do have working-class and bourgeois jobs, the Marxist concept of class does not account for women's domestic labor. Housewives, in the Marxist framework, are an invisible class of workers.

Because they do not produce goods for profit, they are eliminated from the otherwise illuminating analysis of the class system that Marx provides.

This discussion of sociological concepts shows how the study of women causes us to rethink and redefine some of the basic elements of sociological thinking. The following section reviews the contemporary economic status of women by detailing their earnings and occupational distribution. In addition, we look at some of the explanations given by sociologists for the persistence of economic inequality between women and men.

The Contemporary Status of Women

Sociologists use the term *discrimination* to refer to the practice of singling groups out for special treatment. Sex discrimination refers specifically to the unequal and harmful treatment of individuals or groups because of their sex (Benokraitis and Feagin 1986). Sex discrimination is, of course, compounded for women of color by racial discrimination — a situation described by many as "double jeopardy." Public opinion polls indicate that as late as 1985, 75 percent of women in the United States and 64 percent of men believed that women do not receive the same pay as men for doing exactly the same job (Harris Survey 1985).

The facts show them to be correct. On most measures of economic equity, including income, unemployment, and occupational distribution, women fare worse than men. And, when accounting for race as well as sex, the economic disparities grow. In fact, despite the increased presence of women in the pair labor force in recent years and positive changes for women in some segments of the labor market, serious problems of economic equity between women and men persist.

Labor Force Participation Rates

Social myth has it that women do not work. Yet, in 1986, 55.3 percent of all women were in the paid labor force compared with 76.3 percent of men (see Table 5-1). Moreover, women's labor force participation has increased over time, notably in the last twenty years. The increase in the number of women workers is especially marked among women with children. Between 1960 and 1984, married women with children under six nearly tripled their labor force participation. In 1984, 65.4 percent of women with children between 6 and 17 years of age were working; 51.8 percent of women with children under 6 were working (U.S. Department of Labor January 1985). These increases in the number of working mothers mean that whether or not a woman has children is no longer an accurate predictor of whether she will be engaged in paid labor (Almquist 1977).

TABLE 5-1   Labor Force Participation Rates, by Race and by Sex, 1986

	Percent in Labor Force			
	All	Whites	Blacks	Hispanics
Men	76.3%	76.9%	71.2%	81.0%
Women	55.3	55.0	56.9	50.1

Source: U.S. Bureau of Labor Statistics, *Employment and Earnings.* Washington, D.C.: U.S. Government Printing Office, January 1987.

Public opinion often assumes that women work because of freedom or a search for fulfillment. Although that belief may be true for a small number of women, most women are employed out of economic necessity. That is, 41.5 percent of the women in the paid labor force are single, divorced, or widowed, and, although the majority of employed women are married, married-couple families where the wife is not working fall below the national median income level (see Table 5-2). Opinion polls also show that only 37 percent of American women want to be married without a full-time job (Gallup Poll 1985). Most women work for wages either to support themselves or their family or to bring in extra money (Roper Organization 1985). This finding is particularly evident when we consider the high number of female-headed households; they constituted more than one-quarter of all American households in 1985 (see Table 6-1 in the next chapter).

TABLE 5-2   Median Income for Families and Individuals, 1985

	All	White	Black	Hispanic
All families	$27,735	$29,152	$16,786	$19,027
Married couples	31,100	31,602	24,570	22,269
— with wife in paid labor force	36,431	36,992	30,507	22,132
— wife not in paid labor force	24,556	25,307	15,129	17,116
Female householders (no husband present)	13,660	15,825	9,305	8,792
Male householders (no wife present)	22,622	24,190	16,416	19,773
Persons*				
— Males	16,311	17,111	10,768	11,434
— Females	7,217	7,357	6,277	6,020

*working year-round and full-time.

Source: U.S. Bureau of the Census, Current Population Reports, Series P60, No. 154. *Money Income and Poverty Status of Families and Persons in the U.S., 1985.* Washington, D.C.: U.S. Government Printing Office, August 1986.

Employed women have, in the past, been stereotyped as career women —the assumption being that they are somehow different from other women in the population. Employed women are now younger, better educated, more likely married, and more likely to be minding children than their predecessors. But, unlike the social stereotype, women engaged in paid labor closely represent the female population as a whole (Blau 1979).

Black and other minority women are even more likely than white women to be employed, although the gap between the two groups is narrowing. In 1986, among women aged 20 years and older, the labor force participation rate for black women was 58.9 percent, for Hispanic women 51.7 percent, and for white women 54.9 percent (U.S. Bureau of Labor Statistics January 1987). However, despite their more positive attitudes toward working, black women's labor force participation is not increasing as fast as that of white women. This is explained by the fact that there are inadequate employment opportunities for black women, especially those from lower socioeconomic groups (Jones 1986).

The labor force participation rate for Hispanic women is inflated somewhat by the high percentage of Cuban employed women. Because the label *Hispanic* includes Cubans, Puerto Ricans, Mexican-Americans, and other groups of Spanish origin, the aggregate statistics on Hispanic workers misrepresent the experience of any one of these groups. For example, in 1986, the labor force participation rate of Puerto Rican women in the United States was 38.1 percent, for Mexican-American women 50.8 percent, and for Cuban women 56.9 percent (U.S. Bureau of Labor Statistics January 1987).

Occupational Distribution

Most women work in sex-segregated jobs. That is to say, women work in jobs where most of the other workers are women, and women constitute a minority of workers in jobs that have been traditionally identified as men's work. Women also work in fewer different occupations than men and, within occupational categories, women tend to be concentrated in sex-typed jobs.

Sociologists use the term *occupational distribution* to refer to the location of workers in different occupations. The occupational distribution of women workers shows that women are most heavily concentrated in those jobs that have been the most devalued — both economically and socially. As late as 1986, 47.6 percent of all women workers were employed either in clerical or service jobs. Within various job categories, women also occupy sex-typed jobs. Table 5-3 shows, for example, that women (both black and white) are more likely than men to be working in professional specialties. However, more detailed surveys of occupational distribution show that of the 14.6 percent of women in professional work, over 60 percent are em-

TABLE 5-3   Occupational Distribution of the Labor Force, by Race and Sex, 1986*

Occupational Category	Total		Men		Women	
	Black	White	Black	White	Black	White
Managerial/professional specialty	14.7%	25.2%	12.8%	16.7%	16.7%	24.6%
—Executive, administrative, and managerial	6.1	12.2	6.2	13.9	6.0	10.0
—Professional specialty	8.7	13.1	6.6	11.9	10.7	14.6
Technical, sales, and administrative support	27.0	31.9	15.9	20.3	38.3	46.7
—Technicians	2.6	3.1	2.0	3.0	3.1	3.2
—Sales	6.9	12.7	5.2	11.9	8.7	13.7
—Administrative support, including clerical	17.5	16.1	8.6	5.4	26.5	29.8
Service occupations	22.9	12.2	17.6	8.5	28.3	17.0
—Private household	2.2	.8	.1	.1	4.3	1.6
—Protection service	2.5	1.6	4.2	2.4	.8	.4
—Other service	18.3	9.9	13.4	6.0	23.2	14.9
Precision production, craft, and repair	9.3	12.6	16.0	20.7	2.6	2.3
Operators, fabricators, and laborers	23.9	14.7	34.0	19.8	13.7	8.2
—Machine operators, assemblers, and inspectors	10.8	6.8	11.0	7.4	10.6	5.9
—Transportation and material moving	5.9	4.0	10.8	6.5	1.0	.8
—Handlers, equipment cleaners, helpers, and laborers	7.2	4.0	12.2	5.9	2.1	1.5
Farming, forestry, fishing	2.1	3.3	3.7	4.9	.4	1.2

*The Bureau of Labor Statistics does not report separate data on the occupational distribution for those of Hispanic origin; they appear in both the categories of black and white, depending on their self-identification.

Source: U.S. Bureau of Labor Statistics, *Employment and Earnings.* Washington, D.C.: U.S. Government Printing Office, January 1987.

ployed either as nurses or elementary and secondary school teachers while men are more broadly distributed across the professions and are located in higher-paying professions.

So, although a greater proportion of women than men hold professional jobs, men are still more likely placed in more prestigious and better-paid professional work. Table 5-3 also shows the concentration of women in service work. This job category is so sex-segregated that it has come to be called the "pink-collar ghetto" (Howe 1977). Almost half of all women in this category work as waitresses, cooks, nurses' aides, maids, and hairdressers.

Studies of occupational segregation show that there has been a convergence in recent years between black and white women's experience in the labor market, in the sense that black and white women's occupational distribution has become more similar and there has been a lessening of the pay gap between them. Asian-American women are even more likely than black or white women to be in the labor force but, although their educational levels are relatively high, 70 percent of them are concentrated in clerical, service, and blue-collar work jobs (U.S. Bureau of the Census 1984).

The experience of women of color in the labor force is described as double jeopardy because they face the inequities of both race and gender. Black women have always been present in the labor force. In fact, they were rarely able to remain in their own homes as housewives. Although they have carried the double burden of wage labor and housework, they did not have the privilege of "feminine weakness and wifely submissiveness" that is associated with white, middle-class housewives (Davis 1981). Because of the necessity to work, black women are less likely to experience conflict over the choice of family and job than are white women (Epstein 1973), and they do not learn to regard career interests as unfeminine (Ladner 1971).

The majority of employed Mexican-American women are concentrated in clerical, operative, and nonhousehold service occupations (Moore and Pachon 1985), and their median income is less than that of any other group except native American women. The proportion of Mexican-American women who are farm laborers (4 percent) is also higher than that of any of the other groups, reflecting the large proportion of migrant farm workers in the Southwest who are Mexican-American. This figure, of course, probably vastly underestimates the actual number of women working as migrant laborers who never show up in government statistics.

Puerto Rican women are heavily concentrated in operative labor; 40 percent of those employed work as operatives and another 30 percent work in clerical work and 13 percent in service occupations (Almquist and Wehrle-Einhorn 1978). Cuban-American women are more likely to be employed than Mexican-American and Puerto Rican women, in part because of their higher educational level. Still, an extraordinary proportion (43 percent) work as operatives, and smaller proportions than white and other nonwhite women are clerical workers (26 percent), private household workers (1 percent), and nonhousehold service workers (11 percent).

Among native American women, only 35.3 percent are in the labor force. One-quarter are in clerical positions, 26 percent in nonhousehold service, and 19 percent in operative jobs. Japanese-American, Filipino-American, and Chinese-American women have an occupational distribution similar to that of white women, although their income is less than that of white women (Almquist and Wehrle-Einhorn 1978).

The experience of minority women workers underscores the complexities of a society that discriminates against women based on their sex, race, and class. In spite of the myth that minority are highly sought after by employers wanting to meet affirmative action guidelines, their experience in the labor force lags behind that of the white majority (Almquist 1979). Black, Hispanic, Asian-American, and native American women live and work in a society and a labor market that are divided by race and by gender. Yet, their experiences and their consciousness do not separate one from the other. For feminists this complicates the issue of sisterhood among women, for it means not only that we cannot generalize from the experience of white women, but also that women are situated in different experiences that are structured by their race, class, and gender.

The situations faced by women in the labor market vary depending on actual occupation. The following section briefly describes the conditions faced by women in a selected sample of jobs. Although these job types are by no means exhaustive of women's occupations, they point to the variety of circumstances that women face in the paid work they do. Moreover, these summaries illustrate the effects of gender in the social and economic organization of work.

Women in the Professions. Women who work in the professions have the advantage of holding the most prestigious and highly paid jobs in the labor market. Although women professional workers are still a minority of professional workers (see Table 5-4), their numbers in the professions are increasing. Women are 17.6 percent of physicians and they are now nearly one-third of medical school students. In 1986, women were 36 percent of college and university teachers and 18 percent of all lawyers, though they were only 6 percent of engineers — an increase from 2.9 percent in 1979 (Vetter and Babco 1986).

But within the professions, women are concentrated in the lower ranks and in less prestigious specialties. In universities, for instance, where women constitute 36 percent of all faculty, they represent only 6.6 percent of full professors (the top rank), but they are 50 percent of all instructors —positions which are usually one-year, nontenured, and often part-time appointments. In medicine, women are heavily concentrated in the usually less prestigious fields as pediatricians, obstetricians, gynecologists, and general practitioners. Additionally, in universities, medicine, law, and the scientific professions, women tend to earn less than their male colleagues (Hornig 1980).

Recent surveys show that women Ph.D.s earn about 23 percent less than men regardless of their field of work, their experience, the nature of their jobs, and the quality of their training (Babco 1981; National Research Council Committee 1981; Vetter 1981). Moreover, minority Ph.D.s, including both men and women, have lower median salaries than white Ph.D.s, in part because they are disproportionately clustered at the lower

TABLE 5-4   Employed Persons in Selected Professional Occupations, by Race and Sex, 1985 (as Percent of Total)

Occupational Category*	Percent Female	Percent Black	Percent Hispanic
Managerial and professional specialty occupations	44.4%	9.9%	6.6%
—Executive, administrative, and managerial	36.8	5.2	3.7
—Professional specialty	49.4	6.7	3.3
—Engineers	6.0	3.7	2.5
—Architects	9.7	3.2	4.1
—Mathematicians/computer scientists	36.2	7.2	2.5
—Natural scientists	22.5	2.5	3.2
—Physicians	17.6	3.3	4.1
—Dentists	4.4	5.5	2.0
—Registered nurses	94.3	6.7	2.4
—Teachers			
—college/university	36.0	4.0	3.2
—other	73.4	9.5	3.6
—Librarians	85.9	7.5	1.7
—Lawyers	18.0	2.9	1.8

*Because these are selected occupations, percentages will not total 100%.

Source: U.S. Bureau of Labor Statistics, *Employment and Earnings.* Washington, D.C.: U.S. Government Printing Office, January 1987.

ranks (Maxwell 1981). And among Ph.D.s, the unemployment rate of minorities is twice that of nonminorities and is also higher for minority and nonminority women than for white men (Maxwell 1981).

Public myths also have it that black women advance rapidly in the professions because of their double minority status. Yet research does not bear this out. Black women are not being promoted more rapidly than other workers; in fact, they encounter the same limits to mobility that other workers do plus additional limits posed by race and sex discrimination. Specifically, black women are less likely to have corporate sponsors, thereby limiting their opportunities in corporate firms. Also, black women managers report that individuals in corporations who control the distribution of work, promotions, and performance reviews put informal ceilings on their upward mobility in organizations (Fulbright 1986).

Public myths about employed women seriously distort our understanding of women's experiences in the labor market. Many believe for example, that women do not advance in the professions because of their family commitments; but women lag behind men in the professions regardless of their marital status, the presence of children, and whether they are primarily involved in research or teaching.

Clearly, women and minorities who work in the professions do not receive the same objective material rewards as men. But women's work in professional careers is also influenced by more subjective features of professional organizations. Professions are socially organized like communities, and, as such, they involve informal roles and practices, as well as tending toward homogeneity and exclusionary relations (Epstein 1970; Goode 1957). Social control in professional life, as well as access to rewards, typically operates through a sponsorship system that feminists have labeled the *old boy network*. Within the network, social relations with one's peers and mentors can bring access to jobs, promotions, opportunities, and status.

The woman professional who is excluded from the protégé system is likely to find herself at a disadvantage when it comes to professional opportunity. Additionally, the information and colleaguality shared by those in the network are likely to give professional advantage to those who are "in the know." Whether by exclusion or personal choice, women who are not part of the old boy network are likely to find their careers detrimentally affected (Epstein 1970).

This professional culture has encouraged women professionals in most fields to establish alternative networks of support — both for professional advancement and for personal encouragement. Groups such as the Association for Women in Science, the Society of Women engineers, Sociologists for Women in Society, and the Association for Women in Psychology, to name only a few, have flourished in recent years. As both professional networks and local support groups for women professionals, these organizations encourage the development of alternative networks to promote the status of professional women.

Women as Clerical Workers. Women make up 80 percent of all administrative support workers, an occupational category of the U.S. census that includes clerical workers. Women are 98.2 percent of all secretaries, stenographers, and typists; and while over the last century the number of clerical workers has drastically increased, their prestige has declined.

Prior to the mechanization of office work by the invention of the typewriter in the late nineteenth century, skills such as shorthand and accounting were male trades, and relatively prestigious trades at that. An 1888 book titled *How to Succeed As a Stenographer or Typewriter* was addressed to men, saying, "There are comparatively few verbatim reporters, and the young shorthand writer who has reached that distinction should consider that it gives him the rank of a scholar and a gentleman" (Baker 1888, cited in Benet 1972:39). Yet the introduction of mechanized switchboards and typewriters and the corresponding need for new workers brought the rapid introduction of women workers to these jobs. Whereas capitalist owners saved money by tapping the cheap, large female labor market, women workers experienced a decline in the wages and prestige associated with office work.

To this day, the median weekly earnings for women clerical workers are low, especially compared with those of male clericals. In 1986, full-time male clerical workers earned $403 per week; women clerical workers in the same period earned $284 per week (U.S. Department of Labor Statistics, January 1987). A huge supply of women clerical workers is also provided by temporary clerical services, where workers have low wages, little control of their work, minimal social relationships with co-workers, and highly alienated attitudes toward their jobs (Olesen and Katsuranis 1978).

Full-time secretaries, except those who work in large typing pools where work is heavily routinized, are tied to individual and patrimonial relationships with their bosses. Their status is then contingent on that of the boss, whose power may determine their own. Although studies find that secretaries most resent doing personal work for their bosses, bosses expect their secretaries to appreciate and provide nonmaterial rewards such as emotional intimacy, praise, and affection. Moreover, loyalty and devotion to their employer are often the basis for secretaries' rewards at work (Kanter 1977).

Clerical work, of course, varies in different settings, but in large companies where there is the most extensive automation and use of a secretarial pool, clerical work is becoming "proletarianized." That is, work is becoming organized more around manual than mental activities, tasks are externally structured and controlled, and relationships among workers become more depersonalized. Automation in the form of electronic data processing and word processing means that computers now perform many clerical functions, decreasing the autonomy of workers and increasing fragmentation among clerical workers (Feldberg and Glenn 1979). The development of word processing increases productivity, at the same time that it increases surveillance of clerical work (Machung 1984). The proletarianization of clerical work leaves workers less control over the work itself, as well as making relationships between workers and supervisors more impersonal. This process also has serious implications for the development of solidarity among clerical workers. As working groups become less interdependent and more physically separated, it is more difficult for workers to know if they share common conditions and occupy comparable positions in the office hierarchy. Though the strains associated with more mechanized work can create cooperation among the workers, the strains also increase workers' vulnerability, sometimes decreasing workers' desires for personal ties with others (Feldberg and Glenn 1979).

Women in Blue-Collar Work. Among blue-collar workers, women have been entering the skilled trades at a rapid rate — faster, in fact, than men in recent years — though women still constitute only a small percentage of those in the more highly skilled trades. Women in blue-collar work are more likely to be employed as operators than as skilled craftworkers (see Table 5-3), and within the occupational categories in which they work, women earn less than men. For example, in 1985 male craft and repair workers had a weekly median income of $408; women earned $268. Among operators, men earned $325 per week; women $216. And in farm labor, men earned $216 per week; women $185 (U.S. Bureau of Labor Statistics, January 1986). Moreover, the unemployment rate for women in blue-collar labor exceeds that of men.

Women in blue-collar work also find sex segregation on the job. Even when women are employed in the same occupational category as men, they tend to be located in different industries. Women are more likely to be employed in the nondurable-goods sector whereas men are more likely employed in manufacturing, where wages and job benefits have traditionally been higher. Although the job crises that men in these industries face cannot be ignored, women (especially minority women) tend to be located in the poorest quality blue-collar jobs available.

Women in blue-collar jobs are much less likely than men to be protected by labor unions. Though women's union membership increased during the 1970s, the percentage of all workers represented by unions has declined more recently to only 17.5 percent of employed persons in 1986. Moreover, only 12.9 percent of employed women are represented by unions, compared with 21.5 percent of employed men. Because of their concentration in blue-collar occupations, black and Hispanic men and women are more likely to be represented by unions than are white men and women. Women in service occupations and clerical work tend not to be unionized, leaving them subject to the discretionary practices of individual companies and employers.

Despite low rates of union membership, being in a union is significant for employed women and men. Not only does it increase the likelihood of due process and job protection, but also, median weekly earnings for those represented by unions exceed earnings for nonunion members. For example, women who were members of unions in 1986 had median weekly earnings of $368, compared with $274 for nonunionized employed women (U.S. Bureau of Labor Statistics January 1987).

Within blue-collar labor, male supervisors' sex stereotypes and discomfort at the presence of women shapes women's experiences at work. Supervisors may believe, for example, that women should be excluded from some jobs so they do not get hurt; their paternalistic attitudes put supervisors in the position of gatekeepers where they maintain the status quo by assigning women to sex-typed jobs. Often, their reservations about women are not overt and hostile but are, instead, paternalistic. This can make it difficult for women in such jobs to identify or document sexism, for it appears subtle or trivial. Nonetheless, such attitudes and behaviors do create barriers to women's mobility; moreover, supervisors' paternalistic attitudes also communicate to male co-workers that sexist behavior is acceptable (Padavic and Reskin 1986). Studies of desegregation in blue-collar work do show, however, that supervisors often lose their reservations about women's work after supervising more women. Consequently, one mechanism for eliminating sexism in these occupations is to increase the number of women workers in these jobs (Padavic and Reskin 1986).

Women in Domestic and Service Work. Women who work in domestic labor, both public and private, are among the lowest paid of employed women. In 1986, the median weekly earnings for all service workers were $284 for men and $191 for women (U.S. Bureau of Labor Statistics January 1987). Although poorly paid, domestic work is often the only work available for incoming groups of immigrant women, women with little education, and women with little choice of occupation. Public service workers, although poorly paid, at least have the advantage of unionization and more job benefits. But women in private domestic labor are left in the hands of individual employers, who are unlikely to provide health and retirement benefits or paid sick leave. Private-household workers often have the advantage of negotiating their own work schedules and, thus, may have greater flexibility than workers in the public sector, but they pay the price in terms of low wages and little job security (Katzman 1978).

In 1986, women in private-household work earned only $119 per week, a decline from the median of $130 in 1985. Among private-household workers, white women's earnings are actually less than those of black women ($80 per week for white women and $110 per week for black in 1979). This surprising reversal in black and white women's earnings is perhaps best explained by the fact that 60.2 percent of white private-household workers are employed in child care, compared with 10.5 percent of black household workers. Black women are more likely employed as cleaners and servants. These positions account for 73 percent of black household workers and 30.3 percent of white household workers (Grossman 1980).

Women who work as domestic workers do regard the independence and autonomy of the job as a positive feature of the work, but, since domestic workers typically do not have co-workers, loneliness, especially for live-ins, is the most difficult part of the work (Rollins 1985). Rollins's study of black domestic workers in the Boston area identifies maternalism as structuring the relationship between domestics and their employers. Rollins, who holds a Ph.D. in sociology, hired herself as a domestic worker as part of her research design. Through her own experiences and her interviews with black domestic workers she shows that, because the domestic work is based on personal relations, it is both psychologically and economically belittling. While employers may act caring and protective, the job is still structured as a power relationship. Patterns of deferential behavior, such as referring to the domestic as "girl" and treating the domestic as if she is invisible, reveal the subordination and exploitation in this work.

Rollins describes one incident from her own employment that aptly illustrates this. An employer had expressed some hesitancy about hiring Rollins because she seemed so well-educated. Wanting not to lose the job, Rollins appeared at the employers' home dressed particularly shabbily and feigning exaggerated subservience. She writes;

> I said almost nothing, asked the few necessary questions in a soft unassertive voice, and responded to her directions with "Yes, Ma'am." I was rather shocked at her obvious pleasure over and total lack of suspicion about this performance. . . . To me it felt like an absurd and transparent caricature of Stepin Fetchit; her mind, however, was clearly eased of the apprehensions she had had about my suitability for the job . . . . My behavior now expressed my belief in my inferiority in relation to her and thus my acceptance of her superiority in relation to me. (1985:165)

Women who work as domestics develop an astute consciousness of the employer that emerges from their subordinate status. Thus, while appearing deferential is part of the work, domestics maintain a sense of self-respect and independence in their work and their understanding of themselves. Glenn's (1986) study of Japanese-American domestics also shows that women workers are not just passive victims of exploitative conditions. The independent incomes that the women in her study earned liberated them to a degree from the traditionally subordinate roles for women in the family and from their husbands' direct control.

Women in Farm and Migrant Labor. Changes in the social and economic organization of farming have radically altered the work of women farm workers. In the 1940s, nearly one-quarter of the U.S. population lived on farms. Now the farm population is less than 2.5 percent of the U.S. population (U.S. Bureau of the Census *Statistical Abstracts* 1986). Small family farms have been particularly hard hit by the development of corporate farming as the average farm has increased in total acreage.

The transformation of farming from a family enterprise to agribusiness has specifically eroded the position of women in farming. Whereas much farm labor was originally performed by women, men now control and operate the technological equipment of farm production. Typically, women's farm work is now described as that of a helpmate; men, who have taken over the business and technology of farming, work in more sophisticated jobs that bring them higher incomes and more social status. The introduction of more sophisticated farm technology has produced a more complex hierarchy of farm jobs, with women relegated to the bottom. Women receive low wages for assembly-line jobs in farming, whereas the higher wages are given to men who work as operatives and managers (Hacker 1980).

Migrant workers are at the very bottom of the agribusiness ladder, where they face physically demanding jobs, poor working conditions, and extremely low wages. Migrant women, like other women workers, also work a double day — first in farm fields and then in their own families. Research on the family life of migrant laborers shows that the dominant pattern of decision making in migrant families tends to be more egalitarian than we might assume. The same researchers find that women in migrant families tend to be less dependent on their husbands than they might have been within more traditional cultures (Hawkes and Taylor 1975).

Women as Part-time Workers. The data on employed women would be incomplete without considering the situation of part-time women workers. These women face problems in the labor market that are particular to their part-time status. Women are more likely than men to be employed part-time, and in some occupations, part-time work for women is more common than full-time employment. Almost half of the women in craft and operative jobs are employed part-time; seven out of ten in service jobs work part-time (Baker 1978). Either because they are unable to find full-time work or because of home responsibilities, these women do not usually get the employee benefits of health insurance, retirement plans, seniority, training, and promotion that are often available to full-time workers. The working conditions for these women are poor and largely subject to the discretion of employers. Students who have worked as part-time waitresses or in household service jobs know that the personal whims of an employer can make these jobs both financially insecure and psychologically degrading.

In 1986, female part-time workers earned $101 per week and men earned $88 per week. The relative though slight advantage of part-time women workers compared with men may seem surprising, given other economic inequities for employed women. But these figures do not reflect the number of hours worked, nor do they differentiate between part-time workers dependent upon this income and those who are employed for other reasons. Data do show that women employed part-time and maintaining families earn $108 per week, while men maintaining families and employed part-time earn $128 per week (see Table 5-5).

These descriptions of the different occupations of women do not, of course, include all the work that women do. As we have come to take women's work more seriously, scholars have also begun to produce excellent ethnographies of the different occupations constituting women's work. But across these occupations, research shows systematic inequities in the distribution of resources, the opportunities for mobility, and the subjective experiences of work for women and men. This is especially clear in looking at the pay inequities for male and female earners.

TABLE 5-5 Median Weekly Earnings by Sex and Race, 1986 (for Workers Aged 16 and Over)

	Full-time Workers		Part-time Workers	
	Men	**Women**	**Men**	**Women**
Whites	$433	$294	$ 93	$102
Blacks	318	263	92	93
Hispanics	299	241	107	100
All men	$419		$ 93	
All women	290		101	

	Full-time Workers	Part-time Workers
Men who maintain families	$397	$128
Women who maintain families	$290	108

Source: U.S. Bureau of Labor Statistics, *Employment and Earnings*. Washington, D.C.: U.S. Government Printing Office, January 1987.

Unemployment and Job Displacement

Unemployment rates among women also reveal women's disadvantage in the labor force, although unemployment is influenced by race as well as gender. In 1986, among those 16 years and over, white men had an unemployment rate of 6.0 percent; black men, 14.8 percent; and Hispanic men, 10.5 percent. White women had an unemployment rate of 6.1 percent; black women, 14.2 percent; and Hispanic women, 10.8 percent (see Table 5-6). It should be pointed out that unemployment has risen for women and minorities since 1981 and that the official statistics on unemployment far underestimate the actual extent of joblessness. Unemployment statistics include only those looking for work or waiting to be called back to a job from which they were laid off. Many who are jobless are discouraged workers who have given up looking for work and, therefore, do not show up in the official government statistics on unemployment.

Social myth claims that high unemployment among men is a result of women's entry into the labor force. Research, however, shows that the unemployment rate does not vary directly with changes in women's labor force participation (Scholzman 1979). Moreover, because most women (especially those returning to the labor force) work in sex-segregated jobs, it is hardly reasonable to think that they are taking jobs from men. When unemployed, women, like men, experience the hardship of economic need, and unemployment is complicated for women by the fact that they are less often eligible for unemployment than men and are less likely to be cushioned by insurance or union benefits (Scholzman 1979). Recent layoffs in the federal government and in public service jobs have also disproportionately affected women and minorities (Sacks 1984).

The two primary reasons for unemployment among women are, first, job loss and, second, reentering the labor market. In addition to having higher rates of unemployment, data show that women are unemployed longer than men. And, when women have lost their jobs because of plant closings, they have lower rates of reemployment than do men displaced in the same company. Not only do women have greater difficulty finding other jobs, but when they are rehired, they are more likely than men to be hired in lesser jobs. In other words, men are more likely to retain jobs as craftworkers or operatives while women skid downward into jobs with lower wages and fewer benefits. Men, on the other hand, experience a greater wage drop with reemployment than do women, but this is explained by the fact that displaced men, even those who are classified as semiskilled, are more likely to have lost jobs in the higher paying durable goods sector; therefore, they earned more in the job from which they were displaced than women who are displaced (Nowak and Snyder 1986).

Studies of the effects of plant closings show that job loss is a source of economic and psychological strain for both women and men. And, in the regions where job displacement has been highest, there is often little opportunity for reemployment. Following plant closings, workers may find it difficult to move because they own homes in a depressed real estate market or because they have ethnic and familial roots in the community and rely on kin and community friends for psychological and economic support. These and other factors impede the geographic mobility that is often necessary to find reemployment. Women, however, report having even less geographic mobility after job loss because they are often responsible for elderly relatives in their home communities (Nowak and Snyder 1986).

TABLE 5-6   Unemployment Rates by Race and by Sex, 1986

	Whites	Blacks	Hispanics
All, 16 years and over	6.0%	14.5%	10.6%
Men	6.0	14.8	10.5
—aged 16–19 years	16.3	39.3	24.5
—20 yrs. and older	5.3	12.9	9.5
Women	6.1	14.2	10.8
—aged 16–19 years	14.9	39.2	25.1
—20 yrs. and older	5.4	12.4	9.6

Source: U.S. Bureau of Labor Statistics, *Employment and Earnings.* Washington, D.C.: U.S. Government Printing Office, January 1987.

Poverty

One of the consequences of women's inferior status in the labor market is the high rate of poverty among women and, also, their children. The poverty line is an index developed by the Social Security Administration. It is calculated based on the lowest cost for a nutritionally adequate food plan (as developed by the Department of Agriculture). The poverty line (based also on family size) is calculated by multiplying the cost of this food plan by three (assuming that a family spends one-third of its budget on food), adjusted by the Consumer Price Index. In 1985, the official poverty line for a family of four was $10,989.

Especially among female-headed households, the poverty rate among women in recent years has been steadily increasing. In 1985, the median family income for all families was $27,735 (see Table 5-2); for all female-headed households, median family income in this year was only $13,660. Moreover, women's racial status adds to the likelihood they will be poor. In the same year, median family income in households headed by white women was $15,825; for households headed by black women, median income was $9,305, and for households headed by Hispanic women, $8,792 (U.S. Bureau of the Census, August 1986). As Table 5-2 shows, the most prosperous families are white families with both husband and wife present and the wife working. However, as we can see in the next chapter, although these families in some ways define the American ideal, they are by no means the statistical norm in contemporary American society.

In 1985, 34.0 percent of all female-headed households lived below the official poverty line; 50.5 percent of black female-headed households and 53.1 percent of Hispanic families headed by women lived below the poverty line (see Table 5-7). One consequence of increasing poverty among women who head families is an ever-growing number of children who are poor. In 1985, 43.4 percent of black children, 39.9 percent of Hispanic children, and 15.9 percent of white children lived in poverty. Data collected in 1983 also show that for children in families headed by women, the poverty rates are even higher (see Table 5-8).

Limited opportunities for women in the labor market are a major cause of poverty. And in addition to their secondary employment status, women's continuing responsiblities for child rearing, in the absence of adequate day care and other social supports, tend to leave them poor (Pearce and McAdoo 1981). Moreover, poverty among women is exacerbated by the high rate of divorce, since women's economic status after a divorce drastically deteriorates; wives' postdivorce income is 24 percent of previous family income, while men's is 87 percent (Weitzman 1985).

Public myths and federal policymakers often incorrectly assume that women are poor because they do not want to work. Yet, at any given point in time, 16 percent of women receiving welfare assistance through Aid to

TABLE 5-7 Poverty Status of Families and Individuals, 1985 (Percent Below the Poverty Line, $10,989)

	All	White	Black	Hispanic
All families	11.4%	9.1%	28.7%	25.5%
Married-couple families	6.7	6.1	12.2	17.0
Female householder (no husband present)	34.0	27.4	50.5	53.1
Male householder (no wife present)	12.9	11.2	22.9	18.4
All persons	14.0	11.4	31.5	29.0

Source: U.S. Bureau of the Census, Current Population Reports, Series P60, No. 154. *Money Income and Poverty Status of Families and Persons in the U.S., 1985.* Washington, D.C.: U.S. Government Printing Office, August 1986.

Families with Dependent Children are working; over the period of one year, one-half of these women are employed and over a period of five years, 92 percent of women receiving public assistance also work. Thus, the majority of women on welfare do work for pay and there is plenty of evidence that women on welfare like men, have positive attitudes toward work, want to get out of poverty, and have an attachment to middle-class values (Power 1984). Federal policymakers have claimed that the key to success is family, work, and faith (Gilder 1981); in this spirit, they have argued that the problem of poverty lies in having made the male provider role optional for men. But as our analysis of economic trends pertinent to women's status shows, only policies designed to improve women's status, not just reinstate that of men, are likely to alleviate the serious social problems now being generated by women's employment and household status.

TABLE 5-8 Children in Poverty, 1983 (Based on Cash Income Only)

Rates/100	White	Black	Hispanic	All <18
Total	17.3%	46.7%	38.2%	22.2%
Female-headed families	47.6	68.5	70.5	55.8
With mothers,				
— never married	71.3	77.2	85.8	75.1
— separated/divorced	47.3	66.8	70.1	53.5
— widowed	27.9	60.7	38.9	41.1
Male-present families	11.9	23.8	27.3	13.5
(Poverty line = $7,938 for family of three in 1983)				

Source: Congressional Research Service and Congressional Budget Office, *Children in Poverty.* Reported in *Washington Post* (May 23, 1985): 1 ff.

Work Environments for Women ⎯⎯⎯⎯⎯⎯⎯⎯⎯⎯⎯⎯

Sociologists study work organizations by looking at both the structure and the culture of the organization. Within an organization, one's access to power and one's ability to succeed depend, in part, on the structural constraints and possibilities in the organizational structure and climate. In this section we briefly examine three factors affecting women's work in organizations: the sex ratio, sexual harassment, and women's culture in the workplace.

Tokenism

Kanter (1977) has suggested that the experience of women in organizations is influenced by the proportions in which they find themselves. She identifies four types of groups, based on the numerical proportions in which different kinds of people are represented. The first is the uniform group, which has only one kind of person (for example, all men or all white). Skewed groups are those in which there is a great preponderance of one type of person over another, for example, a group that is 85 percent men and 15 percent women. In skewed groups, those in the numerical minority are identified as tokens. Third are tilted groups where there are less exaggerated differences, but in which one group still forms a clear majority (for example, a group where men constitute 65 percent of the group population and women 35 percent). Kanter argues that in tilted groups, minority members have the opportunity to form alliances with each other and can form coalitions and can begin to affect the culture of the group. Finally is the balanced group, one close to a 50-50 proportion of social types. Kanter suggests that only in balanced groups will organizational outcomes for individuals depend more on structural and personal factors than on the dynamics established by the group itself.

Most women entering traditionally male-dominated occupations find themselves in skewed groups where they are tokens. In such groups, tokens stand out in contrast to other members of the group; group dynamics will usually reflect these contrasts. The presence of tokens heightens the boundaries between different groups; in the presence of tokens, members of the dominant group become more self-conscious of what they have in common and they may "test" tokens to see how they respond, for example, to male culture. This means that in skewed groups, the contrast between tokens and the majority becomes exaggerated in social interaction. Also, in skewed groups, tokens receive extra attention and are more easily stereotyped than are those found in greater proportions in social groups. Kanter argues that these perceptual tendencies — visibility, contrast, and assimilation — put more performance pressures on tokens, as they live life in the limelight.

Tokens respond to these performance pressures in a variety of ways. One response is overachievement in which tokens try to gain more control over the extra attention given to their actions; this may, however, be difficult to accomplish, especially for those who are new to organizations. It also involves creating a delicate balance between doing well and not causing too much resentment among the majority. Tokens may also try to turn the notoriety of their uniqueness to advantage, for example, by flaunting their "only woman in the company" status. Kanter argues, however, that this strategy of response reinforces the dynamics of tokenism and disadvantages other women. Third, she says that tokens may respond to performance pressures by trying to become socially invisible, perhaps through dressing "like a man," keeping a very low social profile, working at home, or avoiding risks.

Kanter's research shows that a mere shift in numbers has the potential to transform the working experience of all members of an organization. Her work also shows, in a unique way, how the structure of groups themselves influences the organizational structure and climate of occupational settings.

Sexual Harassment

Sexual harassment is defined as the unwanted imposition of sexual requirements in a context of a relationship of unequal power. Sexual harassment was first defined as constituting illegal discrimination by Title VII of the Civil Rights Bill of 1964. A landmark Supreme Court decision in 1986, *Meritor Savings Bank* v. *Vinson*, rules that sexual harassment does violate federal laws against discrimination. This decision makes sexual harassment unlawful.

There are a number of social myths about sexual harassment, including the myths that it only affects few, that women ask for it, and that charges of sexual harassment are usually false. Because of these myths, women may find it hard to speak out against sexual harassment since the myths establish the tendency for others to blame her. Often, when women have spoken out about harassment, they are ignored, discredited, or accused of misunderstanding the intentions of the other (Project on the Status and Education of Women 1978). But the unveiling of sexual harassment as a serious issue affecting work environments for women has forced employers to create policies designed to deal with sexual harassment; the recent federal ruling has made it clear that sexual harassment is a violation of the law.

Though accurate counts of the extent of sexual harassment in the workplace are difficult to establish, surveys of working women indicate that as many as 50 percent say they are currently being harassed at work; 80 to 90 percent say they have been harassed at some point in their career (Safran 1976). Sexual harassment occurs in every kind of work setting and can deeply influence women's perceptions of themselves as workers (Carothers and Crull 1984). Especially in an unsupportive context, victims of sexual harassment may experience feelings of helplessness, guilt, fear, empathy for the harasser, and ambivalence about the incident (Kaufman and Wylie 1983). One recent survey reported that graduate students who were harassed typically did not think of the experience as coercive at the time; however, in retrospect they did see the relationship as coercive, unethical, and costly to their careers (Glaser and Thorpe 1986).

Researchers also find that the experience of sexual harassment varies depending on whether it occurs in an area of traditional women's work or in areas where women are entering traditionally male oocupations. In "women's" occupations, sexual harassment is characterized by the threat of losing a job for failing to comply with sexual demands; the harasser in these settings is typically a supervisor. On the other hand, when harassment occurs where women are entering male domains, harassment seems to be a form of retaliation directed against women for threatening male economic and social status. In these settings, harassment expresses men's resentment of the presence of women. It can be more difficult for women workers in these jobs to bring charges of harassment since their harassers are more likely to be co-workers. In female work settings where the harasser is a supervisor, women who are harassed may have less internal conflict about bringing up charges and are more likely to be able to garner support from other women for bringing charges (Carothers and Crull 1984).

Women's Culture in the Workplace

In addition to the social structural characteristics of women's work on the employed labor force, feminist scholars are also interested in the cultures women create at work. Work environments shape the experience of women (and men) at work, just as objective rewards can shape one's work experience. Learning about women's work cultures also helps us see how women resist exploitative conditions at work and reveals how women's culture shapes their work activities and environments. Despite the myths about women's work, women workers are not docile and passive (Sacks 1984).

Melosh (1982) and Benson (1978) define women's work culture as the ideology, rituals, and practices through which women forge a relatively autonomous sphere on the job. By sharing photographs, celebrating birthdays, elaborating informal norms among themselves about office procedures and norms, and developing other forms of women's culture at work, women exercise some control over the meaning and character of their work.

Women's culture in the workplace can be the basis for political organization, resistance to oppression, and the creation of solidarity among workers. Recognizing and studying women's culture in the workplace shows how groups that lack power collectively define their positions and use their informal relations to adapt to or resist powerlessness. While these informal relations may soften exploitative work conditions by humanizing the work force (Lamphere 1985), they can also be the basis for militant job actions (Costello 1985). And, as Zavella's (1985) research on Chicana women cannery workers shows, in a labor market where workers are divided along race and sex lines, women's culture can create both ethnic and racial solidarity while also generating gender consciousness of exploitative work conditions.

Explaining Economic Inequality

Within almost every occupational category, women earn less than men. For example, women professional and technical workers earn 68 percent of the income of men in that category; female clerical workers earn 69 percent of male clerical earnings; female sales workers earn 52 percent of male sales earnings; female craft and repair workers earn 65 percent of what men earn in the same occupational group; and female service workers earn 68 percent of what male service workers earn (U.S. Bureau of Labor Statistics January 1987).

Occupational segregation explains some of the wage gap between men and women, as women in traditionally female occupations do earn less than women in traditionally male occupations. But a recent survey by the Department of Labor shows that even in jobs where women do the same work as men, they receive substantially less pay (*New York Times*, March 5, 1982).

Differences in earnings by sex are further complicated by race, as the following data show. In 1986, the median weekly earnings for full-time white male workers were $433; for white women, $291; for black men, $318; for black women, $263; for Hispanic men, $299; and for Hispanic women, $241 (see Table 5-5). It is important to see that the status of women relative to men varies among racial groups. Specifically, the earnings gap between women and men is greater in racial groups with the most economic resources. In other words, there is greater gender equality within those racial groups who have the fewest economic resources and more inequality in those groups with the greatest resources (Almquist 1986). This reminds us that gender per se is inadequate to explain the economic earnings potential of either women or men and it underscores the importance of considering race as equally important to gender in predicting one's life chances.

There are various explanations of the income differences between men and women both in the public and among academic researchers. For example, one popular explanation is that women are paid less than men because their careers are shorter and frequently are interrupted by family responsibilities. But unmarried women also earn less than their male counterparts, casting doubt upon this popular assumption. This idea assumes that women's lesser earnings power is a result of their own choices and that these choices disadvantage them in the labor market. In academic work, the theory that the characteristics of workers explain wage differentials is known as human capital theory.

Human capital consists of the things workers can do to make themselves more productive. The assumption of human capital theory is that, in a competitive economic system, wage differences reflect differences in human capital (Stevenson 1978; Stromberg and Harkess 1978). According to this perspective, the quality of labor supplied by men and women varies because of their different patterns of labor force participation (Mincer and Polachek 1974; Polachek 1975). Presumedly, high turnover rates, interrupted careers, and shorter participation in the labor force among women lead to their lesser productivity and, therefore, lower wages (Blau and Jusenius 1976). Additionally, human capital theory looks at the investments workers make in their own work (such as education and special skills training) as indicative of the value of different groups.

Critics of human capital theory point to its inadequacies on both empirical and theoretical grounds. First, research shows that women's returns on investment in education do not equal those of men. And within similar occupational levels, women tend to have higher education than men (Stevenson 1975). Moreover, even when women are more highly educated, they receive lower pay than men. Black women are lower paid and have less education than white men, but the percentage differences in pay exceed the percentage differences in education. Other research finds that in occupations employing an equal number of men and women, women still earn 8 to 18 percent less than men, controlling for age, seniority, education, and experience (Rees and Schultz 1970). Other research finds an unexplained wage gap of 38 percent even after controlling for male-female differences in education, occupational status, year-round full-time work, and lifetime work experience (Suter and Miller 1973). And with regard to the question of intermittent work patterns and the effect of work experience on wage differentials, other research finds that prior work experience has a greater effect on wages in some occupations than others; consequently, prior work history does not fully explain the wage gap (Jusenius 1976). Moreover, the casual relationship of work experience and wages is far from clear because low wages encourage many women to leave the labor force for unpaid housework. It is equally likely that women leave work because of low wages as it is that they receive low wages because of interrupted work histories (Stevenson 1975).

The theoretical grounds of the human capital perspective "assume an open, fully competitive market process in which individual characteristics are identified and rewarded according to their societal value" (Horan 1978:536). Status attainment research in sociology reveals several problems with this assumption. Sociological research finds that women are not rewarded for increased social status with higher incomes to the same extent as men (Featherman and Hauser 1976; Treiman and Terrell 1975), nor do women and men with similar occupational prestige have similar incomes or similar authority in the workplace (Featherman and Hauser 1976; Treiman and Terrell 1975; Wolf and Fligstein 1979).

An alternative approach to explaining wage differentials by sex is suggested by *dual labor market analysis*. This perspective sees the labor market as organized around both a primary and a secondary internal market. Jobs in the primary labor market have more stability, higher wages, better working conditions, chances for advancement, and due process in the administration of work roles. The primary labor market restricts entry to a relatively few low-level entry jobs but is organized around long promotion ladders, worker stability, good working conditions, and job security (Blau and Jusenius 1976).

Disadvantaged groups such as women and minorities are employed primarily in the secondary market, which is less internally structured than the primary market and is characterized by numerous points of entry, short or nonexistent promotion ladders, less worker stability, little job security, arbitrary work rules. The secondary labor market has jobs with low wages, few or no fringe benefits, poor working conditions, high turnover, few chances for advancement, and often arbitrary and capricious supervision (Doeringer and Piore 1971).

Within the secondary labor market, the firms where women are employed have lower capital investments, low profit margins, irregular personnel practices, higher turnover, and lower pay (Baker 1978; Smuts 1959), leaving women more at the mercy of economic fluctuations. Even in the less marginal industries where blue-collar women work, the jobs that women hold tend to have the characteristics of the secondary labor market (e.g., poor wages, poor fringe benefits, and unstable employment). Yet, the steady supply of women workers discourages employers from paying women wages that would be equivalent to men's (Baker 1978).

The dual labor market perspective causes us to look at the occupational distribution by sex as a major factor in the earnings gap between men and women and leads us to conclude that where people work, not what their individual characteristics are, is a better predictor of income differences (Beck, Horan, and Tolbert 1978). This conclusion seems to be supported by the fact that women tend to earn more in establishments that hire men and women for the same occupation than they earn in establishments that hire women only (McNulty 1967).

Policies for Economic Equity

The Equal Pay Act of 1963 was the first federal legislation enacted requiring equal pay for equal work; it has been extended by various executive orders and civil rights acts to forbid discrimination on the basis of sex. Title VI of the Civil Rights Act of 1964 forbids discrimination against students on the basis of race, color, or national origin in all federally assisted programs. Title VII of the Civil Rights Act of 1964, amended by the Equal Employment Opportunity Act of 1972, forbids discrimination on the basis of race, color, national origin, religion, or sex in any term, condition, or privilege of employment. This law was amended in 1972 to cover all private and public educational institutions, as well as state and local governments. Title VII was a path-breaking law for women, as it established the principle of equal rights in federal law and opened the door for women's participation in education, employment, and athletics, to name some of its major areas of impact. Title IX of the Education Amendments of 1972 forbids discrimination on the basis of sex in all federally assisted education programs in all institutions, public and private, that receive federal monies through grants, loans, or contracts. The impact of this law may have been diluted, however, by a Supreme Court decision in 1984, *Grove City College* v. *Bell*. This decision stipulated that Title IX applies only to programs or activities that receive direct federal support. If Congress fails to pass legislation to once again broaden the interpretation of Title IX, some forms of discrimination that were originally ruled illegal by Title IX could once again become legal (Benokraitis and Feagin 1986).

Although federal laws do forbid discrimination in employment, feminists have argued that, because women tend to be located in different occupations than men, equal pay for equal work will by itself be adequate to eliminate wage inequities in the paid labor force. Comparable worth is the principle of paying women and men equivalent wages for jobs involving comparable levels of skill. Assessing comparable worth requires measuring the skill levels of comparable jobs and developing correlated pay scales, regardless of the sex of the job occupants. The first legal test of the principle of comparable worth came in the state of Washington, where a federal district judge ruled in 1983 that the state of Washington had discriminated against women employees who had received lower wages in sex-typed occupations. However, a Federal Appeals Court overturned this ruling in 1985, although, following the appeal, the state of Washington announced it would spend $42 million for pay equity adjustments in 1985 alone. Comparable worth is an important concept for women workers and one that organizes workers for collective action against wage discrimination (Blum 1986).

Affirmative action is also needed to remedy the continuing underrepresentation of women and minorities in the labor market. Affirmative action refers to the positive efforts needed to end discrimination and race and sex typing of jobs. It includes such actions as notifying women's and minority groups about job openings, advertising jobs rather than relying on word of mouth and old "white boy networks" to recruit able applicants, and developing uniform recruitment procedures. Contrary to popular opinion, affirmative action does not set rigid quotas for jobs, though it does set goals or targets for different fields, depending on the number of qualified women and minorities available in the applicant pool. The legality of affirmative action has been upheld by several Supreme Court decisions. The court ruled in 1986 (in *Local 28* v. *Equal Employment Opportunity Commission* and *Local 93* v. *Cleveland*) that race-conscious remedies, including goals, could be used when employers have engaged in persistent discrimination. In another 1986 decision, *Wygant* v. *Jackson Board of Education*, the Supreme Court ruled that racial preferences could be used in hiring and promotions in order to remedy employers' past discrimination. And, in March 1987 the Supreme Court ruled in *Johnson* v. *Transportation Agency* that employers may sometimes favor women and minorities over men and whites in hiring and promotion as a means of achieving better balance in the workplace. This decision strongly upholds the principle and practice of affirmative action as a method of eliminating the vestiges of discrimination.

Sex, Gender, and Economic Trends

Demographic projections and current economic trends give us some indication of what to expect about women's and men's work in the future. Future projections indicate that blacks will account for a larger share of future labor force growth (20 percent of the total) than whites, but the women (including white, black, and other women) will account for 60 percent of labor force growth in the future. By 1995, 80 percent of women between the ages of 25 and 44 are expected to be in the labor force, compared with 70 percent in 1984 (Fullerton 1985). For men, labor force participation is expected to decline across all age groups.

As women continue to outlive men and as a larger proportion of the population becomes older, more women will be supporting themselves and, perhaps, living in poverty. By the year 2030, when those born in 1965 or earlier will be over 65, 17 percent of the population (compared with 11 percent now) will be 65 years of age and over (Hess and Markson 1980:11). By the year 2000, there will be 154 women for every 100 men over 65. Currently, 81.9 percent of the men between 65 and 74 are married and live with their spouse, compared with 69.4 percent of women. These figures are not expected to change (Markson and Hess 1980). Without major changes in the social and economic value placed on older persons in this society, these men and women will likely experience not only increasing impoverishment but also the psychological difficulties of being perceived as socially and economically useless (Markson and Hess 1980; Rosow 1965).

But we do not have to look that far into the future to see increasing difficulties in economic life. American families, and especially American women, are already facing the realities of an economic crisis marked by rising inflation, increased work, and a decline in the standard of living. From 1970 to 1985, median family income rose from $9,867 to $27,735. Yet, despite increases in the absolute dollar amount of median income, when we control for the real value of the dollar, family incomes and the resulting standard of living have declined (Currie, Dunn, and Fogarty 1980). Discretionary income (that is, disposable income minus expenditures for necessities) declined by about 5 percent between 1973 and 1979. Living standards have been maintained only by increased labor. Incomes of families with one earner earned only $24,556 in 1985 and have fallen behind the cost of living (Currie, Dunn, and Fogarty 1980).

The greatest economic declines (in terms of layoffs, and number of jobs available) in recent years have occurred in occupations where relatively highly paid men have predominated; concomitantly, job growth is primarily in lower paying sex- and race-typed jobs. Also, as companies simplify the production process through mechanization and automation, they will use more unskilled workers, undercutting the position of skilled workers in industry (Sacks 1984). These trends signify potential deterioration of workers' position in the labor force and also show that current realignments in the economy will have differential impacts for women of different classes and races (Power 1984). Moreover, the increased labor force participation of women will have profound effects on the organization of work and household life.

The consequences of this situation for women are not only their increasing need to work and their possibly deteriorating status in the labor market, but also the fact that they maintain two jobs — a paid job outside the home and unpaid household labor. For those who can afford it, the tasks of child care and housework are being pushed into the private labor sector —usually other women. The fast-food industry, as well, benefits from the push of this work out of the household. But especially for those who cannot afford outside services, "social speedup" (Currie, Dunn, and Fogarty 1980) results from the decline in leisure and the increased amount of time involved in work (including domestic services). Most of the extra work caused by speedup falls on women who have not been freed from unpaid labor in the home. As we can see in the next section, the amount of time women spend on unpaid household labor has not declined since it was first measured in 1920 (Vanek 1978).

The Political Economy of Housework

Feminist studies of housework have shown that we cannot conceive of women's work only in terms of paid labor. Because our concept of work has been tied to the idea of paid employment, women's work as housewives has long gone unrecognized as work, even though it is socially and economically necessary. The work that housewives do not only takes care of people's basic needs — food, shelter, and clothing — but also socializes new members of the society. Some argue that housewives' labor benefits employers, too, because housework sustains workers, making it possible for them to return to the labor force (Benston 1969). But social myths about housework show us the contradictions that pervade our images of the work women do in the home. On the one hand, to be a housewife is idealized as a desirable goal for women; at the same time, however, housework is depicted as drudgery and menial labor. Both images obscure the fact that, for most women, housework is time-consuming as well as physically and psychologically demanding, even though it can also be a source of satisfaction.

The glamorous image of the housewife is perpetrated in commercials, where women are surrounded by happy families and a wealth of material goods. The housewife in these ads is usually cheerful, buoyant, and smiling, although pathologically obsessed with cleanliness and food. Three-quarters of all television ads using females, in fact, are for products found in the kitchen or bathroom (Dominick and Rauch 1972), clearly giving the image that this is women's place. Still, the use of male "experts" in the voice-overs in these commercials makes it appear that men know best when it comes to household matters. So, although housework is seen as glamorous, housewives are also ridiculed as scatterbrained, lazy, and disorganized. Anyone who has seen comic strip and greeting card depictions of a housewife standing bedraggled with rollers in her hair, an apron around her waist, a broom in her hand, and a cigarette dangling from her mouth has seen one facet of the contemporary myth about housework. The other is that of the lady of leisure whose only concern in life seems to be how clean her husband's shirts are.

The artificial picture these myths create about housework is unsupported by social and economic research. To begin with, the role of the housewife is multidimensional and is experienced by women in different ways (Lopata 1971). Many housewives are overwhelmed by the isolation of their work and by the repetitiveness of their tasks. As a result, many of them experience prolonged depression and anxiety. Betty Friedan's early book, *The Feminine Mystique* (1963), was based on the alienation of middle-class housewives, whose emotional state was such that they could not even identify their anxiety. "The problem that has no name" was, to Friedan, a state of mind in which the alienation of housewives was so pervasive that they experienced only vague anxieties and intense feelings of powerlessness.

But it would be a mistake to see the housewife role as totally oppressive, for many women find this work both creative and satisfying, especially when compared with the jobs most women occupy in the paid labor force. Historians suggest that housework is less alienating than paid labor because it is task-oriented rather than ordered by the timed structures of industrial activity (Thompson 1967). Because women's work at home is oriented to the needs of others, allows for some personal flexibility, and provides some autonomy, many women prefer it to the alienating labor they would likely encounter in the paid labor force.

Sociological studies of housewives confirm this point. Research finds that housewives dislike the monotony and routinization of their work, but they like the autonomy that housework provides (Oakley 1974). Others find that housewives' work as volunteers also provides them with an independent source of satisfaction and personal expression, although their contentment in these roles is to a large extent dependent on their husbands' affluence (Andersen 1981). These studies of housewives' roles tell us that the role is both complex and fragile. Many housewives are satisfied with the work they do; others find it stultifying and unsatisfying. Many women see being able to be a full-time housewife as a privilege. Many black, Asian, Hispanic, and working-class women have never been housewives only, for they have worked at two jobs to support their families — one job in the paid labor force and the other in the home (Davis 1981). Moreover, even for women in privileged classes, the role of affluent housewife is precariously based on the continued economic and emotional support of their husbands. A sudden death, divorce, or economic need can quickly change even the happiest housewife to an anxious and possibly poor woman who must find a way to support herself and her family (Weitzman 1985).

The emotional experience of housework is, however, only one side of the issue. Whatever the woman's response to housework, her work is real, although traditionally it is unrecognized and unpaid. The most detailed pictures of housework have emerged from time-budget studies that record the tasks that make up housework and measure the amount of time used in household labor. These studies show that the contemporary full-time housewife works an average of fifty-seven hours per week on household tasks by preparing and cleaning up after meals, doing laundry, cleaning the house, taking care of children and other family members, shopping, and keeping records (Hartmann 1981).

Housework is organized in the modern economy as a private service, one that women provide for men and children. Housework is organized around a gender division of labor in which women not only do more work than men, but also do different tasks. The gender division of labor in housework is evident when we look at the tasks that different members of the family do. These tasks can be categorized into two types: work internal and work external to the home. The work that men, including male children, do most frequently is largely external — mowing the lawn, carrying out garbage, raking leaves, and some shopping; the work that women and female children do includes washing and drying dishes, preparing meals, cleaning the house, and doing the laundry. Compared with the fifty-seven hours wives report spending per week on housework, husbands spend about eleven hours. Children are reported to do about the same amount as husbands (Walker 1970). A 1975 study finds that, out of a sample of 340 couples, only 26 percent of the husbands spent some time cleaning, compared with 86 percent of wives; 27 percent of the husbands contributed 2.5 hours per week cooking, whereas 93 percent of the wives contribute 8.5 hours. Only 7 of 340 husbands did laundry, compared with one-half of the wives (Meissner et al. 1975).

Recent time-budgeted studies also show that the husbands of wives who work for wages do not spend more time on housework than the husbands whose wives are full-time housewives (Hartmann 1981a), although men do report spending more time on housework (Pleck 1979). Women who work for wages spend fewer hours on housework (about 33 hours per week) than full-time housewives, but, of course, their total work week is then longer, contributing to the social speedup problems discussed in the previous section. In families with a child under 1 year of age, the full-time houseworker spends about seventy hours per week in housework, thirty hours of which are devoted to child care. Husbands in these families increase the amount of time they spend in child care to about five hours per week, but they spend less on other housework, leaving their total contribution to housework about the same (Hartmann 1981a). Hartmann concludes from this data that "husbands may require more housework than they contribute" (1981a:383). This conclusion is further supported by the finding that, controlling for the size of families, single women spend less time on housework than married women (Hartmann 1981a; Morgan 1978). A 1985 survey also shows that 42 percent of women, compared with 26 percent of men, believe that husbands should have to pay for housework (Virginia Slims American Women's Opinion Poll 1985).

The sexual division of labor in the family helps perpetuate sexual inequality in the labor market, as evidenced by the research finding that, for both sexes, there is an inverse relationship between time spent in domestic labor and wages (Coverman 1983). Researchers also find that the greater womens' domestic burdens are, the lower their occupational attainment and status (Chafetz 1984).

Contrary to social myth, the advent of modern technology and household appliances has not significantly reduced the time women spend in housework (Hartmann 1976, 1981a). The earliest information on time spent in housework was gathered in the 1920s under the guise of the new science of home economics and its emphasis on rational management (Vanek 1978). These studies show that then, as now, women spent approximately fifty-two hours per week doing housework. Although the amount of time spent on housework has not changed, the actual character of housework has.

In 1900, most American homes had no electricity and no running water; in 1920, one-third of American families still lived on farms. By the 1930s, approximately 60 percent of American homes had electricity, opening the way for mechanical refrigerators and washing machines, and gas and electric ranges. Also in the 1920s, a variety of canned and processed foods had become available, reducing the time a housewife spent producing and preparing food. By 1940, 70 percent of American homes had indoor plumbing; in the 1950s, automatic washers replaced wringers; and in the 1960s, women's laundry work was changed by the introduction of dryers and wash-and-wear fabrics (Cowan 1976; Vanek 1978). In the 1970s, the fast-food industry offered to take the work of the housewife out of the home, although microwave ovens, food processors, and computerized home management systems increased the expectations of women's laboring within the home.

Although these technological and commercial developments create the potential for reducing women's work as housewives, ideological changes, as well as actual changes in the requirements of housework, contribute to the demands on the housewife's time. For instance, between 1920 and 1980, the amount of time spent on food preparation, cleaning, and sewing and mending decreased. However, the introduction of cheaper clothing and linens meant that there was more clothing and linen per household, and consequently, the time spent doing laundry increased. The invention of the automobile and the development of suburbs mean that the housewife spends more time transporting family members and shopping. Housewives' managerial tasks in the household have increased as financial and medical records, grocery lists, deliveries, and repairs have become routine work (Vanek 1978). And finally, as child care has become more the work of individuals, not extended families, the amount of time spent on child care has increased.

The evolution of changes in household labor is part of the more general changes that have occurred in the relationship of the household to the economy and is also related to changes in the economic structure of life.

The isolation of women's work as housewives is not inevitable; instead, it is a historically specific development that is tied to the modern structure of economic and household relations. Cross-cultural evidence demonstrates that women are not inevitably domestic. In many societies, even when women are engaged in childbearing and child rearing, their role in child care is accommodated to their role in the public economy — not the other way around (Friedl 1975; Malbin-Glazer 1976). In such societies, women's contributions to production are recognized and valued. Anthropological evidence indicates that women have more egalitarian roles in those societies where individuals are directly dependent on the well-being of the society as a whole, where there is no structural dichotomy between the public and domestic worlds, and where those who make decisions also carry them out (Leacock 1978). The modern role of the housewife, isolated and dependent in the private home, is a specific consequence of the historical transition to industrial capitalism. This transition and its consequences for women's roles in families and households is discussed in the following chapter.

Summary

The work women do has been obscured by social myths that devalue women's work both socially and economically. This history of women's work in industrialized societies is characterized by a shift from the family-based economy to the family-wage economy and, contemporarily, the family-consumer economy. The history of black women's work in America follows a different course. Under slavery, black women's work benefited both their owners and their own families and communities. Ideological changes in the definition of women's work justifies the exploitation of women as wage workers and as houseworkers. The idealized image of women is situated by race and class.

Feminist perspectives on women's work have transformed sociological concepts such as class, status, and work. Gender stratification refers to the hierarchical distribution of economic and social resources along gender lines. Gender stratification intersects and overlaps with the system of racial stratification.

The contemporary status of women is marked by their increasing labor force participation, sex segregation, occupation, and income inequality. The experience of women workers in the paid labor force is further complicated by the intersection of race, class, and gender. Women are more likely unemployed than men and are disproportionately affected by job displacement in troubled industries. Poverty is increasing among women, especially among those who head households. The causes of poverty for women are their status in the labor market, their roles in child rearing, and the rising rate of divorce.

Sexual harassment is a form of discrimination and is defined as the unwanted imposition of sexual requirements in the context of a power relationship. Women's culture in the workplace can generate resistance to exploitation and gives women workers some degree of control over their work conditions.

Current economic trends indicate that women's labor force participation will continue to increase, as will demands for their work both in the paid labor force and in the family. This results in increased stress and social speedup for women workers. Women's work as housewives, though unpaid, constitutes a form of work. Women continue to spend far more time doing housework than do men, including men whose wives work for wages. Housework shows the interrelationship of economic and family systems.

CHAPTER 6

Women, Families, and Households

Introduction

An 1889 housewife's guide proclaims:

> Our boys are, in another score of years, to make the laws, heal the soul and
> bodies, formulate the science, and control the commerce of their generation.
> Fathers who, recognizing this great truth, do not prepare their sons to do
> their part toward accomplishing this work, are despised, and justly, by the
> community in which they live. Our girls are, in another score of years, to
> make the homes which are to make laws, heal souls and bodies, formulate
> science, and control the commerce of their generation. (Harland 1889:202)

The home is woman's place, so the historical legacy tells us. In the period
when this guide was published, the glorification of the home and family was
at its historical peak. The home was considered a moral sanctuary, and
morality, which flourished in the home, was considered the work of women.
It was women who would shape future generations. Thus, although their
place was ideally limited to the domestic sphere, within that sphere they
were charged with preserving and creating the moral fiber of society.

Today's families may seem quite different from this ideal because the
family is one of our most rapidly changing social institutions. Today, for
example, only about 13 percent of American families fit the supposed ideal
of a two-parent family in which the man works and the woman stays home
to care for the children (Ramey 1978). The vast majority of American

families are now either two-earner families, female-headed or single-parent households, postchildbearing couples, or those who have no children. And if we consider families to include more alternative forms of household organization, cohabitors, gay and lesbian couples, singles, and various kinds of communal or cooperative living arrangements have to be included in our picture of contemporary families. Moreover, 50 percent of all children can now expect to live in one-parent homes for part of their lives.

Still, the social ideals of the family remain quite different from the realities of contemporary households. The family is still idealized as a private world — one in which family members are nurtured and prepared for their roles in the outside world. The family is also still perceived as the world of women — a place, where, even if women are employed in the public sphere, they are still expected to tend children and manage the everyday affairs of the household. The realities of contemporary households and the persistence of the family ideal, then, create a series of contradictions — especially for women. On the one hand, the family is idealized as women's world. It is glorified, isolated, and assumed to be detached from public life, as well as being seen as an enclave for the development of family members' personalities and for the gratification of their physical and emotional needs. But at the same time, families have been undergoing rapid social changes, making it clear the families are situated within the larger context of political, economic, and social conditions — all of which are structured in accordance with the gender relations of society.

Thus, although we experience our family in terms of personal, intimate relationships, those relationships are conditioned by events that extend far beyond immediate family life. Yet, the family takes on great significance in the development of our individual lives. It is where we first encounter social expectations, where our physical needs are met, where our primary emotional bonds are first established, and where we first encounter systems of authority, power, and social conflict. Although the family seems to be a personal experience, many of the strains associated with family life can be seen as stemming from the conflicts posed by the family's relationship to other social institutions. For example, unemployment, divorce, women's employment, and the welfare state are all experienced within the family, although they are also a part of broader social conditions.

The relationship of the family to other social institutions is also seen by the importance we give to the family as central to all other social institutions. Pleas for strengthening the family and for so-called pro-family policies signify the threat that contemporary transformations in families pose to traditional ways of life in this society. While appeals to pro-family policies at times stem from genuine concern about troubled families, they also represent a conservative view that desires the return of women to the authority of husbands in the family and that regards the appearance of new, and allegedly deviant, family forms as symbolic of all that has gone wrong with the erosion of male authority and traditional values in the society.

Historical Perspectives on Modern Families

Twentieth-century families in the Western world are characterized by an emphasis on child rearing, an assumed separation of home from work, and the idealization of the home as women's world. In addition, in the late twentieth century the family is also idealized as a private world — one where conflicts are supposed to be self-contained, without the intervention of the state. In reality, of course, the family is heavily entangled not only with economic institutions but also with the political state and its various social agencies. In fact, some have argued that the intervention of the state in family policies results in the "policing of families" (Donzelot 1979; Foucault 1967). Most feminists support the idea of public intervention in family policy, because they believe that new policies and agencies (such as battered wives' shelters and programs for displaced homemakers) are necessary to support women in transition.

The history of the Western family reveals the events that have molded contemporary families. Discussion of this history shows how modern families emerge from more traditional forms; how family structures are interwoven with the economy and the state; and how the family mediates between individual or personal life and the public collective realm of society (Wermuth 1981). Moreover, without historical analysis, we tend to see the family as an abstract form, void of its real context and social changes (Dobash and Dobash 1979; Weber 1947). Knowing the history of a contemporary institution is like knowing the biography of a good friend — it helps you understand the present.

It is impossible to pinpoint the exact time in history when the modern family first emerged. One could trace the patriarchal household to the early Roman family, one of the strongest patriarchal systems known. Or one could look to the medieval period as an era when courtly love and chivalry marked gender and class relations between men and women. Patriarchal households — defined as the rule of men over women — are found throughout Western history. But the modern household in Western society is generally depicted as having its origins (at least in the Western world) in the transformations of economic and political life found in the postmedieval period, roughly beginning in the fourteenth century.

Philip Aries (1962) locates the origins of the modern Western family in a series of gradual transformations that began in the fourteenth century and culminated in the seventeenth and eighteenth centuries. Starting in the fourteenth century, the wife's position in the household deteriorated as she lost the right to replace her husband in the management of household affairs in the event of his death or insanity. By the sixteenth century, the wife was placed totally under the authority of her husband; any acts she performed without the authority of her husband or the law were considered null and void. At the end of the sixteenth century, the Church recognized the possibility of sanctification outside of the religious vocation. In other words, it became possible for institutions outside the church to be seen as sacred at this point, and the family became an object of common piety. The marriage ceremony itself, in the seventeenth century, took on a religious form by becoming like a christening in which families gathered around the bride and groom.

Also in the sixteenth and seventeeth centuries, new importance was placed on the family as attitudes toward children changed. Greater intimacy between parents and children established a new moral climate and, although the extension of school education made education increasingly a matter for the school, the family began to center its emotional life on that of the child. By the eighteenth century, the family began to hold society at a distance, thereby initiating the idea of the family as an enclave of private life. Even the physical character of the household changed. Homes became less open; instead of being organized around large communal spaces, they became characterized by several rooms, each specialized by function (Aries 1962). This change is explained as the result of homes' becoming more organized around domestic work as commerce and production became increasingly located in the public workplace.

It is important to note that this evolution of family life was specific to the noble and middle classes and wealthy artisans and laborers. Even as late as the nineteenth century, the vast majority of the European population was still poor and lived like the medieval family, with children separated from their parents and the idea of the home and the family, as described above, nonexistent. But beginning in the nineteenth century and continuing through the present, the concept of the family, as it originated in the well-to-do classes, extended through other strata of society. Still, the concept of the family as we know it today—a privatized, emotional, and patriarchal sphere—has its origins in the aristocratic and bourgeois classes.

By the late eighteenth and early nineteeth centuries, these historical transformations led to what American historians have labeled the *cult of domesticity* (Cott 1977; Kraditor 1968). The ideology of domesticity gave women a limited and sex-specific role to play—namely, responsibility for the moral and everyday affairs of the home. This ideal, coupled with economic transformations in family life, limited women's idealized experience to the private world of the family. In actuality, of course, large numbers of women, especially from the working class, also performed wage labor. But the definition of womanhood as idealized femininity stemmed from the bourgeois origins of the cult of domesticity. The cult of domesticity also provided the conditions for women's involvement in moral reform movements and, ultimately, feminism because it encouraged women's nurturance to be turned toward social improvement (Cott 1977). But in the context of the family, the cult of true womanhood limited women's experience to affairs of the heart, not the mind. This ideal glorified women's role as homemaker at the same time that it fragmented the experience of women and men.

The idealized domestic role of women followed the transformations in women's labor that were described in the preceding chapter. To review briefly, prior to the seventeenth century, the work role of women was not marginal to the economy or the household. In fact, as late as the seventeenth century, the household and the economy were one, the household being the basic unit of production. Domestic life in the earlier period was not splintered from public life, and households, as the basic units of economic production, consisted not only of individuals related through marriage but also of individuals with economic relationships, particularly servants and apprentices. In such a setting, women's labor, as well as that of children, was publicly visible, equally valued, and known to be economically necessary.

The emergence of capitalism, with the related rise of mercantilism, industrialization, and a cash-based economy, eroded the position of women by shifting the center of production from the domestic unit to the public workplace. This separation not only devalued women's labor in the home, but it also made them more economically dependent on men (Tilly and Scott 1978). The emergence of a family-wage economy, as distinct from a family-based economy, transformed not only women's work but, equally important, the family and women's role within it.

When the workplace became separated from the home, the family, although still economically production, became in the long run a site largely for the physical and social reproduction of workers and for the consumption of goods. As more goods were produced outside the home, the value of workers became perceived in terms of their earned wages. The social value of women, especially those left unpaid housewives, was diminished.

In addition, the status of women in the family was radically altered not only by changes in the economic organization of the household but also by political changes in the relationship of the family to the state. The displacement of large feudal households by the modern state enhanced the power of the husband over his wife. For example, in sixteenth-century England, the state assumed the powers of justice, punishment, military protection, and regulation of property originally assumed by feudal estates. At the same time, a massive propaganda campaign was initiated in support of the nuclear family. Family members were required to be loyal, subservient, and obedient to both the king and the husband (Stone 1975, cited in

Dobash and Dobash 1979). Thus, the patriarchal family became the cornerstone — the basic social unit — for the emergence of the modern patriarchal state (Aries 1962; Foucault 1967). As capitalism has developed further, there has been a shift from private patriarchy within the family to public patriarchy centered in industry and government (Brown 1981). Although individual men may still hold power in families where they are present, the patriarchal state ensures that all women are subject to a patriarchal order. Thus, in contemporary society, social welfare systems, education, family courts, and reproductive policies are all controlled by men, even though their primary effect is upon women and children.

Historically, the patriarchal family and, ultimately, the state was hierarchically structured around the power of men and morally sanctioned by the patriarchal church. With the Protestant Reformation, an ever-increasing amount of religious socialization occurred within the home. Whereas Catholicism had sanctioned family life reluctantly (and thus forbade it to the clergy), the Puritans embraced the family as an exalted and natural (God-given) order. The Protestant ethic, as it emerged, blessed the family as a unit of material labor. The ideal that one could do God's work in secular vocations encouraged a view of the family as sacred and as the place for spiritual life (Zaretsky 1976). In the end, the self-consciousness and individualism encouraged by the Protestant ethic helped ensure the subjective importance of the family. With the rise of capitalism, women's lower status in economic production was counterbalanced by their exalted status in the family as God's moral agents.

The split between work and home established by capitalism is related to a second schism — that between personal and public life. Modern capitalism depends on individual consumerism; thus, it encourages modern families to emphasize individualism, self-consciousness, and the search for personal identity. Yet, when personal identity is viewed as detached from objective material conditions, it becomes mystified. One can come to believe that personal liberation can occur without a change in the objective conditions of economic relations. The "plunge into subjectivity" (Zaretsky 1976:119) and its emphasis on life-style, consumerism, and personal awareness is a form of consciousness specific to and consistent with the ideological and economic needs of capitalist economies.

Modern families are also regulated by the patriarchal authority of the state and its various agencies. Especially in poor and working-class families, state agencies and reformers seeking to eliminate deviance regulate personal and family life through the work of professional experts. Even in the middle class, professional experts claim to know more about personal life, thereby defining individual and family needs and the character of contemporary social problems (Ehrenreich and English 1978; Illich 1977).

The development of family structures does vary depending upon the specific historical experiences of given groups in the society. Working-class families, ethnic families, black American families, and families of other racial groups do not develop in exactly the same fashion as do white middle-class households, as we will see in a subsequent section on racism and families. However, transformations in white middle-class households do set the ideals by which other groups have been judged, and the historical development of racial and ethnic families and working-class families are also affected by the same transformations in economic and family systems. This historical account of transformations in the family life paints only a broad picture of the emergence of family live over time. Specific family histories, like other social experiences, are nested within the class, race, and gender relations of any given historical period.

The family is an institution that is interconnected with economic and political institutions of society. Though we tend to think of families and personal life within them as relatively autonomous social forms, we cannot understand the sociological character of families without studying the interrelationships of families, the state, the economy, and gender, race, and class relations.

Feminist Perspectives on Families and Households _____

All societies are organized around some form of kinship system, although the definition of *family* changes in different cultural and historical contexts. Certain common characteristics of the family have been used to define the family. These include economic cooperation, common residence, socially approved sexual relations, reproduction, and child rearing (Gough 1975). Anthropologists also add that, in most kinship systems, "marriage exists as a socially recognized, durable, although not necessarily life-long relationship, between individual men and women" (Gough 1975). It also appears that, in most societies, men have higher status and authority in the family than women (Gough 1975). Commonsense definitions of the family also define the family to mean blood ties, although as we can see in the following section, many contemporary families do not meet this criterion. Nor, in fact, do many contemporary families meet the criteria of common residence, socially approved sexual relations, reproduction, child rearing, or marriage, as the standard definition implies.

As in the case of work, feminist thinking about families and modern transformations in family and household life have forced some rethinking of the meaning of family. Feminist scholars have suggested a number of revisions in perspectives on the family, including the following: (1) the family is a social, not a natural, unit; (2) primary emotional commitments occur outside, as well as inside, the family; (3) men and women experience the family in different ways; (4) families are economic as well as emotional and reproductive units of society; (5) the family ideal is an ideological concept that does not necessarily reflect the variety of family forms found in contemporary society (Rapp, Ross, and Bridenthal 1979). We discuss each of these revisions in turn.

Families as Social Units

Feminist scholars insist that the family must be seen as a social, not a natural, phenomenon and argue that the study of family life in the past has been biased by assumptions that define it as a natural unit. Feminist perceptives on the family lead in several directions, a major one viewing the family as being in a state of constant transformation as it influences and is affected by the larger social world.

The assumption that families are natural or biological units prejudices our conceptions of the family by making it appear to be universal and detached from the influence of other social institutions. Nonetheless, the idea that the family is "natural" is strongly held by some groups, especially conservative, religious groups, and is often used to argue that women should remain in the family under the authority of men.

In fact, the meaning and character of family systems vary widely. Both historically and in contemporary families, persons designated as kin may extend beyond blood relations; adoption is a case in point. And as in the case of illegitimate children, blood relations may sometimes be excluded from the social network of the family. The traditional assumption that family relations are natural also stems from the ethnocentric attitude that the ideals of our own culture are universally the most appropriate social form.

However, even a cursory look at cross-cultural studies of kinship systems reveals a great variety of family forms. For example, in poor rural villages of the Dominican Republic, although single-mate patterns are the dominant ideal, women usually have multiple partners, live on or near the land of their own families, and have their children tended by maternal kin (Brown 1975). Among the Chuckchee of Siberia, adult women are allowed to marry boys two or three years of age. The women care for the boys until they are adults, because the Chuckchee believe that parental care will cement the marriage bond (Robertson 1977). And in contemporary Iran, under the rule of Shiite religious leaders, women are defined as dangerous and destructive if they are not controlled by men. When the Shiites took power over Iranian society, they lowered the age of marriage so young girls would be under the control of husbands; children are considered the sole property of a husband and women who commit adultery are guilty of a capital crime (O'Kelly and Carney 1986).

Within our own culture, the meaning and character of *family* vary over time and among different groups in the society. Carol Stack's (1974) work on the poor black family has shown, for instance, how extended kin networks in the black community function as systems for social and economic exchange. Kin are recognized as those who share and meet socioeconomic obligations, regardless of blood ties. Among some native American groups, traditionally, ancestry would be traced through maternal descent, young couples would reside with the woman's parent, and, wherever they lived, the women assumed control of the household — including the distribution of game that her husband caught (Axtell 1981).

Emotional Experiences and the Family

A second assumption that has biased traditional views of the family is the idea that the person's most significant emotional contracts take place primarily within the family. Although emotional life within the family is surely a powerful experience, we may have underestimated the emotional connections that exist between nonfamily members. Especially for women, we have assumed that their primary emotional tie is to their husband and children. Recent research on women's friendships reveals that this may not be true. New historical work shows that in the nineteenth century, female friendships included passionate and sensual relations (Cott 1977; Smith-Rosenberg 1975). It appears that the very ties that bind women to the home and to the emotional world of compassion and nurturance also bind them to each other. In contemporary life, because we have not asked the question, we are only now beginning to discover the powerful emotional bonds that women and men experience outside of their immediate family relations.

Men's and Women's Experiences of Family Life

Third, scholars have incorrectly assumed that men and women (as well as children) experience the family in similar ways. Yet, as Bernard's (1972) research shows, marriage provides different experiential realities for wives and husbands and, we might assume, children. The assumption that families share and live in a harmony of interests is shattered when we consider the differences in family members' power (Blood and Wolfe 1960), the psychological conflict of parent-child relationships (Mitchell 1971; Weinstein and Platt 1969), and the vast extent of domestic violence (Dobash and Dobash 1979; Martin 1976). The assumption that all members of the family experience home life in similar ways is probably a reflection of our bias in studying the family primarily from the point of view of the dominant belief system.

Research on expectations about marriage shows that men and women hold different expectations of marital roles, with men tending to have somewhat more traditional expectations than women (Komarovsky 1973; Mason and Bumpass 1975; Osmond and Yancey 1975). However, men and, especially, women have come to prefer less rigid gender roles in the family and in the labor market (Mason 1976; Parelius 1975). A 1983 survey has found that 84 percent of couples agreed with each other that child care should be shared, although only 38 percent agreed that housework should be shared (Hiller and Philliber 1986). More husbands than wives want to maintain traditional roles in money matters, while more wives than husbands believe that the wife should be responsible for domestic matters. And, in this survey, 43 percent of couples agree that money earning is the husband's job, and, although two-thirds of the husbands like (or would like) their wives to have a job, 58 percent of husbands feel it is important for them to earn more than she does. The researchers take these results to mean that few husbands or wives want to give up the prerogatives of traditional roles, yet some are interested in expanding their activities into nontraditional roles. It is also important to note that this study is based only on self-reports of husbands' and wives' expectations for marriage and household duties; it does not study who actually does the household work.

Economic and Family Systems

The popular conceptualization of the family as a refuge from the public world hides the fact that families serve economic purposes, as well as reproductive and emotional ones. As we have already seen in the previous chapter, housework, although financially unrewarded, is economically productive activity. If we had to pay for all the services that houseworkers provide, we would see this quite clearly. In fact a 1973 estimate of the economic value of housework placed it at $13,000 per year (Malbin-Glazer 1976); at today's rates, the value would likely exceed $25,000.

In addition to housework, family organization both reflects and reproduces the economic system of society. The availability of work for different family members will affect the family's form, pattern relationships within the family, and shape the family's lifestyle. And the economic resources available to family members will also determine much about their experience in the family, in schools, at work, and at play. But just as economic arrangements influence families, so do families influence economic arrangements. In the family, people learn values and personality characteristics that make them suitable as workers; families shape our understanding of economic systems and our aspirations and definitions of ourselves within them. Furthermore, the role of the state in shaping family life cannot be underestimated. Particularly for the poor, state intervention in family life is an everyday reality, just as economic policies (through, for example, the tax system) can shape the type of family one creates. In sum, as the preceding history of Western families shows, neither families, economic systems, nor the state can be fully understood with knowing their interrelationships. At the same time that there is an interrelationship between family and work, there are also conflict and competing demands, many of which fall on women, who bear that brunt of the different demands and needs of the work place and home (Ferree 1984).

Ideology and the Family

Finally, feminist scholars have argued that the label "the family" has a specific and ideological meaning — in particular, "the family" implies a monolithic and unchanging entity. The ideology of the family assumes that all people do or should live in nuclear families, that women have husbands to support them, and that motherhood is women's major role. Furthermore, this ideology of the family mystifies women's work in families and, as a result, reinforces their economic exploitation (Thorne 1982).

Feminist scholars suggest instead that we think of the idea of the family as distinct from actual households, since each word, *family* and *household*, has a different and distinct connotation. We tend to think of families as involving blood ties; households, on the other hand, imply the existence of a material (or economic) unit. Households are residential units that cannot be analyzed apart from their socioeconomic context. As Rapp, Ross, and Bridenthal describe them, "households are material units within which people pool resources and perform certain tasks. It is within households that people enter into relations of production, reproduction, and consumption with one another, and on one another's account" (1979:176).

This concept leads to the final point in feminist perspectives on the family. *Family* connotes a particular social ideal and, because of its singular form, the word implies that there is one dominant form of family life. Whereas *household* underscores the connection between residential units and the economic structure of society, *family* carries ideological significance as well (Rapp, Ross, and Bridenthal 1979). Distinguishing households from families allows us to recognize the diversity in people's lived experience and frees the discussion of household life from the traditional assumptions that have biased our study of families. Because most households no longer meet the family ideal, it seems appropriate to think of new language and concepts to describe this change. But old traditions die slowly, and it seems likely that the word *family* will remain in our consciousness and our analysis. Thus, this preceding discussion should point out the importance of recognizing that traditional concepts of the family are no longer adequate to describe the social facts of most people's family experience.

Portraits of Contemporary Households _____

What do American households look like? Statistically, among Western industrial nations, the United States still has the highest rate of marriage. In 1984, 63.2 percent of the American population was married. Single persons made up 21.8 percent of the population; 7.8 percent were widowed, and 7.3 percent were divorced (see Table 6-1).

The changing character of families is especially visible in divorce statistics and statistics about teen births and single female–headed households. The United States has the highest divorce rate of any country in the world; in 1985, one-half of all marriages in that year will likely end in divorce. In 1984, 13 percent of all white births were to single mothers; 59 percent of black births were to black single mothers. In 1985 there were 2 million cohabiting but unmarried couples, and only 28 percent of all households were married couples with children under 18 years of age living at home.

Comparing men and women, men are more likely to be married than women (65.8 percent of men are married versus 60.8 percent of women), although a greater proportion of men are also single — 25.5 percent compared with 18.4 percent for women. The longer life expectancy of women also helps explain the fact that more women than men are widowed; 12.5

TABLE 6-1   Households by Type and Race, 1984 and 1970

	All Groups	Whites	Blacks	Spanish-Origin
1984				
Family households	72.6%	72.0%	72.3%	82.5%
—married-couple families	58.6	61.2	37.3	60.3
—male householder	2.4	2.2	3.8	3.5
—female householder	11.6	9.1	31.1	18.7
Nonfamily households*	27.4	27.5	27.7	17.5
—male householder	11.4	11.2	13.1	8.9
—female householder	16.0	16.3	14.6	8.6
1970				
Family households	81.2	81.6	78.0	87.0
—married-couple families	70.5	72.5	53.3	70.0
—male householdeer	1.9	1.8	2.9	3.7
—female householder	8.7	7.2	21.8	13.3
Nonfamily householders	18.8	18.4	22.0	13.0
—male householder	6.4	6.0	9.1	6.6
—female householder	12.4	12.4	12.9	6.4

*Includes single-member households.

Source: U.S. Bureau of the Census, Current Population Reports, Series F–20, No. 398. *Household and Family Characteristics: March 1984.* Washington, D.C.: U.S. Government Printing Office, April 1985.

percent of the female population in 1984 were widowed, compared with 2.6 percent for men. Also, women are more likely to be divorced (8.3 percent) than men (U.S. Bureau of the Census, *Statistical Abstracts of the U.S. 1986*, 1986).

One of the most significant facts of household patterns is the large number of households headed by women, although changes in the definition of heads of household by the Bureau of the Census make this number difficult to assess and even more difficult to compare with the past. The bureau now distinguishes between families (defined as a group of two or more persons related by birth, marriage, or adoption and living together) and nonfamily households (households maintained by a person living alone or with nonrelatives only). It has also recently redefined the concept of a head of household.

Prior to 1980, the national census routinely classified the husband as the head of the family if he and his wife were living together. But as household responsibilities have become more equally shared, the Bureau of the Census has responded to social change by replacing the term *head of household* with *householder*. This term is given simply to the person in the household whose name appears first on the census form. Although it is not an accurate measurement of who actually supports the household, it is intended to provide a better indication of the roles of women in the family.

In 1984, 11.6 percent of all households were families with female householders. Among blacks, families with female householders constitute 31.1 percent of all households; in Hispanic families, 18.7 percent of the total. Moreover, the number of nonfamily households with female householders is a significant percentage of the total number of households (see Table 6.1). In total, the proportion of American households with women as householders is 25.4 percent of all white households, 45.7 percent of all black households, and 27.3 percent of Hispanic households. Again, given problems in the census definition of householder, these data should be interpreted with caution. But nevertheless, they do indicate the vast number of American households in which women take primary responsibility for household affairs.

Recent changes in the marital status of the population can also be seen among the young. Although people still marry at a rate similar to that of the past, they marry at a later age. In 1985, the median age for women at first marriage was 23.3 years; for men, 25.5 years. In 1960, women's age was 20.3 years; men's 22.8 (U.S. Bureau of the Census, *Statistical Abstracts of the U.S. 1986*, 1986; U.S. Bureau of the Census, September 1981). One result is that a larger proportion of the young population is single. In 1984, 56.9 percent of women and 74.8 percent of men between the ages of 20 and 24 were single; in 1960, only 28 percent of that age group were single (U.S. Bureau of the Census, *Statistical Abstracts of the United States 1986*, 1986).

It is also well known that marriages do not endure, as the ideal implies.

TABLE 6-2 Marital Status of the Population 15 Years and Over, March 1985

	Total	Men	Women
All persons			
Single, never married	26.2%	30.0%	22.7%
Married, spouse present	56.1	58.7	53.6
Married, spouse absent	3.2	2.8	3.5
Widowed	7.4	2.4	11.9
Divorced	7.2	6.0	8.2
Blacks			
Single, never married	39.8	43.3	36.9
Married, spouse present	34.7	38.9	31.2
Married, spouse absent	7.9	7.3	8.5
Widowed	8.9	3.5	13.3
Divorced	8.7	7.0	10.2
Whites			
Single, never married	24.3	28.2	20.7
Married, spouse present	58.9	61.3	56.6
Married, spouse absent	2.5	2.2	2.8
Widowed	7.3	2.3	11.8
Divorced	7.1	6.0	8.0
Spanish-origin			
Single, never married	31.2	36.6	26.0
Married, spouse present	51.3	50.6	51.9
Married, spouse absent	6.6	5.8	7.5
Widowed	4.7	2.1	7.2
Divorced	6.2	4.9	7.4

Source: U.S. Bureau of the Census, *Current Population Reports; Marital Status and Living Arrangements: March 1985.* Series P-20, No. 410. Washington, D.C.: U.S. Government Printing Office, November 1986.

The divorce rate in 1985 was 5.0 per 1,000 persons in the population, compared with 2.5 per 1,000 in 1965 (U.S. Bureau of the Census 1986). In the past, the remarriage rate has tended to equal the divorce rate, although since 1970 the remarriage rate has dropped, whereas the divorce rate continues to climb (Skolnick 1978). Men, however, still tend to remarry sooner and more often than women (Glick and Norton 1977).

Thus, although marriage is still an experience shared by a majority of the population, it is fraught with conflict and dissolution. Moreover, an ever-growing portion of the population finds itself living in family situations that deviate from the traditional family structure. Recent studies find that 16 percent of American homes are single-parent households; 23 percent are child-free or postchild-rearing marriages; 16 percent are dual-career families; and 4 percent are cohabitors (Ramey 1978). These and other alternative households patterns are now becoming more typical than the traditional family.

Recent increases in women's labor free participation have made dual-career couples a more common phenomenon. As we have already seen, the majority of women with children are working in the paid labor force. Moreover, 12 percent of all white children, 20 percent of Hispanic children, and 50 percent of all black children are raised in homes maintained by women (Levitan and Belous 1981).

These changes are also reflected in the aspirations of the young. In 1967, 50 percent of women college students stated that a career was important to them in addition to being a wife and mother (Lozoff 1972). By 1971, 81 percent of college students held this view, including 91 percent of male students, who said they wanted a wife with a career (Lozoff 1972). Also, 60 percent of male and female students thought that both parents should spend equal amounts of time with the children; 44 percent believed that household responsibility should be equally shared; and 70 percent of females and 40 percent of males thought that both persons should contribute equally to the family income. By 1985, 38 percent of American women believed the most satisfying and interesting lifstyle for them would be to be married and with a full-time job (Gallup Poll 1985).

In fact, however, women's and men's beliefs in shared household responsibilities are rarely realized, even among dual-career couples. Although wives who work for wages spend less time on housework than nonemployed wives, husbands of working wives spend no more time on housework than husbands of wives who do not work (Hartmann 1981a). When wives are working in paid employment, it appears that children contribute the additional labor for household chores (Poloma and Garland 1971). Moreover, wives who work in full-time paid employment (based on 1977 data) contributed 36.7 percent of the family income (Bryson and Bryson 1980). Wives' paid work has become an economic necessity, with two-earner families maintaining the highest median income of all families.

The experience of dual-career couples often puts strains on their relationship because of the adaptations they must make in household responsibilities and decision making. Especially when a traditional marriage evolves into a dual-career marriage, all members of the family (including the children) may have difficulty adjusting to new roles. But at the same time that couples face these new issues, there are also positive effects in changing traditional roles. Wives tend to experience greater satisfaction with their jobs, and research indicates that children develop more flexible and less stereotypic gender expectations in dual-career families than in traditional ones (Nadelson and Nadelson 1980). Such findings are a direct contradiction to the idea, widespread in popular thought, that the children of working mothers experience maternal deprivation. The assumption that working mothers, but not working fathers, deprive their children of emotional bonding is further evidence of the extent to which the family is idealized as the responsibility of women.

Some dual-career couples, both married and unmarried, find it necessary, because of their job locations, to maintain separate residences. These *commuter couples* also experience problems posed by their long-distance arrangements, not the least of which are considerable transportation and long-distance telephone expenses. However, researchers find commuter marriages to be less stressful for older couples who have been married longer, where at least one partner has an already established career, and where they are free from child rearing (Gross 1980). Women also seem to be more comfortable with the commuter arrangement than men, probably because this relationship involves a recognition of their right to independence and a career of their own (Gerstel and Gross 1984; Gross 1980).

Regardless of the strains imposed on dual-career couples, research on marital strain shows no effect of wives' employment or degree of interest in their work on their marital adjustment or companionship (Locksley 1980). Wives' employment seems detrimental to marital adjustment mostly in families in which there are preschool children and the wife did not graduate from high school (Staines et al. 1978). But overall, researchers report that wives' employment in itself does not create marital dissatisfaction. In fact, women who work out of economic necessity seem to have more power in family decision making (Ferree 1984).

A current portrait of families and households must also include household relationships other than those of married couples. Single persons constitute a growing proportion of the population; in addition, the number of single-parent households has increased substantially. Single persons constituted 21.8 percent of the population in 1984; among black and Hispanic persons, the number of single persons is even higher (see Table 5.1). Single-parent households now constitute 2.6 percent of family groups with children under 18 years of age (U.S. Department of Commerce, Bureau of the Census 1985).

Recent trends among single persons include a profound increase in the numbers of persons who are cohabiting outside of marriage. Since 1970, the number of unmarried persons living together has tripled, with researchers now estimating that soon a majority of persons will experience this lifestyle at some point in their lives (Macklin 1978). Although the number is difficult to determine, there were approximately 2 million unmarried cohabiting couples in 1985, forming 4 percent of all couples living together. Twenty-eight percent of cohabiting couples have children present; the others live with no other person present. About half of cohabitors have been previously married and 8 percent live with someone other than the person to whom they are currently married. Cohabitation is more common among the young, as two-thirds of cohabiting men and three-quarters of cohabiting women are under 35 years of age (Spanier 1983).

Compared with married couples, those who are living together are more likely to reside in metropolitan areas; half of cohabiting couples live in large metropolitan areas compared with 35 percent of married couples. Blacks are more likely to be living together than whites, although the difference between the two groups has diminished since 1975 (Spanier 1983). Although research on cohabiting couples is sparse, it appears that most of these relationships do not differ significantly from traditional marriages in terms of the household division of labor, gender roles, and egalitarian behavior (Macklin 1978; Stafford, Backman, and Dibona 1977).

In addition, households in which persons live alone have also increased in recent years, in part because of demographic changes in the proportion of aged persons in the population. In 1980, 58 percent of of all households included a husband and wife present, and 23 percent of persons lived alone. This pattern represents an increase of 40 percent merely since 1970, and the figure is expected to rise (Glick and Norton 1977). Moreover, two-thirds of one-person households are maintained by women; half of one-person households are those of persons over 65 years of age. Like single-parent families, many of these persons also live in poverty; in 1984, 12.4 percent of all persons over 65 lived below the poverty line. Again, aging and poverty are complicated by race. Among black persons over 65, 33.2 percent live below the poverty line. For Hispanics, 27.4 percent of this age group are poor. For whites, the proportion of poor elderly persons is 10.1 percent (U.S. Department of Commerce April 1986).

Gay and lesbian households have seldom been investigated, and the research that has been done is often biased by the prejudice against homosexuality in this culture. Much of the traditional research on gay men and lesbian women assumes that homosexuality is pathological behavior, although new perspectives are beginning to show a more objective picture of gay and lesbian existence (Rich 1980; Swerdlow et al. 1980; Vida 1978).

Research on lesbian experiences finds that lesbian women tend to form extended networks of support that operate at local and national levels. In a sense, these support networks function like a large family except that, unlike patriarchal families, they tend to be nonauthoritarian and nonhierarchical (Lewis 1979). Within couples, lesbian relationships tend to be more companion-oriented and more flexible in social roles than are traditional couples (Tanner 1978). Moreover, lesbian households are less bound by traditional gender divisions of labor (Tanner 1978), and they tend to be more egalitarian (Taylor 1980).

Research discloses that children of lesbians (and we can assume also of gay fathers, though this has not been reported in the research literature) are usually accepting of their mother's lifestyle, but they are concerned about external reactions from peers and neighbors (Lewis 1980). Some research also shows that lesbian mothers are actually more child-oriented than heterosexual mothers and that lesbian mothers are more concerned about the long-range development of their children (Miller 1982). Research on black lesbian mothers shows that the quality of their relationships with their daughters is contingent on the extent to which mothers have been able to develop intimate relationships, find satisfaction in their work, and acquire a sense of competency and self-worth (Joseph 1984).

There are no accurate statistics on the number of homosexual couples living together because public discrimination forces them into secrecy. Lesbian mothers may have to protect the custody of their children, although they have won the right to do so in some recent lawsuits by arguing that the quality of parenting, not sexuality, is the most important issue. Feminists argue that, when lesbian mothers have left unhappy marriages, the children may be more nurtured in lesbian households, where two women (or more) share the work of child care (Swerdlow et al. 1980). Fewer children live in male homosexual households, in part because women are still more likely to get custody of their children, but also because fewer male homosexuals live in long-term unions than do lesbian couples (Vida 1978).

These alternatives to traditional family life are indicative of the social changes influencing the contemporary character of the household. Demographic patterns and economic changes both contribute to the ever-changing portrait of the American family. Although some describe the family as the institution most reluctant to change (Lasch 1977), clearly the family is marked by both change and stability. In the next section we examine the historical changes that have led to the development of modern family forms.

Parents in Contemporary Families ⸻⸻⸻⸻⸻

In its modern form, the family serves the functions of reproduction, emotional development, economic consumption, and caring for the young. Within the family, women's roles have traditionally been organized around these functions, whereas men's roles (at least in the ideal) have been defined as located in the public sphere.

Young adults now leave home earlier and marry later than in the past and this development has implications for their sex role attitudes. Especially among young women, those who live away from home prior to marriage are more likely to change their sex role attitudes, values, plans, and expectations and are more likely to move away from a traditional family orientation (Waite, Goldscheider, and Witsberger 1986).

Changes in labor force participation for women have affected their roles in the family and have created more possibilities for women's and men's lives. However, as our discussion of housework has already shown, for most working women, being in the paid labor force is simply added on to their work in the family. Still, research finds that holding multiple roles reduces distress and increases self-satisfaction, despite the demands these multiple roles pose (Thoits 1986).

Motherhood

The child-centeredness of modern families has tended to distract us from thinking about mothers; yet, an examination of motherhood as a social institution reveals both the objective and subjective dimensions of this experience. Women's roles as mothers are idealized in our culture as all-loving, kind, gentle, and selfless. Yet, the objective conditions of motherhood in this society fill the role with contradictions, conflicts, and pleasures. Motherhood is, in fact, a social institution — one that is controlled by the systems of patriarchy and the economic relations in which it is embedded (Rich 1976). Like other institutions, motherhood involves a complex set of social relations organized around specific functions. Once established, institutions also involve a system of power relations, a division of labor, and the distribution of resources.

Viewing motherhood as an institution distinguishes motherhood as a social practice from the potential relationship between a women and her children (Rich 1976). In this society, motherhood is specifically characterized by its isolation. Thus, although most young girls are socialized to become mothers, they are seldom prepared for the solitary activity of actually caring for children in the home. Jessie Bernard (1975) suggests, in fact, that when women marry, their early socialization for dependency is reversed, because as wives and mothers they are expected to be responsible for both their husband and their children. The experience of motherhood than becomes a mixture of satisfaction and pleasure plus anger, frustration, and bitterness (Rich 1976). The contradictions also appear for children since, as Rich says, "most of us first know both love and disappointment, power and tenderness, in the person of a woman" (1976:11). Because motherhood is a role exclusively reserved for women, women's identities develop in ways that reproduce mothering qualities.

Nancy Chodorow has explored this issue by asking how the psychological structures of gender emerge from the "asymmetrical organization of parenting" (1978:49). Chodorow notes that the role of women as mothers is one of the few seemingly universal elements of the sexual division of labor. But instead of relying on explanations that see motherhood as a natural fact, she asks why the psychological characteristics of motherhood are reproduced so that women, and not men, want to be mothers and develop the capacity of nurturing others. According to Chodorow, "women, as mothers, produce daughters with mothering capacities and the desire to mother. These capacities and needs are built into and grow out of the mother-daughter relationship itself. By contrast, women as mothers (and men as not-mothers) produce sons whose nurturant capacities and needs have been curtailed and repressed" (1978:7).

Chodorow explains this process as the result of both the gender division of labor and the psychological processes it inspires. Both boys and girls, in order to become their own person, must separate — psychologically — from the parent. Because the parent most often present is a woman, the process of individuation is complicated by gender identity. Boys, who identify with the gender of the father, learn that their gender role is one of detachment and distance, because the father is seldom present in the home. Girls, on the other hand, identify with the gender of the mother; thus, their own psychological process of separation and individuation is less complete. Girls, then,

> are more continuously embedded in the mediated by their ongoing relationship with their mother. They develop through and stress particularistic and affective relationships to others. A boy's identification processes are not likely to be so embedded in or mediated by a real affective relation to his father. At the same time, he tends to deny identification with and relationship to his mother and reject what he takes to be the feminine world; masculinity is defined as much negatively as possible. . . . Feminine identification processes are relational, whereas masculine identification processes tend to deny relationship. (1978:176)

As a consequence, gendered personalities both reflect and re-create the gender division of labor in the household. Women become mothers because this role is consistent with their acquired psychological being; the fact that they are mothers, then, re-creates similar personality structures of nurturance in their daughters. In sum, the social organization of parenting creates psychic structures that orient the person to his or her social behavior. To reverse this process, so that men as fathers become more nurturant, will require that men be placed in the household on an equal basis with women. But because the organization of parenthood is tied to the organization of economic production, both the family and the economy must be transformed if we are to eliminate gender inequality.

Chodorow's analysis is psychoanalytic in its orientation; thus, the evidence for her argument is clinical evidence. As her critics point out, clinical evidence is weak because it rests on patients' accounts and psychoanalysts' interpretations of those accounts (Lorber et al. 1981). But, beyond these methodological criticisms, some sociologists are concerned that Chodorow overemphasizes psychological processes in lieu of social structural conditions as the source of women's choice to become mothers. It is ideologically normal in our society for women to become mothers; furthermore, given the inequality in men's and women's incomes, it is reasonable for fathers, not mothers, to be the primary wage earner in the family (Lorber et al. 1981:484).

Other questions about the class, race, and culture bias of Chodorow's explanation can also be raised, for she assumes that the mother in the gender division of labor is a devalued woman. Although this is true in many cultures, including the dominant American culture, it is not universally true. An important test of her theory would involved the study of boys and girls who are raised by men or in cultures where women are not devalued and parenthood is more equally shared. We also need to consider the fact that the psychoanalytic perspective may not account for variations in the actual practices and relationships of mothers who are raising children. The mother's own personality, as well as the child care arrangements she makes, may alter the degree to which her sons and daughters separate or do not separate themselves from her, and it certainly alters their relationship with her. But Chodorow's analysis gives us a provocative account of the formation of gender identity and its relationship to the social structure of the family.

Most importantly, Chodorow points out that the family is "a primary constituent of the male dominant social organization of gender and, as such, is as fundamental a constituent feature of society as a whole — of 'social structure' — as is the economy or the political organization" (Lorber et al. 1981:502). One is not dependent on or contained by the other, people live in families, just as they live in societies. Chodorow's analysis has led us to see the importance of understanding "the gender politics of infancy" (Harding 1981) and the connection of masculine and feminine personalities not only to the social organization of families but also to self-other distinctions that constitute the basis for domination relations (Chodorow 1981; Harding 1981). In sum, although the cross-cultural evidence for Chodorow's work remains to be studied, she provides an insightful explanation of some of the effects of nuclear family relations, in which the woman's work as a mother is isolated from that of other persons and is founded on the norm of exclusivity.

Fatherhood

Fathers' roles in the family have traditionally been defined as instrumental. That is to say, fathers were to be the primary breadwinner and source of authority in the family, while mothers were to fulfill the emotional needs of family members. But, just as women have found their traditional roles to be limiting and one-sided, many men have tried to redefine their roles as fathers to include more primary care of children. In fact, researchers have learned that role flexibility within the family is necessary to preserve the well-being of all family members (Spiegel 1983).

Research on fathers has traditionally been based on the assumption that fathers have a limited role in families (Robinson and Barret 1986), though as fathers have assumed more responsibilities in family life, new research has emerged. Still, the research shows that, following the birth of a baby, most fathers tend to help out rather than share child care and they continue to view caring for the baby as the mother's work (La Rossa and La Rossa 1981). Men do express a willingness to help with child care, but not equally (Liss-Levinson 1981). Moreover, mothers say they are unwilling to force the issue because they perceive the price to be too great (Robinson and Barret 1986). Thus, although the adjustment to parenthood for both men and women is considerable, fathers experience less stress in adapting to parenthood than do mothers (La Rossa and La Rossa 1981).

Some men who make intellectual commitments to transformed roles in the family have negative emotional reactions when they find themselves isolated from other men and having little in common with male peers (Levine 1976). Despite the increase in the number of single and divorced fathers, as well as the greater involvement of many men in their roles as fathers, there are few social support networks for men. Many men continue to feel pressure to put their jobs and careers first and, although employers give lip service to increased family involvement, workers perceive that choices have to be made between family and career (Colman and Colman 1981).

Sociological perspectives on fatherhood see fathering, like mothering, as a role, not just a biological connection to one's offspring. In fact, neither kinship nor household membership is always necessary for a man to perform the psychological and instrumental functions associated with a father. Gershenson (1983) indicates that among adolescent parents, the man who fulfills the role of father may be the mother's current boyfriend, the biological father of the child, or any combination of the significant men in the child's life. In fact, he points out that fathering, like mothering, can be done by more than one person.

Men who have worked to include more expressive and caretaking work in their roles as fathers do report considerable rewards in creating fuller relationships with their children. They report more discovery and recognition of their inner lives (Fein 1974), though they also note that society provides little emotional, practical, or financial support for men to spend time regularly with their children. Moreover, gender stereotypes that label child care as women's work continue to influence public reactions to men who care for children either in their own homes or as paid workers (Seifert 1974).

These accounts of men involved in child care indicate that social change in our roles in families are part of a process of discovering the full range of our human qualities (Garfinkel 1985). Yet, the full realization of these qualities will require societal support in the form of paternity leaves, new work arrangements for parents, and transformation in our attitudes about gender and parenting.

Families and Social Problems ──────────────

Violence in the Family

This discussion of the family shows that isolation is both an ideological and a structural characteristic of the modern family. We have already seen the contradictions and dilemmas that isolation poses for mothers. But the effects of isolation and the ethic of family privacy are no more vividly seen than in the high incidence of violence against women in the family. Wife battering, child abuse, and incest have only recently been brought to the public's attention, but all of them make the tensions of family life clear. Violence in families also reveals the continuing presence of patriarchal relations within families.

Only in recent years has the sanctity of the private household been breeched so that these issues have come to our attention. What were once hidden problems now seem disturbingly common. Although accurate measures of the extent of family violence are difficult to establish, researchers estimate that the problem is widespread across families in all classes and races. (Dobash and Dobash 1979; Strauss, Gelles, and Steinmetz 1980). With regard to wife battering and child abuse, indirect evidence of their extent also comes from police records of domestic disturbances (Martin 1976), hospital emergency room files, family court records, homicide rates of women killed by husbands and lovers (Wolfgang 1958), and the great number of divorces that cite violence as the primary reason for ending the marriage (Chester and Streather 1972; Levinger 1966). Information on incest is even harder to obtain because social taboos against it make it one of the most hidden of social problems. But as victims of incest have spoken out, we have begun to see its high incidence across class and race. While we have tended to think of violence as most prevalent in lower classes and among minority groups, it is important to point out that it occurs in all groups, although the middle and upper classes have more ability to keep it secret.

Battered Women. Studies indicate that the overwhelming amount of domestic violence is directed against women (Dobash and Dobash 1979). Coupled with the idea that violence is purposeful behavior, this fact leads to the conclusion that violence against wives is a form of social control — one that emerges directly from the patriarchal structure and ideology of the family (Barry 1979). Historically, wife beating has been a legitimate way to express male authority. Scholars contend that the transformation from the feudal patriarchal household to the nuclear family had the effect of strengthening the husband's power over his wife by placing systems of authority directly in the hands of individual men, not in the indirect rule of the state. Thus, throughout the seventeenth, eighteenth, and nineteenth centuries, men could, within the law, beat their wives, and there was little community objection to their doing so as long as the method and extent of violence remained within certain tacit, and sometimes formally documented, limits. For example, eighteenth-century French law restricted violence against wives to "blows, thumps, kicks, or punches on the back if they leave no traces" and did not allow the use of "sharp edged or crushing instruments" (Castan 1976, cited in Dobash and Dobash 1979:56–57). One ancient code, from which we get the phrase *rule of thumb,* allowed a man to beat his wife with a stick no thicker than his thumb (Dobash and Dobash 1977).

The historical context of wife beating provides a perspective with which to view the contemporary problem. Now, although wife beating is socially abhorred, it is at the same time widely legitimated through its humorous portrayal and through attitudes protecting privacy in marriage. Additionally, the attitude that victims bring violence on themselves (by not leaving) seems to discourage social intervention in violent relationships. As a result, the phenomenon of violence is widely misunderstood. Dobash and Dobash's (1979) study of Scottish wives gives us some understanding of how violence emerges in marriage and how it is tied to the social isolation of women in the family.

Dobash and Dobash traced the course of 109 relationships that resulted in battering, beginning with the initial courtship phase. During the period when couples first met, both maintained separate lives, including an independent social life with friends and individual commitments to their family, jobs, and education. As the couples' commitment to each other increased, the partners modified their social lives, although women did so more than men. One-quarter of the women studied went out with their own friends once a week or more, compared with nearly half of the men. The more serious the relationship became, the less time women spent with their own friends.

Prior to marriage, the women reported that sexual jealousy was the major conflict in the relationship, although arguments over jealousy seem to have had the purpose of confirming the couple's commitment to each other. The women became increasingly isolated from their friends prior to the marriage, and they reported believing that love would take care of any problems that existed in the relationship.

Both partners entered marriage with ideals about how the marriage would work, although after a time it was clear that the husband's ideals would rule. Marriage, for the wife, involved an extreme constriction of her social world, and the husband began to believe that he could monopolize his wife, although she could not put similar demands upon him. He, as the representative to the outside world, was supposed to have authority, independence, and freedom; she could not question his movements.

In this study, 41 percent of the wives experienced their first attack within six months of the wedding; another 18 percent experienced an attack within the first year of marriage. The wives response was one of surprise, shock, shame, and guilt, although both partners treated the incident as an exception and assumed, without discussion, that the issue had been resolved. Yet, as the marriage continued, conflicts repeatedly surfaced. Nearly two-thirds of the couples reported sexual jealousy and expectations about domestic work as the source of conflict leading to violent episodes. The women reported that their social world moved more apart from their husband's as the marriage went on. The wives were mostly involved in the everyday matters of household management and child care, whereas the husbands were involved in their own work. However, the husbands still expected their wives to meet their immediate needs.

What is striking about these cases studies is how common the patterns in these relationships are. Clearly, wife battering emerges from institutional arrangements that isolate women in the home and give men authority over them. Moreover, once a pattern of violence is established, wives believe they have no options. Most will, at some point, leave — even if temporarily (Dobash and Dobash 1979) — but their feeling that they have no place to go is usually a realistic assessment of their economic situation and their powerlessness to effect changes within the relationship (Martin 1976). When wives do stay in abusive relationships, they tend to rationalize the violence to themselves. Research on women who did not leave after battering finds that they use several types of rationalizations, including believing that the man can be "saved" and denying the battering by seeing it as the result of external forces.

In the courts, battered wives are faced with the problem of having to prosecute a man who is both their husband and, possibly, the father of their children. Moreover, even if the wife brings charges, when the husband is released he returns to the home — perhaps more angry than when the violence began (Martin 1976). The movement to establish refuges for battered women has assisted many victims in responding to battering, and such centers have proliferated in communities throughout the country. But difficulties in funding such centers have caused many to close, and current cutbacks in social services funding seem likely to pose additional setbacks. Finally, the attitude that family problems are a private matter, to be resolved between two equal partners and within the confines of the home, creates resistance to social changes that could assist battered wives.

Marital Rape. Marital rape is defined as "forced sexual activity demanded of a wife by her husband" (Frieze 1983). Legal definitions of marital rape vary from state to state, and in many states forced sex is not considered a crime in marriage. Nonetheless, studies of marital rape show it to be a serious problem, affecting probably 10 percent of all married women (Finkelhor and Yllo, 1985; Frieze 1983; Russell 1982).

Marital rape is most commonly associated with other physical violence in the relationship (Pagelow 1980). Victims of marital rape, like other rape victims, experience rape trauma syndrome (see Chapter 9), including physical injury, anger, depression, fear, and loss of interest in sex (Burgess and Holmstrom 1978).

Studies of marital rape find that wives who have several children, who have never been employed before marriage, and who have less formal education are more likely to be raped in marriage, compared with battered wives who are not raped. Husbands who rape their wives are more dominant in the marriage relationship and are also more likely to have drinking problems. Marital rape is more likely to occur also where husbands associate sex with violence, have extramarital affairs, and are unreasonably jealous (Frieze 1983). One of the most disturbing findings in the research on marital rape is that one of its causes is a husband's anger that his wife has been raped by someone else.

Wives in these marriages have few resources of their own to draw on, exacerbating their powerlessness in this situation. Moreover, the belief that sexual access is a right in marriage makes it appear that they have not been raped. Nonetheless, the evidence on marital rape shows the extent to which the definition of women as the property of men continues to affect marital relationships.

Incest and Sexual Abuse.   Accurate estimates of the extent of incest and sexual abuse are very difficult to establish. Man–girl incest is said to involve at least 1 percent of all girls, although one in five girls and one in eleven boys say they have had sexual experience as a child with a much older person (Finkelhor 1979).

Feminist clinicians who have studies incest have challenged traditional Freudian assumptions about incest that children lie or fantasize about incestuous sexual encounters. Incest victims do try to stop the incest by seeking help or striking back, though often they are not believed. Research from feminist clinicians has shown that families where incest occurs tend to share several characteristics, the most significant of which is the estrangement of mother and daughter.

Mothers may be aware of incestuous abuse, but they are typically powerless to stop it. A mother may become a silent bystander because her emotional and/or economic dependence on her husband prevents her from confronting the situation (Armstrong and Begus 1982). Particularly in families where mothers are unusually powerless because of battering, disability, mental illness, or repeated childbearing, there is an especially high risk of sexual abuse, especially among daughters who have taken on the household responsibilities; in such families, the daughter is often led to believe that she must comply with the father's demands if she is to hold the family together (Herman and Hirschman 1977). Moreover, molested daughters in this situation are still dependent upon their fathers for care and, since this may be the only affection they receive, victims often report warm feelings for their fathers, who make them feel special (Herman 1981).

This research finds that the father/assailant feels no contrition about his behavior. When mothers were incapacitated, fathers did not take on the nurturing functions, nor did they express nurturing feelings for the victim or understand the destructiveness of the incest. Fathers typically blamed their wife or their daughter for the incest and, distressingly, Herman finds that daughters often reinforce this view, blaming the mother and herself, while exonerating the father (Herman 1981).

This portrait of incestuous behavior underscores that the intersection of power and gender relations in families is a contributing fact in incestuous behavior. Researchers also are only now beginning to see the multiple consequences of sexual abuse. A study of female prostitutes and drug users finds that as many as 44 percent were sexually abused as children (MacFarlane 1978). Sexually abused female runaways are also more likely than nonabused female runaways to engage in delinquent and criminal activities (McCormack, Janus, and Burgess 1986). These findings also suggest that sexual abuse is important for practitioners to consider when developing treatment programs.

Feminists have pointed to violence as the logical result of both women's powerlessness in the family and a male culture that emphasized aggression, domination, and violence. The modern form of the family leads women to be dependent on men economically and emotionally, and, as a result, the traditional family is a source of social conflict and a haven only for men (Hartmann 1981a). The phenomenon of violence in the family shows clearly the problems that traditional family structures create for women. Feminist criticism of the family rests, in part, on the psychological, physical, and economic threats families pose for women. And it is for these reasons that feminists argue for a change in traditional family structures. These changes, intended to empower women, would not necessarily abolish the family, but they would create new values regarding women's work in the family and new rewards for women in the family, regardless of whether they are also working in the public labor force.

Racism and Families

Women of color share many of the problems of white women in families, but racism and the unique experiences of minority groups also shape the organization of families among racial and ethnic groups in society. Many of the assumptions made in studies of minority families have been biased by the belief that these families are normal only when they conform to dominant groups norms (Staples and Mirandé 1980). Minority families have been targeted as being the source of social disorganization in minority communities (Moynihan 1965) and as contributing to a lack of achievement among minority persons. These assumptions stem from confusing ideology and objective social science research and demonstrate the extent to which racism has pervaded sociological research (Ladner 1971).

When minority families are studied on their own terms, a more objective picture of their character emerges — one that forces a reexamination of the assumptions we make about family life. The revisions in scholarship on minority families have come especially from studies of the black family in society and history, although recent work has also revised contemporary interpretations of Hispanic, Asian-American, and native American families.

Black families in America tend to be larger than white families. Blacks also marry later than do whites, but the divorce rate of blacks is higher than that of whites. Also, a large and increasing proportion of black families and households are headed by women. When two spouses are present, black wives are more likely than white wives to work, and they contribute a larger share of the total family income.

Although these aggregate data give a partial portrait of the black family, they do not tell us about the actual content of these relationships and family systems. Discussions of black families are often contaminated by value-laden terms such as *disorganization, maladjustment*, and *deterioration*. In fact, much of the discussion of black families has emerged from confusion over the use of the term *matriarchy* to refer to the fact of female-headed households. *Matriarchy* is defined as a social structure in which power is held by women. In black families, in which women are often the head of the household, they still have little power within the society; thus, the term *matriarchy* is misleading. It confounds the study of the family with racial and gender stereotypes of the black woman as dominating, castrating, and overbearing and, thus, distorts the reality of family life and black women's lives (Staples 1971).

Because the dominant family ideal in this culture is the patriarchal family, much of the research on black families has attributed problems in the family to its women-centered organization. The infamous Moynihan report, *The Negro Family: The Case for National Action*, published as a federal study of the black community in 1965, cited the family as the cause of social disorganization in black America. In Moynihan's own words, "at the heart of the deterioration of the fabric of Negro society is the deterioration of the Negro family" (1965:5).

Moynihan's report attributed the origins of the family problem to the period of slavery and the social disorganization it created. Other studies of the black family have also cited slavery as creating female-headed families through the separation of family members by slave sales, the practice of slave breeding, and the disrespect paid to the black slave community (Frazier 1948). Others have traced the structure of black family life to its African origins, where polygamy and birth out of wedlock were more common (Herskovits 1958). Recent scholarship on the black family questions both of these conclusions, noting that locating the causes of contemporary family structure in the past downplays an analysis of family life within contemporary economic and social structures (Ryan 1971).

Herbert Gutman, a historian, argues that, if Moynihan was right in concluding that the structure of black families has its origins in the past, then we should expect the family to be less stable as we move backward in time. To test this assumption, Gutman traced five generations of kin as they adapted to the changes of postslavery American society. Part of his research is based on 1925 census data from New York City that show that 85 percent of kin-related black households at that time were double-headed; 32 of the 13,924 families had no father present; and five or six children under age 6 lived with both parents (Gutman 1976:xix). Based on this information, he concluded that female-headed households are a contemporary phenomenon, not just remnants of the past. His historical research is complemented by that of Genovese (1974), who believes that slave owners used the family as a form of social control. Genovese recognizes that separation of families occurred, but he suggests that it was often to the benefit of slave owners to maintain stable families as a way of preventing slave revolts. The slave family, according to Genovese, was subordinated to the economic interests of the owner. If it benefited him, he would break up families for sale; in fact, most slave owners broke up families when they were under economic pressure (Genovese 1974:453).

Both Genovese's and Gutman's analyses indicate that slave families faced oppressive conditions that tested the adaptive capacities of men and women. Within slave communities, a subculture of resistance emerged in which family relations and women's role fostered resistance to dominant white institutions (Davis 1971, 1981). Because of the gender division of labor, black women in slavery provided domestic labor not only in the white household but also in their own. The labor they provided for their own family was the only labor not claimed by the ruling class; it was for the benefit of the slave community. As a result, black women's labor in the slave community "lay the foundation for some degree of autonomy" (Davis 1971:5), and the black woman became essential to the survival of the slave community. Moreover, because of her indispensable labor in the household of the oppressor, she developed a practical awareness of the oppressor's dependence on her. As Davis says, "The master needs the slave for more than the slave needs the master" (1971:6). Black women's consciousness of their oppression benefited the slave community, as women were responsible for the socialization of future generations. Thus, the women in their roles in the family and community passed on a culture of resistance to oppressed kin (Caulfield 1974).

The picture of the black family emerging from these revisions is one of strength and resistance. In fact, Ladner (1971) suggests that traditional myths of the black matriarchy confuse black women's strength with domination. Because of racism, the black woman has not been subjected to the ideals of femininity, as have white women (Davis 1971). One result is found in the strong self-concept and higher educational and occupational aspirations that black women have for themselves compared with white women (Dill 1980; Epstein 1973; Myers 1975; Wilson 1980).

Instead of explaining patterns in black families as the result of slavery or individual pathology, it makes sense to analyze the origins of black family life in terms of the patterns of urbanization, industrialization, and poverty in twentieth-century society (Billingsley 1966; Frazier 1948; Staples 1971). In the early twentieth century, racial discrimination in the labor force denied black persons employment using the skills they had acquired in slavery. As a result, men could find only unskilled, often seasonal, and always underpaid employment; women were more likely to find steady, although also severely underpaid, employment in private domestic labor. In 1920, 41 percent of black women worked as servants and 20 percent as laundresses (Katzman 1978:74). Black women's labor thus made them steady providers for their family. As the twentieth century developed, continuing patterns of unemployment, the elimination of black men through war and imprisonment, and the conditions established for households by the social welfare system encouraged the formation of female-centered households.

The contemporary structure of black households must be understood in terms of both racism and sexism and the economic context in which they are embedded. As we look at black families without racist and sexist assumptions, we see that even in the poorest of families, systems of cooperation and social exchange characterize the organization of family life (McCray 1980; Stack 1974). The social and community ties that people generate in the face of poverty and oppression, in fact, appear stronger than some of the ties of nuclear families. This fact shows us that black families are not necessarily disorganized, but that they are not always organized according to dominant group ideals. Seen in this way, the role of women in the black family can be seen for the strength it creates, not the social destruction it allegedly causes. Black women continue to work to support their families (Rodgers-Rose 1980) and to hold high ideals for their children's future (Dill 1980). Higginbotham's (1981) studies of educated black women show that those educated women from the lower middle class are less likely to be married than educated black women from middle-class families because parents in the lower middle class are more likely to encourage their daughters to become educated than to get married. Different from popular images of working-class black families, parents have positive aspirations for their children and hope they will receive more education than the parents themselves have achieved (Wilkinson 1984). Black working-class families view the education of their children as providing a way to overcome racial discrimination, whereas white working-class families worry that highly educated children will no longer honor family customs and maintain cohesion with their relatives (Willie 1985).

Black middle-class families promote among their children and through their community activities a strong sense of building a just and equitable society, whereas white middle-class families are likely to encourage family members to become individually better informed and enriched. Willie also points out that a significant difference between white and black middle-class families is the greater likelihood of middle-class black mothers' being in the labor force; in fact, her contribution to family income is essential in maintaining the family's standard of living. This tends to create greater egalitarianism within black families and promotes the greater participation of black husbands in child care and household management (Willie 1985).

Eliminating pejorative assumptions about minority families has transformed our knowledge of black families, as well as of Chicano and Puerto Rican families. As with the study of black families, past studies of Chicano and Puerto Rican families have been founded on the assumption of pathology. Machismo in Hispanic families has been assumed to encourage aggressive, violent, authoritarian behavior in men and saintly, virginal, submissive behavior in women (Staples and Mirandé 1980). But some researchers see machismo as a more benevolent feature of Hispanic families, encouraging honor, respect, and dignity among family members (Mirandé 1982; Murillo 1971). Research shows that Hispanic families are more egalitarian than the ideal of machismo suggests (Baca-Zinn 1976; Cromwell and Cromwell 1978; Mirandé 1979; Ybarra 1977), and that the Hispanic family is more woman-centered than prevailing stereotypes suggest (Baca-Zinn 1976).

Chicano families have been characterized as close-knit kinship systems, typically explained as a consequence of Chicano culture. However, scholars now recognize that these family patterns represent adaptation to a hostile society that excludes Chicanos from full participation and keeps them socioeconomically marginal (Baca-Zinn 1986). Especially for women, close kinship networks provide social exchanges and support that is not available elsewhere, particularly considering that Chicana workers are restricted to employment primarily in domestic work, cannery and packing jobs, the textile industry, and in agricultural labor. The fact that there is greater egalitarianism among Chicano couples where both partners are in the labor force (Ybarra 1982) suggests that the power of persons within the family rests on resources external to the marriage, not on the culture or individual attributes of persons within the marriage. In discussing machismo among Chicano men, Baca-Zinn says that because white maleness is highly valued, but also denied to minority men, their gender identity may be difficult to establish. Though Chicano men do not appear "super masculine" in comparison to black or Anglo men (Senour and Warren 1976), Baca-Zinn suggests that "it may be worthwhile to consider some expressions of masculinity as attempts to gain some measure of control in a society that categorically denies or grants people control over significant realms of their lives" (Baca-Zinn 1982a:39).

Research on Asian-American and native American families is sparse and, in both cases, assimilation and acculturation are key concepts in understanding the transformations in family life. There are approximately 1.5 million individuals of Chinese, Japanese, Korean, Filipino, Vietnamese, Cambodian, Thai, and East Indian ancestries living in the United States (Yamauchi 1979, cited in Staples and Mirandé 1980). Although these persons conform more closely to middle-class American family norms than do other minorities, their family systems are marked by the tensions of generational changes in traditional cultures. American-born children may adapt American values, whereas their parents and grandparents may adhere to the more traditional and conservative family mores of their culture. Within Asian-American communities, ethnic cohesiveness and continuity through generations may be difficult to maintain, and families may experience conflict as a result (Staples and Mirandé 1980).

The stability of racial-ethnic families must be seen, however, in the context of racist policies that discourage strong and cohesive families (Glenn 1983). For Asian-Americans the history of immigration policies discouraged family unity. The Naturalization Act of 1870 and the Chinese Exclusion Act of 1882 forbade the entry of wives of Chinese laborers into the United States. Until passage of the Magnuson Act in 1943, the Exclusion Act of 1924 forbid alien-born wives to enter the United States (although their children could). Moreover, until ruled unconstitutional in 1967, anti-miscegenation laws barred marriages between whites and "Mongolians" or laborers of Asian origins (Chow 1987). Such policies make it difficult for stable Asian-American families to form and show that, as with black American families, family stability is as much a factor of racist policies and practices as it is of the choices and characteristics of members of the minority group.

Among native Americans, family life-styles vary widely, as diversity among groups is a key element of culture. Also, the attempt to impose Western family forms on these people complicates the picture of native American family life. Interference in these cultures by social workers, the federal government, and other outsiders may have done more to promote family and cultural disorganization than to assist these groups. Among native American families, urbanization contributes to high rates of unemployment and dependence on public welfare (Miller 1975). Left to their own culture, native American families tend to rely on extended family networks to fulfill family functions (Redhorse et al. 1979; Staples and Mirandé 1980). The imposition of Western standards on these traditional forms creates stress for the community and the family, because adapting to both traditional and dominant societal values poses difficulties for both individuals and families.

The problems faced by minority families underscore the point that families do not exist in a cultural and economic vacuum. Economic changes, racial and cultural conflicts, and gender relations interact to product family systems. In sum, we can see that no single model of family life characterizes *the* American family, in spite of ideological beliefs to the contrary. Even the feminist perspective that family life is debilitating for women seems questionable when we consider the role of the family in the cultural resistance of minority groups. Sociological perspectives on family life should be sensitive to the interaction of the family with other social institutions and should keep in mind that the ideology of the family often, if not always, departs from the actual structure of both dominant- and subordinate-group family systems.

Adolescent Pregnancy

The increase in poverty among children is due almost entirely to the growth of single-parent families, many of whom are teenage mothers. By the time of their eighteenth birthday, 22 percent of black females and 8 percent of white females have given birth; by their twentieth birthday, 41 percent of black females and 19 percent of white females have given birth (Moore 1985). In 1985, teens accounted for 13 percent of white births and 59 percent of black births (U.S. Department of Commerce, Bureau of the Census 1986). Although the birth rate for white teens is increasing and the birth rate for black teens has slightly declined, the overall rate of teen births is very high — especially for black teens (Ladner 1986).

Marriage rates for teens have also dropped, meaning that most of these babies will be raised by single mothers. In 1985, 90 percent of births to black mothers under 20 years of age were to single women. Teen mothers face higher medical risks in pregnancy and are more likely to have low-birth-weight babies, which, in turn, is a major cause of infant mortality. The recent increase in infant mortality rates, which had previously been on the decline since 1940, is probably due in large part to the increase in teenage pregnancy.

But, in addition to the health problems, teenage parents face chronic unemployment or, when they work, low earnings and low-status jobs. In 1986, the unemployment rate for black teenage males was 39.3 percent; for white teenage males, 16.3 percent; and for Hispanic teenage men, 24.5

percent. For teenage females, unemployment was 39.2 percent for blacks, 14.9 percent for whites, and 25.1 percent for Hispanics (see Table 5-6). It is little wonder that, despite the fact that teens parents initially perceive welfare only to be a temporary means of providing for their children, the fact is that their situation encourages long-term welfare dependency (Ladner 1986).

Approximately 85 percent of teenage mothers continue to live with their families, many of whom are themselves single female heads of household who were also teenage mothers. Ladner's study of two generations of teenage mothers (where grandmothers are only in their thirties, though one is 29) shows that they feel resigned to their plight. Compared with a similar population whom Ladner studied twenty years ago, these women's futures are harsher and bleaker than those of their earlier counterparts who had high hopes for positive and productive futures (Ladner and Gourdine 1984).

The high rate of teenage pregnancy has caused much concern over the issue of birth control and the sexual behavior of the young. Since the early 1970s, birth control has become widely available and evidence shows that an increasing number of women and men now engage in sexual intercourse prior to marriage. By age 16, one-fifth of all American teenagers have had intercourse; by age 19, two-thirds have had intercourse. Moreover, one in ten women has had at least one pregnancy by age 17, and one-quarter of all women have had one pregnancy by age 19. Of these, eight in ten are premarital pregnancies (Zelnik, Kim, and Kantner 1979). But, why, now that birth control is available, are these young women not using effective contraceptive methods?

Studies show that teenagers typically wait for several months after initiating sexual activity before using contraceptives (Zelnik and Kantner 1978). One recent study indicates that one-third of teenage patients make their first visit to contraceptive clinics after they suspect that they are pregnant. Only 14 percent make the visit before they become sexually active; the remainder arrive after initiating sexual intercourse, and most of these girls do not seek contraceptive advice until after they have been sexually active for at least three months (Zabin and Clark 1981). This knowledge is particularly unsettling because it is known that one-fifth of first premarital pregnancies among teenagers occur within the first month of sexual intercourse; another half occur within the first six months of intercourse (Zabin, Kantner, and Zelnik 1979). There is also a decline in use of birth control pills and the IUD among teenagers because many believe that the bill and IUD are themselves risks to health (Meriwether 1984).

Many have argued that a sociological reason for the nonuse of birth control among young women is that the regular use of contraceptives requires conscious recognition of oneself as sexually active (Luker 1975).

Teenage sex tends to be episodic; for a young woman to make calculated plans for contraceptive protection requires her to see herself as a sexually active person. Cultural and legal proscriptions that encourage the denial of sexuality to young women seem likely only to exacerbate this situation.

Many also argue that sex education does not filter down to adolescents before they start having sex. Girls often have little or no information about their bodies and are often seriously misinformed about sex (for example, believing they cannot get pregnant if they're standing up during intercourse!) The fact that mothers, not fathers, talk to their children about sex also spreads the message that men have no responsibility in this area, discouraging young men from being responsible for birth control and resting the decision to avoid pregnancy only on young girls (Meriwether 1984). Researchers find that pregnant teens romanticize the demands of motherhood and many believe they can give their babies a better deal than they received. Moreover, since adolescent pregnancy disproportionately affects poor and minority youth, having children may be their only way of achieving masculinity or femininity in a society that denies them the expression of these traits in adult roles (Ladner 1986).

Adolescents who do get pregnant are more traditional in their sex role orientation than other sexually active young teens. They perceive themselves as competent in highly sex-typed activities, have lower aspirations and grades, and have less of a sense of personal control. Also, teenagers who get pregnant are also more likely to rely on God to determine the course of their lives, indicating that both traditional gender roles and religious beliefs influence the problem of teenage pregnancy (Ireson 1984). This should lead us to conclude that programs and policies designed to alleviate the problems of teenage pregnancy must recognize the importance of gender relations in understanding the character of this growing social problem. It has been demonstrated that more egalitarian gender role attitudes are associated with the belief in contraceptive use; moreover, young men with egalitarian gender role attitudes are more likely to use contraceptives in premarital intercourse than are young men with more sexist attitudes (MacCorquodale 1984).

Child Care

Child care in American society is, by virtue of the character of the family, largely a system of private care. The parent-child unit is allegedly self-sufficient and, given the gender division of labor, the responsibility for child care falls almost exclusively on individual women. The experience of mothers (or other caretakers) and children is isolated within the home and is based on the assumption that children are best cared for by their biological mother. Exceptions to this design do exist, although even then the arrangements for child care are usually managed by the mother, and it is other women who do the work. So, although it is more and more impractical to do so, mothers usually have nearly exclusive responsibility for the everyday care of their children.

The privatized and exclusive character of child care seems especially inappropriate when we consider the labor force participation rate of mothers. As already noted, recent increases in the labor force participation rate are highest among women with children, especially women with children of preschool age. By 1985, 65 percent of all women with children worked; 52 percent of those with children under 6 years of age worked. Yet, among children aged 3 to 13, 83 percent were cared for in their own home; 70 percent of these children were cared for by their parents or another relative. In fact, it is estimated that only 1.7 percent of American children are tended in group care (Baxandall 1979).

These facts make it imperative that we imagine new models and policies for child care in society. Historically, as Baxandall points out, depression and war have provided the major impetus for establishing public child care facilities in the United States. Although there was an expansion of child care facilities in the early 1970s, since then the availability of such facilities has decreased. In fact, licensed and voluntary child care centers in the United States now care for only one-sixth the number of children cared for at the end of World War II. This situation exists despite that fact that the labor force participation rate of women at that time was 38.1 percent compared with 55.3 percent today (Blau 1979; U.S. Bureau of Labor Statistics January 1987).

Public child care in the United States first originated in the Works Progress Administration (WPA) of the New Deal. In the 1930s, WPA day-care and nursery schools were designed to provide employment for needy teachers, child care workers, cooks, janitors, nutritionists, and clerical workers during the Depression. By the end of the Depression and the beginning of World War I, when jobs were no longer in short supply, the WPA nurseries were eliminated. However, in 1941, the Lanham Act (also known as the Community Facilities Act) was passed by Congress to meet the day-care needs of mothers in war-time employment. The Lanham Act made matching federal funds available to states for the expansion of day-care centers and nursery schools. Following World War II, when women were no longer needed in the labor force, Congress withdrew funds for day care and most of the Lanham Act nurseries closed (Baxandall 1979).

Since World War II, federally funded day-care programs have been established for the poor. For example, Project Headstart, funded through the Office of Economic Opportunity, was designed primarily for children from families below the poverty line. In the past, public attitudes toward funded child care were stigmatized by the association of federally supported child care with welfare services. But support for increased availability of child care services now runs high, with 81 percent of women and 79 percent of men favoring public support for child care centers (Roper Organization 1985).

But the myth persists that only the biological mother can best care for the child. This is evidenced in the attitude that children cared for in the absence of mothers suffer from maternal deprivation. The fact that child care is defined as women's work is revealed by noting that, in spite of the relative absence of most fathers from the everyday life of the home, no one has suggested that children of working fathers suffer form paternal deprivation. Yet, the wear and tear that sole responsibility for child care imposes on the woman, limiting her ability to be a good mother, is only now being recognized. Few have considered that there may be beneficial effects on children who receive a wide variety of stimuli from different persons — no one of whom can maintain the same level of activity, enthusiasm, and curiosity as the child. Yet, in most situations, the structure of the contemporary family discourages shared child care arrangements, leaving isolated mothers to draw on their own resources to make whatever arrangements are possible for the care of their children.

Summary

Historical legacies glorify the home as a refuge, while also idealizing women's role within the home. Today, the family is a rapidly changing institution and the traditional family ideal is realized by only a small minority of American families.

Modern families are characterized by an emphasis on child rearing, assumed separation of work from home, and idealization of the home as women's world. The emergence of capitalism affects family structure by shifting economically valued labor outside of the home and into public workplaces. Patriarchal societies regulate women's role in the family by making men the basis for authority. The historical development of families is situated in race, class, and gender relations in the society.

Feminists distinguish between families and households to emphasize the economic functions of households. The family is an ideological concept. Feminist also see families as social, not natural, units and note that men and women experience families in different ways.

Contemporary American households are characterized by high rates of divorce and an increase in the number of households headed by women. Households consist of married couples, cohabitors, dual-career couples, gay and lesbian couples, and singles. Each of these types of household has a unique sociological reality that shapes the experience and consciousness of its members.

Mothering roles in this society are filled with contradictions, conflicts, and sources of gratification. The asymmetrical organization of parenting in households reproduces gender identities in men and women that are associated with attachment in women and detachment in men. Fatherhood is being transformed as more men take on primary child care activities.

Family violence, including wife beating, marital rape, and incest, emerge from women's powerlessness in society. Racism also shapes the organization of family life. Black, Chicano, Puerto Rican, and Asian-American families have been characterized in terms of pathology, but studies of these families from their own point of view lend a more positive picture of family structure in minority communities.

Adolescent pregnancy is a major cause of the increase in poverty among children and single women who are heads of households. Teenage mothers and fathers face chronic unemployment and poverty. Teens' willingness to use contraceptives during premarital intercourse is related to their gender role attitudes. Child care in American society remains largely a system of private care, the work of which falls almost exclusively on women. Resistance to day care stems from the belief that only biological mothers can best care for children.

CHAPTER 7

Women, Health, and Reproduction

Introduction

Physical health is one of the most basic of life's privileges. Although we tend to think of our bodies as best cared for by personal hygiene and individual diet and health habits, in fact, physical health is heavily influenced by sociological factors. As one of those factors, gender plays a significant part in determining physical well-being and in influencing our bodily experience.

For instance, the likelihood that one will encounter stress, become overweight, experience hypertension, or become chronically ill is significantly affected by one's sex. National health statistics show that hypertension is more common among men than women until age 55, when the pattern is reversed (Hess and Markson 1980). National data also show that, under age 35, men are more likely to be overweight than women, although the reverse is true after this age (National Center for Health Statistics 1985). Women are more vulnerable to chronic and acute diseases than are men, although men are more likely to become disabled by disease (Hess and Markson 1980). And in all cases, along with gender and age, racial status is a complicating factor in each of these conditions. For example, blacks are far more likely to experience disability, to develop hypertension, and to suffer from poor nutrition (Hess and Markson 1980). And, with regard to life expectancy, only half of all nonwhite males and two-thirds of nonwhite females born in 1974 can expect to live beyond age 65. Two-thirds of white

185

males born in that year will live beyond age 65; four-fifths of white females will (Hess and Markson 1980).

These data indicate that physical health is mediated by social and cultural organization. For this reason, gender roles influence not only what we will become but also how long our lives will be and how we are likely to die. The first section of this chapter reviews research on sex roles and health, showing how gender roles influence the distribution and experience of health and illness. This section is followed by a discussion of health and work, because where one works has many influences on physical well-being. Gender also influences the development of social problems of eating disorders and substance abuse, as we will see.

In addition to influencing the health of populations, gender relations in the society are reflected in institutional patterns of health care systems. As the feminist movement has shown (Ruzek 1978), health care institutions in this society are dominated by men, even though healing and caring for others have traditionally been defined as the work of women. Because of the sexist structure of health care in this society, women have had little control over their own reproductive lives. The next section of this chapter discusses the politics of reproduction, especially surrounding the issues of abortion, pregnancy, and birth control. This section is followed by a review of the historical emergence of health care institutions and the process by which male domination in health care was established. Finally, the contemporary status of women in medicine and the feminist health care movement are discussed. Throughout this chapter, we will see that gender relations are important in determining the character of health and reproduction in contemporary American society.

The Social Structure of Health

Gender Roles and Health

Historically, patterns of male and female health change according to the social arrangements of the time. For instance, in the late nineteenth century, illness was quite fashionable for women — at least those of the upper middle and upper classes. Women in these classes were expected to be idle and faint; consequently, retiring to bed because of "nerves" was not only acceptable, but actually encouraged by medical practitioners (Ehrenreich and English 1973).

Differences in life expectancy for men and women did not emerge in American society until the beginning of the twentieth century. Even now, longer life expectancy for women occurs primarily in highly industrialized Western societies (Hess and Markson 1980). In America, death rates for both males and females have declined drastically since 1900, but there has been a trend toward a larger sex mortality differential (Ortmeyer 1979). Decreases in maternal mortality rates (death during pregnancy and child-birth) explain part of the increase in the sex mortality differential, but by far the greatest part of the difference is attributable to men's greater susceptibility to infectious diseases.

For both sexes, mortality caused by infectious disease has declined since 1900, but researchers cite differences in male and female roles and cultural practices as contributing to higher male death rates caused by infection. In particular, male occupational roles, more frequent travel and contact with strangers, and greater exposure to more people have been cited as contributing to the higher male death rate caused by infection (Graney 1977). In addition, health studies indicate that 75 percent of the increase in mortality differences by sex can be explained by increases in cigarette smoking, particularly among men in the twentieth century (Ortmeyer 1979). Cigarette smoking is known to contribute to greater cardiovascular and respiratory disease — a fact that, given changes in women's smoking patterns, may significantly alter the sex mortality differential in the future. Recent reports show a convergence in the number of men and women who are currently smoking and beginning to smoke; moreover, the evidence also shows that more men than women quit smoking and that more teenage girls than boys are initiating smoking. As a result, we might expect to see cardiovascular and respiratory diseases increase among women.

Particular health problems faced by men and women can be seen as consequences of their respective sex roles. The male role, for example, poses a number of hazards to physical health. Not only are men more likely than women to contract infectious disease and cardiovascular and respiratory illnesses, but they also have higher death rates caused by accidents, suicides, and homicides. Men commit suicide three times as often as women, although women make four times as many attempts. The male-female suicide rate also increases with age. Four times as many men as women commit suicide at age 65, but at 85 years of age, twelve times as many men as women commit suicide. Men are also four times more likely to be homicide victims than are women; black men are six times as likely to die by homicide as white men. Black women are four times as likely to die by homicide as white women and are slightly more likely than white men to die by homicide (See Table 7-1). These patterns demonstrate the risks and stresses that are created by both racial and gender statuses in the society.

To summarize, it would appear that the work-oriented, ambitious, aggressive, and competitive life-style associated with the male role tends to produce heart diseases along with other health problems. Yet, the patterns of women's health reveal other problems, many of which are a function of women's status within both the society and the health care system. Women have higher rates of acute and chronic illness and a higher incidence of sick

TABLE 7-1 **Mortality Rates From Suicide, Homicide, Accident, by Sex and Race, 1985**

	Suicide	Homicide	Accident (Excluding Motor Vehicle)
White men	19.3	8.4	51.8
Black men	10.5	53.8	66.2
White women	5.6	2.8	18.3
Black women	2.1	11.2	21.9

Source: National Center for Health Statistics, U.S. Department of Health and Human Services, *Health, United States 1985.* Washington, D.C.: U.S. Government Printing Office, December 1985.

role behavior, as measured by the number of days of restricted activity and bed disability (Nathanson 1975). And although no sex differences are found in compliance with doctors' orders (Waldron and Johnston, 1976), women utilize the health care system more than men (even when controlling for pregnancy).

Women's Roles and Health

Women's health, like men's, varies according to the sociological features of their lives. In fact, much of the recent research on women and health reveals a direct link between women's roles and the likelihood of leading healthy lives. Several studies indicate that there are higher rates of reported illness among housewives than among women working outside the home (Nathanson 1980), indicating that employment generally has positive effects upon women's health. Moreover, housewives who have never worked outside the home are healthier than those who once worked but dropped out of the labor force to become full-time homemakers (Welch and Booth 1977). Employed women are also less likely than housewives to act out a sick role, and when employed women are sick, they tend to return to normal activities more quickly than do housewives (Nathanson 1980).

Some have interpreted these variations in health between housewives and employed women as indicating that feelings of self-esteem and accomplishment are the result of working in a society where paid work is the major basis of self-esteem (Nathanson 1980). However, most women's jobs certainly do not afford them the achievement and gratification traditionally associated with men's work; thus, this assumption must be cautiously considered. However, the housewife role in our society is devalued, which is likely to have serious repercussions for women in this position.

Recent research also shows that mental health follows gender patterns in society. Most studies indicate higher rates of mental illness for women than for men, at least as indicated by hospital admissions, clinical treat-ment, and the duration of treatment. Some explain this finding as a result of women's secondary status in society, which, because it produces stress, makes women more mentally ill than men. Others argue that high rates of mental illness among women reflect the fact that women are more likely to report mental problems, seek help, and think of themselves as emotional and lacking self-control. This explanation interprets women's higher mental illness rate as the consequence of learned sex role behavior. Both explanations are probably correct, underscoring the point that mental as well as physical health is connected to the status of persons in society. These data suggest the need for change in women's traditional status — a point that is underscored by a study showing that women living in nontra-ditional relationships are less depressed than women living in traditional ones. Men living in nontraditional relationships are more depressed than comparable women (Rosenfeld 1980), which may indicate the personal needs and services that women in traditional relationships provide for men but not for themselves.

Racism and Health

Racial oppression in this society further complicates patterns of health in men and women, and stereotypical thinking and adherence to racial myths on the part of clinicians and physicians is a necessary part of under-standing the health care that minority groups receive. A study of white male psychiatrists finds that two-thirds of them agree that blacks have impaired self-images as a consequence of racial attitudes toward blacks; almost half think there is a high degree of self-hatred among blacks; over three-quarters believe the matriarchal structure of family contributes to identity problems for black males. This high degree of acceptance of racial myths among white therapists indicates that they themselves have been culturally conditioned and that they do not understand behavior as adap-tive to conditions of oppression (Wilkinson 1980).

Although the health of the black population has improved since 1950, death rates from cerebrovascular disease, homicide, and diabetes are still considerably higher for blacks than for whites. Black women are also much more likely than white women to succumb to cancer, heart disease, strokes, and diabetes. Maternal death from reproductive complications has de-creased since 1960, but it is still three times higher among black than white women. This can be attributed both to the higher birth rate and the greater frequency of high-risk pregnancies among black women (Headen and Headen 1986).

In the 45 – 64 age cohort group, black women die at twice the rate of white women. And, though the incidence of breast cancer is lower among black than white women, the mortality rate from breast cancer is higher among black women. Black women also have double the incidence rate of cervical cancer and are three times more likely to die while pregnant than are white women (Cope and Hall 1986). Black women's double jeopardy because of their race and gender status is also reflected in the data on hypertension. Between 1976 and 1980, 25 percent of black women were diagnosed with hypertension, compared with 11 percent of white women) and 43 percent of black women heading their own households who were also diagnosed as having high blood pressure (McGhee 1984).

Accidental death also occurs in different patterns comparing blacks and whites. Among black men, for example, death caused by accident is greater than among white men, except by motor vehicle accidents. Suicide rates among black men are lower than for white men, although suicide among black men has been increasing in recent years. Suicide rates for black women are half those for white women. It would appear that, although violent death is more common for black Americans, cultural values and the economic dependence of families on black women's work influences the lesser degree of suicide among blacks (and black women, in particular).

Native American health is also affected by the degree of oppression they experience. Their mortality rates are one and a half times higher than those of the general population and, in the three-year period between 1980 and 1982, 37 percent of native American deaths occurred among those under age 45, compared with 12 percent of deaths at this age in the general population. Moreover, native Americans are twice as likely to die by homicide than are others in the general population (U.S. Office of Technology Assessment 1986).

Among women, race and social class significantly affect chances for good health and for exercising some degree of control over their own bodies. For example, race is an important indicator of maternal mortality risk. Up to age 40, nonwhite women are twice as likely to die in childbirth as white women, and nonwhite women aged 25 – 29 experience the same risks in childbirth as white women ten years older (Daniels and Weingarten 1979). Moreover, poor and black women do not have the same expectations as white women of being able to alter their birth experiences. As a result, they are less likely to question some of the obstetrical practices (such as separating the mother and newborn baby) that white, middle-class women have challenged (Hurst and Zambrana 1980).

In 1985, infant mortality — one of the major indices of the health of a population — was still twice as high for blacks as for whites. Also, though infant mortality rates had been decreasing over recent years (1965 – 1982), in 1983 new concern was expressed as the rate of decline in infant mortality, especially among blacks, slowed (Mann 1986). Black and Puerto Rican Americans are also more likely to have low-birth-weight babies (National Center for Health Statistics 1985), a fact that contributes to infant mortality and represents the health problems faced by these mothers.

Both historically and now, women of color and poor women have been denied control over their reproductive lives. Studies indicate that very high percentages of poor and minority women have been sterilized, often without their knowing consent. Thirty-nine and eight tenths percent of all black women had been sterilized in 1982, including 35.6 of those between 25 and 34 years of age; 25.4 percent of white women and 20.6 percent of white women aged 25–34 had been sterilized by 1982 (National Center for Health Statistics 1985). One study, conducted in the 1970s, found that 42.3 percent of the women living in East Harlem had had either a tubal ligation or a hysterectomy. In most cases, the doctor had recommended it to the patient but had given her incorrect information about the consequences (Hurst and Zambrana 1980). Other studies indicate that among samples of welfare mothers, approximately half have been sterilized (Corea 1977); welfare women have had approximately one-third more sterilizations than other women (Gordon 1977).

Sex differences in health indicate that our physical well-being is highly dependent on the conditions we face in our social environment and as part of our social roles. This fact is particularly evident when we look at occupational roles and the effect of work on our physical and mental health. And because, as we have seen in Chapter 5, work experience is a function of gender, women's health issues must be seen in the context of their place in the work force.

Women, Work, and Health

The mythology of work in this culture is that it provides an avenue for self-expression and the realization of personal goals. In fact, we are coming increasingly to see that work can be hazardous to both physical and mental health. Recent public attention to the toxic chemicals produced in industrial environments has heightened our awareness of the ways in which work environments pose hazards for workers. But until recently, most of the attention to this issue has focused on male workers, just as the male work role has often been cited as a source of anxiety and stress. Investigations by the Occupational Safety and Health Administration (OSHA) have resulted in increased information about the effects of toxic agents, carcinogens, and occupational accidents on the health of workers. Yet, when attention is given to women workers, the major focus is usually on only the dangers to their reproductive health. Studies of occupational health hazards have alerted us to many issues, but there is much to be learned, particularly about the effect of work on physical health.

Work Environments and Health

Gender-biased definitions have caused us to ignore the work environments of many women. One telling example comes from recent national surveys of cancer mortality in various occupational groups. These studies typically do not consider housework to be an occupation. Consequently, they have provided no data comparing cancer among housewives and other workers. A recent study shows, however, that housewives have a far greater death rate by cancer than any other occupational group of women (Morton and Ungs 1979). The work that women do in the home exposes them to a wide variety of toxic substances; moreover, none of these substances are subject to the control systems advocated for use in industrial settings, nor are the workers who use them instructed to wear protective equipment or to be periodically screened for toxic contamination. Additionally, although these substances are often used together during household cleaning, no one knows about their potentially hazardous combination. Because housework is seldom considered to be real work, little public attention has been given to the carcinogens and toxic substances used, nor has the high death rate by cancer among housewives been widely discussed.

Obviously, the health risks for both male and female workers are great. OSHA reports that 70,000 chemicals are being used in the workplace and that 2,000 new chemicals are introduced annually (Bell 1979). A 1978 government survey found that 20 percent of all cancer, heart, and lung diseases were attributable to chemicals and pollutants in the work environment and its products (Ortmeyer 1979). This estimate was probably a conservative one because it counted only those cases that could be directly attributed to this cause.

Both men's and women's work involves stress and physical dangers other than toxic risks. Job-related stress leads to an increased risk of disease even without direct physical hazard on the job, and stress can be caused by a host of factors, including monotony, human relations, lack of control over one's work, time demands, insecurity, and relative powerless (Stellman 1977).

The increasing use of video display terminals (VDTs) in the workplace, for examples, poses new questions about workers' health. As of 1986, 15 million workers in the United States used VDTs and their numbers are increasing at a very rapid rate. Given the fact of gender segregation in jobs where VDTs are most extensively used, the majority of workers using VDTs are women. Video display terminals are known to cause eye, back, and hand strains, when work conditions and the physical work site are not properly adapted and designed. Some researchers also see possible hazards in the exposure of workers to the steady emission of low levels of radiation from video display terminals; to date, there are no federal standards limiting exposure to radiation from VDTs. And, though the studies are as yet inconclusive, there is preliminary evidence suggesting an increased risk of miscarriage among pregnant women working with VDTs (McNulty 1986; Stellman and Henifin 1983). Especially in industries like banking, insurance, and airlines, where use of VDTs is common, there is growing concern among occupational health activists about the potential consequences of VDTs for workers' health. Many are calling for federal policies to regulate video display terminals, though to date the companies producing VDTs have actively resisted such legislation (Brown 1985).

Reproduction and Protective Legislation

When considering issues of work and health, it is easy to see that work and gender are closely bound together. Concern about women's work and health has almost exclusively focused on women's reproductive health. Interestingly, however, few ever consider how reproductive hazards for men are related to their work (Wright 1979), leading to the erroneous conclusion, based on sexist premises, that only women reproduce. Clearly, occupational toxic agents and carcinogens can equally affect male sperm; yet protective legislation against reproductive hazards is almost always aimed at female workers. Both the history of protective legislation and its contemporary status reveal this fact.

In the 1920s, the Women's League for Equal Opportunity staunchly opposed the protective legislation proposed by groups such as the Women's Trade Union League and the Consumer League of New York. They argued that consumer restrictions on the conditions of labor should be based upon the nature of the industry, not on the sex of the worker (Stellman 1977:36). Yet history shows that protective laws apply specifically to women workers. The Supreme Court decision in *Muller* v. *Oregon,* for example, held in 1908 that it was consititutional to restrict the work day to ten hours for women only. Protecting workers from long work days and unhealthy environments is a reasonable action, but when applied only to women, these laws exclude women from jobs under the benign guise of protection (Chavkin 1979).

Contemporary protective legislation has also been used to exclude women from work in trades in which the hazards seem no greater than those in some traditionally sex-segregated female occupations. For instance, Title VII of the 1964 Civil Rights Act prohibited employment discrimination on the basis of sex, race, color, religion, and national origin. Yet it also provided for bona fide occupational qualification (BFOQ), which made it lawful to hire on the basis of sex when sex is a reasonable qualification for performance on the job (Hill 1979). For instance, the BFOQ clause allowed women to be excluded from jobs exceeding weight-lifting limitations set only for women. That weight restrictions on women's work are based on gender stereotypes is clearly shown by the fact that such restrictions do not appear in occupations that are typically female (such as waitressing) and that involve strenuous physical effort. Subsequent court cases made it clear that the BFOQ clause could only be applied in a very restricted way. In both *Weeks* v. *Southern Bell Telephone and Telegraph Company* and *Rosenfeld* v. *Southern Pacific Company,* the courts ruled that individual women, like individual men, have to be given the opportunity to show that they are physically qualified for a job (Hill 1979). Overall, however, Title VII has been the basis for eliminating much protective legislation.

The contradictions in protective labor legislation are expecially clear in the case of policies alleged to protect women's reproductive health. An increasing number of working women are raising children at the same time. Moreover, more than 40 percent of women who have given birth in recent years also worked during their pregnancies (Hendershot 1977; Petchesky 1979). Arguments in favor of protective laws for women workers rest on the assumption that pregnant women and fetuses are especially susceptible to toxic chemicals, radiation, and other risks. Although there is little doubt that these hazards do affect pregnant women and fetuses (Hunt 1979), the issue is whether they affect the reproductive health of men as well. Legislation or company practices that apply to women only seem to rest on the faulty assumption that only women reproduce. Yet we have evidence of the damaging effects of lead poisoning on male sperm, the excess of chromosomal aberrations among male vinyl chloride workers, and the causal relationship between the pesticide dibromochloropropane (DBCP) and male sterility (Wright 1979). Moreover, wives of male chloride workers have excessive rates of stillbirths and miscarriages (Infante 1975). Removing only women from jobs in which they may be exposed to these substances clearly does not protect the reproductive health of the population.

Gender-biased assumptions in protective regulations are intricately bound to the sex-segregated character of the labor force. Concern for women's health has not caused companies to remove workers from jobs traditionally considered women's work—in spite of known risks from mutagens, teratogens, and toxic substances that are found in occupations employing mostly women. For example, women who work in hospital operating rooms as nurse-anesthetists, anesthesiologists, and scrub personnel have higher rates of miscarriages and birth malformations than other groups of workers, but no one has argued that women should be excluded from these jobs (Hunt 1979; Wright 1979). Protective policies that restrict women from hazardous jobs seem to emerge only in higher-paying and traditionally male occupations in which women are now beginning to be employed (Chavkin 1979). Other occupations that pose equally serious hazards, but yet are poorly paid and filled by women, are usually excluded from protective legislation. Similarly, risks to the male reproductive system seldom are used to restrict their employment opportunities. In fact, one bizarre suggestion has been made that male workers exposed to sterility-causing DBCP might consider it a novel form of birth control (Wright 1979)!

To limit occupational health hazards solely to women or solely to reproductive effects is to overlook the complexities of work and the various health hazards it creates. Job policies are needed that will protect all workers from health hazards posed by their jobs. Included would be policies that protect the reproductive health of men and women and provide a good system of reproductive leave for both sexes (Wright 1979). Moreover, toxic substances and radiation have a hazardous effect not only on workers in industrial plants but in surrounding communities as well. As Supreme Court Justice Felix Frankfurter said in 1916:

> Once we cease to look upon the regulation of women in industry as exceptional, as the law's graciousness to a disabled class, and shift the emphasis from the fact that they are *women* to the fact that it is *industry* and the relation of industry to the community which is regulated, the whole problem is seen from a totally different aspect. (1916:367, cited in Hill 1979)

Discussion of women's health and work also cannot ignore the fact that, in spite of real risks to health posed by contemporary jobs, employed women, as far as we can tell, are healthier on the average than women who are unemployed. Only the future will reveal the long-range effect of carcinogens, toxic substances, and radiation on human life, but current data indicate that employment has positive effects on women's health. There are higher rates of illness among housewives than among women who work for wages, although it is also true that the presence of children in the home makes women less likely to adopt a sick role (Nathanson 1975, 1980). Even with the additional burden of the double day, women who work for wages have better physical and mental health than women who do not.

In sum, research on women's health and their work environments reveals a host of social problems. Although the specific hazards that workers face will vary depending on the type of work and the specific work conditions they face, there is a serious need for careful study of work-related health hazards. Policies that single out women as a restricted class cannot solve this problem, nor can ignoring the complexities of gender relations in the workplace. In the end, safe workplaces, both in industry and in the home, must be constructed for men and women alike.

Gender, Health, and Social Problems ─────────────

Women, Weight, and Food

The culture that we live in is one that is obsessed with weight and thinness. In fact, one survey showed that, when asked to identify their greatest fear, one-fifth of those surveyed said their greatest fear was getting fat (Chernin 1981). Women, but men as well in this culture, are taught to dislike their bodies; no matter what their shape, size, or form, women's bodies can never meet the cultural ideal, especially as it constantly changes over time.

Beginning in the twentieth century, our culture began to regard fleshiness as not sexy. Sexy bodies are depicted as thin ones; in fact, cultural images of weight have projected an increasingly thin image, resulting in a very high rate of anorexia among models and actresses who portray these ideals. Being thin is also increasingly associated with wealth and class, since idealized sex objects also portray class images (Millman 1980). In an odd sense, only rich women can "afford" to be thin, since poor women are much more likely to be overweight. Fat on women and men also violates gender roles, as we tend to think of overweight women as having improperly indulged themselves, and overweight men are derided for seeming passive, vulnerable, and soft (Millman 1980).

One consequence of this cultural obsession with weight and thinness is the high rate of anorexia nervosa, bulimia, and compulsive eating among women and, increasingly, men. While anorexia nervosa generally occurs among white, adolescent females, men, and minorities are increasingly being affected. Black women, however, are still more likely to be overweight, undernourished, and calcium deficient than white women.

Anorexia nervosa is characterized by severe weight loss; anorexics also have delusions about their body image, thinking of themselves as fat when they are, in actuality, dangerously thin. They typically do not recognize signs of nutritional need and may, literally, starve themselves to death.

Feminist psychotherapists who work with anorexic clients have shown that these are women who have fully internalized cultural ideals of womanhood. Seen in the context of a whole array of practices designed to reduce women's body size, such as stomach stapling, diet fads, breast reduction surgery, and other extreme procedures, anorexia is even to be expected in a culture so obsessed with thinness (Bruch 1978; Chernin 1981, 1985; Lawrence 1984).

Other eating problems, such as bulimia and compulsive overeating, also stem from the culture's definition of idealized womanhood. Bulimia, the syndrome in which women (typically) binge on huge amounts of food and then purge themselves by vomiting, use of laxatives, or extreme fasting, seems to be rapidly increasing, especially among the young and college students (Boskind-White 1985). Researchers estimate that 4–18 percent of college students are bulimic (Boskind-White 1985). A 1984 national poll of women found that while only 25 percent were actually overweight, 41 percent were unhappy with their bodies, 80 percent felt they had to be slim to be attractive to men, and a majority were ashamed of their stomachs, hips, and thighs. It is no wonder then that the survey also revealed women's intense desperation about weight control and found that half of the respondents had used diet pills, 27 percent used liquid formula diets, and 18 percent used diuretics for weight loss (*Glamour* February 1984:198–201)

Feminists also point out that one of the origins of women's problems with food lies in the fact that the food industry targets women as a population. Women are regarded in the culture as responsible for food and, though they are supposed to provide it for others, the thin models of the food and fashion industry also deny women the food they are meant to provide for others.

Gender and Substance Abuse

With the widespread use of drugs in American culture beginning in the 1960s, it was generally believed that "the drug revolution" would eventually eliminate differences in patterns of substance abuse between women and men. People assumed that as women took on more "male" roles, such as working in the paid labor force, women's use of alcohol and drugs would more nearly approximate men's. This has not occurred.

With regard to alcohol, men drink more frequently than women and drink more on any given occasion. Men are also three to four times more likely to be classified as problem drinkers. In drug use, men use marijuana, inhalants, cocaine, hallucinogens, PCP, and heroin more than do women. Women do exceed men in the use of mood-modifying drugs that are medicinal and legal, such as prescribed medications, tranquilizers, barbiturates, antidepressants, and over-the-counter drugs (Colten and Marsh 1984). In fact, two-thirds of the prescriptions for psychotropic drugs are written for women. The only illicit substances used equally by young women and young men are amphetamines (Johnston, Bachman, and O'Malley 1982).

Among women, the frequency of drinking and the volume of consumption increase with education (Parker et al. 1980). National surveys find that the highest rate of drinking problems among women are found among those who are unsuccessfully looking for work, followed by women who, because of their position in the labor force, face the stress of dead-end, low-income jobs (Sandmaier 1980). Still, women drink less than men do and drinking is less likely to become a problem for them. According to the National Center for Health Statistics (1985), nearly half of all women abstain from alcohol altogether, compared with 21 percent of men; and 21 percent of women are moderate or heavy drinkers, compared with 48 percent of men.

When women do drink, they are more likely to drink alone, in private, or with a spouse. Women also tend to be introduced to alcohol by men and are encouraged by men to drink. There is some evidence that employed women drink more than unemployed women, though no association has been found between drinking and the role conflicts experienced by women who are married and working for wages (Parker et al. 1980). In fact, despite the popular image of housewives who are alcoholics, marital status does not predict alcohol use for women. Housewives, in fact, are less likely to be problem drinkers than are other groups of women, although housewives are more likely to use mood-altering drugs than are working women and are more likely to mix alcohol and other drugs (Sandmaier 1980).

The most marginal female alcoholics are skid row women, whose downward paths seem to begin with marital crises, compared with skid row men, who are more likely to begin their downward mobility following the loss of a job (Garrett and Bahr 1976). It is important to see, though, that in spite of these associations between employment and drinking, the greatest amount of female problem drinking occurs among women aged 18–20 years. Moreover, drinking among young women has dramatically increased in recent years, nearly closing the sex gap between male and female drinkers (Sandmaier 1980).

Most women receiving drug treatment are being treated for barbiturate, sedative, and tranquilizer use, though women make up a small (25 percent) proportion of those treated for drug abuse. Women are approximately 20 percent of the heroin addict population, but, though they are a minority of heroin addicts, they tend to be in more difficult situations. Women heroin addicts, compared with men, are more likely to be unemployed, unmarried, and with dependent children. They also have lower self-esteem than male heroin addicts and have more symptoms of depression and anxiety, and they are more likely to have other health problems (Colten and Marsh 1984). Women's careers as addicts also narrow their life options more than occurs among male addicts (Rosenbaum 1981).

One explanation of the differential patterns of substance abuse among men and women is that gender roles encourage different social responses to drug and alcohol use by men and by women. There is no evidence that confusion about one's sex role identity is a cause of substance abuse; in fact, for both men and women, it would appear that patterns of substance abuse are consistent with images of masculinity and femininity in the culture. But, according to traditional gender roles, women are not expected to drink and use drugs to the same extent as men. Indeed, women who become alcoholics tend to be perceived as more masculine and "hard" than other women, indicating that this violates expected roles for women. Women heroin addicts are also seen as more deviant, more reprehensible, and less treatable than male addicts. So, while traditional sex roles may protect women from substance abuse, they also pose constraints on the treatment and societal reaction to women with substance abuse problems.

The problem of drug abuse is not just a problem with illegal drugs. Women are more likely than men to be prescribed tranquilizers, sedatives, and amphetamines; in fact, health professionals estimate that between 1 and 2 million women are addicted to legal drugs (Wolcott 1979). In part, high rates of legal drug use among both men and women are attributable to the belief that technological advancements make relief available for every condition and disease (Klass 1975), but the particularly high rates of prescribed drug use among women also require a gender-specific explanation.

Some suggest that women are more often prescribed tranquilizing drugs because they are more likely to seek help for their problems than are men (Nathanson 1975). According to this explanation, women are more free, because of their social roles, to report pain, both physical and emotional, than are men; physicians are also likely to expect women to be emotional, while they tend to regard men as more stoic (Cooperstock 1971). Others say that, because of structured inequality, women's roles are more stressful and, as a result, women have more real complaints (Fidell 1973).

While both of these are plausible explanations, we should also remember that powerful economic and political interests capitalize on women as a market for drugs that bring massive profits to their producers. In 1975, for example, it is estimated that the raw materials for Valium, one of the most heavily prescribed drugs to women, cost $87 per kilo; packaging and production cost an additional $487 per kilo. But the final retail price for one kilo was $11,000 — 140 times the cost of material and 20 times the total production cost (Pekkanen 1975). A large part of this cost was the cost of promotion; drug companies spend well over $3,500 per physician per year in promoting their products (McKinley 1978). In the case of Valium, 98 percent of the wholesale price went to promotion and profit (Pekkanen 1975).

The Politics of Reproduction: Birth Control, Abortion, and Childbirth

Feminist Perspectives on Reproduction

The issues of abortion, birth control, and pregnancy are at the heart of feminist politics and are core issues around which feminist analysis has been built. Contemporary feminists see women's right to control their own bodies as essential to the realization of other rights and opportunities in society. As the Boston Women's Health Book Collective has written, "Unless we ourselves can decide whether and when to have children, it is difficult for us to control our lives or participate fully in society (1984:291).

Whether a woman experiences pregnancy, abortion, or birth control as stressful or traumatic is at least partially due to the ways in which they are socially organized. Reproduction, although it is a physiological event, stands at the junction of nature and culture (Oakley 1979). Women do not simply get pregnant and give birth in the physical sense alone; they do so within a definite set of social relations (Petchesky 1980). These social arrangements vary not only historically but also cross-culturally. Feminist arguments about the social control of reproduction clearly take this fact into account. As Margaret Mead wrote following her early study of seven Pacific Island cultures:

> Whether childbirth is seen as a situation in which one risks death, or out of which one acquires a baby, or social status, or a right to Heaven, is not a matter of the actual statistics of maternal mortality, but of the view that a society takes of childbearing. Any argument about women's instinctively maternal behavior which insists that in this respect a biological substratum is stronger than every other learning experience that a female child faces, from birth on, must reckon with this great variety in the handling of childbirth. (Mead 1962:221)

Female control of reproduction is cross-culturally and historically the dominant social arrangement (Oakley 1979). Yet, in modern Western societies, reproduction is controlled by men. Moreover, traditional social theories have largely ignored the question of reproduction, as if assuming that it is irrelevant in analyses of human experience and social organization.

Feminist perspectives on reproductive issues assert women's right to control their own bodies. Feminists see the medical profession as unresponsive to women's needs and as treating women's bodies as objects for medical manipulation. Not only are feminists distressed by the demeaning treatment women receive in medical institutions, but they are critical of the fact that it is men (either in medicine or in politics) who make decisions about reproductive issues (Ruzek 1978). The feminist position is that it is women's right to choose their reproductive status. Not only do feminists believe in individual rights on reproductive issues, but they also see that reproduction is embedded in systems of social power and social control (Petchesky 1980). The history of reproductive issues and their contemporary manifestations also shows that reproduction is directly entangled with class and race relations, in addition to relations of gender. Recent cutbacks in federal spending on abortion, a recurring history of sterilization abuse, and the manipulation of powerless women for medical experiments are all evidence of the powerlessness of women to control reproduction. This section reviews the politics of reproduction focusing on three contemporary issues: birth control, abortion, and pregnancy.

Birth Control. Birth control, although a personal matter, is also controlled by decisions of the state, the social organization of scientific and medical institutions, and the normative system of public values and attitudes. Because birth control regulates sexual activity and population size, its significance extends beyond the individual relationships in which it is actually practiced. Moreover, the availability, form, and cultural significance of birth control bear directly on the role of women in society (Gordon 1977).

Many young women today probably take birth control for granted, although it was not long ago that the right to practice birth control was established in law, especially for the unmarried. A 1965 Supreme Court decision (*Griswold* v. *Connecticut*) established the first constitutional precedent that the use of birth control was a right, not a crime. However, this decision extended only to married persons; not until 1972 (in *Eisenstadt* v. *Baird*) were laws probibiting the dispensing of contraceptives to any unmarried person, or by anyone other than a physician or pharmacist, held unconstitutional (Goldstein 1988). This decision was introduced following an incident in which Bill Baird, a long-time birth control activist, handed a package of vaginal foam to an unmarried young woman during a lecture on contraception at Boston University. Baird, in violation of a Massachusetts law that prohibited the distribution of nonprescribed contraceptives, was arrested and convicted of a felony before the case reached the Supreme Court.

Prior to the establishment of the constitutional right to birth control, laws varied from state to state and, even in those states where the distribution of birth control devices was legal, actual dispensing depended on the discretion of individual doctors. The effect was to shift the decision regarding birth control from women to men in the medical and judicial professions.

Current policies on birth control are also being shaped by a political context that puts control over these issues into the hands of men and the government. For example, the Adolescent Family Life Law, passed by Congress in 1981, mandated the development of "caring services" to counsel pregnant teenage girls. However, the bill prohibited the use of funds from its budget for research on contraceptive development and it barred recipients from providing abortion counseling or services. Research funds allocated by this bill also could not be used for any research on abortion except research that demonstrates its consequences — the strong implication being that research could only be supported when it was to show the negative consequences of abortion.

Adolescent reproductive rights have also been a recent area of judicial rulings. In 1976, the Supreme Court (in *Planned Parenthood of Central Missouri* v. *Danforth*) struck down a Missouri statute requiring every unmarried minor to have parental consent before having an abortion. The Court argued that minors, like adults, have a constitutional right to abortions; thus, blanket regulations of parental consent are unconstitutional. In 1979, this principle was reaffirmed in *Bellotte* v. *Baird* when a Massachusetts law requiring minors to have the consent of both parents or the authorization of a court, if they refused, was ruled unconstitutional. More recently, however, in a 1981 ruling (*H. L.* v. *Matheson*), the Supreme Court ruled that it is constitutional for a state to require physicians to notify parents of a minor seeking an abortion if the minor is living at home and is dependent on them for support, if she does not claim to be mature enough to make the abortion decision on her own, and if she offers no special reasons why her parents should not be told (Donovan 1981). And in 1983 the Court cases *Akron* v. *Akron Center* and *Planned Parenthood of Kansas City* v. *Ashcroft* reaffirmed *Bellotte* v. *Baird* by ruling that the state cannot make a blanket judgment that all minors are too immature to make decisions about whether to have an abortion; these cases do, however, uphold provisions that parental and judicial consent may be required in some cases. Thus, though there is flexibility on the issue of a minor's rights to choose abortion, these decisions still place young women in the situation of potentially needing the approval of parents or a court to proceed with an abortion (Goldstein 1987). Court delays make the timeliness of such decisions critical, but, more fundamentally, such decisions clearly take the control of the woman's body out of her hands.

These directions in law are especially troubling when we consider the research on teenage sexuality, contraception, and parental relationships. Procrastination is the teenager's most frequent reason for delay in initiating contraceptive use and the second most frequent reason is fear that parents will find out. One-third of all teenagers delay going to a clinic for fear their parents will find out (Zabin and Clark 1981). Regulations that limit the options available to young girls (or anyone else) seem unlikely, then, to solve the problems associated with teenage pregnancy.

Abortion. Women's rights to choose abortions were established by the 1973 Supreme Court decision in *Roe* v. *Wade*. This decision held laws unconstitutional that prohibited abortion except where such laws are restricted to the last three months of pregnancy or to the stage of fetal viability (Goldstein 1987). The Court's decision acknowledged that on the issue of abortion, separately legitimate social concerns collided: (1) the constitutional right to privacy, (2) the right of the state to protect maternal health, and (3) the right of the state to protect developing life. Thus, the Court divided the gestation period into thirds and argued that in the first trimester the woman's right to decide her future privately, without interference from the state, took precedence over the other two rights. In the second trimester, the state cannot deny an abortion, but it can insist upon reasonable standards of medical procedure. In the third trimester, abortion may also be performed to preserve the life or health of the mother.

The majority of American women and men support women's rights to choose abortion. Recent surveys show that 70 percent of the American public support a woman's right to decide, with the consultation of her physician, whether to have an abortion in the first trimester of pregnancy; 56 percent of the American public support the *Roe* v. *Wade* Supreme Court decision (see Table 7–2). Interestingly, the public supports a woman's right to decide even though a slight majority also believe that abortion is equivalent to murder. This indicates that although many people believe

TABLE 7-2   Public Opinion on Abortion, 1985

Question: Do you agree or disagree that any woman who is three months or less pregnant should have the right to decide, with her doctor's advice, whether or not she wants to have an abortion?

	Agree	Disagree	Not Sure
1985	70%	28%	2%

Question: Do you favor the 1973 Supreme Court decision on abortion?

	Favor	Oppose	Not Sure
TOTAL	56%	42%	2%
White Protestant	54	44	2
White Catholic	53	45	2
Jewish	91	9	—
Moral majority (white)	39	59	2

Question: Do you favor or oppose a constitutional amendment to ban abortions?

	Favor	Oppose	Not Sure
TOTAL	38%	58%	4%
White Protestant	41	55	4
White Catholic	46	49	4
Jewish	4	91	5
Moral majority (white)	56	41	3

Question: Do you agree or disagree that to perform an abortion, even during the first three months of pregnancy, is the equivalent of murder because fetus's life has been eliminated?

Agree	Disagree	Not Sure
52%	44%	4%

Source: The Harris Survey. Orlando, Florida: Tribune Media Services, February 4, 1985.

that abortion is morally wrong, they are in favor of leaving the choice to the individual concerned.

Other surveys show that support for abortion varies depending on the reason it is needed. In 1980, 80 percent of the population supported abortion in cases where the mother's health was seriously endangered; 83 percent where pregnancy resulted from rape; 83 percent where there was a serious chance for birth defect; 53 percent where the woman was from a low-income family and could not support any more children; 48 percent in cases where the woman was not married and did not want to marry the man; 47 percent if the woman was married but wanted no more children; and 41 percent for any reason. Moreover, this study shows that support for abortion has risen in the last fifteen years (Granberg and Granberg 1980).

Although federal regulations on the availability of abortion are rapidly changing, feminists still insist that abortion should be an option for women who want them. Although many feminists may not choose abortions for themselves, they believe that it should be a woman's choice. Moreover, for those who believe that abortion is inherently immoral, feminists point to the historical and cross-cultural record, which indicates great variation in the social meaning and practice of abortion.

TABLE 7-3 Abortion Rates by Selected Characteristics, 1982 (Women, Aged 15–44; Rate = per 1,000)

	All	White	Black and Other
1972	13.2	11.8	21.7
1981	29.3	24.3	55.9

Distribution of abortions, by selected characteristics, 1981:

Age:		Prior	Live Births:	Prior	Abortions
<15 years	1.0%	0	57.8%	0	64.9%
15–19	27.5	1	19.8	1	24.7
20–24	35.2	2	13.9	2+	10.4
25–29	20.0	3	5.4		
30–34	10.6	4+	3.1		
35–39	4.4				
40+	1.3				

Gestation Period:		Marital Status:	
<9 weeks	51.4%	Married	18.9%
9–10	26.9	Unmarried	81.1
11–12	12.9		
13+	8.8		

Source: U.S. Bureau of the Census, *Statistical Abstracts of the U.S., 1986.* Washington, D.C.: U.S. Government Printing Office, 1986.

In some societies (such as those of Japan and some eastern European countries), abortion is a major method of population control (Luker 1975). And in America, abortion was not viewed as morally wrong (if performed prior to quickening at four or five months) until the second half of the nineteenth century. Prior to that time, abortion was a common practice and was often performed using drugs, potions, techniques, and remedies made popular in home medical guides. Abortion was viewed as relatively safe and was commonly assisted by midwives, "irregular" physicians, and physicians of the period. The earliest laws governing abortion were not enacted until 1821 and 1841, but these laws placed guilt only on those who used particular methods of inducing abortion that were feared unsafe. None of these laws punished women for having abortions; they were intended as regulations to ensure safe methods (Mohr 1978).

In the mid-nineteenth century, abortion became an increasingly widespread phenomenon, especially among white, married, Protestant women. During this period, abortion also became increasingly commercialized. One noted woman entrepreneur, Madame Restell, earned an enormous income from her abortion products and spent as much as $60,000 per year on advertising alone (Mohr 1978). As both the drug industry and the medical profession grew in the second half of the nineteenth century, more profits could be made by companies seizing control of the abortion market. Thus, in addition to eliminating midwives from the practice of abortion, the medical profession created laws and spread propaganda that altered the perception and practice of abortion.

These changes were additionally fueled by shifts in the class, racial, and ethnic structure of American life. The emerging new class of physicians were not only incensed by the flagrant commercialization of abortion, but they expressed the fear that the growing rate of abortion among the middle and upper classes would cause immigrants, blacks, and the poor to outbreed them. Spurred by the growth of Social Darwinism and an increasing nativist movement, the anti-abortion crusade appealed to racist fears and portrayed abortion as the work of criminals, backward medical practitioners, and immoral social agents (Mohr 1978). Thus, beginning in the period between 1860 and 1880 and continuing through the first two-thirds of the twentieth century, anti-abortion policies included strict criminal laws about abortion and put absolute control of abortion in the hands of the medical profession. By these laws, women seeking abortions and their accomplices were defined as guilty of murder, abortion was defined as a criminal act, and the distribution of abortion and birth control information was deemed illegal. The public moralizing about abortion that we see in the late twentieth century has come historically from the emergence of new professional groups seeking to control abortion. Only very recently has abortion been seen as a moral issue stemming from religious beliefs.

Racism and Reproduction. The reproductive issues of abortion, birth control, and sterilization have particular significance for women of color. Although the majority of minority women support women's rights to abortion and birth control, history also shows that the birth control movement has been closely linked with racist movements for population control.

In the early twentieth century, when Margaret Sanger was organizing the birth control movement, white birth control reformers were campaigning to prevent so-called racial suicide by allowing the overpopulation of blacks, immigrants, the poor, and social misfits (Davis 1981; Gordon 1977). The campaign for birth control was interwoven with genocidal movements to eliminate racial groups, and appeals for birth control were clearly intended to limit what was perceived as overbreeding among the poor. Sanger herself made this appeal part of her campaign and, thus, seemed to support the racist goals of the eugenics movement.

In the contemporary record, information on the sterilization of minority and poor women confirms that birth control and population control are often linked. As we have already seen, sterilization rates are highest among black and Puerto Rican women and female welfare recipients. In addition, a 1976 study reveals that 24 percent of all native American women of childbearing age have been sterilized (Davis 1981). These data raise the issue of the blurred distinction between forced and voluntary sterilization. Although forced sterilization is illegal, reports indicate that doctors and clinics do give misleading information to minority and poor clients. Although clients may technically agree to the procedure, they have frequently been misled or misinformed.

A noted example is found in the case of Minnie and Mary Alice Relf, 12- and 14-year-old black girls. In 1973, their mother was told by the family planning clinic in Montgomery, Alabama, to sign a form authorizing shots for them. The girls had already been given the drug Depo-Provera as a birth control measure, but the Montgomery clinic ordered that they be sterilized when this drug was found to cause cancer in animals (Davis 1981). The mother was led to believe that, in signing the authorization form, she was agreeing to more shots, but when it was learned that they had been permanently sterilized, a suit was filed against the clinic. The Southern Poverty Law Center, filing suit, contended that the agency had performed the operation because the girls were allegedly "mentally retarded" and that, with "boys hanging around," sterilization was the most convenient method to prevent pregnancy (Corea 1977).

Subsequent federal investigations revealed a high incidence of sterilization of minors in other government-sponsored clinics. These incidents and a general history of the association among racism, sterilization, and birth control raise serious questions about contemporary findings that the hysterectomy rate among never-married black women is three to four times higher than that of never-married white women and that the hysterectomy rate for all women is highest in the South (Gutmacher Institute 1981). The politics of sterilization, coupled with the experimentation on Third World women for contraceptive development, indicates that racism is institutionalized in the health care system. Birth control, including abortion, is a necessary condition for the emancipation of women, but from a feminist and nonracist perspective, it must be a matter of choice. Reproductive issues are central to feminist analyses for change, and they are a clear case in which decisions made by men in the political, scientific, and medical communities take power away from women to direct their own lives. The next section reviews the history of the medical profession and its control of female reproduction. The chapter concludes with a review of the contemporary institution of medicine and the role of women within it.

The Politics of Birth: Pregnancy and Childbirth

Historical Perspectives on Childbirth. The emergence of modern medicine is usually seen as a conquest of ignorance and a triumph over superstition. Modern medical men are imbued with high status in our society and are perceived as learned, rational, and wise. Women also tend to view their doctors as explorers, pioneers, or therapists (Wolfson 1970), thus creating an image of the doctor as caring and adventurous at the same time that he is all-knowing and authoritative. Yet, there was a time when healing was almost solely the province of women. Particularly in matters of birth and childrearing, women were perceived as the experts and birth was a female-centered, home affair (Dye 1980). Until the nineteenth century in this country, women presided over most births, in the presence of female friends and kin who provided comfort and aid to the childbearing woman (Wertz and Wertz 1977).

Because childbirth was originally placed in the hands of women as midwives, developments in the history of childbirth provide a case study in which what was once a female-oriented process has come to be dominated and controlled by men. Although this section focuses primarily on childbirth, it also reveals more general patterns in the emergence of modern medicine. In the end, we will see how particular characteristics of medicine as an institution still take control of reproduction away from women.

Childbirth has a distinctive social history and one that is tied to the emergence of medicine as a profession, as well as to changes in the ideology and structure of women's roles in society. In colonial America, childbirth occurred in the home and in the presence of female family members and friends (Dye 1980; Scholten 1977). During this period, six to eight pregnancies were typical for women, as was a fear of pain and the possibility of death in childbirth. Female midwives who attended births generally practiced noninterventionist methods of delivery and, along with the other females present, provided comfort and emotional support for the laboring mother (Wertz and Wertz 1977). Records of the midwives' practices, successes, and failures are hard to find in this period, so it is difficult to know exactly how skilled or knowledgeable they were. Yet, information and experiences about childbirth were shared by women, and there is little indication in the historical record that midwives posed dangers for childbearing women. There are no recorded epidemics of puerperal fever, such as those that killed thousands of women when birth was moved to hospitals, and there are few recorded instances of midwives' incompetence in the colonial period (Wertz and Wertz 1977). Without romanticizing midwives and the process of birth, it appears that, unlike images of midwives that appeared later with the advent of scientific medicine, "the stereotype of the midwife as a curse upon women seems unfitting for colonial midwives" (Wertz and Wertz 1977:13).

Nevertheless, the pain associated with childbirth was a significant factor in women's desire for alternative practices. New interventionist techniques promised by the male founders of medical science appealed to women who sought relief from long and difficult labors. So, beginning in the mid-eighteenth century, a slow transition occurred in which birth was shifted from female to male control. American medical men took their lead from French and English physicians, who described the body as being like a machine and developed instruments or tools to intervene in natural bodily processes. Tools (such as forceps) promised to shorten labor and to make difficult labors more manageable, although such techniques were generally resisted by American and English women midwives, who believed that these techniques introduced new dangers and unsafe procedures to the natural process of birth.

In the mid-eighteenth and early nineteenth centuries, there was an open market for both female midwives and the medical men who were developing new birth techniques. Advances in knowledge about the physiology of labor, as well as various birth techniques, were taught in medical colleges —most of which were located in England and France. American men learned from these colleges but, because the government provided no financial support for medical education, women, with fewer financial resources than men, did not attend. However, medical education during this period was notoriously poor (Dye 1980), and many have argued that female midwives continued to have greater skills in birth, based on their practical experience, than did medically trained men (Ehrenreich and English 1978).

By the mid-nineteenth century, medical men had adopted an increasingly interventionist approach toward birth, whereas female midwives relied more upon the normal course of delivery. As an aside, Mary Wollstonecraft (1759–1797), an outspoken English feminist whom we study in Chapter 10, deplored the takeover of childbirth by men and insisted that her daughter, Mary Shelley (author of *Frankenstein*), be born with a woman attendant. When the placenta was not delivered, a male midwife was called in, who, upon inserting his hand to withdraw it, caused Wollstonecraft to hemorrhage and later to die of puerperal fever. (Flexner 1972; Wertz and Wertz 1977). Studies indicate that, although physicians gained greater control of childbirth during this period, as late as the early twentieth century, midwives had high status in their communities (Litoff 1978), maintained their own apprenticeship systems (Mongeau, Smith, and Maney 1961), and had better mortality records than medical men (Dye 1980).

Transformations in childbirth that ultimately resulted in the medical model of contemporary birth were accelerated in the mid-nineteenth century, when obstetrics was first developed as a medical specialty and when Victorian cultural attitudes transformed bourgeois notions of female sexuality. During the Victorian period, pregnancy was treated, in the middle and upper classes, with shame and concealment. Because the Victorian period severely restricted women's sexuality and because pregnancy directly acknowledged their sexual activity, it became an event to be hidden and concealed. For example, it is reported that Susan B. Anthony's mother was embarrassed by her pregnancy (Wertz and Wertz 1977). Like other bourgeois Victorian women, she disappeared from public view when she was pregnant.

At the same time, the emergence of the medical profession provided status to those who could afford new medical treatments. Families who could pay for it, especially in urban areas, began to go to medical specialists. Obstetrics was one of the first of these specialties, although most women continued to employ women midwives because they were more trusting of their noninterventionist techniques and more comfortable in their modesty with other women (Bogdan 1978). Physicians themselves stated that medical midwifery was the key to a successful practice because, if they could eliminate midwives, it would be a dependable market and its uncharted knowledge provided a chance for the expansion of the physician's career (Barker-Benfield 1976; Scholten 1977). In keeping with the Victorian sensibilities of the time, the typical obstetrician (so renamed from male midwives to symbolize their alleged professionalism) draped his client in cloth and avoided looking at her body. Consequently, obstetrics with middle- and upper-class clients was commonly practiced by touch alone. Obstetricians thus gained little knowledge of their female patients and relied upon experiments on poor and black women to advance their field. Following the Civil War, maternity hospitals were established as charitable asylums for poor and unmarried pregnant women. Stating that such places would provide a more moral and sanitary environment than their own homes, doctors provided free medical treatment for poor women (often servants of the upper classes) in return for using these patients as research subjects (Wertz and Wertz 1977). Because the physicians would have violated the "ladylike" codes of the period by actually examining an affluent woman's body, poor, black, and immigrant women in the charity hospital became research subjects for medical treatment and observation.

One of the most outrageous cases of experimentation is found in the practice of J. Marion Sims, originator of gynecology and early president of the American Medical Association. One of his early claims to fame was the discovery of ways to suture tears that occurred between the vagina and bladder and the vagina and anus. He developed these techniques by purchasing black female slaves, whom he kept in hospital quarters that he built in his own yard (Axelson 1985). Because he saw black slaves as enduring, passive, and helpless, he performed countless experimental operations on them without anesthesia. The pain he inflicted on them had to create unimaginable agony, yet this seemed not to faze him in his obsessive search for techniques to build his own career (Barker-Benfield 1976). Nor did it seem to bother upper-class women, who later erected a statue to him in Central Park because of their gratitude for his surgical method! (They, of course, experienced it only after the development of anesthesia.)

Sims, like other medical men of his day, believed that women's psychology stemmed from their sex organs, and he was anxious to perform clitoridectomies and oophorectomies (removal of the clitoris and ovaries). His drastic use of the knife seemed intended not for the betterment of women, but for the enhancement of his own career, because an aspiring specialist, then as now, made his name through the invention and publication of new techniques. Indeed, as one historian has noted, the operating rooms where female surgery was performed in the nineteenth century were essentially "an arena for an exchange between men" (Barker-Benfield 1976:101). Sims, in fact, developed gynecological procedures as if he were an explorer charting new frontiers; his own writings clearly show this to be his own metaphor about his work. He was the first to develop the speculum and says of it, "Introducing the bent handle of a spoon, I saw everything as no man had ever seen before. . . . I felt like an explorer in medicine who first views a new and important territory" (Barker-Benfield 1976:95). Other medical men, too, declared his "speculum to be to diseases of the womb . . . what the compass is to the mariner" (Barker-Benfield 1976:95).

The removal of childbirth from the home and the control of women contradicted the Victorian point of view that birth was a private matter, to be conducted in secrecy and within the domestic world. So, initially, delivery by men was seen as a breakdown of moral standards and an offense to female delicacy (Donegan 1978). But over time, as doctors promised safer and less painful births, women began to desire the new techniques they were offered. Most women wanted less painful childbirth, although in the late nineteenth century, the absence of pain in childbirth was associated with supposedly precivilized women — especially Indians and blacks. Racism in the middle and upper classes defined more "primitive" peoples as closer to nature and, therefore, unlikely to experience childbirth pain. Thus, from the racist perspective of the bourgeois class, to experience pain and, therefore, to need relief from it became a sign of one's civilized nature. Needing relief from childbirth pain was also an indication of the social distance of the upper and middle classes from other strata of the society. Pain, then, became a mark of the "truly feminine" — a fact with its own paradoxical truth because childbirth pain and complications were greatly increased by the "civilized" practices of tight corsets, lack of exercise, fashionable illness, and airless rooms (Wertz and Wertz 1977).

Nonetheless, rather than change their cultural habits, middle- and upper-class women sought relief from childbirth pain and, thus, became more interested in the promises of modern medicine. But promises were all many of these techniques gave, for although they may have alleviated extreme pain, there is little evidence that childbirth was made any safer by medical men of the early twentieth century. Puerperal fever, later found to be caused by infections generated by unsanitary hospital procedures and interventionist techniques, became a major cause of maternal death (Wertz and Wertz 1977). Epidemics of puerperal fever killed thousands of women who sought painless deliveries through hospital births.

The number of births occurring in hospitals increased rapidly after the 1930s. Prior to this time, hospital birth had been primarily an urban phenomenon and, even there, had occurred on a large scale beginning only in the twentieth century. In 1930, only about 25 percent of all births took place in hospitals; by 1970, over 95 percent of all births occurred in hospitals (Wertz and Wertz 1977). Hospital births represent the ultimate transformation of birth from a female-centered, home activity to one that is male controlled and medically defined. The prevalence of hospital births followed a direct assault on women midwives in the second half of the nineteenth century, when propaganda to make women fear pregnancy and legislation to eliminate midwives combined to generate new definitions of women's place in childbirth and, more generally, in medicine (Barker-Benfield 1976). Legislation between 1900 and 1930 made licensing for midwives a necessity. However, to obtain a license, midwives were required to get vouchers of their moral character from a member of the medical profession, to have their homes and outfits inspected by a physician's nurse, and to have attended births under the supervision of a physician. Because few physicians would provide these credentials, the number of practicing midwives radically declined. In New York City, for example, the number of practicing midwives declined from 3,000 in 1908 to 270 in 1939, 2 in 1957, and 1 in 1963 (Barker-Benfield 1976). Moreover, in most cases, women were excluded from medical schools and, if they wanted to enter the health care system, were relegated to secondary status as nurses (Ehrenreich and English 1978). Childbirth and, more generally, women's health had effectively been placed in the hands of male physicians.

The movement of childbirth to hospitals and medical men was further increased by popular racist fears of contagion and germs that were associated with poor, immigrant, and black people. The fads of genetic science and Social Darwinism of the 1920s and 1930s increased middle-class fears of associating with those from the lower strata of society. Coupled with the home economics movement of the 1920s that defined home environments as sources of germs and disease (see Chapter 6), popular opinions laced with racist and class ideologies further generated a social definition of childbirth as a scientific event to be placed under the authority of medical men.

The Medicalization of Childbirth. Physicians now routinely define pregnancy and birth as medical events and, because of this model, they are more likely to prescribe drugs during pregnancy and birth, set strict limits on what is considered a "normal" pregnancy, and define medical intervention as essential during birth. Midwives, on the other hand, define pregnancy as a healthy and normal condition — one that is optimized, not by intervention and technological management, but by providing the best possible environment for the pregnant woman (Rothman 1982). Conflict between the medical and midwifery models of childbirth lies at the heart of current political and economic struggles over the control of childbirth, including political conflicts over the licensing of midwives and the establishment of nonmedical birth settings (Weitz and Sullivan 1986).

The dominance of the medical model in controlling pregnancy and childbirth can be seen in the way that pregnancy and childbirth are routinely handled by the medical profession. Birth is most likely located in hospitals, were doctors and the staff, not the mother, have control and authority over the delivery procedures. Even in the birthing rooms which some hospitals have more recently established, ultimate authority lies with the physician, who may (and does) intervene in the birth process at any point. Reinharz (1986, 1988) has also shown how the medical model permeates physicians' treatment and women's understandings of miscarriage.

Interventionist practices characterizing the rise of male control over childbirth continue to dominate women's childbirth experiences. This fact is especially evident in the dramatic increase in the number of cesarean sections being performed in hospitals throughout the country. Since 1965, cesarean sections have increased from 4 percent of all births to 20 percent in 1983 (Taffel, Placek, and Moien 1985). Some hospitals report that as many as one-quarter of all births are performed by cesarean section (Corea 1980). In an age when childbirth is supposed to be safer and less threatening than in previous years, how do we explain the high proportion of births using a process that clearly increases the risks to both mother and child?

Researchers cite the routine practices of technological monitoring of birth as contributing significantly to the increase in cesarean births. Although some also mention physicians' greed for higher compensation and their desire for predictable schedules as contributing to the incentives to perform cesareans, it seems most likely that the social organization of childbirth around technological intervention is responsible for the increase. Typically, the process of labor is now observed by an electronic fetal-monitoring device that not only replaces the monitoring originally performed by nurses but also keeps the laboring woman passively strapped to the device and immobile throughout the course of labor. Even though changes in the baby's breathing and heartbeat are routine features of the birth process, the close detection of these changes by the electronic fetal monitor results in a high number of false indications of fetal distress (Corea 1980). Because of this situation, which is complicated by doctors' fears of malpractice if an actually distressed fetus is missed, doctors seem to react quickly to the slightest indication of change in the fetal condition by performing a vast number of unnecessary cesarean sections.

Other practices in the obstetric management of birth have also been criticized, including the separation of the mother and infant immediately following birth (Rossi 1977), the overuse of anesthetics that affect the infant's nervous system, and the widespread use of birth positions that immobilize the mother and increase the incidence of episiotomies (Wertz and Wertz 1977). All of these practices contribute to better hospital management, but they pose clear risks for mothers and their children. Thus, it appears that in modern medical practice, the social organization of hospital routines takes precedent over maternal and infant well-being. Moreover, the expectation is that maternity clients should maintain a passive attitude while trusting in the doctor's authority and knowledge.

Women have become increasingly critical of the conditions surrounding childbirth, and many groups have organized to create out-of-hospital birthing centers, more licensing and increased use of midwives, and greater consumer education to enhance women's control over childbirth (Weitz and Sullivan 1986). Although some reforms are being introduced, feminists argue that the process of childbirth still remains one of the fundamental ways in which women's reproductive abilities are subordinated to the definitions, practices, and controls of men. In the concluding section, we look at the character of the modern medical profession and women's place within it.

Reproductive Technology

New reproductive technologies, including artificial insemination, in vitro fertilization, embryo transfer, and genetic engineering, raise new concerns and questions about women's control of their bodies. Feminists point out that, while some of these technologies seem to offer liberating possibilities, at the same time they make women new targets for the manipulation of reproductive engineers (Arditti, Duelli-Klein, and Minden 1984).

Donor insemination, for example, means that lesbian women or women who want children without men can become pregnant. In vitro fertilization makes it possible for those who are infertile to have children. Amniocentesis and an array of other tests now allow for prenatal evaluation of the embryo, meaning that characteristics such as sex, disability, and disease can be determined prior to birth. While these may appear to be laudable developments, they also raise disturbing questions. Why, for example, is biological parenthood so important that we would go to such lengths and cost to bear children? What are the implications of determining sex prior to birth, especially in cultures where female infants are less valued than males? And what does it say about the oppression of disabled people and our prejudices against them if we screen for disabilities prior to birth?

The eugenics movement in the United States in the earlier part of the twentieth century, like that of Nazi Germany, sought to apply the principles of genetic selection to improve the offspring of the human race. In both Nazi Germany and the United States, it was explicitly racist, including, for example, compulsory sterilization of those defined as "unfit" or "defective." Many feminists equate the contemporary development of reproductive technology with the possibility for a new eugenics movement — one that, though it may not appear blatantly racist, is still embedded in a racist, sexist, and homophobic culture. Would reproductive technology be used, for example, to control the fertility of those deemed unworthy? To whom are reproductive technology and, therefore, choice over reproduction most likely made available?

Although new reproductive technologies appear to give women choices over how and when they will have children, these technologies do not affect all women equally (Corea 1985). Though women may have "rights to choose," the choices women have are structured by race, class, and gender inequality (Petchesky 1980; Rothman 1982). Reproductive control can, in fact, become a façade for population control and, in the context of racism, population control is often a mechanism for more social and political control (Corea 1985; Rothman 1982).

Such questions make the question of power central to any discussion of reproductive technology. Feminists do not necessarily believe that reproductive technology should be eliminated altogether. But they argue that, as long as it is controlled by men, women are still denied the rights to control their bodies. Only organized resistance to the control of women's bodies by men will ensure that these technologies do not become a new means for the oppression of women.

Women and the Health Care System

When a woman seeks medical care from a physician, there are 87 chances out of 100 that the person she sees will be a man (U.S. Bureau of the Census, *Statistical Abstracts of the United States* 1986). This fact is especially significant because women utilize the health care system more than do men, as measured by physician visits, hospital admissions, and the prescription of drugs (National Center for Health Statistics 1985). Women's health care is intricately interwoven with the power of men in medicine and with the profit structure of modern medicine. These factors influence the client-physician relationship, the quality of care received, and the status of women workers within the health care system. Feminist criticism of medical institutions is a response to this political and economic structure.

Doctor-Patient Relationships

The most immediate context in which power relations can be seen in medicine is the doctor-patient relationship. Because women are more likely to make physician visits and 87 percent of doctors are men, this doctor-patient relationship is likely to reflect the gender roles in society as well as the roles of professionals and their clients. Both the doctor and the patient are likely to have expectations of the other that are conditioned by the status each occupies. We have already seen that women tend to see their doctors as explorers, pioneers, or therapists; doctors, on the other hand, are likely to see illness among their women patients as psychologically based (Wallen 1979). These definitions reflect gender role expectations because they indicate that male doctors are not taking women patients seriously, whereas women tend to view their doctors as all-knowing. In fact, an early study determined that clinicians (in this case, psychiatrists, psychologists, and social workers) held different standards of health for men and for women. Their concepts of healthy men were similar to their concepts of sex-unspecified healthy adults. But their concepts of healthy women were that they were submissive, not independent or adventurous, unaggressive, easily influenced, excitable, easily hurt, emotional, conceited about their appearance, and not objective (Broverman et al.

1970). If these definitions guide physicians' treatment of their clients, we would expect physicians to cure them according to gender role expectations that they think are appropriate.

Complicating this possibility is the fact that in medical schools, physicians are trained to view their patients as individual cases, not as representatives of their social structural milieu. Consequently, doctors sometimes advise patients based on their conventional wisdom (Barrett and Roberts 1978). Particularly because the physician's background is likely to entail gendered assumptions about male and female patients, the advice he gives is influenced by sex-stereotypic roles and norms. Studies indicate that male doctors encourage male patients to see their problems as stemming from job stress, while locating women's problems in their family roles. Moreover, doctors are prone to view women's complaints as psychosomatic, leading them to prescribe psychotherapy instead of situational or structural changes that might alleviate their difficulties. Because of the physicians' tendencies to view cases as individual pathologies, neither male nor female patients are encouraged to consider the social structural origins of their difficulties (Barrett and Roberts 1978; Lorber 1975).

Other research reveals similar problems in doctor-patient consultations. Observations of consulting patterns reveal that women are given less complete and shorter explanations of their medical problems than are men, in spite of the fact that women ask more questions of their doctors. Because they are more inquisitive but receive less information, women experience frustration in their encounters with doctors. Because doctors see female illness as psychologically caused, they are also more pessimistic about the patients' recovery and, thus, give them less information about their condition (Wallen 1979).

The stereotypic attitudes of male doctors toward their women patients are consistent with the images of women encouraged in medical schools and in medical advertising. Medical texts, particularly in the area of gynecology, depict women as nuturing, passive, and powerless (Scully and Bart 1973). Medical advertisements typically show women as depressed, sullen, and afraid. There is also a strong association between the type of illness and the sex of the patient in medical ads. Women are shown as suffering from emotional illness, whereas men are seen as suffering from organic illness (Prather and Fidell 1975). These advertisements also play on cultural stereotypes, with men depicted in work settings and women shown in domestic roles or glamorous fashion poses. Among other things, these images and sex role stereotypes, coupled with the profit structure of medical industries, have encouraged an extremely high rate of prescribed psychoactive drug use among women.

Because women constitute a majority of physician clients, they create a captive market for medical and drug establishments. Because women are reluctant to criticize their doctors, the medical profession is able to maintain its authority, while not challenging the societal basis of sex role stereo-types and the profit structure of medical practice. In sum, the problems of women's health care are manifested in the doctor-patient relationship but, ultimately, have their basis in the power of men in medical institutions and the profit structure of the medical profession.

Women as Health Care Workers

The interaction of male power and profit systems is even more clear when we consider the status of women workers in the health care field. Women constitute 87 percent of health care workers (Walsh 1977), yet they are systematically found in the least prestigious and most poorly paid positions in this field. Among doctors, women constitute a 7 percent minority; among nurses, women are 98 percent of registered nurses, 10 percent of whom are black (Grimm 1978). Black and Hispanic women in health care are concentrated in the lowest paying of these occupations (McKinney 1986).

Women who are nurses do not face the problem of existing in a male-dominated occupation, but their position relative to that of male professionals creates its own set of problems. Moreover, minority women and men in these fields also face the problems of racism and discrimination, which hamper their career development. Studies indicate that male physicians tend to think of themselves as leaders and of nurses and paramedics as their employees (Bates 1970). Consequently, nurses and other health care workers are put in a position in which male professionals hold authority over them, in addition to receiving greater material benefits. Moreover, men who do enter nursing tend to progress to higher echelons than women within the profession (compounding the problem of sexism that women in this field face) (Grimm and Stern 1974). Research also shows that salaries in the nursing profession tend to be insensitive to the amount of experience one has had; for example, one survey finds that the difference between starting and maximum median wages for all status levels within nursing does not exceed 20 percent (Godfrey 1974).

Some have explained the poor salaries of nurses as a result of their lack of ambition. But this assumption is not supported by surveys that show that although more than half of male nurses believe that men have greater professional dedication than women, only 15 percent of female nurses hold this view (Lynn et al. 1975). Moreover, although men are likely to believe that women nurses prefer male supervisors, 60 percent of female nurses disagree. More male nursing administrators (56 percent) than female administrators (39 percent) believe that the entry of men to nursing will upgrade the profession (Lynn et al. 1975). Moreover, female nursing administrators are more likely aware that men are paid more than women for the same work. Women nursing administrators are also more likely to believe that women are just as effective as men (Lynn et al. 1975).

These data suggest that women nurses face sexist attitudes that define their work as less valuable than that of men. Moreover, on the job, nurses are subordinate to the doctor's authority; countless accounts have described the sexist putdowns, innuendoes, and insults that some doctors direct toward the nursing staff. More generally, physicians maintain a monopoly over medical knowledge and medical practice, even though nurses have more actual contact with hospitalized patients (Ehrenreich and English 1973).

The subordination of the nursing profession to the authority of doctors has resulted in a split between the activities of curing and caring. Stereotypically, nurses are alleged to provide nurturing, whereas doctors maintain the expertise in healing. Such a myth not only belittles the professional knowledge of nurses but also creates an atmosphere that may not work in the best interest of patients. As alternative medical practices have shown, a patient's health involves a complex configuration of physiological, emotional, and social systems. It would appear that a more useful system of medicine is one that integrates the process of healing with the complexities emerging from the interaction of these systems.

Among women who enter higher-status jobs (such as that of physician), most end up in the least prestigious specialities, such as pediatrics, obstetrics/gynecology, and general practice. There is, however, evidence of a recent change in this regard. By 1983, women made up 33 percent of first-year medical students. In fact, between 1971 and 1983, the number of women in medical schools nearly tripled; since 1959, the number of women in medical school has increased 700 percent (Walsh 1977). Because of the long period of training, internship, and residence, the impact of these changes on the composition of practicing physicians may not yet have been felt. Some data also show a growing tendency for women to enter traditionally male specialities (Kehrer 1976), although the percentage of women on medical faculties has increased only 1 percent since 1975 (Vetter and Babco 1986).

Some see these changes as signs of major breakthroughs for women in medicine, but this generation is not the first to witness such changes. At the turn of the twentieth century, women were a much larger proportion of all physicians, with some cities reporting almost 20 percent of all physicians to be women (Walsh 1977). The entry of women to medicine is historically closely aligned with feminism and the new opportunities it encouraged for women. Although the feminist movement at the turn of the century was quite different from contemporary feminism, it did encourage women, at least of the upper and middle classes, to use their skills, especially in areas perceived as helping professions. Since the turn of the century, women have been excluded from medicine through overt discrimination denying them entrance to medical schools and professional assignments and through informal practices whereby they received encouragement or support, were channeled into nursing schools, encountered hostility from peers, and were excluded from the old boy network that placed persons in their careers.

Women's lower status in the medical profession is often explained as the result of conflicts they experience in their family and work roles. For instance, some claim that women choose less prestigious specialities to accommodate their families, by working fewer hours and with less professional commitment. Yet, data on this point are contradictory (Lorber 1975), and recent surveys show an increase in full-time employment among female physicians (Mandelbaum 1978).

More pertinent to the status of women as physicians is a consideration of the structure of medical education and medical work as creating obstacles to women's advancement. Research cites the lack of sponsorship, sexual tracking systems, nonsupportive peer environments, and overt ridicule as contributing to the demise of women's medical careers (Lorber 1975). Yet, recently, there has been a reduction in women's attrition rates in medicine (Walsh 1977) as government policies prohibiting sex discrimination have disrupted the autonomy of male-dominated professional enterprises. Moreover, the current women's movement has helped create a climate of mutual support among women students and professionals, leading to the creation of an environment more conducive to women's success. Only the future will show us if these recent changes will continue to be effective in enhancing women's status. The historical record of women's decline in medical careers indicates that none of these gains can be taken for granted. Continual lobbying, network building among women, and federal support for women's medical education are all necessary for stabilizing the role of women in this profession.

The Women's Health Movement

The women's health movement has suggested various alternatives to traditional medical care, ranging from more consumer information to feminist self-help clinics (Ruzek 1978). As a social movement, the women's health movement is founded in reaction to the sexism of the medical profession and on criticism of traditional medical practices that deny women control of their own reproductive lives and physical health.

Numerous groups in the women's health movement are also organized to provide health care to women without the high-handed authority of traditional medical practitioners. Many of these organizations disseminate health care information, some offer direct services, and others work primarily as lobbying organizations, attempting to create changes in the health care system and its policies.

Altogether, the women's health movement has the goals of reducing differences in knowledge between patient and practitioner, challenging the mandate of physicians as the sole providers of health care, reducing the professional monopoly over goods and services, increasing the number of women practitioners, and organizing clients around health issues (Ruzek 1978). Whether the women's health movement can be successful in its goals remains to be seen. But its emergence is indicative of the dissatisfaction women have faced in health care institutions and over issues involving reproduction and health. As this chapter has shown, feminist perspectives on health and reproduction insist on women's right to control their own bodies. As long as the power to control women's bodies remains in the hands of men, feminists are likely to continue organizing on these issues.

Summary _____

Physical health is influenced by gender roles. Patterns of male and female health change according to historical conditions. Health studies indicate that mortality and illness rates are associated with gender roles in society. Racial and class oppression also influence the likelihood of physical health and illness, as well as the likelihood of death by accident, hypertension, and other diseases.

Occupational health and safety must also be seen in the context of gender relations. Women and men workers are exposed to a wide variety of occupational health hazards; health hazards vary according to occupation. Protective legislation against reproductive hazards has typically been aimed at female workers, though reproductive hazards are incurred by male workers as well. Protective legislation has often been used to exclude women workers from high-paying, high-status, traditionally male occupations.

Social problems associated with health are also conditioned by the culture's gender expectations. Cultural obsession with thinness creates a high rate of anorexia, bulimia, and other eating problems. Women's gender roles also influence their use of alcohol and drugs. Women are less likely to engage in alcohol and substance abuse than men.

Feminists believe in women's right to control their own bodies. Female control of reproduction has been historically and cross-culturally the most prevalent social arrangement. Modern Western cultures have put reproductive control in the hands of male medical authorities. Birth control is a right that women have achieved through judicial reform. Abortion was made legal by the 1973 Supreme Court ruling in *Roe* v. *Wade*. Public support for abortion has increased in recent years. Population control and sterilization abuse have been used to exploit women of color.

Childbirth occurs in this culture within institutions that are controlled and organized by men. The medical model defines childbirth as a medical event requiring intervention and technological supervision. Interventionist practices have resulted in an increase in the number of cesarean section births. New reproductive technologies raise liberating possibilities for women and men but, to date, have not been controlled by women. Reproductive technologies also can be linked to eugenics movements for population control.

Gender relationships influence the doctor-patient relationships, since the majority of doctors are men and the majority of patients are women. Women's treatment by the medical profession stems from stereotypes physicians may hold about women clients. Gender stratification in the health care system keeps women, for the most part, in lesser-status jobs and gives them less control than men over medical decisions and medical knowledge. The women's health care movement is a social movement that is critical of male control of health care systems and that is organized to help women resist medical exploitation.

CHAPTER 8

Women and Religion

Luther S?.

Introduction

In 1895, Elizabeth Cady Stanton, a passionate feminist, close friend of Susan B. Anthony, and founder of equal rights and suffrage associations during the first wave of feminism in the nineteenth century, wrote,

> From the inauguration of the movement for women's emancipation the Bible has been used to hold her in the "divinely ordained sphere," prescribed in the Old and New testaments. The canon and civil law; church and state; priests and legislators; all political parties and religious denominations have alike taught that woman was made after man, of man, and for man, an inferior being, subject to man. Creeds, codes, Scriptures and statutes, are all based on this idea. The fashions, forms, ceremonies and customs of society, church ordinances and discipline all grow out of this idea. (Stanton 1895:7)

Eighty-seven years later, Sonia Johnson, a Mormon woman excommunicated from the Mormon Church in 1979 for her political efforts on behalf of passage of the Equal Rights Amendment (ERA), echoed Stanton's thoughts on religion. Johnson has stated, "Patriarchal religions are male supremacist bodies. They are bodies that believe that men rule because of divine right, divine right to rule, to tell the rest of the people, who are women, how to be. A ruling class always has privileges, that's what it means to be one of the ruling class, to have privileges." (Langlois 1982:12)

Although the Mormon Church denies that Johnson was excommuni-

222

cated for her support of the ERA, the church vehemently opposed passage of the Equal Rights Amendment. Ironically, Johnson attributes the birth of her feminism to the church. She recalls a day when her ward bishop read a priesthood directive saying that women could no longer pray in sacrament meetings. Johnson remembers that at the time she wondered to herself, "What have women done to deserve this?" (Langlois 1982:9). Her subsequent discussions with church officials, her private reflections on women in the church, and the church's vociferous protests against the Equal Rights Amendment made her deeply question the patriarchal order of the church. Her commitment to passage of the ERA and her growing feminist beliefs stemmed from these critical experiences.

Stanton's *The Woman's Bible,* Johnson's excommunication, and numerous other feminist critiques of religion make it seem that religion is indeed the foe of women's liberation. The Judeo-Christian tradition in the United States provides the foundation for laws governing marriage, divorce, contraception, abortion, and sexuality that feminists argue have oppressed women. Feminists also contend that the church provides the basis for the double standard of male and female sexuality. Female role models in the Christian church are defined through women's sexual behavior and dichotomize women into two polar types: Eve the temptress and Mary the virginal mother (Burlage 1974).

Sexism in traditional religious teachings and the exclusion of women from positions of religious authority indicate that religion is a powerful source for the subordination of women in society. And yet, across the years religion has also been an important part of the feminist movement and other social and political movements for human liberation. This is particularly evident in the black community, where religion has been a powerful instrument for social change and where women's roles in the church have provided black women with opportunities for leadership, education, and the development of organizational skills. Moreover, religious belief in the black community rests on a strong faith in justice, fairness, and equality.

Thus, while religion has been a repressive force in women's lives, it has also been a source of liberation. Bernice Johnson Reagon, black feminist, performer, and director of the Black American Culture Program at the Smithsonian Institution, reflects on her religious experience in childhood, writing in her autobiography,

> Everybody in church talked about/Miss Nana's relationship with God/People thought she had a sort of audacity/Everybody else would say/"Now, Lord, here comes me your meek and undone servant and you know me and you know my condition"/This was a way of saying/"Now Lord, I don't even need to go over my situation/Let us start now with where I am and what I need today"/ . . . /Miss Nana was grateful for what she got but she didn't let up on God for what she wanted/God had already given her a soul, right?/

But then she'd say,/"That ain't all I need, Lord/You are not off the hook/I expect you to be here on time tomorrow night." (Reagon 1982:90–91)

For women, the church has a dual reality as both oppressor and potential liberator. Our understanding of these dual tendencies will be best developed through exploring sociological and feminist perspectives on religion. In the sections that follow, we explore several themes in the feminist critique of religion, including the historical relationship of women, religion, and feminism; women's religious beliefs and status within churches; the role of the church in minority communities; and new perspectives inspired by feminist spirituality and theology.

Sociological Perspectives on Religion

For most persons, religion is something they hold dear, sometimes so much so that they see it as the only possible view of the world. Paul Tillich, a liberal theologian, defines religion as the expression of humanity's ultimate concerns, the articulation of longing for a center of meaning and value and for connection with the power of being (1957). Sociologists who study religion take another approach. They are not so much interested in the truth or falsity of a religious belief system, but in how belief systems and religious institutions shape social behavior and reflect the collective experience of society's members (Hess, Markson, and Stein 1982).

From a sociological perspective, religion provides a culture with powerful symbols and conceptions that are deeply felt and shape a group's view of the world around them. Religious belief is often the basis for cultural and societal conflict and is frequently so strongly felt that people will fight and die for it. Religion is also the basis for in-group membership, sometimes strongly protected by sanctions against interfaith marriages, although by 1985 more than three-quarters of Americans approved of marriages between Catholics and Protestants or between Jews and non-Jews (Gallup Opinion Poll 1985).

Sociological perspectives on religion also take the institutional structure of religion as significant in a variety of ways. Like other institutions in society, religious institutions socialize their members through enforcing group norms that dictate many aspects of everyday life, including what men and women wear; how life events (such as birth, puberty, marriage, and death) are defined and ritualized; and how men and women are defined in terms of home, work, child care, politics, and the law. Religious institutions also include power structures and, like other social institutions, are characterized by a system of stratification, which is clearly demarcated by gender, race, and class. Feminists have also described patriarchal religions as legitimating widespread violence against women, as in the case of Indian suttee, African clitoral circumcisions, and the burning of women as witches (Daly 1978).

Religious belief is a particularly important part of our sexual experience. Researchers find that religion, more than any other sociological factor, plays the strongest influence on women's sexual behavior. The frequency and number of a woman's sexual encounters is highly related to her religious faith. In his classic study of human sexual behavior, Kinsey (1953) shows that the most devout women are those who are the least sexually active, while the least religious are much more sexually active. Sociological studies have also reported an inverse relationship between religious behavior and premarital sexual behavior (Woodruff 1985), meaning that those who are most religious are those who are least likely to engage in premarital sex. Moreover, others have shown how the practice of confessionals in the Catholic Church is used to maintain social control by regulating sexual life (Zaretsky 1980).

These studies indicate that sex and gender are not just a matter of secular social relations. Despite an overall decline in religious faith in American society, religion continues to be a powerful influence on sex and gender relations in contemporary society. For feminist scholars, one of the beginning points of their analysis of religion is the fact that, as measured by a variety of indicators, women are more religious than men in American society. Women are more likely to attend church than men and to attend on a regular basis, and women express higher degrees of religiosity. But, as feminists have pointed out, despite the fact that women outnumber men in religious faith and in attendance at worship services, it is men, regardless of religious denomination, who maintain religious authority. In Christian churches it is men, for the most part, who are the priests and clergy, and they are typically backed up in the institution by men as deacons, elders, and vestry of the church. Orthodox Jews and Roman Catholics still deny ordination to women and, though their numbers are growing, women are a numerical minority in seminaries of all faiths.

These patterns of gender inequality in religious institutions have raised the question of to what extent religious traditions contribute to the subjugation of women; feminist scholars have also examined the alliance between religion and other oppressive social systems (Hargrove, Schmidt, and Davaney 1985). Religion is clearly one of the foremost forces in society to preserve traditions, conserve established social order, stabilize world views, and transmit values through generations. But religion is equally important in social transformation. Religious beliefs can and do frame new sources of human potential and possibility, and organized religious groups can release enormous bursts of political energy (Falk 1985). This is well demonstrated in the history of the Civil Rights Movement, with its organizational center in black churches. The Civil Rights Movement demonstrates that religious institutions can provide liberation movements with the leadership, organizational structure, and values that provide both the support network for social movements and the visions for new futures that such movements need.

Historical perspectives on religion show that religion has been a patriarchal force and has been deeply related to the development of feminism. In the following section we briefly examine these themes in the history of religion.

Patriarchy and Feminism in the History of Religion ————

Religion as a Patriarchal Force: Witchcraft

During the Middle Ages in western Europe, it is estimated that between 30,000 and 9 million women were killed or tortured as witches (Daly 1978). The breadth of this estimate indicates how difficult it is to pinpoint the number of witch persecutions. Toward the end of the seventeenth century in the United States, another twenty persons (seven of whom were men) were tried and executed as witches. Though the scope of the American experience hardly matches that of the witch craze that swept Europe during the period of the Inquisition, the sociological impetus was the same. In both places, witches were believed to be women influenced by the devil, and they were perceived to be threats to social purity.

In western Europe, the *Malleus Maleficarum,* issued by the Catholic church in 1484, defined the church's position on witches. This document defined witchcraft, described the alleged practices of witches, and standardized trial procedures and sentencing for those persecuted as witches throughout Europe. The *Malleus Maleficarum* defined witchcraft as stemming from women's carnal lust; women were seen as instruments of Satan because of their insatiable desire. According to the *Malleus Maleficarum,* "All witchcraft comes from carnal lust, which is in women insatiable. See Proverbs XXX: there are three things that are never satisfied, yea, a fourth thing which says not, it is enough; that is, the mouth of the womb" (*Malleus Maleficarum,* cited in Dworkin 1974:133). People believed that witches collected male organs for use in satanic rituals and stole semen from sleeping men. They were also believed to cast spells over male organs so that they disappeared entirely!

Who were these women and what was happening in history that there was such organized madness to eradicate them? Historians explain the witch hunts as stemming from the historical movement of the Catholic and Protestant churches to establish themselves as supreme authorities over sacred and secular matters. The period of the witch hunts in western

Europe was a period of the solidification of church authority. Women who were singled out as witches were women who deviated from the religious norms of the time; they were healers, wise women, and midwives. Those who had formed witch cults were women who had a strong sense of people as a part of nature and who, because of this belief, gave animals a prime place in some of their rituals. Such a belief system, with its integrated view of human life and nature, was anathema to the patriarchal and hierarchical structure of the church. And, as feminists have argued, since the church was the ultimate representation of male power, witchcraft also symbolized men's fears of female sexuality, its assumed relationship to nature, and its unbounded expression. Feminists describe the witch hunts as a means of men's desire to control women's sexuality (Daly 1978; Dworkin 1974). Women defined as witches also were often widows and spinsters — in other words, single women who were living independently of men (Anderson and Gordon 1978; Szasz 1970). In sum, the witch hunts were a mechanism for ensuring the social control of women by men, as represented in the emerging hegemony of organized patriarchal religion.

The persecution of women as witches is a historical case of the imposition of serious sanctions against women who lived outside the developing control of patriarchal religious bodies and outside the control of men. Modern sociologists see the persecution of witches as the persecution of sexual and religious deviants (Szasz 1970). It is an illustration of the use of social control to regulate women's religious and sexual behavior.

Religion and the Emergence of American Feminism

In American society, the power of the Protestant and Catholic faiths was well established during the colonial period and, though women outnumbered men in the churches, the church hierarchy was exclusively male (Cott 1977). Not until the nineteenth century in the United States do historians typically see the beginnings of significant social change in women's religious roles and the seeds of developing feminism. Two particular developments in the nineteenth century in the United States have major significance for the role of women in religion and the development of the feminist movement — the evangelical spirit of the Second Great Awakening and the widespread belief in the cult of womanhood that defined and restricted women's world to the world of domesticity (Hargrove, Schmidt, and Davaney 1985).

The Second Great Awakening was a social movement in the early nineteenth century that emphasized a revivalist and egalitarian spirit in religion. During this period, ministers and lay persons began to see religion as a route to salvation on earth and they used this belief to teach the restraints they believed were necessary for an orderly society (Cott 1977). Occurring in the aftermath of the French Revolution and in the midst of worries about the destructive influence of growing urban populations and Catholic immigration, the Second Great Awakening had a democratic impulse — reaching out to the urban poor and western frontier residents. The Second Great Awakening created a lay missionary spirit in which conversion and religious benevolence were seen as the solution to the social ills generated by widespread social transformations affecting the fabric of American society (Cott 1977).

During this period, Christianity was softened (or "feminized") and, rather than stressing dogma, it instead exalted meekness. Also, Christians began to reinterpret Christ as embodying these more sex-typed images of love, forgiveness, and humility. The "feminization" of American culture and religion meant that, among other things, by the middle of the nineteenth century, women were the majority in American religion (Douglas 1977; Welter 1976). During this period, women were defined as the keepers of the private refuge of the home — the place where piety and religious spirit were to prosper. In this domestic refuge, women's purity and piety were seen as vehicles for redemption; women were seen in opposition to the aggressiveness and competition of the public sphere that was identified with men. Though these images exalted the traditional status of women, many have suggested that they also provided women with positive roles and images — at least ones that did not degrade and denigrate women's culture. The exaltation of women's culture encouraged women to speak in prayer meetings and congregations and encouraged them to participate in voluntary religious associations.

Women's religious societies were especially successful at fund raising and these societies became the basis for a developing sense of sisterhood among women. Local missionary activities trained women for what was defined as a life of social usefulness: teaching hygiene, citizenship, family values, and social relationships and engaging them in fieldwork in the cities. As a consequence, women's religious activities engaged them in other social reform movements.

Thus during the nineteenth century, women were considered to be more spiritual and more naturally prone to religious observance and piety than men. The belief that women were naturally good also influenced the development of the feminist movement in this period. Women's alleged moral superiority was perceived to have a potentially benevolent impact on the more callous and harsh realities of the public world. Some feminists argued that extending the values of the domestic or private sphere to the public would create a more compassionate public world — a theme now resounded among some contemporary feminists as well (Miller 1977). Throughout the nineteenth-century women's movement, religious faith played an important part in articulating feminist concerns. Women in the Women's Christian Temperance Union, one of the first feminist organizations, extolled the virtues of women and blamed the impersonal and competitive culture of the male public world for a variety of social ills.

Belief in the virtues of women's culture led early feminists to use the values of the home as the basis for crusading in the public world and for demanding women's rights. At the same time, as the suffrage movement developed, men (and some women) also used arguments from the Bible against women's suffrage and other changes in her status. They maintained that the Scripture ordered a different and higher sphere of life apart from public life and that this "higher" sphere was the responsibility and, in fact, nature of women. As a result, many feminists eventually gave up on the traditional churches and turned to experimental religious societies, such as the Quakers, for more inner-directed spiritual experiences.

But for most early American feminists, religious faith was a significant part of their feminist ideology. Elizabeth Cady Stanton was herself relatively alone in seeing the domination of women as having religious roots. By the late nineteenth century, when Stanton first published *The Woman's Bible,* the influence of Darwin's thought was also paramount in American culture. Stanton had likely been influenced by the more relativistic view of culture that Darwin's work inspired. Darwin's work had encouraged the development of anthropological relativism — a system of thought that saw ideas in society as emerging from culture. Such a belief made it possible to doubt that the Bible had been divinely inspired. While Stanton herself seemed to be influenced by this developing social consciousness, other feminists of the period did not share her perspective.

The first publication of *The Woman's Bible* in 1895 (reprinted in 1898) reflected Stanton's belief that domination of women had deep ideological and religious roots. Other feminists, however, did not share her sense of its importance. Members of the National American Women Suffrage Association, with the exception of Susan B. Anthony and a few others, repudiated any connection with it (Hole and Levine 1971). After this, *The Woman's Bible* went into obscurity, not to be rediscovered until the 1970s during the second wave of feminism in the United States.

Historians of religion have since asked why Christianity was a basis for women's progressive movements in the nineteenth century when, in the twentieth century, Christianity is more often perceived as an enemy to feminists than a friend (Reuther and Keller 1986). The answer lies in observing the social transformations occurring in the nineteenth century. Throughout the nineteenth century, the process of industrialization meant that men had entered a new secular world. Even when women worked in the industrial sector, the cultural ideology of the time defined women's world as being in the home. Religion was defined as a part of women's culture, although, for women, religion was one of the few dimensions of public culture in which they were allowed to participate.

By the early twentieth century, women's winning of the vote coincided with shifts in the boundaries between religious and secular domains. Women in the twentieth century entered the public world with men. Feminist social reformers of the 1920s and 1930s were more likely to use the language and philosophy of social science than they were to use theology to articulate their concerns. In the twentieth century, religion for women, if they believed it at all, had become more a private culture. At the same time, secularization resulted in the increasing conservatism of churches on women's issues. Churches, particularly Evangelical and Catholic churches, perceived secularism as having a pernicious influence on society. As a result, the churches politicized religious culture by using religious doctrine as a platform against women's equality and their social, legal, and reproductive rights.

By the time of the emergence of the second wave of feminism in the 1970s, women's religious roles had changed dramatically. Though many feminists were still active in religious life, their critical distance from religious institutions and their understanding of religion's deep sexist roots created a new basis for feminist criticism of religion and a new basis for feminist transformation of religious thought. We now look at the images of women in traditional religious texts and see the implications of these images for women's religious participation and faith.

Women, Religiosity, and the Church

Images of Women in Religion

Contemporary feminists have contended that the traditional view of women in most religious faiths idealizes and humiliates women (Daly 1978). Images of women in religious texts reflect and create stereotypical sex roles and legitimate social inequality between men and women. The New Testament of the Bible, for example, urges women to be subordinate to husbands, thereby fulfilling the assumed proper hierarchy of women as subordinate to men as men are subordinate to God. And Jewish feminists have also repudiated the traditional Jewish morning prayer in which a man blesses God for not creating him a woman, while a woman blesses God for creating her in accordance with his will.

The humiliation of women through religious texts is especially clear in religious depictions of female sexuality, defined by both Christianity and Judaism as a dangerous force to be feared, purified, and controlled by men. In Orthodox Judaism the myth that women are unclean during menstruation and seven days thereafter also reflects a negative view of female sexuality. Feminists see misogyny, meaning the hatred of women, depicted in the creation stories in male-dominated cultures which assign women responsibility for evil. In most of these legends women are seen as sexually alluring, curious, gullible, and insatiable. The biblical story of Adam and Eve is, of course, the classic example. Eve is depicted as cajoling Adam into eating the apple, thereby dooming them to live in a world of trouble and evil. And Hebrew myth depicts Lilith, the first woman as equal to Adam in all ways, but she refused to do what he wanted her to do. As this myth goes, in response to Adam's demands, the Lord created Eve from Adam's rib and made her inferior and dependent. One version of this legend in Hebrew tradition is that it is Lilith who persuades Eve to eat the apple from the Tree of Knowledge. Feminists suggest that this creates dual stereotypes of woman — one as evil, the other as gullible. Either way, women are defined through these myths as bad (McGuire 1981).

Religious Texts as Interpretive Documents

Whether or not a group of religious believers accepts their religious tradition as literally true and divinely ordained by God or whether the group sees their religious text as subject to interpretation influences the group's acceptance of transformed religious roles for women. Sociologists see all religious texts, including the Bible and the Torah, as cultural and historical documents. That is to say, sociologists see these texts as not containing truth per se, but as cultural artifacts — records of particular cultural beliefs, historical practices, and societal legends. The legends and beliefs that the texts communicate are the basis for what Durkheim called the "collective consciousness" of a society — the system of beliefs in a society that create a sense of belonging to the community and the moral obligation to live up to its demands. Thus, sociologists see these histories and texts as neither true nor false, but as symbols, powerful as they may be, of group belief and collective consciousness. Consequently, they are subject to interpretation and symbolic use by religious groups.

This is probably the most contentious point between sociologists of religion and those with strong and traditional commitments to religious world views. But it is well illustrated in the history of Christianity and its dual interpretation in the historical context of slavery. European explorers who traveled to African cultures in the sixteenth century encountered societies with religious practices and beliefs quite unlike the Christian traditions of western Europe. Their response to such practices was to define African people as heathens and savages who worshipped pagan gods (Jordan 1968). Europeans' identification of Africans as heathens led them to believe that black women and men were lustful, passionate, and sexually aggressive; this became the basis for racial and sexual stereotypes of black men and women. White beliefs in black men's sexual prowess created fears among white men that were the basis for extreme measures of social control throughout American history, including lynching. Also, the identification of black women as lustful established white men's belief in their rights to sexual relations with black women.

Christian beliefs played a central role in legitimating the exploitative treatment of African people. Slave traders and owners believed that blacks needed Christian salvation. Slaveowners saw their exploitation of slaves as the justifiable and necessary conversion of heathens, even going so far as to think that the slaves could not take care of themselves. Therefore, slaveowners reasoned, it was their Christian duty, though a burden, to care for the slaves (Genovese 1972).

While Christianity was a tool of the oppressing class, used to justify and legitimate the economic and cultural exploitation of millions of Afro-American slaves, it also reinforced slaves' own belief in their rights as human beings. As a result, Christianity provided the basis for slaves' political resistance to exploitation. The slaves came to believe in the Christian values that slaveowners taught them and, therefore, continued to believe in their own humanity and their rights to social justice. So, while Christianity was interpreted by slaveowners to justify slavery, for the slaves Christianity was a source of salvation.

Understanding the relationship between Christianity, slavery, and emancipation also helps us understand why feminists who reject the misogynist traditions of religious beliefs and institutions sometimes also see Christianity as providing the theological and philosophical basis for advocating women's liberation. In the sections that follow we examine more carefully the role of women in religion and the new ways in which feminist theologians have transformed traditional theology to generate new meaning systems intended for the liberation of human beings.

Sex, Gender, and Religious Beliefs

As we have already seen above, studies show that women are more religious than men, both in expressed religious faith and women's participation in worship services (Nelson et al. 1985). This difference has persisted over time, despite the fact that church attendance has declined in American society. In 1984, 57 percent of all Americans identified themselves as Protestant, 28 percent as Catholic, and 2 percent as Jewish. Four percent claimed other religious preferences and 9 percent said they had no religious preference (see Table 8-1).

Also, in 1985, 71 percent of the American population said they were members of a church or synagogue, though many fewer said they had attended church within the last seven days, including 47 percent of women and only 36 percent of men (Gallup Poll, December 22, 1985). Since more people report church membership in polls than the churches themselves report to data-gathering agencies, poll data are not totally reliable. Nonetheless, the poll data indicate the public importance people attribute to religious affiliation; they are also likely to be a sound measure of where people place their religious identification.

In 1985, 66 percent of the public said that they have a lot of confidence in

TABLE 8-1   Expressed Religious Preference, by Sex and by Race, 1984

	Protestant	Catholic	Jewish	Other	None
All	57%	28%	2%	4%	9%
Men	55	27	3	3	12
Women	59	28	2	4	7
Whites	55	29	3	4	9
Blacks	82	7	—	3	8
Hispanics	18	70	—	2	10

Source: Gallup Report, *Religion in America 50 Years: 1935–1985.* Princeton, N.J.: Gallup Poll, May 1985.

the church as an institution (Gallup Poll, July 14, 1985); and women have more confidence in the church as an institution than do men. Furthermore, 61 percent of the public said they believed that religion could answer all or most of today's problems. This is an increase from 56 percent in 1984, although it is a significant decrease from the 81 percent who believed so in 1957 (Gallup Poll, May 30, 1985).

Clearly, despite the historical decline in religious faith and attendance at worship services, religion still plays a significant role in our society. Religious belief influences a wide array of other social attitudes and behaviors. As we have previously discussed, this is especially evident on matters involving sexual attitudes and behaviors. For example, a majority of men and women who say that religion is very important in their lives believe that premarital sex is wrong, while 80 percent of those who say religion is not very important to them also believe there is nothing wrong with premarital sex (*Gallup Poll,* 1985). In addition to sexual attitudes, religious belief and affiliation also affect a broad range of opinions on social and political questions, with those of the Jewish faith typically being more socially and politically liberal. Church attendance and fundamentalist Protestant religious identification also tend to preserve more traditional sex role attitudes while youth, labor force participation, and educational attainment contribute to more egalitarian views (Thornton, Alwin, and Camburn 1983). And religion influences the perpetuation of sex differences in occupational choices, with the most sex-segregated preferences appearing among males and females in religious denominations with the greatest degree of gender inequality in the church (Rhodes 1983).

Attention to women's religious beliefs shows, however, that women may have a slightly different understanding of religion than do men. The General Social Survey, a national opinion poll taken among American men and women in 1983, asked people to identify their images of God. The population as a whole ranked their images of God in the following order: creator, healer, friend, redeemer, father, master, king, judge, lover, liberator, mother, and spouse. But, on closer look, men were more likely than women to emphasize the paternal images of God (for example, father, master, king), whereas women were more likely to identify with the more feminine images of God (such as healer, friend, lover, mother, and spouse). And in recent years, the more feminine images of God have become more popular among the entire population, though for both men and women they are still secondary to paternal images (Roof and Roof 1984).

These data suggest that women's understandings of religion may differ from those of men and that women may adopt those aspects of religious belief that speak best to their situations (McGuire 1981). The data also raise the question as to whether women see themselves as their religion sees them. Although the traditional image of women in religious texts is one that sees women as more passive, docile, and pious, women may be more active agents in the construction of their religious identity and beliefs than has typically been assumed. Though sexist images in religious thought remain, it may well be that women adapt them to their own circumstances, indicating that women's religious faith is not as passive or meek as the images in religious texts suggest. Such a perspective sees women not as mere victims of religious and gender roles, but as active agents in constructing their own religious world views.

Some suggest that this is less true in evangelical denominations and sects that cling to the most traditional views of womanhood. During the 1970s and continuing into the 1980s, there has been a dramatic resurgence of traditional evangelical Christianity. Evangelicals, popularly known as "born-again Christians," are those who claim to have been born again through conversion, who accept Jesus as a personal savior, who believe the Scriptures are the authority for all doctrine, who feel urgency in spreading their faith, and who claim to have had a dramatic witnessing of the presence of a divine spirit (Flowers 1984; Pohli 1983). By 1984, 22 percent of the American population identified themselves as evangelical Christians, an increase from 17 percent in 1981. The resurgence of this movement has created a consequent rise in the political power of this group. In the national population as a whole, slightly more women than men identify themselves as evangelical Christians; women are 62 percent of all evangelical Christians (Pohli 1983). Though the vast majority of evangelical Christians are white (74 percent), 36 percent of all nonwhites are evangelical Christians, compared with 16 percent of whites. Also, compared with the rest of the national population, evangelical Christians are less educated, older, and more likely to live in small communities. Thirty percent of those who have completed only grade school are evangelical Christians, 19 percent of those with high school diplomas, and 12 percent of those with college degrees. And 22 percent of those over the age of 50 are evangelical Christians, compared with 13 percent of those between the ages of 18 and 24 (Gallup Poll, July 7, 1980).

Careful examination of the world views and social attitudes and experiences of women in the evangelical churches finds that women's opinions in these faiths are "received ones," meaning that women are more likely to internalize religious views imposed by others. Studies of evangelical women find that becoming an evangelical Christian involves the narrow constriction of women's world views and opinions about the world and social issues (Pohli 1983). As we will see in a subsequent section, belief in evangelical Christianity among women is also a source for their anti-feminist political activities.

Women's Status in the Church

Women's Roles in Religious Institutions

Measures of church attendance and identification alone do not fully reveal the extent of women's religious participation. While observers can easily document that women have been excluded from positions of religious leadership, nonetheless it is women who constitute the vast bulk of church activity. Although many of these activities are difficult to measure numerically, observations of women's activities in religious organizations show that women run the church bake sales, dinners, and bazaars. Women also teach Sunday schools, babysit during religious services, visit the sick, join prayer circles, and arrange and staff church social events. In fact, women have historically been those who raise funds for churches and temples. And, although Orthodox Judaism defines women's religious role as centering on the home, in Reform temples women participate fully in the life of the temple and they engage in a wide array of volunteer religious, educational, and philanthropic activities (Hargrove, Schmidt, and Davaney 1985).

These activities in different religious organizations make important social ties for the women, but they also reflect a gender division of labor within religious institutions. In Protestant churches, women rarely preach, serve as trustees, control funds, or make decisions about the pastor, church, or church programs. In Roman Catholic churches, men have held all the positions of religious authority. This patriarchal structure is so pervasive that Roman Catholicism has even been described as a sexual caste system. This means that, despite the greater participation and faith of Roman Catholic women, the organizational structure, beliefs, ritual expressions, and prescribed norms of the Catholic Church are patriarchal (McGuire 1981).

Gender segregation in religious institutions is also evident in the non-traditional religious cults. In the Hare Krishna, Sikh, and Divine Light Mission religious cults, women's roles have been described as those of housemother. These cults are male authority systems where women serve the men in exchange for the rewards of emotional gratification. Moreover, the very intense nature of commitment in these nontraditional groups leads to extremely repressive aspects. Women in these cults typically have domestic obligations required as demonstration of their religious commitment and they are often expected to engage in sexual relations with the men of the cult. Whereas male devotees have access to positions of power as a means of bonding and sustaining their group affiliation, love and devotion are seen as leading to spiritual fulfillment for women in these movements. Moreover, women in these cults are often subjected to psychological, physical, and sexual abuse, as they are expected to be devoted to the religious leaders. Those who have studied women who leave such movements have noted, in fact, that the destruction of romantic idealism is a significant part of the women's decision to leave these movements (Jacobs 1984).

Despite the patriarchal structure of religious institutions, women develop organizational and leadership skills through their work in religious institutions. And, though their contribution is often trivialized, there is a heavy dependence on women's labor in religious organizations. However, in most churches and temples, it seems that women are in the background. They play the support roles, but not the leadership roles. The Catholic Church, for example, relies heavily on the work of nuns in the church, the schools, and the community, but, until 1970 when Vatican II modernized the role of nuns by allowing them to discard their habit and take on a more public role, nuns were cloistered and kept a silent majority in the Catholic Church. Now they are among the active women within the church and are urging that women be ordained and given access to real power in the Catholic Church.

Women as Clergy

The restriction of women to support positions in the church and their exclusion from policymaking has led women to organize for the ordination of women in all the major denominations. In 1970, among non-Catholic clergy, men outnumbered women clergy thirty to one, but between 1970 and 1980, female clergy increased by 146 percent. The main line Protestant denominations accounted for the largest share of this increase, though more women are also being ordained as rabbis. (In 1972, Sally Preisand was the first woman to be ordained as a rabbi.)

The entry of women to the clergy is not entirely new, though its magnitude is certainly unprecedented. But throughout the nineteenth century women were licensed as evangelists, and, beginning in the 1880s, black women began to press for ordination in the main-line Protestant denominations. The African Methodist Episcopal Zion Church ordained women as early as 1884 and the African Methodist Episcopal Church began ordaining women in 1948. But Harvard Divinity School did not even open its doors to women until 1955.

Of the 2,000 women ordained between 1977 and 1981, the United Methodist Church alone accounted for 1,000 women clergy (Carroll, Hargrove, and Lummis 1981). Holiness and Pentecostal denominations ordained fewer women during the 1970s, but they still account for the largest share of all clergywomen. The Salvation Army, for example, claimed a third of all women clergy; another third are found in Assemblies of God (Jacquet 1978).

Those who have examined women's role as clergy in Holiness and Pentecostal churches claim that the higher status of women as clergy in these churches stems from the faiths' rejection of the practices of the main-line churches, including their role definitions for women. Furthermore, the emphasis on charismatic or prophetic ministry, rather than the more "priestly" ministry of male-dominated religious institutions, means that the ministry is more open to women's participation (Barfoot and Sheppard 1980; Carroll, Hargrove, and Lummis 1981). However, as these churches evolve into more traditional and bureaucratic organizations and away from more spiritual symbolic roles, the proportion of women in positions of clerical leadership does decrease (Barfoot and Sheppard 1980).

Evidence of the increasing role of women in the clergy is also seen by the substantial increases in their enrollments in divinity schools. In 1972, women were only 10.2 percent of divinity students, compared with 25.8 percent in 1985. These increases reflect more than an increasing proportion of women as divinity students; they reflect large increases in the absolute numbers of women in divinity school (Baumgaertner 1986). By 1985, women were 20.8 percent of preordination degree students in divinity schools, while they were only 11.5 percent in 1975. Black and Hispanic enrollment in divinity schools has also increased. In 1972, black student enrollment was only 3.2 percent of the total; in 1985, though still a small proportion of all divinity students, black students had increased their enrollment to 5.4 percent, 26.4 percent of whom were women. In 1972, there were 264 Hispanic students in divinity school — a number too small to calculate except as a miniscule percentage of the whole. But by 1985, Hispanics were 2.5 percent of the total, 22.4 percent of whom were women. This is still a tiny proportion, but it represents an increase of 550 percent (Baumgaertner 1986). By 1980, a third of all students at the Reform Jewish seminary were women, indicating the greater acceptance among Reform Jews for women's participation in rabbinical roles.

Sociologists have pointed out that the more conservative denominations discriminate the most against women (Rhodes 1983). And, the more priestly the conception of the ministry in a given denomination, the slower to ordain women the denomination will be. Still, feminists point out that the role of a pastor is quite consistent with women's roles as nurturers and supporters. Some preliminary evidence shows that women in clerical roles are more democratically oriented and more likely to involve the laity in significant levels of church life than are men (Carroll, Hargrove, and Lummis 1981).

Still, in 1983, women were only 6.3 percent of the total labor force of clerics and theologians; other minorities (blacks, Hispanics, and Asians, including minority women) were also 6.3 percent of this labor force (Vetter and Babco 1986). And, although the number of ordained women and women enrolled in seminaries has increased, women who are ordained tend to be underemployed and paid lower salaries, and they are less likely to be considered for the better positions — as, for example, an assistant pastor who has responsibility for children's programs (Verdesi 1976).

In mainstream churches, resistance to women clergy stems from the fact that women clergy are perceived as a threat to organizational maintenance (Lehmann 1982). But sociologists have also argued that the receptivity to women clergy depends in large part on lay attitudes toward the changing role of women in society (Lehmann 1980). Thus, as the women's movement has generated changes in the public's perception of women's roles, the resistance to women clergy has eroded slightly over time.

Religion, Racism, and Social Change ⸺⸺⸺⸺⸺⸺

The Role of the Church in Black Communities

Within black communities, the church has historically provided a buffer against segregation, discrimination, and bigotry. Some sociologists have also suggested that black churches provide for the release of emotion that cannot be expressed in the dominant white racist society (Blackwell 1985). Most recognize that within the black community the church is, along with the family, the most important institution in black society. It is the one institution over which blacks have their own control (Frazier 1964) and it is an important source for social cohesion in the black community. Black churches are often described as the organizational and expressive core of black culture and community (Dodson and Gilkes 1986), and within the black community the church performs a variety of social and community functions (Blackwell 1985).

Black churches are instruments for the development of black leadership and they provide a cohesive institutional structure within black communities. They are also the basis for community action and act as charitable institutions on behalf of black people. Because of the churches' many functions in black communities, black ministers (and, when the ministers are men, their wives) play roles as both social workers and political, personal, and religious advisors. Moreover, the black church has a function of supporting education for the black community and being an institution for the transmission of community values, historically stressing the value of the family, mutuality, and responsibility. The educational function of the black church is illustrated by the fact that more than one-half of all black colleges are funded by religious bodies. The church in black communities can also be an agency for the development of black business ventures, especially well illustrated by the economic entrepreneurship of Black Muslims. Finally, the church also provides an index of social class within the black community (Blackwell 1985).

Women's Role in Black Churches

Within the black community, as in white communities, it is the work of black women that holds the church together. It is estimated that black churches are 75 percent female. And, in the Sanctified church, the term within the black community used to refer to Holiness and Pentecostal churches, women are 90 percent of the congregation. Women's activities are crucial to black churches, and Gilkes (1985) contends that all black churches have been influenced by the militancy of women in the Sanctified church. Gilkes also points out that historically men have rarely matched the financial contribution of women in the Sanctified church.

Black women, like white women, seem to have greater participation in decision making in churches with smaller, not larger, congregations (Grant 1982). And interviews with black male ministers reveal continuing prejudices against black women in the ministry, resulting in unfair expectations and unjust treatment of women ministers whom they encounter (Grant 1982). Thus, although black women's role in the church has been central, they too have been excluded from many positions of authority and leadership.

Gilkes's studies on the role of women in the Sanctified church gives us a detailed picture of black women's participation in religious activity and institutions. The Sanctified church elevates women to roles as heroines, both as spiritual and professional role models. Gilkes identifies a feminist infrastructure in the Sanctified church that has its origins in women's racial uplift movements of the late nineteenth and early twentieth centuries. She also shows that the collectivist orientation of these churches has emerged from the relationship of black culture and its churches to the dominant culture. They have rejected the patriarchal organization of major denominational churches which has, in turn, encouraged a cooperative model of gender relations and pluralistic political practices within the church (Gilkes 1985). In this sense, they provide a feminist model of institutional organization and practice for the larger society.

Religion and Social Justice

Black women's and men's religious experience also must be seen in the context of their culture and community (Dodson and Gilkes 1986), as the role of black churches is multidimensional and includes religious, as well as social and political, work. Because the central theme of black theology is liberation (Flowers 1984), black churches serve as meeting places for protest strategy and have been highly significant in the historical development of black protest. The liberatory function of the black church is evidenced by the fact that blacks define the education of both oppressed people and oppressors as central tasks of Christian missions. Black spirituals and sermons are full of protest symbolism. The musical ministries of black women have advanced and institutionalized their forms of creative expression (Dodson and Gilkes 1986). There is, in fact, enormous cultural significance to black church music, almost every popularly recognized indigenous musical style in United States has antecedents in the oral tradition of black worship services.

Despite the liberatory functions of the black church, sociologists have also shown that religion can serve as an "opiate" for social protest. In other words, sociologists describe black churches as both encouraging and discouraging social protest. Some sociological research has shown that, despite the connection of black theology to movements for social justice, there is an inverse relationship between religious piety and political militancy (Marx 1967).

Still, for racial and ethnic groups, religion is often the basis for group identity. For Jewish women and men, religious and ethnic identity are fused as a public and political culture. And, for native Americans and black Americans, religion is one way to affirm one's ethnic subculture, while creating a basis for political and social organizing. Once again we see that religion has plural tendencies. Religion is the basis for racial and ethnic identity and it provides an organizational basis for movements of social liberation. At the same time it has a conservative influence on those who are the most orthodox.

Religion as a Basis for Anti-Feminism _____

The New Right and Anti-Feminism

The rise of the New Right over the last several years has generated a new period of religious activism. The Right to Life movement and, in the 1970s, the Anti-ERA movement centered in part on deeply held religious beliefs and depended on organizational support and financing from many church organizations. In addition, recent attempts to ban feminist books (along with other books objectionable to the Christian right) from classrooms indicates that some aspects of religion remain powerful foes to women's liberation and the feminist movement. For example, a 1986 court decision in Tennessee ruled in favor of parents who objected to having their children learn from books in the public schools that showed women as engineers; the parents contended, among other things, that these books did not promote the proper role of women as being in the home (*New York Times,* October 24, 1986).

The New Right is a coalition of various groups from the religious and political right, the most well-known of which is Jerry Falwell's Moral Majority. In 1980 the Moral Majority alone had 400,000 persons on its national mailing list and a huge budget of $1.2 million. Activities of the New Right are also supplemented by the memberships and budgets of other groups, some of which have budgets exceeding $1.5 million. The National Right to Life Committee has over 11 million members (Conover and Gray 1983).

The religious right has been a major source for mobilization on anti-feminist activities. Those in the New Right see the church as the defender of public morality; they perceive feminism, liberalism, and humanism as threatening to Christian values of family life and as violating the hierarchy of God-man-woman. Women, they believe, should be subordinate to their husbands. So, for example, the Eagle Forum, a national organization of women and men headed by Phyllis Schlafly, define themselves as a group "who believe in God, Home, and Country, and are determined to defend the values that have made America the greatest nation in the world" (Eagle Forum, cited in Conover and Gray 1983:74). The National Right to Life Committee takes as its motto, "For God, for Life, for the Family, for the Nation."

The anti-feminist activities of the religious right have been particularly well organized in the campaign to stop passage of the Equal Rights Amendment and in the anti-abortion movement, but they are also opposed to reproductive freedom, sex education, and pornography; they support prayer in the public schools, preferred tax status for Christian schools, and other policies that would ensure women's subordination to male authority.

The New Right views the battle over family values as "the most significant battle of the age-old conflict between good and evil, between the forces of God and forces against God, that we have seen in our country" (*Conservative Digest* 1980:15, cited in Conover and Gray 1983). One of the reasons the New Right has been so politically effective is that it has established an organizational infrastructure through the support of Protestant and Catholic churches. The support of evangelical churches makes available a massive communication network through television preachers. And, in 1975, the National Conference of Catholic Bishops approved a document titled the "Pastoral Plan for Pro-Life Activities," which provided for the political implementation of the Catholic Church's position against abortion. Moreover, the religious appeal to a sense of urgency about their goals fuels the activism of New Right members by adding to their belief that they are acting in God's will.

Sociological and political scientists who have examined the New Right have investigated the extent to which religious faith predicts people's support for the New Right. One study of New Right activists found, for example, that those who oppose abortion and the ERA have more traditional moral codes, support traditional sex roles in the family, and place responsibility for women's status on individual women (Conover and Gray 1983). A survey of anti-feminist activists also showed that, of those opposed to passage of the Equal Rights Amendment, 85 percent believed it would result in unisex toilets and 90 percent believed it would lead to homosexual marriages, alter basic family structure, change relationships between the sexes, and result in women's being drafted (Tedin 1980). Membership in Catholic or fundamentalist Protestant churches per se does not predict support for New Right attitudes, but there is a strong relationship between church attendance in these groups and New Right attitudes (Tedin 1980).

The Abortion Debate: The Conflict of Religious World Views

One of the most active programs of the New Right has been its organized opposition to abortion rights for women. Spurred by the 1973 Supreme Court case *Roe* v. *Wade* (see Chapter 7), many women who had previously not been politically active were prompted into anti-abortion activism. These were predominantly women with high school educations (and occasionally some college), who were married, had children, were not employed outside the home, and tended not to have been politically active in other groups or unions. Most had not been active in the PTA, church groups, scouting, or other activities typically associated with their traditional homemaker roles. These are women who believe that men and women are intrinsically different and that women are best suited to raise children, manage homes, and love and care for their husbands. Men, on the other hand, they believe are best suited for the public world of work.

The sociological literature identifies several explanations for anti-feminist activities. Kristin Luker's work, based on a study of California pro-choice and anti-abortion activists, depicts the debate over abortion as a debate over conflicting world views. Anti-abortion activists tend to believe that giving women control over their fertility (through abortion or birth control) breaks up the set of relationships in traditional families, where women care for the home and children and men go into public work. Anti-abortion activists also define sex as sacred and are disturbed by social changes in values that secularize and profane sex. Unlike pro-choice women, they believe that one becomes a parent by being a parent and that the purpose of sexuality is to have children. Their world view also includes the idea that the availability of contraception only encourages teens to have sex; therefore, to halt teenage pregnancy and what they believe is immoral behavior, we should eliminate sex education and birth control.

The world view of pro-choice women, on the other hand, is one that sees women's control over reproduction as essential for women to have control over their lives. Pro-choice women do not see reproduction as the primary purpose of sex; instead, they think of sex as a means of communication between partners and, if they think of it as sacred at all, it is because they see sex as a mystical experience that breaks down the boundaries between self and other. Also, pro-choice activists see nothing natural about masculinity and femininity. Rather, they see persons and their sex roles as learned and emergent, just as they see parenthood as a learned role. To pro-choice activists, parenting means giving a child emotional, psychological, social, and financial resources, not just biologically bearing a child.

Pro-choice and anti-abortion activists differ not only in their world views, but also in their sociological characteristics. Pro-choice activists are better educated and less likely to be married than those against abortion. Anti-abortion activists have less income than pro-choice activists (whose income also tends to be their own). Pro-choice women are much more likely to be working in the paid labor force and, if married, their husbands also have above-average incomes. In fact, the incomes of pro-choice women place them in the top 10 percent of women earners, while those few anti-abortion activists who do work are situated in the lowest income groups and are employed in traditionally female occupations.

Luker (1984) finds that the single most dramatic difference between these two groups is in the role religion plays in their lives — a fact supported by other research (Himmelstein 1986). Three-quarters of the pro-choice people in Luker's study say that formal religion is either unimportant or completely irrelevant to them. Only 25 percent ever attend church, and these do only on occasion. In contrast, 69 percent of those opposed to abortion say that religion is important in their lives; 22 percent of them say it is very important. Half attend church once a week; 13 percent, more often. Only 2 percent of the activists opposed to abortion never attend church.

Eighty percent of the women active in the pro-life movement are Catholics, and many are converts to Catholicism. Only 1 percent are Jewish and 9 percent are Protestant; 5 percent claim no religion. On the other hand, 63 percent of the pro-choice women claim no religion, 22 percent report that they are vaguely Protestant, 3 percent are Jewish, and 9 percent say they have a "personal" religion.

Luker argues that those who are actively against abortion see a societal decline in religious commitment and, more broadly, a decline in the sense of a common community. They believe that the absence of belief in a Supreme Being leads to a "do your own thing" attitude, whereas the pro-choice world view is one centered around the belief in the highest abilities of human beings. The struggle over abortion, in Luker's thinking, is a struggle over the meaning of motherhood itself. She writes that abortion "strips the veil of sanctity from motherhood" (1984:205).

Luker and others depict anti-abortion activism and anti-feminism as stemming from the status anxiety some groups experience when social and economic changes in the society threaten their social and cultural status (Ehrenreich 1983; Luker 1984). Anti-feminism is not just seen as a direct function of socioeconomic variables like age, education, and class, but is explained by the fact that some groups are especially vulnerable to the social, cultural, and economic changes that feminism and the transformation of men's and women's roles in society have generated. Their anxiety about these threats to their status is the basis for their support of right-wing movements (Himmelstein 1986).

This helps explain a fact that has puzzled many—that so many of the activists in anti-feminist causes are women. While some suggest that women in these movements are the "footsoldiers," not the leaders, it is clear that women are a large portion of anti-feminist activists. Seeing their anti-feminist activities as a result of status anxiety explains why anti-feminism is more prevalent among women who are the most vulnerable to and dependent upon men. Their pro-family position is one that sees the traditional family, in fact, as a fortress that protects women from men's declining commitment and ability to meet their traditional breadwinner role (Ehrenreich 1983).

Religious activism has not, however, been restricted to the New Right. While most feminists do not express or act on strong religious beliefs, some have developed their feminist politics through religious faith. For them, while they have been critical of patriarchal religion and its subordination of women, their reexamination of religious faith has created the framework through which their feminist world view has been constructed. In the concluding section of this chapter we review the work of feminist theologians who are actively working to construct new forms of faith and spirituality that are intended to provide the grounds for women's liberation.

Faith, Feminism, and Spirituality

Feminism and Religious Reform

The feminist critique of religion has at its heart a deep-felt sense of injustice (Christ and Plaskow 1979). This is particularly evident in the personal accounts some feminist scholars have written of their experience in divinity school. Judith Plaskow, a noted feminist theologian, describes the reaction of her thesis advisor at Yale Divinity School when she said she wanted to do her thesis on theology and women's experience. "Fine," he told her, "it was a good subject as long as she dropped all the references to women" (Christ and Plaskow 1979:i–ii). Both she and Carol Christ, another feminist theologian and scholar, were told by divinity faculty that the history of Christian attitudes toward women was not an important area for study (Christ and Plaskow 1979).

Theologians like Christ and Plaskow nonetheless persisted in their studies of women and religion. The first feminist analyses of religion during feminism's second wave in the 1970s criticized the explicit statements of female inferiority found in religious texts, the subordination of women in the church, and the exclusion of women from ministry. Christian women, for example, rejected the biblical teaching that women must be subordinate to their husbands as indicated in, among other things, the passage in wedding ceremonies that women must obey their husbands. They also criticized the image of God as male and have developed new images for feminist worship. Feminists came to believe that the church and theology will only transcend sexist ideologies when women are granted full spiritual, theological, and ecclesiastical equality. And they are not hesitant to acknowledge the interest-laden character of feminist theology, since they have openly declared the commitments out of which it emerges.

However, beyond this reform position lies a deepening analysis of the androcentrism, or male-centered view, of traditional theological views. This developing analysis is one that is critical of the theological world view of biblical faith and that sees sexism in religion as integrally tied to the dualistic and hierarchical mentality of traditional Christian theology (Reuther 1979). From this perspective, feminist transformation of patriarchal religion will take more than eliminating or changing sexist images in religious thought and admitting women to positions of religious leadership. The more radical feminist critique suggests that the male models of patriarchal religions cannot be simply rehabilitated to include women. Instead, the radical perspective understands the exclusion and domination of women to be fundamental to the very nature of patriarchal systems of religious thinking. The radical view sees sexism as so deeply embedded in the theology of patriarchal religion that reforms alone could never create the postpatriarchal future that feminist theologians seek (Christ and Plaskow 1979).

This position in radical feminist theology sees the need for revolutionary changes in religious thought, practices, and organizations and refuses even to accept the possibility of the male messiahs of Christian tradition. Whereas many feminists believe that traditional religions can be reformed by identifying sexist language and symbols and giving women full status in places of worship, more radical feminist theologians say that women should simply discard patriarchal religious traditions and forge new visions of women's spirituality — ones that are distinctively based on women's experiences.

Radical Feminist Theology

Several themes emerge from this radical theological stance: that patriarchal religions rest upon and re-create the domination of women by men; that women, like nature, are degraded and seen as needing control; that patriarchal religion forms the basis for other patriarchal institutions; that patriarchal religion has emerged historically through the suppression of female power; and, finally, that spirituality based on women's experience is the only way of reclaiming a fully human faith and liberatory vision of the future.

Two of the most noted radical feminist theologians are Rosemary Reuther and Mary Daly. Reuther (1979) has articulated the feminist view that Christian theology is centered on a domination model. She argues that traditional Christian theologies depict the soul and spirit as opposed to the human body, flesh, matter, and nature. This world view sees human beings as standing between God and nature and teaches human beings that they must subdue the irrational desires of the flesh to spiritual life. This creates a model for domination — one that sees human life as dominated by God, just as some human lives are dominated by others. Furthermore, because Christianity depicts the desires of the flesh as needing suppression, the domination model of Christianity has justified the historical domination of those seen by Christians as more carnal (including Jews, blacks, and native Americans). Moreover, Reuther contends that Christianity encourages a world view characterized by dualisms — such as the ethnocentric "we/they" view of the world that sees one group as superior and all others as inferior and in need of salvation and civilization. Thus, the missionary spirit of Christianity feeds the historical development of racism and the development of imperialistic power by seeking to create a monolithic empire.

Similarly, Daly argues that the "widespread conception of the 'Supreme Being' as an entity distinct from this world but controlling it according to plan and keeping human beings in a state of infantile subjection has been a not too subtle mask of the divine patriarch" (1979:56–57). Unmasking the patriarchal character of religious traditions causes us to see the powerful alliance between religion and oppressive social structures. Patriarchal theologies have in this way directly contributed to the oppression of women.

This more radical feminist critique of patriarchal religion leads to more fundamental changes in feminist visions of faith and spirituality — ones that are stimulated by asking what it would mean if women's experience were the basis for theological and religious world views. Experience is the key term in this developing feminist analysis. Feminist religious scholars take experience to mean the fabric of life as it is lived. In keeping with the feminist practice of consciousness raising and defining the personal as political, they believe there is something unique about women's experience and that women's faith and spirituality should be centered on those experiences (Saiving 1979).

This has also led such thinkers to distinguish between religion and spirituality. They claim that religion is that which is historically associated with established and institutionalized structures and ideologies, whereas spirituality suggests a vital, active, and energizing interior perception of the power of being (Yates 1983). This vision of spirituality is exemplified in the frequently cited lines of Ntozake Shange's play, *for colored girls who have considered suicide/when the rainbow is enuf:* "i found god in myself/& i loved her/i loved her fiercely" (1975:63).

Because religion has such a deep hold on the human psyche, radical feminist theologians believe we cannot afford to leave it in the hands of men. They see that men's control of religion emerged only with the suppression of female power and symbolism through the historical demise of Goddess worship. They argue that there is nothing natural about patriarchal religion, pointing out that the introduction of male gods and messiahs occurs at specific historical points in the development of human experience and that, prior to the introduction of male messiahs, goddess worship was a nearly universal phenomenon. The earliest artifacts of human culture, they suggest, are female statues and symbols, indicating the awe our ancestors felt for women and their bodily mysteries (Spretnak 1982).

The creation of new symbols, legends, myths, and rituals centered on women's experiences is central to new forms of feminist worship. For contemporary women spiritualists, reclaiming the goddess has become symbolic of the affirmation of female power and the female body, the celebration of female will, and the recognition of women's bonds and heritage (Christ 1979). Positive attitudes about women's bodies are an essential dimension to this new feminist spirituality, and affirmation of the female body and the life cycle expressed in it have become the basis for new feminist rituals. Also, the positive value of female will is expressed by newly celebrated practices like women's spellcasting and witchcraft.

According to Christ, reclaiming goddess imagery is a way of acknowledging female power as beneficent and independent. This is, of course, in radical contrast to the patriarchal perception of women's power as inferior and dangerous. The significance of the goddess for reevaluating women's bonds and heritage is, according to Christ, that "as women struggle to create a new culture in which women's power bodies, will and bonds are celebrated, it seems natural that the Goddess would reemerge as symbol of the newfound beauty, strength, and power of women" (1979:285).

In sum, the emphasis in radical feminist theology is not just to point out the androcentric bias of traditional religious world views, but to fundamentally change theology and religion to represent women's experience in all its forms. Some have criticized radical feminist theology as reflecting a white, middle-class, and Christian or post-Christian perspective, and Jewish women have criticized some feminist theology for its anti-Semitic framework (Hargrove, Schmidt, and Davaney 1985). However, the many attempts to re-create systems of faith to acknowledge the presence and power of women are indicative of the far-reaching attempts of feminist thinkers to create new visions and world views that will provide the foundations for building a feminist society.

Summary

Religion is a powerful source for the subordination of women. At the same time, religion has historically been a powerful instrument for social change. For women, religion has a dual tendency to be both oppressing and potentially liberating.

Sociologists see religion as a system of beliefs and an organized institution that provide groups with symbols and concepts that define their world view and shape other social institutions. Religion provides group norms that influence the everyday behavior of members of a society. Religion is strongly associated with sexual attitudes and behaviors and can operate as a system of the social control of sexuality.

The burning of witches during the European Middle Ages represents the growth in the authority of the church and its takeover of women's traditional power. Women who were persecuted as witches were those who were sexual and religious deviants. In the United States, religious belief has played a strong role in the development of feminism. During the nineteenth century, women were believed to be more pious and spiritual than men and religion was used to justify their exclusion in the domestic sphere. Religion also was important to some of the early feminists, although others saw religion as a source of women's oppression.

Images of women in religious texts produce stereotypical sex roles and have defined women as subordinate to men. Whether a religious group defines its religious tradition as literal or interpretive is related to the group's acceptance of nontraditional religious roles for women. Christianity has historically been used to justify slavery and the sexual exploitation of black men and women. At the same time, Christian theology was used by blacks as the basis for strong beliefs in social justice.

Gender inequality in religious institutions has segregated women into the least powerful and influential religious roles, even though women are the majority of church participants and tend to be more religious than men. Women play a support role in most church activities. Religious beliefs influence a wide array of social attitudes and behaviors. Women are more likely than men to see feminine images of God. Evangelical Christianity defines traditional roles for women. Gender segregation in houses of worships for different faiths has given women secondary status in religion, though the number of women clergy in most denominations has increased in recent years. Black churches provide cohesion and fulfill important sociological functions in the black community. Black women's work in the church holds the church together.

The New Right has become especially politically active on anti-feminist issues in recent years. Anti-feminists in the New Right hold different world views about sexuality and women's role than do activists who are pro-choice on the issue of abortion. Religious identification is one of the major distinctions between those who are pro-choice and those who are against abortion.

Some feminist theologians have a reform perspective on religion. They believe that eliminating sexism in religious images of women in religious texts and admitting women to positions of religious leadership can transform religious institutions and belief systems. Radical feminist theologians have constructed new theologies that begin with women's experience and construct new rituals, legends, myths, and spiritual practices based on women's experience. Both reform and radical feminists see faith as an important dimension to the construction of a new feminist society.

CHAPTER 9

Women, Crime, and Deviance

Include Room – 272-?

Introduction

Sandra is a hustler. As described in Eleanor Miller's *Street Women* (1986), she is a white woman, 23 years old, who grew up in a strict family household. When she was 9 years old, her father, a heavy drinker, accused her of being a whore. His fury and her mother's passivity led her to run away from home. By the time she was 12, a juvenile court had labeled her "uncontrollable" and she was sent to a delinquent home for girls.

She repreatedly ran away from institutions in which she was placed and, as a young teenager, started working the streets as a prostitute. When one of her girlfriends was found dead, she started paying a pimp for protection. She used drugs with him, but when he was high, he beat her and the other women who worked for him. After beating one woman to death, he was given a life sentence. Sandra paid the maitre d' of a hotel so she could safely work the hotel as a prostitute. She also worked in a topless bar for a while, but her big success, in her eyes, came through an escort service she established with a female partner.

They accumulated a lot of money through their entrepreneurship and Sandra began hanging out with a gambler. When he was arrested, she and the woman working with her were also arrested and their attorney's fees wiped them out financially. Sandra went to work for a house of prostitution, where she earned money she sent to her boyfriend's lawyer. She then became involved with another man who was a heavy drug user and became a serious drug user herself. She is pregnant and in prison, having been busted for marijuana and carrying a concealed weapon (a knife).

She plans to enter the state university on her release from prison. However, she says she doesn't think she'll stop hustling. In her words, "If the opportunity comes up and someone offers me enough money, I'll do it. . . . I don't think I'll ever walk the stroll again, but I'll do anything else. If I have to feed my baby, I will, you know? I know I can. I know I can survive anywhere" (Miller 1986:54).

Is Sandra a serious criminal? Did she have other options for how she would support herself? What does her case tell us about gender relations between women and men? Can we imagine a society in which Sandra's life would be different? Is her case typical of female crime?

Her case indicates that patterns in female crime are strongly connected to gender relations in society. And, though Sandra is white, women of color are also quite likely to be in her position. What does this tell us about race, class, and gender in the commission of crime and the distribution of justice in this society?

This chapter begins with a review of sociological perspectives on crime and deviance, particularly as they have been developed to explain criminal and deviant behavior among women. Two sections follow that discuss women and social deviance and women and crime, respectively. As each of these sections shows, many of the assumptions made about female crime and deviance are based on gender expectations about women's roles in society. Furthermore, patterns of gender relations are also reflected in the actual crimes that women commit. The feminist movement has called attention to the fact that gender relations in this society generate a high degree of violence against women. The fourth section of this chapter reviews information on women as victims of crime and discusses the theoretical perspectives used to explain violence against women. Finally, women's position within the criminal justice system is discussed, particularly as the system treats women offenders. Throughout this chapter, we can see how crime is defined in relationship to gender and is also complicated by race and social class.

Origins of Deviance Theory

Female crime and deviance have only recently come to the attention of academic scholars. A few early studies (Lombroso 1920; Pollak 1950; Thomas 1923) of women's crime and deviance appear in the sociological literature, but most of them depict female deviance as rooted in their biological and psychological predispositions. Contemporary feminist research has taken a critical examination of these assumptions as a starting point for analysis. Examining these early assumptions, thus, introduces the contemporary issues surrounding crime and deviance among women.

Lombroso's work in the 1920s, although by now discredited, was one of the earliest studies of female crime. His highly racist and sexist ideas viewed crime as based on biological differences between women and men, whites and blacks, the fit and the unfit. Lombroso believed that crime represented the survival of primitive traits; his theory was explicitly linked to popular racist and sexist notions of the time (Higham 1965). He explained female crime by arguing that women (and nonwhites) are less highly evolved than white men and, thus, are more susceptible to primitive urges. He also depicted women as less varied in their mental capacities and, generally, more passive and sedentary than men (Klein 1980). As he said, "Even the female criminal is monotonous and uniform compared with her male companion, just as in general woman is inferior to man" (Lombroso 1920:122, cited in Klein 1980:78).

In Lombroso's work, the cause of crime is located within individuals and their biology, not within their social circumstances. W. I. Thomas, an early sociologist, paid more attention to the role of social circumstances in producing crime. Thomas's work on the significance of meaning in attributing deviance to persons is of great importance to sociological thinking, although his work on female deviance is seriously flawed. Like Lombroso, he traces female crime to biological differences between the sexes to deep-seated psychological "wishes" that are unique to young girls. In his early work, Thomas claims that females are biologically *anabolic* — motionless and conservative — whereas males are *katabolic* — destructive of energy, yet creative because of the outward flow of this drive. (As an aside, Thomas also sees monogamy as an accommodation to these basic urges because he believes that through monogamy women become domesticated and men become leaders!)

Thomas's later work (*The Unadjusted Girl,* 1923) contains an important sociological insight — that female delinquency is a normal response to certain social conditions. But he still emphasizes that social behavior is a result of "primary wishes" that are derived from biological instincts. He identifies these wishes as the desire for new experience, security, response, and recognition; for women, there is the added wish for maternalism. In Thomas's view, middle-class people are less likely to commit crimes because they are more likely to control their natural desires. But delinquents are driven to crime because they long for new experiences. Girls, in particular, he says, engage in deviance to manipulate others, and their maternal instincts lead them to crimes, such as prostitution, in which he claims they are seeking love and tenderness (Klein 1980).

In sum, Thomas attributes motivational differences between males and females to internal, even biological, differences between the sexes. Although this biological explanation for sex differences is inadequate (see Chapter 3), Thomas did recognize differences in the attitudes of males and females and attempted to use these differences to explain patterns of delinquency and crime. His work, though seemingly crude to us now, has left an important message for more recent sociological work.

He attempts to find a behavioral basis for sex differences in male and female delinquency, and he tries, even if unsuccessfully, to relate those differences to attitudes that we now see as reflecting sex role socialization. Whether patterns of female crime can be properly attributed to sex role socialization is an important question that we explore further in this chapter. But this suggestion opens the door for other sociological investigations.

The major problem in Thomas's work, other than the crude gender stereotypes he uses by seeing women as more manipulative, more emotional, and more desirous of love and tenderness than men, is that he portrayed sex differences as internal to individuals, not as a product of their social environment. But he had an important insight even on this point because he thinks that internal wishes and motivations can be directed by socialization and manipulation of the social environment. Thus, his work provides a foundation for the liberal tradition in criminology that sees individual rehabilitation as the best solution to problems associated with deviant behavior. The liberal solution "requires that individual offenders be treated as undersocialized, as not fully adapted to the social values of society which represent their interests, and ultimately as being 'sick' rather than inherently evil or rationally opposed to the dominant values of society" (Smart 1977:37). The efficacy of such a view can, in fact, be questioned, but no doubt it is fundamental to many of the rehabilitative programs and treatment modes of contemporary practitioners.

More recently, the work of Otto Pollak (1950) also provided the basis for early and sexist assumptions about female deviance. Like Lombroso and Thomas, Pollak traces women's deviance to their biological and psychological being; however, he reduces women's criminal behavior to sexuality and to what he assumes to be the natural character of sexual intercourse (Klein 1980). Pollak claims that the basis for female crime is women's passive role in sexual intercourse. According to Pollak, women are able to conceal their sexual arousal from men and because of this physiological manipulation, women become socially deceitful. His major concern with female crime is the "masked" character of female criminality; he argues that the real extent of female crime is hidden from the public's view. Women, he contends, are deceitful and duplicitous; he sees them as the masterminds behind crime, manipulating men into committing offenses while they remain immune from prosecution. Pollak sees women as liars and interprets the hidden nature of their criminality as a reflection of their cunning behavior (Smart 1977). Moreover, in Pollak's view, men have been so duped by women that they protect women through chivalry and thus fear to charge and convict them for their crimes.

Although the views of Lombroso, Thomas, and Pollak appear quite outlandish now, the issues they raised continue to be addressed in current research and theory. Many still assume that delinquency can be traced to different emotional states in men and women, and they have looked to sexual character as the root of female criminality. Some who interpret female crime as a rebellion against sex roles want to decrease women's crime by restoring them to their "proper" place in the social system (Klein 1980; Smart 1977). And there is even a revival of biological explanations of crime which, though resting on highly questionable suppositions, has received much attention in the public media.

Biological Explanations of Crime ──────────────

Wilson and Herrnstein argue that social scientists overly rely on social and environmental causes of crime and ignore genetic predispositions toward criminal behavior. They insist that sex differences in crime among men and women must be understood as a function of aggression, which they see as rooted in the hormonal constitution of the sexes. They write, "Knowledge has not yet advanced to the point where it can be said positively that human sex differences in aggression have been directly traced to differences in hormones. Yet, the evidence for some sort of connection is stronger than the . . . objections may suggest" (1985:119)

Why do women commit fewer crimes than men? In their words, "Our best guess centers on the difference in aggression and perhaps other primary drives that flow into the definition of sex roles" (1985:124). And, while they do admit that social and cultural arrangements may have some influence on the gender gap in crime, they see biological differences as establishing differences that go deeper than social structure. They write, "The underpinnings of the sexual division of labor in human society, from the family to commerce and industry to government, may not be rigidly fixed in the genes, but their roots go deep into the biological substratum that beyond certain limits they are hard to change" (1985:125).

Wilson and Herrnstein's work has been soundly criticized by other scholars for its simplistic view of biology and culture as opposing systems, its misuse of scientific research, its confusion of genetic correlates (such as sex and race) with genetic cause, and its omission of white-collar and corporate crime in their definition of crime (Kamin 1986). But the popularity of recurring arguments about the genetic basis for criminal behavior cannot be ignored. As we have already seen in Chapter 3, biologically reductionist arguments tend to flourish in periods marked by radical changes in traditional social relations. Biologically based explanations of female crime need to be understood in this political context.

Sociological Perspectives on Crime and Deviance _____

New research and theory on crime and deviance provide new directions for understanding the significance of gender in exploring criminal and deviant behavior. Several questions are the basis for this work, including some of the same questions asked by early theorists. Answers to these questions now typically take quite a different direction in relating women's and men's crime and deviance to gender relations.

One beginning question is, Do women commit less crime than men and, if so, why? Are there distinctive characteristics of female deviants? How has criminological research been influenced by sexist assumptions? Why is female deviance typically seen as sexual deviance and women's crime seen as caused by physiological differences or internal motivations?

From a feminist perspective, female crime and deviance must be seen within the context of societal gender relations; otherwise, any account of crime that is produced is liable to be misleading. Although feminists recognize that individual women may commit crimes or engage in deviant behavior, they see these acts as related to the status of women in society. Thus, any explanation of crime that views individual behavior as causally significant overlooks the more complex origins of deviant and criminal behavior. Moreover, feminist perspectives on crime and deviance are also beginning to see the influence of gender relations on men's criminal and deviant behavior.

From a feminist perspective, the traditional questions that sociologists ask about women's crime and deviance are incomplete. For example, prior to the feminist movement, few criminologists asked about the experience of women as victims of crime, and they did not inquire about how societal gender relations generate crimes committed specifically against women (such as rape, wife battering, and incest). In fact, traditional studies of women as criminals and deviants have largely been limited to topics that feminists do not see as crime and deviance, such as prostitution, teenage promiscuity, and lesbianism. As we have seen in discussing the meaning of work and families, feminist analyses and questions have also led us to reexamine the meaning of crime and deviance. The following sections discuss these concepts and theory and research about them more thoroughly.

Women and Social Deviance _____

Although deviance is a concept with many popular connotations, sociological definitions of deviance are based on three primary points: (1) deviance is social behavior that departs from conventional social norms; (2) deviance involves a process of social labeling; and (3) deviance becomes recognized within the context of social institutions that reflect the power structure and gender, race, and class relations of society. We examine each of these ideas in turn, noting also some of the common assumptions that sociologists make about deviant behavior.

Defining Deviance

From a commonsense point of view, we might think of deviance as behavior that is bizarre, unconventional, and perhaps hard to understand. But from a sociological perspective, this definition is inadequate and misleading. First of all, what is unusual in one situation may be quite ordinary in another; second, even the most extraordinary behavior can often be understood if we know the context in which it occurs. Thus, sociologists define deviance as behavior that departs from conventional norms, noting that norms vary from one situation to another. Consequently, sociologists see deviance as located in a social context. Knowing and understanding this context is essential to understanding deviant behavior.

Although deviance is defined as behavior that departs from conventional norms, deviant behavior, like conventional behavior, is often guided by norms and rules, both formal and informal. In fact, deviance may be practiced in subcultures in which the social norms of the group encourage members to engage in deviant acts. One example comes from the research on gang rape, which shows that violence escalates when there is peer pressure to show off one's "masculinity" through increased aggression and abuse of the victim (Brownmiller 1975).

Another commonsense definition of deviance is that it is behavior that people disapprove of. But this idea, too, is inaccurate because deviance is subject to social definition, and whether it is approved or disapproved depends upon who is doing the defining. Because deviance is situationally specific, it is sometimes difficult to distinguish deviant behavior from conventional behavior (Matza 1969). In fact, there is probably more overlap between deviant and conventional behavior than one might think. Most people engage in deviant behavior, sometimes on a regular basis. But whether they become identified as deviant may be a function of their social standing (including their sex, race, and class), the context of their deviant acts, and their ability to maintain a conventional identity.

For example, many would consider that the enjoyment of pornography is deviant behavior. It offends many people's moral sensibilities (including that of feminists, who see it as portraying women in a degrading and dehumanizing way). Yet, the easy availability of pornography, its widespread consumption, and its appearance even in the most respectable settings make it seem that pornography is a normal feature of everyday life. Moreover, whether one is perceived as deviant for reading or watching pornography depends upon one's social standing and the social context in which pornography is viewed. This fact is evident when we consider the deviant label attached to a frequenter of peep shows or pornography houses, in contrast to the socially legitimate label afforded to the young bachelor who keeps a copy of *Playboy* on his coffee table or bathroom reading rack. Moreover, when we analyze pornography as an economic industry, we see that its social organization is very similar (although perhaps more coercive) to that of other industries in which workers are exploited for profit and products are marketed by the use of women as sex objects.

Labeling and Social Deviance

This discussion brings us to the second major point that sociologists make about deviant behavior: Deviance involves a social labeling process (Becker 1963). One cannot be called deviant without being recognized as deviant, and sometimes persons become labeled as deviant regardless of whether they have actually engaged in deviant behavior. Becoming deviant involves societal reactions to one's behavior — or alleged behavior. The labeling perspective in deviance theory emphasizes that some groups with the power to label deviance exercise control over what and who is considered deviant. Police, courts, school authorities, and other agents of the state thus wield a great amount of power through their control of institutions. So, for example, social workers, psychiatrists, or other agents of the state who define a woman as mentally ill can have a drastic effect on her behavior, identity, and options.

Sociologists who work from the labeling perspective point out that in the absence of a deviant label, actual deviant behavior may have no consequences at all. But the process of being labeled as deviant may involve real changes in a person's self-image as well as his or her public identity. So, sociologists note that once one is labeled a deviant, it is likely that one becomes a deviant. But this new identity usually does not emerge suddenly or as the result of a single act. Instead, it involves a process of transformation wherein one adapts his or her self-image and behavior to the new identity being acquired (Lemert 1972). For example, in becoming a prostitute, a woman may slowly change her identity from a nondeviant status as a sexually active woman to a deviant status as a prostitute by exaggerating to herself that the exchange of sexuality for economic favors is typical of nondeviant women (Rosenblum 1975).

Deviance, Power, and Social Conflict

The labeling perspective helps us see that deviance occurs in the context of social institutions. Persons in these institutions have the power to label some persons as deviant and others as not. This fact is especially true to the degree that the official agents of these institutions carry sex, race, and class stereotypes or biases that make them more likely to discover deviance in some groups than in others. These agents include the police, judges, lawyers, prison guards, and others who may enter the official process of labeling deviant behavior (such as psychologists, psychiatrists, counselors, social workers, and teachers). Because these official agents of social institutions have the power to label some groups and persons as deviant and others as not, and because these institutions reflect the power structure and the systems of race, class, and gender relations in the society, deviance tends to be a label that falls most frequently on powerless persons in the society. Thus, the labeling of deviant behavior can be seen as a form of social control.

Sociologists who focus on deviance have suggested that it be studied from the point of view of the deviant actor (Becker 1963; Matza 1969). This method would allegedly prevent sociologists from seeing deviance only through official eyes and would create a more accurate portrayal of the deviant's social world. Many feminists studying deviance share this point of view, adding that, traditionally, female deviance has been viewed through male eyes.

Prostitution, for example, has traditionally been described in terms of male demands for sexuality and females' supply of this service (McIntosh 1978). Although this is an apt description of the economic nature of prostitution, it also makes ideological assumptions about both male and female sexuality. Women are depicted as merely providing an outlet for male sexual needs and remaining sexually passive, while men are defined as having greater sexual urges than women. Prostitution is a sex-specific crime that punishes women, not men, for not subordinating their sexuality to monogamous marital relationships (McIntosh 1978). Were sociologists to study prostitution from the point of view of the prostitute, other questions would likely emerge.

For example, we might ask what the typical relationship between pimps and prostitutes is and how prostitutes view their pimps. One study finds that prostitutes laugh at the notion of having a pimp and say that they only use men to give them back-up protection. The men, on the other hand, thought they were pimps, even though the women did not think so (Pottieger 1981). Another issue that might be studied from the point of view of prostitutes is how they define their sexuality. Young delinquent girls, for example, have a more differentiated set of sexual mores than the simple virgin/whore dichotomy that is usually imposed upon them (Wilson D.

1978). This fact suggests that prostitutes, as well as delinquent and other girls, define their own sexual codes of conduct and negotiate them in social interaction.

A feminist perspective on prostitution also encourages interest in the female subculture among prostitutes. Typically, this subculture is assumed to be competitive and distrustful (Bryan 1965); yet, prostitutes work together and are dependent on each other for safety and support. Instead of assuming that they exploit each other, we might ask how their female group culture is established and maintained (Millman 1975). One study finds, for example, that clusters of four to five call girls maintain emotionally and financially reciprocal relations with each other. An exchange of clients is necessary to cover appointments if they are busy, to provide more than one woman if needed for their clients, or to aid financially troubled friends (Rosenblum 1975). Contrary to the idea that prostitutes have weak and exploitative relationships with each other, this research discovers an essential network existing among these women.

Feminist Perspectives on Deviance

Feminist perspectives on deviant behavior are critical of traditional studies for their content, their omissions, their interpretations of female deviance, and even their assumptions about what counts as deviance. To a large extent, the study of female deviance has been ignored, making it easier for sexist interpretations of deviance to persist. When female deviance is studied, it is often relegated to a few categories of deviant behavior that evoke sexist stereotypes. Thus, studies of female deviance have typically been limited to behaviors that are linked with female sexuality (such as prostitution and promiscuity) or to behaviors seen as stemming from women's alleged inability to control their emotions (such as mental illness, alcoholism, and drug abuse). And interpretations of female deviance have been clearly tied to the sexual status attributed to women in this society. This tendency seems especially true when we compare the alleged defiance of women with that of men. A double standard of morality marks some behaviors as deviant in women that are not considered deviant when performed by men. A good example is the issue of teenage promiscuity — a value-laden concept, yet one that policymakers and official institutions take quite seriously. The double standard of morality marks promiscuity as a social problem only among young girls. Teenage boys are expected, if not encouraged, to be aggressive in their sexual encounters; girls who do the same thing are labeled as "loose" and are likely to be seen by officials as consituting a social problem.

The sexual status attributed to female deviants is also evident in the frequently made assumption (particularly among official agents of correctional and counseling institutions) that all female deviants are sexually deviant as well. For example, women junkies and alcoholics are frequently presumed to be sexually promiscuous as well and, in many jurisdictions, female delinquents charged with nonsexual deviant offenses may be routinely checked for virginity and/or venereal disease (Chesney-Lind 1977; Strouse 1972).

Another assumption that feminists criticize is the idea that females engage in less deviance and delinquency than do males (Cowie, Cowie, and Slater 1968). But if fewer females are detected, it may simply be because we assume that they are less deviant. Therefore, this assumption becomes a self-fulfilling prophecy. Moreover, if women are seen to be usually less deviant than men, then those women whose deviance is detected may be seen as more abnormal than their male counterparts (Smith 1978). This perspective would help explain the fact that when a woman is defined as deviant, more strict sanctions may be brought against her because she has greatly violated her gender role (Smith 1978).

Feminists have pointed out that those who study deviance usually choose topics that are exciting to them. Although they are not critical of this fact, they do point out that much of the research on deviance (because it is done largely by men) focuses on the most titillating aspects of deviant behavior (Millman 1975). Thus, much of the research on deviance (especially that of women) has a voyeuristic quality, particularly as it describes the intricacies of deviant behavior from the perspective of an outsider.

In their studies of deviant behavior, sociologists have often relied on ethnography. This is a descriptive method of investigation in which the recorder details all of the features of social organization of the people he or she is studying. Ethnographies have provided rich accounts of the everyday life of deviant actors because they are a good tool for observing the meanings and behaviors of deviant actors from their own perspective. But often, ethnographers overlook the fact that women occupy some of the same deviant scenes as men. Only recently, as feminists have sensitized researchers to the existence of women, have we begun to get accounts of the everyday activities of female deviants (Prus and Vassilakopoulos 1979). Such studies are valuable for their details of the everyday activities of deviant persons, but they seldom provide any explanatory connection between the individual and the social institutions that perpetuate this behavior.

In studying deviance, sociologists have also tended to ignore issues that may appear mundane but are important in establishing complete accounts of the social world of the deviant. For instance, few have considered the effect that deviance might have on the lives of those in the deviant's social circle (Millman 1975). It is often these people — the family and friends of deviant actors — who must accommodate to the consequences of social deviance (including social stigma, embarrassment, ostracism, or imprisonment). Because sociologists focus on the public aspects of deviance, they ignore its emotional dimension and the accommodations that friends and families make to it.

With regard to female deviance, traditional sociological interpretations have often rested on sexist assumptions about male and female behavior. Many traditional studies of female deviance assume either that female deviants have lost control of their emotions or sexuality, or that they are exploitive, impulsive, or "doing it all for love" (Millman 1975). In addition, female deviance is often equated with female sexual pathology. Thus, the causes of female deviance are often attributed to individual maladjustment or a poor family background. It is true that some female deviance (including sexual deviance) does involve the individual's psychosexual adjustment. Often, in fact, child abuse, particularly sexual abuse by the father or other male kin, results in damage to female self-concepts and sexual identities (Jaget 1980). Consequently, such experiences may provoke a woman to engage in deviant behavior. But these events in her biography (which are by no means true for all female deviants) are not always the sole or the primary cause of deviant behavior.

Routine engagement in deviant behavior involves embarking on a deviant career and, like other careers, involves opportunity and socialization into new roles, as well as some reward (both material and psychological) for doing so. Moreover, individual maladjustment should also be seen as originating within institutional patterns of a patriarchal society. The incest victim is abused, not because of her own psychological derangement, but because of the institutional structure of patriarchal families, where men can demand sexual services, where they can exert power and authority, and where deviant sexual relations can be hidden through family privacy (Herman and Hirschman 1977). Furthermore, when individuals seek assistance for psychological problems, other institutional features of patriarchal society may interfere. The preponderance of male psychotherapists and the sexist assumptions of clinicians, social workers, and juvenile authorities not only prevent positive solutions but may even create further problems for individual deviants. When official agencies are contacted for help, the likelihood is high that the deviant will acquire a new label (criminal, juvenile delinquent, alcoholic, or junkie), and this label will be seen as the problem to be dealt with. In consequence, the origins of the client's conflicts may be overlooked altogether, leading only to a further exacerbation of her problems.

In sum, explanations of female deviance have tended to be sex-specific, particularly because deviance in women, but seldom in men, is seen to emerge from problems in the woman's sexual identity or sexual behavior. This fact underscores the point that female deviance has traditionally been linked to female sexuality, as evident in explanations of female deviance as well as in the topics chosen for study. Nowhere is this tendency more clear than in traditional perspectives on female homosexuality — a subject that is almost always relegated to a deviant category.

The deviant label attached to lesbianism makes it appear that there is something perverted about loving persons of one's own sex. Much of the research on lesbianism and homosexuality assumes that this sexual preference is pathological. Consequently, the prevailing mode of explanation has been one of individual maladjustment. But lesbianism can just as well be seen as conscious resistance to conventional heterosexuality, by which women are defined as the adjuncts of men and female sexuality is seen as passive acquiescence to male demands. The volumes of research asserting that homosexuality needs correction are strong evidence of the compulsory nature of heterosexual institutions in the society (Rich 1980). Lesbianism and homosexuality are deviant, not because gay men and lesbian women are sick, but because they exist outside of the dominant expectations of a patriarchal and heterosexist society. It is the heterosexist structure of institutions that defines lesbians as deviant, invisible, and abhorrent. Inside lesbian-feminist communities, lesbian existence is viewed as a healthy response and a conscious resistance to patriarchal domination.

In conclusion, sociological work on female deviance is only beginning to challenge the sex-stereotypic assumptions that have guided earlier work on the topic. As research emerges from a feminist perspective, we are beginning to see new issues and new perspectives for investigating the social problems that female deviants face. From these revisions, feminists hope to develop more complete and more analytically correct accounts of the experience of female deviants.

Women as Criminals

Women's participation in crime has long been ignored by criminologists. Criminologists are now asking new questions about women's involvement in criminal behavior and its relationship to gender relations. The evidence shows that women commit much less crime than do men and, furthermore, that their crimes tend to be less serious than men's (Datesman and Scarpitti 1980; Simon 1975). However, women's participation in some crimes has increased in recent years, although not at the rapid rate implied by popular accounts. Three central questions asked in the research on women and crime are: Has women's crime increased and, if so, for what types of crime? Is the amount of female crime beginning to approximate the amount of male crime? How is female crime linked to gender relations, and have changes in traditional roles created more opportunities for women to commit crimes?

The Extent of Criminality Among Women

Available information on female crime comes primarily from official statistics (the FBI's *Uniform Crime Reports*), from self-report surveys, and from national victimization and crime surveys. Although each data source reveals different kinds of information, they give a consistent picture of female crime. However, since *Uniform Crime Reports* does not report race and sex simultaneously, it is not possible, using these data, to differentiate women's and men's crimes by race.

Data on arrests show that the proportion of women arrested (as a percentage of all arrests) has increased slightly over the last decade, but that the increase in arrest rates for serious offenses is caused almost entirely by women's greater participation in property offenses, especially larceny (Simon 1975; Steffensmeier 1981a). Arrest data must be interpreted with caution, however, since arrest rates are only a measure of enforcement, not the actual commission of crime. Apparent increases and decreases in crime among different social groups are as much an indication of the law-and-order mentality of the time (Curran 1984) as they are accurate measures of actual crime.

However, contrary to the sensationalized portrait of female crime drawn by the popular media, the proportion of arrests for women committing violent crimes has hardly changed since the 1940s (Simon 1975). Although the percentage increase of violent crime by women does exceed that of men (see Table 9-1), that is because the low absolute rates of crime by women in this category create small absolute increases into large percentage increases (Miller 1986). The proportion of violent crimes committed by women has remained about the same.

In contrast, the gap in male-female property crime rates has narrowed substantially since 1960, as arrest rates for property crimes have increased much faster for adult females than for adult males. Specifically, women make up about one-third or more of all those arrested for larceny, fraud, and embezzlement, although burglary and auto theft remain primarily male offenses (Steffensmeier 1981b). Based on arrest rates, larceny is the most frequent female crime. In 1985, larceny constituted over one-fifth of all female arrests (see Table 9-2). Criminologists point out that the vast majority of female larceny arrests are for shoplifting (Cameron 1964), although male shoplifters take more expensive merchandise (Cohen and Stark 1974). Horwitz (1986) also points out that shoplifting among women is influenced by peer group support and level of commitment to conventional morality, suggesting the influence of female subcultures, especially among the young, on patterns of women's crime.

Some have suggested that other property crimes, such as fraud and embezzlement, have increased for women because there are more opportunities for women to commit these crimes when their status in the labor

TABLE 9-1 Total Arrest Trends, by Sex, 1976–1985

	Women's Crime as Percentage of Men's		Women's Crime as Percentage of Total		Percentage Change 1976–1985	
	1976	1985	1976	1985	Men	Women
Total crime	18.8%	21.2%	15.8%	17.5%	+15.1%	+29.8%
Violent crime	11.7	12.2	10.5	10.8	+15.4	+20.0
Murder and nonnegligent manslaughter	16.9	13.6	14.5	12.0	+ 2.5	−17.5
Forcible rape	1.0	1.1	1.0	1.1	+33.6	+47.5
Robbery	8.0	8.3	7.4	7.6	+ 2.1	+ 5.9
Aggravated assault	15.1	15.7	13.1	13.6	+22.6	+27.8
Property crime	28.7	31.8	22.3	24.1	+ 3.1	+14.3
Burglary	6.1	8.3	5.8	7.7	−17.5	+12.0
Larceny—theft	46.6	45.1	31.8	31.1	+18.1	+14.0
Motor vehicle theft	7.7	10.2	7.2	9.2	−10.7	+17.4
Arson	12.7	15.5	11.2	13.4	+ 5.5	+28.9
Other assaults	16.5	18.4	14.1	15.5	+40.6	+56.9
Forgery/counterfeiting	42.7	49.6	29.9	33.2	+17.0	+35.9

Fraud	57.6	71.8	36.5	41.8	+47.8	+84.4
Embezzlement	38.4	60.2	27.7	37.6	− 1.0	+55.3
Stolen property buying, receiving, possessing)	11.6	13.2	10.4	11.7	+ 5.8	+20.6
Vandalism	9.1	11.1	8.3	10.0	+14.9	+41.4
Weapons (carrying, possessing, concealing)	8.8	8.4	8.1	7.7	+21.8	+15.5
Prostitution and commercialized vice	234.6	237.1	70.1	70.3	+68.6	+70.4
Sex offenses	9.6	8.4	8.7	7.8	+47.6	+30.2
Drug abuse violations	16.4	15.9	14.1	13.7	+26.5	+23.1
Gambling	11.0	17.9	9.9	15.2	−61.7	−37.3
Offenses against family and children	12.1	16.1	10.8	13.9	−29.9	− 6.7
Driving under the influence	9.1	13.2	8.4	11.7	+34.1	+94.1
Liquor laws	16.6	19.2	14.3	16.1	+39.5	+61.4
Drunkenness	7.7	9.9	7.2	9.0	−29.7	− 9.8
Disorderly conduct	20.4	24.0	17.0	19.3	+ 7.2	+25.8
Vagrancy	29.6	12.1	22.8	10.8	−10.7	−63.5
All other offenses, except traffic	17.5	18.3	14.9	15.4	+48.0	+54.6
Suspicion	16.6	18.1	14.3	15.4	−56.6	−52.7
Curfew and loitering	25.3	31.4	20.2	23.9	−33.0	−16.9
Runaways	134.5	135.6	57.4	57.6	−27.4	−26.7

Source: U.S. Department of Justice, Federal Bureau of Investigation, *Uniform Crime Reports, 1985.* Washington, D.C.: U.S. Government Printing Office, 1986.

TABLE 9-2   Total Arrests, by Sex, 1985

	Percentage of All Arrests		
	Total	Male	Female
Violent crime	4.2%	4.5%	2.6%
Murder and nonnegligent manslaughter	0.2	0.2	0.1
Forcible rape	0.3	0.4	*
Robbery	1.2	2.3	0.5
Aggravated assault	2.6	2.7	2.0
Property crime	16.5	15.1	22.7
Burglary	3.7	4.2	1.6
Larceny — theft	11.5	9.6	20.4
Motor vehicle theft	1.1	1.2	0.6
Arson	0.2	0.2	0.1
Other assaults	5.3	5.5	4.7
Forgery/counterfeiting	0.7	0.6	1.4
Fraud	2.8	1.9	6.8
Embezzlement	0.1	0.1	0.2
Stolen property (buying, receiving, possessing)	1.1	1.1	0.7
Vandalism	2.2	2.4	1.2
Weapons (carrying, possessing, concealing)	1.5	1.7	0.7
Prostitution and commercialized vice	1.0	0.4	3.9
Sex offenses	0.8	0.9	0.4
Drug abuse violations	6.8	7.1	5.4
Gambling	0.3	0.3	0.2
Offenses against family and children	0.5	0.5	0.3
Driving under the influence	14.6	15.6	9.7
Liquor laws	4.5	4.6	4.3
Drunkenness	8.1	8.9	4.1
Disorderly conduct	5.7	5.6	6.1
Vagrancy	0.3	0.3	0.2
All other offenses, except traffic	20.8	21.3	18.6
Suspicion	0.1	0.1	0.1
Curfew and loitering	0.7	0.6	1.0
Runaways	1.4	0.7	4.5
Total	100	100	100

*Less than one-tenth of 1 percent.

Source: U.S. Department of Justice, Federal Bureau of Investigation, *Uniform Crime Reports, 1985.* Washington, D.C.: U.S. Government Printing Office, 1986.

market improves (Simon 1975). The evidence shows, however, that although women are approximating men in terms of total arrests for the category of fraud and embezzlement, fraud accounts for the largest percentage of these arrests (Datesman and Scarpitti 1980). Most women arrested for fraud are involved in small-profit offenses such as minor confidence games, welfare fraud, or being an accessory to fraudulent business practices (Hoffman-Bustamante 1973)

Women do account for 37 percent of all arrests for embezzlement, but for women, it is also largely a petty crime. Eighty-one percent of the thefts in this category for women are for sums of money between $1 and $150; male embezzlers account for 70 percent of the thefts over $1,000 (Datesman and Scarpitti 1980). Although changes in women's position in the labor force may explain some of the increase in female embezzlement, large embezzlement schemes are still mostly the work of men, who remain in higher-level occupational positions and, therefore, have more opportunity to engage in white-collar crime. Moreover, a study of employee theft has found that, in the large retail organization studied, males account for 40 percent of the labor force but 56 percent of the thefts. All of the persons in managerial positions committing thefts were males, whereas females accounted for a majority of the thefts in sales and clerical positions (Franklin 1979).

Causes of Female Crime

What, then, can we make of the relationship between female roles and their participation in crime? Many criminologists suggest that patterns of crime among women represent extensions of their traditional female roles. Activities such as shoplifting, credit card fraud, and the passing of bad checks result from the opportunities women have as consumers. Likewise, the crimes that are less frequent for women (such as armed robbery, aggravated assault, and major embezzlement) involve either physical strength or economic opportunities associated with male gender roles.

These associations have led some to conclude that women's involvement in criminal behavior changes when there are changes in their social roles (Adler 1975). Many have, in fact, attributed increases in women's crime in recent years to the development of the women's movement. Adler argues that shifts in sex roles make women more willing to participate in crime and that this explains recent increases in crime among women. Simon (1975) says, on the other hand, that objective changes in women's situation, particularly their greater labor force participation, make more criminal opportunities available to women. Is either of these a valid explanation of increases in women's crime?

To begin with, even with increased economic opportunity for women in the labor force, the vast majority of women remain in low-paid, low-status jobs. Thus, it is an exaggeration to say that women's opportunities for crime are related to women's rapid advancement in the labor force. Second, increases in female crime which show up in the arrest statistics do not necessarily reflect an increase in the actual extent of crime. Rather, these statistics may reflect an increase in the detection of female crime. This increased detection can occur in several ways.

It is possible that the feminist movement has created changes in public attitudes about female crime. So, although the amount of crime may remain the same, the police may be more likely to arrest women for offenses they commit (Datesman and Scarpitti 1980). A second possibility is that changes in the rate of female crime do not result from changes in sex roles per se, but instead from broad structural changes in the economy, technology, legal systems, and law enforcement practices (Steffensmeier 1981b). Greater reliance in the last twenty years on self-service marketing and the use of credit cards have increased the opportunities for crime for all consumers. At the same time, detection systems (including national information systems, technological surveillance, and an expansion of private security forces) have increased the amount of social control and law enforcement. Thus, "the greater willingness of business officials to prosecute, the trend toward computerized records, and improvements in the detection of offenses such as shoplifting, bad checks, credit card fraud, and forged prescriptions would also tend to increase female, more than male, arrests for larceny, fraud, and forgery" (Steffensmeier 1981b:63).

Eleanor Miller (1986) makes the most compelling and reliable argument about the causes of women's crime. She reminds us that increases in crime among women in recent years have been almost entirely in property crimes. Rather than attributing the causes of women's crime to the women's movement and the changes it engenders, she argues that the women's movement coincides with (and, in fact, stems from) other structural changes that best explain women's criminal behavior as well.

Those who have associated increases in female crime with the rise of the women's movement do so because the women's movement and increases in women's crime can be marked in the same period of time. However, according to Miller, those who argue that the rise of the women's movement coincides with the rise in female crime overlook one important fact: that during this period (the mid to late 1960s) unemployment for women relative to men was at its highest. Like Simon, Miller looks to increases in the labor force participation of women as explaining increases in female crime, but Miller's argument is fundamentally different.

The increased labor force participation of women beginning in the mid-1960s was especially marked among better-educated women with children who had never worked before. Yet occupational segregation depresses the wages of all women workers and raises their unemployment rate (Niemi and Lloyd 1975). Consequently, the entry of older white middle-class women into the labor force may disadvantage minority, poor, and younger women at the same time that the unskilled, domestic, and laborers' jobs these women might have held are becoming more scarce. The effect is to create an underclass of women, for whom criminal activity is then the only means of supporting themselves and their children. This argument is also supported by historical evidence that there are significant increases in property crimes by women in periods of economic depression.

Miller also argues that women's crime cannot be understood separately from the crime of the men for whom they often work. Her research on female hustlers shows, as we saw in the opening case of Sandra, that women's crime often benefits men — directly and indirectly. The street hustlers in Miller's study worked in the context of street networks, the controlling members of which are predominantly young black men with lengthy criminal records. For the men, further encounters with the criminal justice system will likely lead to long prison sentences. The men's major source of income derives primarily from the work of the women. Moreover, because the men have increasing contact with the criminal justice system, there are diminishing rewards for crime. The men's creation of street networks in which women do the crime and they take the money maintains men's advantage of criminal activity, without as great a risk of criminal prosecution.

Miller's explanation of female crime locates the causes of women's crime much more in the context of rising rates of poverty among women, thereby also supporting the long-standing association sociologists have seen between poverty, unemployment, and crime. Such an explanation of crime is particularly compelling because it explains women's and men's crime in the context of structural characteristics that involve class, race, and gender.

Defining Crime

Finally, feminist perspectives on crime, like the perspective of radical criminologists, see definitions of crime and the criminal justice system as systems of social control. What counts as crime is established by powerful persons in the society, who define some acts as criminal in order to protect their own interests (Chambliss and Seidman 1982; Quinney 1970). Thus, criminal acts are defined primarily as the crimes of the powerless, particularly crimes against property. Laws defining crime are made by the rich and politically powerful; at the same time, laws are created that allow for the legal acquisition of money by the wealthy.

From this perspective, we might ask why some behaviors are considered crimes and others are not. For feminists, this question is also important. For instance, as the example of abortion shows (see Chapter 7), historical changes in the law sometimes defined abortion as criminal behavior and other times did not. Moreover, these changes in abortion policy benefited medical doctors, who sought to gain control of the abortion market (Mohr 1978). Those who define crime do so for their own interests, and these interests have often worked against the interests of women. Consider, for instance, who would be considered criminal if our definition of crime included the control of another person's body. From this perspective, the normal practices of the medical profession might be considered criminal (see Chapter 7), as would the acts of corporations whose products prove unsafe to women's health. The act of rape provides another case in point because, even now, in a majority of states rape within marriage is not legally defined as rape.

Feminist perspectives on crime and gender take a more broadly based view of criminal behavior than do traditional perspectives in criminology. Whereas traditional criminological research generally asks who committed the crime and why, feminists see crime within a holistic context of social power, gender relations, and economic stratification. Thus, from a feminist perspective, it is inadequate to ask simply why women commit fewer crimes than men. Feminists have directed attention not only to the crimes committed by women, but even more to the crimes committed against women. A discussion of gender and crime is then incomplete without an inquiry about women as victims of crime.

Women as Victims of Crime

Statistics indicate that, overall, women are less likely to be victimized by crime than men; however, there are important qualifications to make about this observation. To begin with, national data on victimization rates come primarily from the National Crime Panel Survey, a project sponsored by the Law Enforcement Assistance Administration. The National Crime Panel Survey is based on a national sample of households and businesses in which persons are asked to report crimes by which they were victimized in the preceding months. Because the surveys include crimes against businesses, they may distort the gap between male and female victimization since men are more likely to own businesses. The surveys are intended to give a more complete picture of crime than analyses based only on crimes reported to the police.

But problems remain, including sampling errors that have been found in the data, the likelihood of faulty recall among some research subjects, and the fact that many crimes still might not have been reported to the survey interviewers (Senna and Siegel 1981). Particularly in the case of rape, it is quite possible that, if a victim never reported it to the police, she might not report it to a researcher either.

Moreover, the National Crime Panel Surveys are restricted by asking only about FBI index crimes — homicide and nonnegligent manslaughter, forcible rape, aggravated assault, robbery, larceny, burglary, and auto theft. The surveys omit homicide, because it is believed that this crime is accurately documented in official records. Even more important, when considering the issue of violence against women, is that the National Crime Panel Surveys include no information about wife beating or incest

—crimes against women that we know are largely hidden from public view (see Chapter 6).

Given these qualifications in the data, how can we characterize the victimization of women by crime? Women are less likely to be victimized by crime than men. However, there are some groups of women and some crimes in which victimization rates are higher for women than they are for men. Also, some women are more likely to be victimized than others, and these categories reveal how victimization by crime is related to the political and economic powerlessness of women in society (see Table 9-3).

Race, Gender, Class, and Victimization by Crime

Black women and women between the ages of 16 and 19 are victimized by crime more than are men in general. Also, women between 16 and 24 years of age are more likely to experience violent crime than are women of any other age. For crimes of theft, women between 12 and 15 are the prime targets, and the victimization rates are inversely proportional to the age of the victim (Bowker 1981b). Surprisingly, elderly women have the lowest rate of victimization by crime, suggesting that the amount of crime against the elderly of either sex has been grossly exaggerated in the media (Markson and Hess 1980).

TABLE 9-3   Crime Victimization, by Race and Sex, 1984 (Rate per 1,000 Persons)

	Male		**Female**	
	White	**Black**	**White**	**Black**
Crimes of violence	38.3	51.1	21.9	33.5
Rape	0.1	0.5	1.4	3.3
Robbery	6.9	14.9	3.3	9.2
Completed	4.3	11.3	2.3	7.0
with injury	1.9	4.2	1.0	2.3
without injury	2.4	7.1	1.3	4.7
Attempted	2.6	3.6	1.0	2.2
with injury	0.6	1.0	0.4	0.9
without injury	2.0	2.5	0.6	1.3
Assault	31.3	35.7	17.2	20.9
Aggravated	11.8	18.8	4.8	7.8
Simple	19.4	16.9	12.5	13.1
Crimes of theft	75.6	78.5	69.4	59.1
Personal larceny				
With contact	2.4	6.6	2.3	4.6
Without contact	73.2	71.9	67.1	54.4

Source: U.S. Department of Justice, Bureau of Justice Statistics, *Crime Victimization in the U.S., 1984.* Washington, D.C.: U.S. Government Printing Office, May 1986.

Regardless of their actual victimization, at every age women have a greater fear of crime than do men. Women's fear of crime increases with age, the most fearful being elderly women who live alone (Burkhardt 1977; Markson and Hess 1980). Fear of rape, however, decreases with age, and young urban women are the most fearful of rape (Warr 1985). Fear of rape affects women especially by restricting their freedom, as the fear dictates when and where they travel (Gordon et al. 1980; Warr 1985).

Generally speaking, black men and women are more victimized by violent personal crimes such as rape, assault, and robbery. Whites are more victimized by property crimes, as blacks and those of Spanish origin experience 15 percent less property crime. However, in recent years, crimes against black, Spanish-American, and white women have increased, and there is little reason to expect that this trend will not continue (Bowker 1981a).

Additional data on victimization rates underscore the idea that crimes against women reflect their powerlessness. Divorced and separated women are more likely to be crime victims than are married women. Women who have never been married are also victimized more than are married women (U.S. Department of Justice 1986). One should not take these data to mean, however, that married women are safe from victimization. Research on violence against wives indicates a high degree of violence within the privacy of the household (Dobash and Dobash 1979; Finkelhor and Yllo 1985). That these events do not show up in public records of crime should not lead us to the complacent conclusion that marriage protects women from crime and violence. Instead, empirical data on women and crime suggest that women's isolation (both inside and outside the home) is a common feature of crimes of violence against women.

Rape

The case of rape illustrates how isolation and powerlessness make women vulnerable to crime. In 1985, the Uniform Crime Statistics reported 87,340 cases of forcible rape in the United States. This is a rape rate of 36.6 per 100,000 women in the population, an increase of 38 percent since 1976. Rape is the fastest-growing violent crime and, because of underreporting, the FBI itself estimates that their official figures represent only one-fourth of the actual cases of forcible rape in that year. Moreover, the Uniform Crime Statistics on rape do not include those that result in death because these crimes are classified as homicides. Depending on the character of the incident, some rapes may be officially categorized as other forms of assault. The official statistics underestimate the actual extent of rape.

Specific data on which women are more likely to be raped show the connection of rape to women's status in society; women of the lowest status are the most vulnerable to rape. Victimization surveys show that black women are slightly more likely to be raped than white women and that divorced or separated women are much more likely to be raped than women who have never been married. Married women are much less likely to be raped than are divorced, separated, or never-married women. For all women, the rape rate is higher for those with incomes under $10,000 per year. Unemployed women and women living in households where they are not family members are seven times more likely to be raped than are wives. The rate of rape is also higher among women who head their own households and is directly related to the amount of time one spends in public places (Bowker 1981a; U.S. Department of Justice 1986). These data indicate that women who are alone are more likely to be raped, but they also show the connection between rates of victimization and women's status in society.

This information gives us a compelling picture of women's experience and its relationship to violence as a system of social control. Explanations of violence against women have usually suggested that its causes lie within the personalities and social backgrounds of individuals who commit violence. But the empirical data on women as victims indicate that the causes of violence lie, not in the characteristics of offenders, but in the social status of their victims. This is not to say that women are responsible for the violence committed against them. Quite the opposite; it locates the causes of violence within the political and economic status of women in society. This finding is revealed in a more detailed examination of explanations of rape, which can then be generally used to understand the causes of violence against women. Theoretical explanations of rape can be broadly categorized into four groups: psychological theories, the subculture of violence theory, sex role learning theory, and political-economic theory (Andersen and Renzetti 1980).

Psychological Explanations of Rape. Psychological theories of rape look to individual characteristics of personality maladjustment and psychosexual development as the origins of men's motivation to rape. Explaining rape as a matter of individual psychopathology conforms to stereotypic notions of rapists as psychopathic and deviant, but it does not fit the evidence. That is, empirical studies have been unable to find consistent personality differences between men who rape and those who do not (Albin 1977). Moreover, because the vast majority of rapists go unidentified by official agencies, there is a tremendous bias in such studies. The men included in the studies are those who are most likely to be detained or incarcerated for rape, and because these men are more likely to be black, Hispanic, or poor, studies of rapists tend to be both class- and race-biased. The suggestion in the psychological studies that only abnormal men rape thus carries an implicit class and race bias that defines these men as deviant and psychologically deranged. At the same time, such studies underemphasize the causal contribution of the social environment to the occurrence of rape.

Subculture of Violence. A second theory of the causes of rape comes from the subculture of violence perspective in criminology. This theory sees the social environment as the origin of violent behavior, but it is extremely biased by its differential emphasis on the behavior of black and working-class men. Susan Brownmiller popularized the use of the subculture of violence theory to explain rape in her best-seller, *Against Our Will* (1975). Adopted from Wolfgang and Feracuti (1967) and Amir (1971), the subculture of violence theory claims that violence is a cultural way of life in working-class and black communities; thus, its members come to take violence for granted, and it becomes a routine feature of everyday life. Male violence and aggression are explained in this perspective as adaptations to poverty, but the emphasis is placed upon the collective psychological maladjustment of minority and working-class populations. The problem with the subculture of violence thesis is not that violence in these communities is not a problem, but that this theory blames the presumedly pathological culture of these people for violent behavior.

Such a perspective begs the question of whether violence is more widespread in poor and working-class communities or whether it is just less hidden. Criminologists have frequently pointed out that the higher rape and violence rates found among minority and poor men largely reflect race and class discrimination in the criminal justice system. It is important to note that the most violent crimes (rape and homicide) show smaller race differences than the less violent crime of robbery (Hindelang 1978). This fact seemingly discredits the subculture of violence theory. Critics of this perspective also point out that violence is equally extensive in the dominant culture; it is just more easily hidden or legitimized as appropriately masculine behavior. In the end, the subculture of violence theory gives us an inadequate explanation of violence against women because, in its focus on society's underclasses, it does not explain why violence is also symptomatic of the dominant culture.

Gender Socialization as a Cause of Rape. The third perspective used to explain rape comes from sex role learning theory. Feminists have suggested that the causes of rape can be traced to the dominant culture and its emphasis on masculinity as a learned pattern of aggression and domination (Griffin 1971). Unlike psychological and subcultural theories that emphasize deviations from the mainstream culture, feminist explanations see rape as an exaggeration of traditional sex roles (Clark and Lewis 1977). Sex role socialization theory provides a perspective on rape that is sensitive to the variety of contexts in which it occurs. For example, a large proportion of rapes are committed by persons who are known to the victim, especially among white and young female victims (Bowker 1981a). Many of these violent events occur in the context of a date or some other relationship between the victim and the rapist. Researchers have noted that heterosexual relations typically involve some degree of seductive coercion on the part of the man, whereas women are expected to resist sexual relations (Clark and Lewis 1977).

There is support in the research literature for this explanation. Men who rape are more likely to have attitudes that see sexual aggressiveness as legitimate and the presence of sexually aggressive friends is also the best predictor of whether a man will act sexually aggressive (Adler 1985), indicating that men's image among other men is an important context for understanding their willingness to rape. This perspective also helps us understand the commonly reported finding that men who rape typically do not think they have done anything wrong. Convicted rapists typically justify rape in a variety of ways. They see the women as seductresses, think that women say no to sex when they really mean yes, think that victims eventually relax and enjoy the rape, believe that nice girls don't get raped, or see what they did as only a minor wrongdoing (Scully and Marolla 1984). Scully and Marolla's research on rapists also shows that men who rape see it as a means of revenge and punishment; their victims are thought to represent all women. Other rapists see rape as an afterthought, like a bonus after a burglary or robbery. Others define rape as recreational and say that it boosts their self-image (Scully and Marolla 1985).

From the perspective of sex role theory, rape occurs because men have learned that forcing women to have sex is legitimate and normal behavior. Understanding rape from this perspective helps us see how traditional gender reactions encourage the high incidence of rape in this culture. But we cannot limit our understanding of rape only to socialization and interpersonal relations. Although it is correct to see rape as connected to learned patterns in the culture, this perspective is inadequate without an understanding of how the cultural concepts of masculinity and feminity emerge from the status of women and men in the society.

Rape and the Political-Economic Status of Women. Feminists suggest a fourth perspective on rape that explains violence against women as founded on the political and economic status of women in patriarchal and capitalist societies. This political-economic theory states that women historically have been defined as the property of men in these societies. For example, the rape of black women by white slaveowners is evidence of the relationship between rape and the property status of women. Although women in contemporary society are no longer explicitly defined as the property of men, their use as sexual objects in advertising reduces their sexuality to a commodity. Moreover, images of violence against women in advertising and the popular media legitimate violent behavior against women and reiterate their status as sexual objects. To become an object is to become a piece of property, and this status, according to feminists, dehumanizes women and makes them an object for male violence.

Also, the fact that most rapists do not believe they have done anything wrong shows that violence against women carries some degree of legitimacy within the society (Clark and Lewis 1977). Those women who are perceived as the least valuable in the society are apparently most likely to be raped. This fact explains why black, poor, unemployed, and unmarried women are the most frequent victims of rape. The evidence is that high rates of poverty and divorce have the strongest relationship to the likelihood of rape (Smith and Bennett 1985). This is a suggestive finding since we have already seen the increasing linkage between divorce and poverty. But it also suggests the lingering consequences of the seemingly antiquated idea that women should remain the property of men.

Cross-cultural evidence discloses that the level of violence against women is lowest in those societies where women have the most social, political, and economic autonomy (Friedl 1975). In patriarchal societies, where men rule women, women lose their autonomy and are encouraged to be dependent on men. Research on rape victims shows that women who are not identified as belonging to a man (i.e., women who are alone in public, single, divorced, separated, or living with nonfamily members) are most victimized by rape. At the same time, as we have seen in Chapter 6, increasing social isolation seems to be a pattern in the phenomenon of wife beating (Dobash and Dobash 1979). And in the case of incest, the isolation of women in the privacy of family life keeps that act a closely guarded secret.

Feminist discussion and research on rape have shattered the myths surrounding the crime. Still, women are told by male experts and authorities that they should not resist, that giving in is safer than fighting to avoid rape. Bart and O'Brien's (1985) research refutes this. Their study of women who had been attacked shows that women who confront rapists, both physically and verbally, and who resist in a variety of strategies are most likely to avoid rape.

Violence against women is based on the economic and political powerlessness of women living in patriarchal societies. Understanding violence against women requires an analysis that shows the relationship of violence to the structure of major social institutions. In this sense, stopping violence against women is intricately connected to the liberation of women from oppressive social and economic relations.

This discussion of women and crime has concentrated on the commission of crime, its victims, and its perpetrators. But the question remains of what happens to women when they enter the criminal justice system either as victims or as defendants. A review of this issue reveals once again how women's experience within particular social institutions is affected by gender relations and the overall status of women in society.

Women in the Criminal Justice System _____

Women in the criminal justice system are treated differently from men both as offenders and as victims. Although justice is symbolized by a blindfolded woman, equality of treatment by the law does not exist for women (Moulds 1980).

Gender and the Courts

Research, particularly in the area of rape, shows that women victims are not equally credible before the law. For example, in many rape trials, the victim's past sexual history is often introduced to discredit her testimony against her assailant. Many states have reformed their legal statutes to make a woman's past sexual history inadmissible as evidence in a rape trial (Bienen 1977). Moreover, in spite of legal reforms, trial evidence indicates that lawyers' allegations about a woman's character may still be used to discredit her testimony or to make her appear to have an illegitimate claim (Randall and Rose 1981). Research also shows that certain characteristics of rape victims or a rape incident are likely to make the victim's testimony seem unsubstantiated. For this reason, police and prosecutors make judgments about the victim's credibility and the prosecutive merit of her case. If she had a prior relationship with her assailant, if she delayed reporting the crime, if she was under the influence of drugs or alcohol, or if she is a prostitute, a black woman, a welfare recipient, or a hitchhiker — her case may be seen as unsubstantiated (Clark and Lewis 1977; Wood 1981).

Recent research also shows that the racial composition of victim-assailant dyads is significant in understanding official reactions to rape. Research shows that black men charged with assaulting white women are not more likely to be arrested or found guilty than white men who rape white women, but, once arrested, they receive more serious charges than other defendants. Moreover, if found guilty, they also receive more serious sanctions. This research suggests that race of the defendant, taken alone, is insufficient in understanding the influence of race in the processing of rape cases (La Free 1980).

Women's perceptions of the criminal justice system clearly influence their willingness to report rape. They are much more likely to report rape when they see a high probability of conviction (Lizotte 1985) and when the rape fits prevailing definitions of a "classic" rape — that is, rape involving use of a weapon, rape by a stranger, rape in a public place, or rape with a break into the victim's home (Williams 1984).

Further research finds gender bias in the courts by looking at women as adjudicators and as defendants. The eighteenth-century legal scholar Blackstone, whose work provides the cornerstone for English and American law, thought women were rightfully prohibited from jury service because of the defect of sex. Though women are now being fairly represented on juries, until very recently they were severely underrepresented on juries and were often permitted exemptions from jury service simply because of their sex. Women are still selected as forepersons of juries much less often than would be expected given their numbers on juries. White men with college degrees, high-status occupations, and previous jury service are much more likely to be selected as jury forepersons (Hans 1986).

Gender bias in the courtroom also affects the disposition of jury cases, though not directly because of the sex of jurors. In cases of rape, jurors' beliefs about rape influence their willingess to convict or acquit. Men are more likely than women to believe in rape myths (Burt 1980), and women tend to have greater empathy for rape victims while men are more likely to see the defendant's point of view (Deitz et al. 1982). As a result, the greater representation of women on juries has resulted in a higher rape conviction rate in recent years. However, women and men do recommend similar punishments for defendants found guilty of rape (Hans and Vidmar 1986).

For women offenders who are brought before the criminal justice system, sexist stereotypes, prejudices against women, and a double standard of morality for men and women may influence the progress of their cases. Further, because women are often not taken as seriously as men in the society as a whole, it is not surprising that this bias appears in police decisions and courtroom trials.

There is an ongoing debate among criminologists as to whether notions of chivalry influence the disposition of cases involving female defendants. The results of research on gender bias and courtroom dispositions toward female defendants are mixed. Some researchers argue that notions of chivalry and paternalism result in more lenient treatment of women offenders than their male counterparts, while others find no difference by sex in judicial discretion (Curran 1983). Female defendants fare better than males in pretrial decisions in that they are more likely to obtain freedom prior to the adjudication of their case. However, scholars explain this as the result of a combination of factors, including the "bench bias" of judges (Kruttschnitt and McCarthy 1985).

Other research shows that women who display gender-appropriate behavior are less likely to be arrested than those who deviate from expected gender roles; however, race and age of the offender are much better predictors than demeanor of whether the person will be arrested (Visher 1983). It seems most reasonable to conclude that no single fact explains the disposition of courts toward female offenders (Kruttschnitt 1984). Moreover, feminists have argued that although paternalistic attitudes may appear to be benign, women offenders are actually harmed by them because they define women who break the law as needing more help than do male offenders. This appears to be substantiated by the fact that, when convicting for the same crime, courts apply more serious sanctions against females than males (Haft 1980). It is also evidenced by the fact that, especially among juveniles, young women are more likely to be incarcerated for behaviors that, when performed by young men, are not considered offenses at all.

Gender and Juvenile Justice

Among both boys and girls, arrest statistics indicate that there has been a decline in delinquency in recent years (Ageton 1983). Moreover, there is a somewhat wider gap in the amount of juvenile crime committed by young women and young men. Male juvenile delinquents are more likely to be involved in serious crime (including property and violent crimes) and in petty property crime, with the exception of larceny. Not surprisingly, arrest rates for female delinquents are highest for prostitution and running away (Canter 1982). And, as we have seen in Chapter 6, research also reveals a much higher rate of sexual abuse in the family among female delinquents than among males (McCormack, Janus, and Burgess 1986). Among young black women, there has also been a decline in juvenile offenses. In fact, young black women commit a smaller proportion of black crime among youth than white women do of the total of white youths' crime (Laub and McDermott 1985).

In the name of protection or guidance, female delinquents are much more readily incarcerated for noncriminal offenses than are male delinquents. Young women are far more likely to be arrested for what are called status offenses than are boys. These offenses include behaviors that are at odds with conventional standards of morality (running away, incorrigibility, waywardness, and curfew violations), as opposed to actual criminal offenses. One study reports that 75 percent of girls compared with 25 percent of boys are brought to the juvenile justice system for status offenses, not criminal behavior. Boys are far more likely to go to court for criminal offenses: burglary, larceny, and car theft (Chesney-Lind 1977).

Evidence from the juvenile system indicates that the court takes more severe sanctions against females than males for noncriminal status offenses, as girls are more likely to be held in jail or sent to juvenile detention facilities (Chesney-Lind 1981). Less severe dispositions are made, however, against girls than boys when criminal offenses are involved (Datesman and Scarpitti 1980). These differences hold for black juveniles as well, although there is somewhat less of a discrepancy in dispositions against black males and females when the charge is a criminal offense (Datesman and Scarpitti 1980).

The emphasis for juvenile treatment is on rehabilitation. In the case of girls, a frequent result is an attempt to bring them into line with traditional sex role expectations of passivity, submissiveness, conformity, and virginity (Haft 1980). In sum, sexual and moral misbehaviors are judged as more serious offenses for girls than for boys. This evidence indicates that the juvenile justice system operates *in loco parentis* and in accordance with traditional sex role stereotyping. For status offenders, the courts attempt to bring female youth into line with traditional moral standards for girls. For criminal offenders, it appears that women are still perceived as less serious, as not responsible for their behavior, and as less dangerous than men.

Women and Prison

Considering all women offenders, women who become incarcerated constitute a small proportion of all prisoners. The proportion of women prisoners has always been approximately 4 percent of the total prison population, but since 1975, the number of women in prison has increased rapidly (Bowker 1981). A national survey of women prisoners finds that they are relatively young; two-thirds are under 30 years old, and their median age is 27. Half of all imprisoned women are black. Over half have been on welfare, 60 percent do not have a high school diploma, and three-quarters of them have children (Leonard 1983). As with male prisoners, race and class biases in the criminal justice system operate to put more black and poor women in prison (Lewis 1981).

The family status of women prisoners shows that 20 percent are currently married, although almost two-thirds have been married at some time. Of the three-quarters who have children, three-quarters of them had children living at home at the time of their arrest. Forty percent were working at legitimate jobs just prior to their arrest (Glick and Neto 1977).

Studies of women in prison find that 43 percent have been charged with violent crimes (Glick and Neto 1977); the remainder have been sentenced primarily for property crimes (29 percent) and drug offenses (22 percent). Other reports indicate that many women prisoners are charged as accessories to crimes committed by men, and they point out that many imprisoned women are charged with relatively minor offenses, such as prostitution, shoplifting, and drugs (Shakur and Chesimard 1978). Also, although it is popularly believed that women generally serve shorter sentences than men, women are sentenced to longer terms than men for the same crimes (Haft 1980).

The situation within prison for incarcerated women is quite different from that of men. As with men, the conditions faced by women in prison often include inadequate facilities, poor health care, separation from their families, and insufficient jobs and educational training (Leonard 1983). But women's prisons are typically smaller than men's prisons and somewhat more informal. There is a tendency for social control to be less rigid in women's prisons. For example, women in prison are often made childlike by pseudo-motherly attitudes on the part of prison guards (Shakur and Chesimard 1978). But although the outward appearance of the women's surroundings seems more benign, there is still strict control of their behavior and movements.

The activities made available for women prisoners often reflect sex role stereotypes, especially in the area of job training. Whereas male prisoners may learn skilled trades that are higher paid upon their release from prison, women are typically encouraged to learn housekeeping, hairdressing, sewing, and clerical skills (Haft 1980). When they leave prison, these skills prepare them only for poorly paid and sex-segregated occupations. Consequently, upon leaving prison, many find that illegal activities are more lucrative, and they may return to crime. It should be pointed out, however, that the recidivism rate for women offenders is less than that for men (Datesman and Scarpitti 1980).

Health facilities in women's prisons are mostly inadequate, particularly in meeting needs specific to women's medical and reproductive care. Many women enter prison with existing medical problems — the most frequent being drug addiction, psychiatric illness, hypertension, and respiratory disease (Novick et al. 1977). Although medical services for male prisoners are also notoriously poor (Goldsmith 1975), what services do exist are set up to deal with men; as a result, women's specific needs (especially for gynecological and obstetric care) may go unheeded. Women's privacy in health care may also be ignored, as in the case of institutions that provide sanitary napkins free of charge but require inmates to pay for tampons (Resnik and Shaw 1981). Even though some women may remain sexually active in prison (through occasional releases or relationships that develop within the prison), it is significant that women may also lose the right to use contraceptives in prison. Many prisons will not permit women prisoners to use particular birth control devices (such as diaphragms and intrauterine devices). For women who are pregnant or become so in prison, long waits for medical evaluations may make abortion a high risk, and some facilities do not allow abortions at all. Should a woman prisoner carry through her pregnancy, she may not receive an adequate diet and prenatal care, and when she gives birth, she may be separated from her child. Nursing is then impossible and, at worst, the child may be placed in a foster home (Resnik and Shaw 1981). There is evidence that, in spite of these problems, women prisoners do attempt to meet their own health needs. They are critical of prison health facilities and, in some cases, attempt to implement home techniques of health care, including herbal remedies and self-examination (Resnik and Shaw 1981).

In sum, the conditions in women's prisons often lead them to fend for themselves. In the face of these conditions, research indicates that women's own social networks in prison are more supportive and affectionate than those formed in male prisons. Giallombardo's early study (1966) found that women in prison form pseudo-families, with prisoners taking different roles in relation to each other (such as mother, daughter, and sister). Her observation has since been replicated by others, although it may be more common among juveniles (Propper 1976). Many have interpreted this phenomenon as a reflection of the external values and cultural expectations that society has for all women. According to this argument, women in prison have external norms, values, and beliefs that define women in stereotypic family roles; these norms and roles are then reflected in prison subcultures.

An alternative explanation emphasizes women's active construction of a supportive subculture, rather than their passive acquiescence to external sex roles. Thus, women prisoners form a conscious culture of resistance like those of other oppressed groups who, in the context of domination, create and maintain networks of mutual support (Caulfield 1974). Cultures of resistance often take the form of conscious affirmation of cultural differences in the face of external domination. Although women in prison do not all come from similar cultural backgrounds, the subcultures they form in prison exhibit resourcefulness, flexibility, and creativity in the social relations they develop. The perspective of a culture of resistance emphasizes that they are not merely passive victims of their situation; instead, they develop adaptive strategies to cope with the conditions they face.

Part of this subculture is reflected in the homosexual relationships that emerge between some women prisoners. Compared with homosexuality among male prisoners, which tends to be founded on coercion or prostitution, women prisoners put more emphasis on love than physical sex in homosexual relations. Because lesbianism in women's prisons occurs in the context of love, sexual coercion is a rare event (Bowker 1981). Moreover, many loving relationships between women emerge in prison subcultures without an overt sexual relationship, whereas such relationships are less evident in men's prisons (Bowker 1981).

Summary

Female crime and deviance historically have been explained as the result of women's biological and psychological characteristics. Early sociologists looked to social circumstances as instrumental in producing crime. Sexist assumptions about women's character still permeate some explanations of crime. Biological explanations of crime, though unsupported by scientific evidence, have recently been revived.

Female deviance should be interpreted in the context of gender relations in society. Sociologists define deviance as behavior that departs from conventional norms and that is labeled deviant. Becoming deviant involves societal reactions to behavior. Deviance occurs in the context of social institutions that have the power to label some as deviant, others not. Feminist perspectives on social deviance look to the point of view of the deviant actor for understanding deviance. Feminists are critical of the sexual labeling of deviant girls. Feminists also point to a double standard in deviant behavior that sees as deviant in women behaviors that are not seen as deviant in men.

Data on crime show some increase in female crime, especially in the category of property crimes. Some attribute the causes of women's increased crime to the women's movement. A more reliable explanation sees the causes of women's crime as located in high poverty rates among women and the development of an underclass of women. Feminists see crime as involving a system of social control.

Women are less likely to be victimized by crime than men, except by rape. Women's victimization by crime varies by race, class, age, and marital status. Women's fear of crime restricts their freedom. Rape is the fastest-growing crime and reflects the powerlessness of women in society. Four perspectives are used to explain rape: psychological explanations, a subculture of violence theory, gender socialization, and the political and economic status of women.

Women in the criminal justice system are treated differently than men as offenders and as victims. Gender bias affects the courtroom process. Juvenile delinquency has been declining among young girls and young boys in recent years. Male delinquents are more likely to be involved in serious crime; female delinquency is primarily for status offenses. Women in prison are a small proportion of all prisoners. Conditions faced by women in prison include poor health care, separation from families, insufficient job training, and lack of educational opportunity. Women's subcultures in prisons reflect adaptive strategies designed to cope with oppressive conditions.

PART III

Feminism and Social Change

CHAPTER 10

Feminism and Social Reform: Liberal Perspectives

Introduction

The women's movement has been one of the most visible and influential social movements in recent history. There are probably few in this country, women and men included, who have not been touched by some aspect of the women's movement. And, though not as many persons call themselves feminists, polls do show that the majority of American people identify with many of the values and programs that the women's movement has encouraged and supported.

Sociologists define social movements as groups that act to promote or resist changes in society. Movements often emerge because of their members' perceived sense of injustice and their wish to effect changes that will redress such injustices (Turner and Killian 1972). Social movements involve the sustained activity of organized groups and they often include a network of organizations that, though they may have different goals and members, have a shared sense of belonging to the movement. Sociologists who study social movements also try to identify the societal conditions that foster the development of social movements. In the case of the contemporary women's movement, the development of feminism can be traced to the development of the nineteenth-century women's movement.

The Women's Movement ⎯⎯⎯⎯⎯⎯⎯⎯⎯⎯⎯⎯⎯⎯⎯

The growth of feminism in Western culture is tied to both intellectual and social changes in western Europe and the United States. As we can see later in this chapter, the social thought of influential European thinkers in the eighteenth and nineteenth centuries, including Mary Wollstonecraft, John Stuart Mill, and Harriet Taylor Mill, lay the basis for contemporary feminist political philosophy and social thought. In both Europe and the United States, the feminist movement emerged in the context of other historical changes of the nineteenth century, including geographic expansion, industrial development, expanding educational opportunities for women, and the growth of other social reform movements (Hole and Levine 1971).

American Feminism in the Nineteenth Century

In the United States, many of the early feminists were women who advocated the equal rights of women to acquire an education. One of the earliest advocates of education for women was Emma Willard, who campaigned actively for the establishment of colleges for women in the 1920s. Frances Wright also was an active spokeswoman for the establishment of equal educational training for women. Education for women, these women argued, would extend the "rights of man" to all persons and, therefore, make for general human improvement. As the result of their efforts, Oberlin College was the first to admit women in 1833. Mount Holyoke College opened in 1837; Vassar, in 1865; Smith and Wellesley, in 1875; Radcliffe, in 1879; and Bryn Mawr, in 1885 (Flexner 1975). Although extending education primarily to women of the upper class, the existence of these institutions nonetheless created an educated class of women, many of whom worked on behalf of women's rights.

But feminism did not just have its origins in the activism of educated white women. Its political origins also lie in the abolitionist movement of the 1830s and the efforts of black and white women and men to struggle for the abolition of slavery and women's rights. Charlotte Forten (1784–1884), a black woman reformer and abolitionist, was a founder of the Philadelphia Female Anti-Slavery Society. She tutored her three daughters, Margaretta, Harriet, and Sarah Louise, each of whom was also active in the abolitionist and feminist movements. The Grimke sisters, Sarah (1792–1873) and Angelina (1805–1879), were daughters of a slaveholding family who traveled and spoke out vigorously against slavery in the 1830s. Both the Grimke sisters and Sarah Forten were delegates to the first Anti-Slavery Convention of American Women held in 1837. The correspondence between Sarah Forten and Angelina Grimke records their friendship and their strong sentiments about both abolitionism and feminism (Sterling 1984).

Frederick Douglass, a former black slave and ardent abolitionist, supported women's rights for many years and was a strong supporter of women's suffrage. He and other male abolitionists believed that women's suffrage was necessary for the full enfranchisement of all citizens, though racism among white women and men in the women's rights movement forced Douglass and other abolitionists to subordinate the issue of women's suffrage to that of black suffrage (DuBois 1978). The abolitionists saw clear links between freedom for slaves and freedom for women, though as the women's rights movement developed, white women discriminated against black women in the movement and used racist appeals to argue for the extension of voting rights to white women.

From their work in the abolitionist movement, women learned how to organize a political movement. They challenged the assumption of the natural superiority of men and understood that suffrage was an important source for self-respect and social power. Historian Ellen Carol DuBois has concluded that

> abolitionism provided [American women] with a way to escape clerical authority, an egalitarian ideology, and a theory of social change, all of which permitted the leaders to transform the insights into the oppression of women which they shared with many of their contemporaries into the beginnings of the women's rights movement. (DuBois, 1978:32)

In 1840, a World Anti-Slavery Convention was held in London. The mere presence of women delegates at this convention generated excitement about the potential power of women, although women were relegated to the galleries and were prohibited from participating in the proceedings. Their exclusion from the proceedings generated an increased awareness among women of the need for a women's movement. When they returned to the United States, two of the women attending the convention, Lucretia Mott and Elizabeth Cady Stanton, continued to meet and discuss strategies for establishing women's rights. On July 14, 1848, they called for a Woman's Rights Convention to be held in Seneca Falls, New York, five days later. Despite such short notice, 300 men and women came to Seneca Falls and there approved a Declaration of Sentiments, modeled on the Declaration of Independence. The Declaration of Sentiments declared that "all men and women are created equal; that they are endowed by their Creator with certain inalienable rights; that among these are life, liberty, and the pursuit of happiness" (Hole and Levine 1971:6). Those attending the Seneca Falls Convention also passed twelve resolutions, one of which resolved to grant women the right to vote.

The Seneca Falls Convention has since been heralded as the official beginning of the women's suffrage movement in the United States. Other women's rights conventions were held throughout the United States, including one in 1851 in Akron, Ohio, where Sojourner Truth, a former slave, challenged the popular doctrine of women's delicacy and physical inferiority. She exhorted,

> Nobody ever helps me into carriages or over puddles, or gives me the best place—and ain't I a woman? . . . Look at my arm! I have ploughed and planted and gathered into barns, and no man could head me—and ain't I a woman? I could work as much and eat as much as a man—when I could get it—and bear the lash as well! And ain't I a woman? I have born thirteen children, and seen most of 'em sold into slavery, and when I cried out with my mother's grief, none but Jesus heard me—and ain't I a woman? (Hole and Levine 1971:191)

In the beginning, the women's movement was not just a single-issue movement. Feminists saw the issue of suffrage as one aspect of women's rights and advocated full equality for women. The momentum of the women's movement was stalled somewhat by the Civil War, but after the war, feminists worked hard to get sex added to the Fifteenth Amendment. The Fifteenth Amendment declares that the right to vote cannot be denied or abridged by race, color, or previous condition of servitude, but it did not extend to women—either white or black. Although feminists' efforts to get sex added did not succeed, this setback furthered their resolve for suffrage; in 1869, Susan B. Anthony and Elizabeth Cady Stanton organized the National Woman Suffrage Association (NWSA), which embraced the broad cause of women's rights. A few months later, Lucy Stone and others organized the American Woman Suffrage Association. This organization restricted itself more narrowly to the suffrage issue, trying to avoid more controversial issues like marriage and the church.

Suffrage, however, was not the only issue for which early feminists fought. The Temperance movement in the late nineteenth century was organized by women with a strong feminist consciousness. The motto of the Women's Christian Temperance Union (WCTU), under one of its early presidents, Frances Willard, was "Do everything!" Willard organized departments in the WCTU, each with its own programs of activity, including work in prisons, in kindergarten, and with the shut-in sick; other departments were concerned with physical culture and hygiene, prostitution, and motherhood. One department, the most effective, worked for suffrage. The Temperance movement pressed for laws restricting the sale and consumption of alcohol; women were encouraged to join because their status as married women gave them no legal protection against abuse or abandonment by a drunken husband (Flexner 1975).

In 1890, the American and National Women's Suffrage Associations merged to become the National American Woman Suffrage Association (NAWSA) and, by this time, the women's movement had become a single issue movement. Feminist efforts were devoted to gaining women's right to vote—a right they believed would open other opportunities and give women full rights as citizens. Shortly after the turn of the century, a second generation of American feminists appeared, including women like Carrie Chapman Catt, president of the National American Women's Suffrage Association. Also, Alice Paul, a young militant woman, became active in the suffrage movement. She formed a small radical group, the Congressional Union, to work solely on federal suffrage for women. The Congressional Union used tactics such as parades, mass demonstrations, and hunger strikes to further their cause. The combined efforts of the Congressional Union, the NAWSA, and local suffrage groups and activists were eventually successful. On August 26, 1920, the Nineteenth Amendment, guaranteeing women the right to vote, was adopted.

With the success of the suffrage movement, the women's movement lost much of its public momentum and, many say, lay dormant for the years between passage of the Nineteenth Amendment and the rebirth of American feminism in the 1960s. Others have shown, though, that feminist activities through this period did not totally disappear. Many women continued to pursue feminist goals in a variety of organizations and contexts; their work provided continuity between the early women's movement and contemporary feminism. While only a few organizations from the 1920s to the 1960s embraced explicitly feminist goals, the birth control and family planning movement, the settlement house movement, the establishment of organizations working to improve working conditions for employed women, and the founding of professional women's groups (including the National Federation of Business and Professional Women's Clubs, the League of Women Voters, and the American Association of University Women) set the stage for feminist developments in later years (Ferree and Hess 1985). Even in the post–World War II period, when cultural ideology strongly defended the idea that women's proper place was in the home, the National Women's Party, organized by Alice Paul, continued to fight for improving the status of women. The National Women's Party had one major plank in its platform—passage of the Equal Rights Amendment (ERA). Since 1923, when the ERA was first introduced in Congress, Paul and other members of this organization worked to garner support from other women's organizations, lobbied Congress, and sought publicity for the amendment. Most other women's organizations opposed passage of the ERA, believing it would legitimate protective legislation for women. Yet, despite their differing goals and philosophies, all of these organizations provided strong female support networks in the particularly hostile environment of post–World War II sexist ideology (Rupp 1985).

The Emergence of the Contemporary Women's Movement _____

Several transformations in women's roles occurring during the 1950s and 1960s influenced the development of contemporary feminism. These included changes in women's labor force participation, a change in women's fertility patterns, increases in women's educational level, and ideological patterns that glamorize women's domestic life. In the 1950s, women were idealized as happy housewifes whose primary purpose was to care for their husbands and children. In this decade, women were marrying younger, but they were also having fewer children because widespread use of contraception gave women control over their fertility. At the same time, white middle-class women were better educated and, although their education was intended to make them better wives and mothers, they were acquiring many of the same skills as men. For women in the home, technological changes in housework simplified physical tasks, but they increased consumption and new patterns of family life in automobile-based suburbs complicated the role of housewives. Although there was less physical labor associated with housework, housewives were supposed to be constantly available to their children. Whatever time was saved by labor-saving appliances was more than replaced by increased shopping, transporting of children, and nurturing of family members. The dominant ideology of housework and motherhood told middle-class women that their work in the home would bring them fulfillment and gratification but, in fact, many found the experience to be depressing, isolating, and boring.

This situation created a crisis for middle-class women in the family that was brought to the widespread attention of the public by the appearance of Betty Friedan's best-seller, *The Feminine Mystique,* in 1963. Friedan identified "the problem that has no name" for white, middle-class housewives — namely, that their isolation in the family was the source of their discontent. Friedan's book critically assailed the establishment (including mass advertising, women's magazines, and Freudian psychology) as contributing to women's problems. The chord she struck was soon repeated by a number of critical assessments of women's roles that appeared in academic and popular literature (Evans 1979).

In addition to experiencing a crisis in domestic life, women were, at the same time, appearing in the labor force in greater numbers. Throughout the 1950s, women from middle-income families entered the labor force at a faster rate than any other group. And they were working not just in the years prior to marriage, but in addition to their marriage and family roles. Although married women's work experience was defined in terms of helping their families, it broadened their horizons at the same time that it made them conscious of discrimination in the workplace. Thus, the decade of the

1950s and the early 1960s created a self-conscious cohort of women who lived in the contradictions of a society that idealized their role and promised them opportunity and gratification while it devalued their labor and denied them self-expression.

Professional women working within established institutions began pressuring politicians to recognize the problems facing American women. Thus, in 1961, although it was likely done for political reasons, President John F. Kennedy appointed a Presidential Commission on the Status of Women, chaired by Eleanor Roosevelt. The commission was charged with documenting "prejudices and outmoded customs that act as barriers to the full realization of women's basic rights" (Hole and Levine 1971:18) and with making recommendations designed to alleviate the problem. The commission report, *American Women,* was released in 1963, the same year that Friedan's *The Feminine Mystique* appeared.

The commission's report made a number of recommendations involving employment and labor discrimination. It was the basis for the Equal Pay Act of 1963, requiring that men and women receive equal pay for equal work performed under equal conditions (Hole and Levine 1971:28ff). Problems in enforcing this law and exemptions that were later attached to it prohibited the act from making the radical changes it implied. Thus, the commission's work had only a moderate effect. Moreover, the commission held steadfastly to the idea that the nuclear family was the foundation of American history and that women's role in the family was an invaluable and necessary resource. Although recognizing the contribution that women made to the home, the commission ignored the effects of home life on women that Friedan's book so strikingly portrayed.

These developments within both the government and the society provide the context for women to begin to question their traditional roles, but it remained for major social movements of the period to crystallize the vague discontent that women felt. Consequently, the birth of contemporary feminism must be seen as also stemming from the Civil Rights Movement and, later, the anti–Vietnam War and student movements.

Feminism and the Civil Rights Movement

The Civil Rights Movement was initiated within black communities of the South during the 1950s as a challenge to public racial segregation and white racial prejudice. But like the nineteenth-century American feminists who developed their feminist politics through participation in the abolitionist movement, white women working in the Civil Rights Movement soon saw their own oppression as similar to the racial injustices against which they were organizing. White women worked in the Civil Rights Movement out of their felt need to remedy the inequities of racial injustice, which they saw as a moral issue calling for their humanitarian participation. For white women and men, joining the Civil Rights Movement required a radical departure from the dominant beliefs and practices of white society. Their challenge to the status quo on racial issues was soon to influence the way they also interpreted other social issues (Evans 1979).

Between 1963 and 1965, white liberals from the North (especially male and female college students) went to the South in great numbers to assist in the civil rights struggle. The nonviolent direct-action projects in which they engaged (voter registration drives, protest marches, and sit-ins) forced them to encounter institutional racism and generated a new consciousness not only of racial issues but of the institutional structure of American society (Rothschild 1979). Most importantly, the Civil Rights Movement's emphasis on examining the roots of oppression caused many white people to look into their own experience so as to comprehend their relationship to dominant institutions. In so doing, white women in the movement began to see the origins of their own oppression — both as they had learned sexism in their own lives and as it was reflected in the public institutions of society.

In spite of a growing feminist consciousness, sexual politics within the Civil Rights Movement divided black and white women for two reasons. First, white women in the movement often proved their social liberalism by having sexual relations with black men. Although this action was encouraged by the permissive atmosphere in the movement, it discouraged solidarity between black and white women (Rothschild 1979). Second, both white and black women believed that the movement had failed to address the issue of sexual inequality. Black women in the Student Non-Violent Coordinating Committee (SNCC) wrote position papers protesting the fact that women in the movement were relegated to clerical work, were not given leadership and decision-making positions, and were belittlingly referred to as "girls." But white women, supporting the idea that the movement should be led by blacks, were reluctant to present their own analysis of sexism, and distrust between black and white women prevented their alliance against male sexism (Evans 1979).

Throughout the summers of 1964 and 1965, the position of whites in the Civil Rights Movement became increasingly precarious. Black disillusionment with white liberals and the ideology of black power eventually resulted in the exclusion of whites from SNCC in 1965. Thus, at the very time that women were becoming more conscious of their ties to each other, both white and black women ended up working in movements that were even more male-dominated and less open to an examination of sex inequality. For black women, the black power movement explicitly appealed to the power of black men and the role of black women as supporters of men. White women, after their exclusion from the black power movement, organized around antiwar and student issues, but in groups that were typically male-dominated. These movements once again relegated them to traditionally women's work and treated them as sexual objects for the pleasure of radical men. By applying the analysis of racial injustice they had learned in the Civil Rights Movement to their own oppression as women, white feminists emerged from the ranks of other activist groups (Evans 1979).

The feminism of black women emerges under similar conditions, though as in the nineteenth century, black women's feminist politics are much more situated in their anti-racist activities. But increasing educational levels and transformation of the employment status of black women throughout the 1960s and 1970s create the sociological conditions through which their evolving feminist consciousness can be seen.

Surveys of black women show that they are more likely than white women to hold feminist values (Hemmons 1980; Malson 1983) though they do not necessarily identify with the feminist movement. Also, black women's political consciousness is often situated in the context of their community work, where they identify themselves as working to empower the black community — through both professional and political work (Gilkes 1980). For black women, the concept of sisterhood has not been the basis for a political identity, as it has been for white women. For black women, political identity has more likely been formed around issue of race, and, as a result, they see feminist issues in a different context than do white women (Dill 1983). Thus, whereas white women see themselves oppressed as a sexual group, black women see race, class, and sex exploitation as intersecting in their lives.

Theory, Politics, and Social Change

By the late 1960s, feminism in the United States had developed as a full-fledged movement, with a variety of organizations, local consciousness-raising groups, and political strategies intended to advocate transformations in women's status in society. The feminist movement has evolved through two major branches — women's rights and women's liberation (Hole and Levine 1971). The women's rights branch of the feminist movement works from an "equal rights" strategy — a strategy of extending equal rights to women particularly through legal reform and anti-discrimination policies. From this perspective, the inequality of women is the result of past discriminatory practices and, thus, is best remedied by creating sex-blind institutions in which all persons, regardless of sex (or race, religious preference, sexual preference, or physical disability), are given equal privileges. The women's liberation branch of the feminist movement, on the other hand, takes a more far-reaching analysis, seeing that transformation in women's status requires not just legal and political reform, but radical transformation of basic social institutions, including, to name a few, the family, sexuality, religion, and education. These two branches of the feminist movement have different perspectives on women's status in society and, therefore, different strategies for social change.

To some extent, the separation between the two is for analytical purposes only since, in fact, there is significant overlap in the membership, organizations, activities, and philosophies of the two. But these different orientations also rest upon quite different assumptions that stem from the political and social theories upon which feminism is built. As we will see, the women's rights approach is more centered in the context of liberal political theory, while the women's liberation branch has its roots in more radical philosophical theory. In the remainder of this chapter, we examine the relationship between feminist politics and feminist theory and their implications for social change.

Frameworks of Feminist Theory

To many people, the idea of theory implies a way of thinking that is highly abstract and perhaps void of any connection to the "real" world. Many tend to think of theories as ideas that hold a certain degree of fascination for intellectuals, but that are not particularly relevant for the ordinary person's understanding of her life or the world around her. However, most of us do have ideas about the way society is organized. Thus, while we may not think of ourselves as theorists, we hold many assumptions, unexamined as they may be, about the organization of society and the possibilities for social change.

Sociological theory attempts to explain the relationship between social facts, like many of those we have observed in preceding chapters, and the social structure of society and culture. Feminist theory, similarly, attempts to situate the everyday events of women's and men's lives in an analysis that links our personal and collective experience to an understanding of the structure of gender relationships in society and culture. Feminists also claim that what we know, both intellectually and practically, is thoroughly infused with gendered assumptions about the character of the social world, its problems, its inhabitants, and its meaning.

The purpose of feminist theory is to help us understand the conditions we face in society and to help us envision the possibilities for liberating social changes. Therefore, theory is not just written and thought for theory's sake, but rather for what it suggests about political change as well. While theoretical analyses may seem complex and sometimes abstract, their purpose is to help understand the character of social structure and, therefore, the possibilities for social change. As we can see by examining the different frameworks of feminist theory and their relationship to feminist politics, different political frameworks in the feminist movement also rest on different theoretical assumptions. Although these assumptions are not always evident in political discourse, understanding them can sharpen political analyses and inform strategies for social change.

For example, since feminism has moved into the mainstream of American life, many people identify themselves as feminists with little understanding of the liberal framework they assume (Eisenstein 1981). Whether one assumes a liberal or a radical feminist stance, examining the intellectual roots of different feminist perspectives provides a more complete understanding of the assumptions of a given perspective, as well as the different programs for social change that given perspectives imply. Consequently, careful study of particular feminist frameworks enables us to answer questions about women's status in society more accurately and, therefore, allows for a better assessment of possible directions for social change.

The theoretical and political frameworks of feminist thought emerge from some of the classical traditions of social and political theory. However, as we will see, in considering issues about women's lives, feminists have revised some of these classical perspectives to better explain the position of women in society. But, like the intellectual traditions from which feminist thought stems, feminist theory is organized around varying assumptions about social organization and social change. These assumptions also guide the way in which we interpret the empirical observations of social research, such as that reviewed in earlier chapters of this book. Depending on the theoretical position used to understand data, the data may take on a different meaning. Facts do not usually speak for themselves; they are interpreted within the context of assumptions one makes about their meaning and their relationship to other facts. Theories guide this interpretation and, therefore, are an integral part of the process of knowledge construction.

To date, three major theoretical perspectives have been developed in feminist theory. They include liberal feminism, socialist feminism, and radical feminism. Liberal feminism emphasizes social and legal reform through policies designed to create equal opportunities for women. In addition, liberal feminism emphasizes the sex role socialization process as the origin of sex differences, thereby assuming that changes in socialization practices and the reeducation of the public will result in more liberated and egalitarian gender relations.

Socialist feminism is a more radical perspective that sees the origins of women's oppression in the systems of capitalism and patriarchy. Classical Marxists, in fact, see the oppression of women as stemming primarily from capitalism, in which women are defined as the property of men and the accumulation of profit necessitates the exploitation of women's labor. Socialist feminists have criticized traditional Marxism for reducing women's status to capitalism alone, noting that women are also oppressed in precapitalist- and noncapitalist-based social systems. Although maintaining the importance of class systems and the economic relations of capitalism in their analyses, socialist feminists see capitalism as interacting with patriarchy to create women's oppression.

Radical feminists, on the other hand, see patriarchy per se as the primary cause of women's oppression. They look to the devaluation of women in all patriarchal societies as evidence of the centrality of patriarchy in determining women's status. Within American culture, they trace women's oppression to the patriarchal control of female sexuality and male domination in social institutions.

Each of these perspectives is detailed more thoroughly. Liberal feminism is the subject of this chapter, and socialist feminism and radical feminism are discussed in Chapter 11. As we will see, no single perspective provides the singularly most correct analysis of women's place in society. As our review will show, each perspective has its own conceptual strengths and weaknesses and, thus, is able to answer some questions better than others. Together, these feminist theoretical perspectives provide a rich and engaging analysis of women in society.

The adequacy of each perspective should be assessed, in part, in terms of its ability to address several fundamental issues in feminist thought. Most importantly, because feminism purports to liberate *all* women, a sound feminist analysis must be able to address the relationship of race, class, and gender. The adequacy of a given theoretical and political framework must be judged according to the perspective on race and class (as well as gender) that it provides.

In addition to explaining how race, class, and gender intersect in women's experience, feminist perspectives must address some of the central issues that are encountered in thinking about women. These issues follow from the topics that have organized the preceding chapters of this book. They include understanding the issue of nature versus nurture (including the process of sex role socialization); interpreting women's status in work and the family; explaining the social control of female reproduction, health, and sexuality; comprehending female crime and deviance and their connection to gender relations; and relating the ideology of sexism to the social institutions in which it is produced.

The Liberal Perspective

The Liberal Basis of Modern Feminism

Our review of feminist theory begins with liberal feminism — the most mainstream feminist perspective. In political and sociological theory, *lib-*

eral has a particular meaning quite different from its common usage to mean open-minded, tolerant, or socially nontraditional. The specific philosophical meaning of liberalism lies behind the political liberalism of certain kinds of activist groups. Liberalism in this sense is characterized by an emphasis on individual rights and equal opportunity. Thus, liberal groups are those that attempt to reform social systems for the purpose of giving all groups equal opportunities.

The liberal politics of the women's movement include a range of organizations and issues, perhaps best exemplified by the National Organization for Women (NOW), founded in 1966. As a national organization, NOW works within the established economic and political systems to advocate for social changes on behalf of women. Other liberal feminist organizations, such as the National Women's Political Caucus and the Women's Equity Action League, also work within the existing political system through extensive lobbying and agendas for legislative reform on a wide range of feminist issues, including fair employment practices. These groups tend to be bureaucratically organized, involve formal leadership, and are constituted through official memberships.

The gains inspired by liberal feminism in recent years have made significant changes in women's lives. On issues ranging from equity in employment to reproductive rights, liberal reforms have resulted in increased opportunities for women and increased public consciousness of women's rights. The fact that liberal feminism works largely within existing institutions has, most likely, contributed to its broad-based support.

Because liberalism is such a popular strand of feminist thought and is fundamental to the assumptions of some feminist politics, it is important that we carefully examine its intellectual roots. The origins of liberal philosophy lie in western Europe and the societal transitions of the eighteenth and nineteenth centuries. By examining this context and the social thought produced within it, we will examine the theoretical tenets of the liberal perspective, as well as show its connection to the evolution of feminist thought. And, although we have already reviewed the growth of American feminism in the nineteenth and twentieth centuries, this historical analysis of liberal thought will give students a more detailed and analytical vision of the liberal basis of some feminist beliefs and politics.

The Origins of Liberalism

The origins of contemporary liberal feminism reach back to the seventeenth- and eighteenth-century Age of Enlightenment in western Europe (also known as the Age of Reason). This period fostered an array of political, social, and intellectual movements, most of them characterized by an explicit faith in the capacity of human reason to generate social reform. As the setting for the early philosophies of feminism, the Age of Enlightenment is noted for its libertarian ideals, its pleas for humanitarian reform, and its conviction that "reason shall set us free" (Rossi 1973).

The philosophy of the period provided the theme for major changes in Western social organization (including the French and American Revolutions), and it set the stage for the eventual development of social-scientific thought and the emergence of sociology as an academic field. The historical context of early feminist thought is found in conditions that inspired more general appeals to social reform through the application of human reason. It is worthwhile to examine some of the transformations that mark the period and that provide the historical arena for the emergence of contemporary liberal feminism.

Sociologists cite two notable developments that influenced broad-scale change in the West: the consolidation and expansion of a world system of capital (Wallerstein 1976) and a decline in the traditional sacred authority of religion (Nisbet 1970). The development of Western capitalism created new systems of inequality marked by the displacement of the poor from rural land and the concentration of wealth in the hands of the new capitalist class. The related developments of urbanization and industrialization also planted the seeds of the social problems that continue to confront us in the late twentieth century — urban crowding and the development of slums, pollution and waste, poverty, crime, and new tensions in family life. But in the Age of Enlightenment, political thinkers who observed these changes also delighted in the decline of the influence of the sacred authority of the church and the secular feudal state. The Enlightenment thinkers fostered the hope that the human ability to reason would provide societies with reasonable solutions to the new problems they encountered.

Thus, one of the central tenets of Enlightment philosophy and the political-social thought it inspired was that free, critical inquiry was to be the cornerstone for the future. At heart, the Enlightenment thinkers were optimists, and they seemed undaunted by the vast problems surrounding them. Although, in retrospect, they can be criticized for their naive faith in human rationality, their work is also praised for its emphasis on nondogmatic discussion and open inquiry (Hughes 1958).

Their libertarian ideals challenged the power of feudal elites and assumed that the future was in the hands of the masses. And, as they considered the development of history, they envisioned a decline in the brutal and "uncivilized" physical abuses of the past (deTocqueville 1945). They believed that the church, identified by most Enlightenment thinkers as the villain of past repression, would continue to decline in its authoritarian influence; modern society would instead be regulated by the rational construction of democratic government.

The influence of the Enlightenment extends beyond the eighteenth century, laying the foundation for the development of social science in the nineteenth and twentieth centuries and influencing later thinkers, such as

John Stuart Mill, in the nineteenth century. Sociology, in particular, is indebted to the Enlightenment for its emphasis on the application of reason and the scientific method to the solution of social problems. Early sociological thinkers, such as Auguste Comte (1798–1857) and Henry Saint-Simon (1760–1825), believed that social knowledge would take the form of social laws, telling us how the social world operated and, therefore, how we could engineer positive changes. The simplicity of their faith in sociology as the ultimate science is now apparent, but their influence on the positivist methods of sociology is immeasurable. The positivism they inspired and that others have developed assumes that the techniques of scientific observation in the physical sciences can be used in the discovery of social behavior. Their insistence on the application of sociological knowledge for engineering social change continues to influence the activities of modern social planners.

Liberal Feminism

The philosophy of liberalism emerging in this period rests on two central principles — one, the concept of individual liberty, and the other, an emphasis upon human reason as the basis for humanitarian social change. In liberal feminism, these philosophical ideals are the basis for the principle of equal opportunity and social reform. Consequently, much of the focus of social change among liberal feminist groups lies in the construction of legislation and in the regulation of employment practices. According to the liberal perspective, the obstacles to equal rights for women (and other groups as well) lie in traditional laws and practices that deny the same individual rights to women that men already have.

The liberal perspective assumes that persons can create humanitarian change through the use of human rationality. Injustice is viewed as due to irrationality and ignorance; reason and the pursuit of knowledge are believed to be the source of social change. Consequently, liberal policies for change rely upon a faith in the process of social reform. Liberal feminists' practical solutions to inequality include programs that prohibit discrimination (such as affirmative action and equal opportunity policies). Liberal feminism also seeks the reform of individuals through, for example, the resocialization of children and the relearning of appropriate social roles for adults. A central emphasis of the liberal perspective is that all persons' abilities are culturally learned; therefore, egalitarian gender relations will follow from relearning traditional sex role attitudes and behaviors.

The popularity of the liberal perspective makes it difficult to identify as a specific social and political philosophy. It is the philosophical backdrop to many contemporary programs for change, and it has been widely adopted by diverse groups working for legal and economic reform. Liberalism also encourages the acceptance of diverse life-styles, because it sees life-style as a matter of individual choice. Within the liberal perspective, persons and the societies they create should be tolerant and respectful of the choices persons make. Because persons have civil rights to exercise their freedom, societies should not erect barriers to individual liberties. The liberal perspective, like other feminist perspectives, rejects the conservative view that persons assume their status in life because of ascribed (biological) characteristics and attributes the different statuses that people acquire to social learning and the denial of opportunity. Thus, liberal feminists (along with other feminists) reject the conservative belief that women are bound to particular roles and statuses because of their biological capacity to bear children.

In sum, the liberal perspective of feminism assumes that the inequality of women stems both from their deprivation of equal rights and from their learned reluctance to exercise them. The goal of liberal feminism is equality — the construction of a social world where all persons can exercise individual freedom. At its heart, the liberal perspective is a philosophy based on the principle of individual liberty. In the liberal framework, every person should be allowed to exercise freedom of choice, unfettered by either public opinion or law. In effect, all persons should be given equal opportunities, and civil rights should be extended to all. The liberal feminist philosophy lies behind the call for reforms such as the Equal Rights Amendment, which, if it were enacted, would amend the Constitution to state: "Equality of rights under the law shall not be denied or abridged by the United States or by any state on the basis of sex."

An Enlightenment for Women?

The legacy of the Enlightenment, as it is recorded in the historical record, was a period characterized by the ascendency of reason over tradition, the outreach of humanitarianism to dispossessed groups, and general improvement in the condition of humanity. Therefore, the Enlightenment period is often interpreted as the origin of contemporary social thought.

We are not sure what the Enlightenment was like for women, because its recorded history has been largely that of men's accomplishments. We do know that women's historical experience differs significantly from men's (Kelly-Gadol 1976) and feminist historians have suggested that the Enlightenment is no exception. They would argue that the Age of Reason is a reference only to the reason of certain men; during this same era, women's work was idealized as belonging in the emotional world of the home. Nevertheless, women's labor (both in the home and outside of it) constituted a major part of the society's economic productivity. Most women still produced marketable goods in the home and, as factories became the site for production, women and children were employed for long hours at low wages.

Seen in the context of women's lives, the period of the Enlightenment takes on a different meaning. Both women and the working class seem to have been left out of the Age of Reason, since the intellectual movement of the Enlightenment was largely based on the thought of bourgeois white men. During this same period in the United States, most black women and men were still enslaved and, although slavery was one of the concerns of the men of the Enlightenment, histories of feminist thought rarely look to the thoughts of black women, slave or free, as an origin for early feminist work. Yet the development of feminist thought cannot be located exclusively in the Enlightenment. Black women such as Charlotte Forten, Maria Stewart, Sojourner Truth, and Ida Bell Wells articulated some of the early principles of feminist thought (Lerner 1973; Sterling 1984). Maria Stewart, a former servant to a clergy family in New England, was the first American woman to deliver a public lecture (in Boston on September 21, 1832). Though rarely recognized in the histories of feminism, her exhortations to women domestic workers and day laborers to improve their minds and talents which she saw as thwarted by women's servitude are clear and passionate feminist ideals. When she left Boston because of hostile public response to her work, she delivered a parting speech ardently defending the right of women to speak in public (Sterling 1984). To exclude women like Stewart and the many other black thinkers and activists of this early period from the history of feminist thought is to take white European and American philosophers as creating *the* history of feminism and to see black women's feminist ideas only as secondary or as a reaction to white thought (Gilkes 1985).

This interpretation does not mean we should disregard the influence of Enlightenment thought on the history of feminism, but it does cast this history in a different light. The legacy of the Enlightenment as the triumph of man's reason is a celebration of the growing preeminence at this time of men's rational power. Women during this period were identified with the irrational and emotional side of life. The ascent of rationality which the Enlightenment celebrates can then be seen as the ascent of male rational power over the presumed emotionality and inferiority of women.

This revision puts the thinkers of the Enlightenment period into a different context and also reveals different aspects of their work. Feminist historians who have studied the major Enlightenment philosophers (Rousseau, Diderot, and Condorcet, for example) conclude that, although the Enlightenment philosophers had the potential to decry the sexist ideas of sacred traditions, most of the Enlightenment thinkers ignored the revolutionary potential of their ideas for change in women's lives (Kleinbaum 1977). Still, the thinkers of the Enlightenment do have a strong influence on the development of modern feminism, although a more complete history of feminist thought, as it also evolves through the work of black women, has yet to be written. White and black women in this period, in both Europe and the United States, produced some of the earliest feminist work, although many of the white women never escaped the class-biased boundaries of their own experience.

Later (in the nineteenth century), John Stuart Mill was to become an exception among male philosophers, as he adopted a strikingly feminist position on the emancipation of women. Together with his collaborator, Harriet Taylor Mill, John Stuart Mill produced a series of essays that have now become the cornerstone of modern liberal feminism. (The Mills's work is studied later in this chapter.) The roots of liberal feminism in western Europe are first traced to the work of Mary Wollstonecraft.

Mary Wollstonecraft

Mary Wollstonecraft (1759–1797) provides part of the philosophical foundation for modern feminism. Her essay, *A Vindication of the Rights of Women,* first published in London in 1792, was so provocative that editions of it quickly appeared in Dublin, Paris, and New York (Poston 1975). So astutely did she outline the position of women that her essay was equally provocative to white middle-class women who discussed it in consciousness-raising groups in the 1960s and 1970s. Her words continue to inspire women almost 200 years after the original edition was published — a testimony to the influence Mary Wollstonecraft has had.

Wollstonecraft left her home as a teenager in 1778. Distressed by her father's excessive demands for obedience and her family's continued poverty, she wandered from town to town in the countryside of Wales and England (Rossi 1973). Her independence and self-sufficiency established a lifetime pattern of refusing to submit to authority — both in her life and in her writings. She later wrote:

> I will venture to affirm, that a girl, whose spirits have not been damped by inactivity, or innocence tainted by false name, will always be a romp, and the doll will never excite attention unless confinement allows her no alternative. Girls and boys, in short, would play harmlessly together, if the distinction of sex was not inculcated long before nature makes any difference. I will go further and affirm, as an indisputable fact, that most of the women, in the circle of my observation, who have acted like rational creatures, or shown any vigour of intellect, have accidentally been allowed to run wild. (Wollstonecraft 1975:43)

Her concern with subservience to authority recurs as a central theme in her work, and it is tied to her argument that learning and socialization are responsible for the formation of mind. Foretelling generations of feminists to come, Wollstonecraft argued that sex role characteristics were the result of education (used broadly in her work to mean all social learning). What appeared to be the natural weakness of women was the result of their lack of liberty and their dependence on men. She writes, "All the differences that I can discern, arises from the superior advantage of liberty, which enables the former to see more of life" (Wollstonecraft 1975:23). She goes on to say:

> It is vain to expect virtue from women till they are in some degree independent of men; nay, it is vain to expect that strength of natural affection which would make them good wives and mothers. Whilst they are absolutely dependent on their husbands they will be cunning, mean and selfish, and the men who can be gratified by the fawning fondness of spaniel-like affection have not much delicacy, for love is not to be bought; its silken wings are instantly shriveled up when anything besides a return in kind is sought. (1975:144)

Throughout her essay, Wollstonecraft emphasizes that blind submission to authority not only limits social and political freedom but also inhibits the development of mental reasoning. Like others in the Enlightenment, she imagines that the downfall of tyranny will occur as society becomes organized around the principle of rational thought. She writes, "Tyrants would have cause to tremble if reason were to become the rule of duty in any of the relations of life, for the light might spread till perfect day appeared" (1975:150).

Wollstonecraft equates the life of a dutiful soldier to that of a well-socialized woman:

> They both acquire manners before morals, and a knowledge of life before they have, from reflection, any acquaintance with the grand ideal outline of human nature. The consequence is natural; satisfied with common nature, they become a prey to prejudices, and taking all their opinions on credit, they submit blindly to authority. So that, if they have any sense, it is a kind of instinctive glance, that catches propositions, and decides with respect to manners but fails when arguments are to be pursued below the surface, or opinions analyzed. (1975:24)

More than other early white feminists, Wollstonecraft was sensitive to the issue of social class and the artificial distinctions among persons that she believed social class created. She directed her arguments especially to leisure-class women, for, she said, it is in that class that women are most dependent on men. She held in contempt the idleness of mind and attention to gentility that she believed wealth produced: "The education of the rich tends to render them vain and helpless, and the unfolding mind is not strengthened by the practice of those duties which dignify the human character" (1975:9). "The preposterous distinctions of rank, which render civilization a curse by dividing the world between voluptuous tyrants and cunning envious dependents, corrupt, almost equally, every class of people, because respectability is not attached to the discharge of the relative duties of life, but to the station" (1975:144). Although she recognizes that her observations are of a particular social class, she gives little, if any, attention to women of other classes and cultures. Thus, although her analysis is sensitive to the issue of class, she develops little perspective on the experience of women in the lower classes.

Wollstonecraft's outspoken portrayals of femininity, authority, and property relations earned her a lifetime of insults and insinuations about her bad character. Her contemporaries indexed articles written about her under the topic "prostitution" (Rossi 1973; Wardle 1951); more recently, her feminist beliefs have raised charges that she was "pitifully weak," "consumed with penis envy," and an "extreme neurotic" (Lundberg and Farnham 1947). These same critics wrote, "Out of her illness arose the ideology of feminism, which was to express the feelings of so many women in years to come" (Lundberg and Farnham 1947:145–159).

Wollstonecraft's work is a powerful criticism of the feminine role and its connection to power and social control. Her writing typifies the passion with which the Enlightenment thinkers pursued their condemnations of traditional authority, and it stands as one of the most persuasive accounts of the effects of women's subservience on their powers of thought, behavior, and self-concept. Her statement that more egalitarian education was needed to liberate women sounds as if it could have been written yesterday. It is a tribute to Wollstonecraft's own capacities for reason and her unchecked passion for justice that her words continue to inspire two centuries after they were written.

Harriet Martineau

Not long after Wollstonecraft's death in 1797, another woman was born who could appropriately be called the mother of sociology. Little recognized in contemporary histories of sociological thought, the Englishwoman Harriet Martineau (1802–1876) was one of the first to use field observation as a method for the development of social knowledge. She was the translator of Auguste Comte's (the father of sociology) *Positive Philosophy;* and, like her counterpart, Alexis deTocqueville, she traveled widely in America, producing a descriptive and analytic account of her observations in her book *Society in America* (1837). Her other book, *How to Observe Manners and Morals* (1838), is the first methodology book in sociology, for in it she details the method of participant observation as she developed it in her own work (Lipset 1962; Rossi 1973).

Like many of the early feminists, Martineau matched her concern for women's emancipation with her support for the American abolition movement. Her outspokenness on the slavery issue, coupled with her daring to travel as a single woman in nineteenth-century America, generated threats against her life. She was eventually forced to restrict her travels to the northern section of the country, but her analysis insists upon the right of women to speak their conscience. She wrote:

> The whole apparatus of opinion is brought to bear offensively upon individuals among women who exercise freedom of mind in deciding upon what duty is, and the methods by which it is to be pursued. . . . The reproach in all the many similar cases I know is, not that the ladies hold anti-slavery opinions, but that they act upon them. The incessant outcry about the retiring modesty of the sex proves the opinion of the censors to be that fidelity to conscience is inconsistent with retiring modesty. If it be so, let the modesty succumb. (1837:158–159)

And, as Marx and Engels were also later to proclaim, she wrote: "If a test of civilization be sought, none can be so sure as the condition of that half of society over which the other half has power" (1837:156).

Feminism, Race, and the Anti-Slavery Movement

The connection Martineau made between the abolition and feminist movements is indicative of the association that early feminists had with the anti-slavery movement in America. White women's dissatisfaction with their position likely led to their involvement in and appreciation for the abolitionist cause (DuBois 1978). Their involvement in the anti-slavery movement taught white feminists how to understand and change their situation.

Black women in the anti-slavery movement were more likely to put racial prejudice at the center of their feminist analyses. Sarah Forten, for example, writing in 1837, discussed the influence of prejudice on her life. She said,

> It has often embittered my feelings, particularly when I recollect that we are innocent victims of it . . . and [I] consequently seek to avoid as much as possible mingling with those who exist under its influence. I must also own that it has often engendered feelings of discontent and mortification in my breast when I see that many were preferred before me, who by education — birth — or worldly circumstance were not better than myself — their sole claim to notice depending on the superior advantage of being white. (Sterling 1984:124).

White women who worked in the abolition movement gained an understanding from black women of the concept of institutional power and adopted the political conviction of natural rights for all individuals, regardless of race or sex. But their analysis of racial and sexual oppression remained at the level of analogy. Early white feminists did not develop an understanding that took account of the historical specificity of the black experience in America, nor did they ever make the kind of analysis that could adequately account for class and other cultural differences among women (DuBois 1978). As a result, the liberal tradition of feminism that was established by leaders such as Elizabeth Cady Stanton (1815–1902) and Susan B. Anthony (1820–1906) began and continued with an inadequate comprehension of race and class issues in women's experience.

Martineau's own analysis of race and class is filled with contradictions. She appealed to justice and freedom, yet maintained the ethnic stereotypes typical of her period. She wrote:

> The English, soon find it impossible to get American domestic help at all, and they are consigned to the tender mercies of the low Irish; and everyone knows what kind of servants they commonly are. Some few of them are the best domestics in America; those who know how to value a respectable home, a steady sufficient income, the honour of being trusted, and the security of valuable friends for life; but too many of them are unsettled, reckless, slovenly; some dishonest, and some intemporate. (1837:171–172)

Martineau's work stands as an example of early white feminist thought, complete with its class and race contradictions. More generally, in spite of appeals to reason, free will, humanitarianism, and liberty, liberal feminism has never adequately addressed the issues of race and class inequality. In stating that racism and sexism are analogous forms of oppression, liberal feminism suggests an analysis that would take race, class, and gender into account. But as the concluding section of this chapter shows, this analysis is not provided by liberal white feminists, leaving the theoretical and political task of comprehending race, class, and gender oppression to other thinkers.

John Stuart Mill and Harriet Taylor Mill

No thinkers have been more influential in the development of liberal feminism than John Stuart Mill (1806–1873) and Harriet Taylor Mill (1807–1858). *The Subjection of Women*, first published in 1851, was the philosophical inspiration for the British suffrage movement and, like Wollstonecraft's *A Vindication of the Rights of Women*, continues to be studied. The analysis that the Mills develop is the philosophical backbone of liberal feminist politics. Their essays go further than Wollstonecraft or Martineau in that they relate women's oppression to a systemic critique of liberty and the relations between the sexes. A review of the Mills's work provides an analysis of the particular assumptions and modes of thinking that are characteristic of liberal feminism.

From an early age, John Stuart Mill was steeped in the rigors of intellectual thought and disciplined study. Under his father's stern supervision, he began a course of study at age 3 that created his intellectual genius at the same time that it apparently robbed him of emotional gratification (Rossi 1970). His life was one of continuous intellectual production mixed with political activism and long struggles with emotional depression. His father's intense emphasis on rational thought left Mill with a long struggle to "cultivate the feelings," an accomplishment perhaps best made though his strong relationship with Harriet Taylor (later to become Harriet Taylor Mill).

The relationship between John Stuart Mill and Harriet Taylor is one that matches romantic commitment and intellectual collaboration with a fervor for individual liberty; so passionate and unusual was their life together that it is still the subject of discussion (Rossi 1970). Through their correspondence and conversation with each other, their published ideas were formed. Mill himself wrote that the ideas in *The Subjection of Women* (published after Harriet's death) belonged to his wife and had emerged from their vast discussions on a topic dear to them both (Rossi 1970). Yet, over the years, scholars have seldom given Harriet Mill the recognition she deserves for her contribution to these works or, for that matter, to her own writing. The fact that Harriet Taylor Mill has so seldom been cited in the many detailed reviews of the Mills's work underscores the sexist character of philosophical criticism and points out how little credit has been given to women thinkers of the past. Alice Rossi makes a convincing case that the Mills's work was a joint effort, even though it was published under his name. She also argues that *Enfranchisement of Women* (published in 1851) was actually written by Harriet Mill (Rossi 1970). Through this review, their works are interpreted as a collaborative effort.

Taken together, the Mills's essays provide the most comprehensive statement of the liberal perspective of feminist thought. The issues they raise can be grouped into several key areas — the logic of inquiry, the issue of sex differences, work and the family, and the process of modernization and social change.

The Logic of Inquiry. The logic of the Mills's arguments is typical of that inspired by the rational perspective of the Enlightenment thinkers. Convictions, the Mills claimed, fare poorly in argumentative debate, for the resistance of conviction to reason makes rational argument impossible. Strong feelings, they maintained, are impenetrable by rational debate. Consequently, those who argue against almost universally held opinions will, most certainly, have a hard time being heard. In discussing the subordination of women, the Mills clearly argued that open inquiry — especially listening to women's voices — is a prerequisite to establishing knowledge of women's lives. They wrote:

> We may safely assert that the knowledge which men can acquire of women, even as they have been and are, without reference to what they might be, is

wretchedly imperfect and superficial and always will be so, until women themselves have told all they have to tell. . . . Let us remember in what manner, up to a recent time, the expression, even by a male author, of uncustomary opinions, or what are deemed eccentric feelings, usually was, and in some degree still is, received; and we may form some faint conception under what impediments a woman, who is brought up to think custom and opinion her sovereign rule, attempts to express in books anything drawn from the depths of her own nature. (Rossi 1970:152–153)

Knowing that their ideas in *The Subjection of Women* would be controversial, the Mills placed the burden of proof to the contrary on those who would oppose human liberty:

The burden of proof is supposed to be with those who are against liberty, who contend for any restriction or prohibition, either any limitation of the general freedom of human action, or any disqualification or disparity of privilege affecting one person or kind of persons, as compared with others. The *a priori* presumption is in favor of freedom and impartiality. (Mill 1970:3)

The starting point of their argument, as well as the central concept in the liberal perspective, is that all persons have equal liberty and, therefore, that human institutions should treat all alike. Their words provide the philosophy behind the modern practice of equal employment opportunity and equality before the law. They wrote, "The law should be no respecter of persons, but should treat all alike, save where dissimilarity of treatment is required by positive reasons, either justice or of policy" (1970:4). They defined human liberty as a natural right and one that should not be denied on the basis of any individual or group characteristics. But as the style of their writing shows, rational style of their argument is coupled with a passionate emphasis on the necessity for liberating social changes.

Sex Differences and Social Learning. The Mills showed how social conditions create sex-specific attitudes and arrangements that their opponents use to discredit the claim of women's equality. By imagining new alternatives, the Mills showed how a change in the relationship of the sexes would likely alter the characteristics usually thought to be natural differences between the sexes. They argued that there is no reasonable defense for the current state of affairs and that the creation of liberty for women would benefit not just women but society as a whole. The social benefits of liberation would include "doubling the mass of mental faculties available for the higher service of humanity" (1970:153), overcoming the selfish attitudes and self-worshiping characteristics of humanity (1970:148), and enhancing the "softening influence" (1970:156) of women's moral tendencies.

What is considered to be natural is only what is taken for granted, they argued. And foretelling the thoughts of contemporary feminists, they wrote:

> Was there ever any domination which did not appear natural to those who possessed it? There was a time when the division of mankind into two classes, a small one of masters and a numerous one of slaves, appeared, even to the most cultivated minds, to be a natural, and the only natural, condition of the human race. . . . Did not the slave owners of the Southern United States maintain the same doctrine, with all the fanaticism with which men cling to the theories that justify their passions and legitimate their personal interests? (1970:20–21)

They went on to say:

> The smallest acquaintance with human life in the Middle Ages shows how supremely natural the dominion of feudal nobility over men of low condition appeared to the nobility themselves, and how unnatural the conception seemed, of a person of the inferior class claiming equality with them, or exercising authority over them. It hardly seemed less so to the class held in subjection. The emancipated serfs and burgesses, even in their most vigorous struggles, never made any pretension to a share of authority; they only demanded more or less of a limitation to the power of tyrannizing over them. So is it that unnatural generally means only uncustomary, and that everything which is usual appears natural? The subjection of women to men being a universal custom, any departure from it quite naturally appears unnatural. (1970:22–23)

Like contemporary social scientists, the Mills saw that what appears natural is primarily the result of social learning. They continued by saying that one can know what persons actually are only by comprehending their social experience. In their words, "We cannot isolate a human being from the circumstances of his condition, so as to ascertain experimentally what he would have been by nature; but we can consider what he is, and what his circumstances have been, and whether the one would have been capable of producing the other" (1970:126).

The Mills believed that because women had been held in such an unnatural state of submission and domination, it was impossible to make claims about natural sex differences. All that we see as masculinity or femininity, they contended, is the result of learned, not actual, differences. So, they wrote, "women have always hitherto been kept, as far as regards spontaneous development, in so unnatural a state, that their nature cannot but have been greatly distorted and disguised" (1970:104–105). They went on, "I deny that any one knows, or can know, the nature of the sexes, as long as they have only been seen in their present relation to one another" (1970:38), and said, "one thing we may be certain of—that what is contrary to women's nature to do, they will never be made to do by simply giving their nature free play" (1970:48).

The Mills made the case for liberty by seeing the detrimental effects of social learning or, in their words, education and custom, under a state of subjection. They assumed that persons construct their social arrangements and social identities, although some may have more power than others to do so. Human beings, they argued, are rational and creative. Only by removing constraints and obstacles to liberty can the free expression of rational choice and humane social development be encouraged. According to the Mills, human beings have a natural right to self-expression that unnatural systems of authority and rule take away.

Thus, the Mills's concept of liberty rests on the idea of voluntary contracts among human actors. Accordingly, they argued that marriage ties should be based on free and voluntary choice and that law, in marriage and other areas, should treat all alike — giving no unnatural advantage to one group or another. The purpose of *The Subjection of Women* is, in fact, to show the following:

> The principle which regulates the existing social relations between the two sexes — and legal subordination of one sex to the other — is wrong in itself, and now one of the chief hindrances to human improvements; and that it ought to be replaced by a principle of perfect equality, admitting no power or privilege on the one side, nor disability on the other. (1970:1)

Harriet Taylor Mill, in her own essay, *Enfranchisement of Women,* argued, in addition, that "we deny the right of any portion of the species to decide for another portion, or any individual for another individual, what is and what is not their proper sphere" (Rossi 1970:100). Although the Mills differed on their opinions about women's place in marriage, their attitude toward the self-determination of the sexes was clearly one that denies the right of one to restrain the other. As they wrote, "The law which is to be observed by both should surely be made by both; yet, as hitherto, by the stronger only" (Rossi 1970:68). This premise in their work is also the foundation for their ideas on women's place in the workplace and the family.

Work and the Family. The Mills's belief in individual liberty is also seen in their arguments on women's occupations. They believed in the *laissez-faire* operation of the economic market, meaning that they favor a nonintervention approach to economic processes. Their assumption was that, if persons are free to choose their occupation, then the best qualified will fill the positions most appropriate to their talent. Then the occupational system will work in the best interests of all.

These assumptions are grounded in the earlier work of the British economist Adam Smith. Smith maintains that the economic market should be based on open competition and a lack of regulation or interference. According to Smith, this *laissez-faire* policy best suits what he thinks are the laws of the market. He identifies the laws of the market as stemming from the self-interest of individuals. Open competition between individuals will establish a harmony of interests as individuals mutually compete to establish reasonable prices for the sale of goods. Because Smith believes this process to be the natural law of the market, he concludes that the most effective policy is a hands-off or *laissez-faire* approach.

Although the Mills did not speak so directly about the laws of the economy, they similarly assumed that free competition is the key to economic equity — at least in terms of occupational choice. So, in *The Subjection of Women,* they wrote:

> It is not that all processes are supposed to be equally good, or all persons to be equally qualified for everything; but that freedom of individual choice is now known to be the only thing which procures the adoption of the best processes, and draws each operation into the hands of those who are best qualified for it. . . . In consonance with this doctrine, it is felt to be an overstepping of the proper bounds of authority to fix beforehand on some general presumption, that certain persons are not fit to do certain things. (1970:32)

But the Mills's arguments about an open choice of occupation have one important qualifier. In spite of their general position on the emancipation of women, John Stuart Mill and Harriet Taylor Mill disagree about women's preferred occupation. John Stuart Mill believed that the occupation women should (and would) choose is marriage. He argued that in marriage, women's work is to be the moral educators of children and to be themselves objects of beauty and adornment. Thus, regardless of his advocacy of an open marketplace, in his correspondence with Harriet Taylor, he wrote:

> It does not follow that a woman should actually support herself because she should be *capable* of doing so: in the natural course of events she will *not.* It is not desirable to burden the labour market with a double number of competitors. In a healthy state of things, the husband would be able by his single exertions to earn all that is necessary for both: and there would be no need that the wife should take part in the mere providing of what is required to *support* life: it will be for the happiness of both that her occupation should rather be to adorn and beautify it. (John Stuart Mill and Harriet Taylor Mill, *Early Essays on Marriage and Divorce,* in Rossi 1970:74–75) (Emphasis by John Stuart Mill)

Later, in *The Subjection of Women,* Mill wrote:

> In an otherwise just state of things, it is not, therefore, I think, a desirable custom that the wife should contribute by her labour to the income of the family. . . . Like a man when he chooses a profession, so, when a woman marries, it may in general be understood that she makes choice of the management of a household, and the bringing up of a family, as the first call upon her exertions, during as many years of her life as may be required for the purpose; and that she renounces, not all other objects and occupations, but all which are not consistent with the requirement of this. (1970:88–89)

In other words, in spite of his general arguments to the contrary, John Stuart Mill thought that women were more self-sacrificing than men and that they would by *nature* want marriage. Only a free market, however, will sort out which individuals have this nature and which do not. Still, he would prefer not to change the traditional activities of women in the family. He wrote, "The education which it *does* belong to mothers to give . . . is the training of the affections. . . . The great occupation of women should be to beautify life" (Rossi 1970:76).

Harriet Taylor Mill seriously disagreed with Mill on this subject, and her arguments show her to be the more radical of the two. In *The Enfranchisement of Women,* she argued, "To say that women must be excluded from active life because maternity disqualifies them for it, is in fact to say, that every other career should be forbidden them in order that maternity may be their only resource" (Rossi 1970:105). And in the same essay, she said, "Let every occupation be open to all, without favour or discouragement to any, and employments will fall into the hands of those men or women who are found by experience to be most capable of worthily exercising them" (Rossi 1970:100–101).

The disagreement between John Stuart Mill and Harriet Taylor Mill indicates one of the shortcomings in this philosophy of emancipation. He stops short of advocating full equality for women, because he does not support major changes in family relations (Goldstein 1980). Harriet Taylor Mill's analysis is more far-reaching because she argues for the unqualified equality of women with men. Both of them, however, fail to make a radical analysis of women's status because their assumptions ignore the limits to individual free choice that are created by the system of stratification.

The Mills's analysis of occupation is characterized by meritocratic assumptions. *Meritocracies* are systems in which persons hold their positions allegedly based on their individual talents and personal choices. Although meritocracies supposedly resist ascriptive hierarchies (i.e., those based on characteristics such as sex or race), they still maintain hierarchical organization (Harding 1979). Because the Mills's analysis ignores questions such as how talent is distributed, how talent is created or recognized, and how merit is defined, they do not analyze how social systems are marked by unequal powers, privileges, and rewards. In short, their analysis does not overcome inequality; it simply replaces educational, occupational, and legal inequality by gender with other forms of distinction.

Because the Mills do not develop a theory of social class or a perspective on racism, their view of the emancipation of women is based primarily on the optimistic belief that social progress is marked by the increased liberty of the individual. As a central tenet in liberal philosophy, this concept of individual liberty leaves unanswered the question of how institutions are structured around collective inequality. At the same time, the liberal perspective implies that individual liberty will result in the social transformation of the whole society.

Modernization and Social Change. The picture of the future that liberalism portrays tends to be an optimistic one. Likewise, its view of history assumes that modern Western civilization is more progressive than in the past because, in the Mills's language, the modern, advanced state leaves behind the tyrannies and repressions of the past. The Mills conceptualized history in terms of progressive improvement, and they imagined the future as lacking the subjugation and repression of the past.

In keeping with the Enlightenment perspective, the Mills assumed that the historical rule of force is ending with the development of modern rationalized institutions. History, they argued, replaces the use of force with the use of reason. Accordingly, social organization is no longer based on ascriptive roles, but rather upon the achieved merit of individuals. The Mills wrote:

> For what is the peculiar character of the modern world—the difference which chiefly distinguishes modern institutions, modern social ideas, modern life itself, from those of times long past? It is, that human beings are no longer born to their place in life, and chained down by an inexorable bond to the place they are born to, but are free to employ their faculties, and such favourable chances as offer, to achieve the lot which may appear to them most desirable. (1970:29–30)

The Mills's attitude toward this alleged change is consistent with their desire for equality of choice. Their plea for the enfranchisement of women was based on the argument that women are the only exception to an otherwise emancipated world. So, they wrote:

> At present, in the more *improved* countries, the disabilities of women are the only case, save one, in which laws and institutions take persons at their birth, and ordain that they shall never in their lives be allowed to compete for certain things. The one exception is that of royalty. . . . The disabilities, therefore, to which women are subject from the mere fact of their birth, are

the solitary examples of the kind in modern legislation. (1970:35; emphasis added)

Although this essay was published following the emancipation of the slaves in the United States, the Mills's arguments reveal naive optimism about the actual disenfranchisement of many social groups. Although broad-scale legislation had struck down many ascriptive barriers in the law, in practice a large majority of society remained oppressed. The Mills's naiveté in considering that inequality of rights was a "relic of the past" (1970:30) rests solely on their belief that rationality provides a new moral base for society. The Mills envisioned the Western world as the most advanced of all forms of civilization. Yet, this view is both *ethnocentric* (meaning that it regards one's own group as superior to all others) and is founded on class-based and race-based assumptions about the desirability of present social arrangements. The Mills's commitment to rationality as a moral basis for society blinded them to the facts of continuing inequality and oppression of underprivileged peoples in the contemporary Western world.

The Mills's optimism about social change also led them to assume that women's status had necessarily improved over time. They wrote:

> Experience does say, that every step in improvement has been so invariably accompanied by a step in raising the social position of women, that historians and philosophers have been led to adopt their elevation or disbasement as on the whole the surest test and most correct measure of the civilization of a people or an age. Through all the progressive period of human history, the condition of women has been approaching nearer to equality with men. (1970:37)

But feminist studies have shown that women's status has not necessarily improved with time (Kelly-Gadol 1975). In Western culture, women's status has fluctuated depending upon developments in industrialization, capitalism, the advent of technology, and transformations in patriarchal relations. The Mills's assumption that the position of women was necessarily improving is a reflection of their sincere commitment to bringing about that change. But because they did not study specific historical developments in women's roles created by capitalism and patriarchy, their analysis of social change has a hollow ring.

However, these criticisms aside, the Mills's arguments for the emancipation of women still stand as provocative, replete with insightful ideas on the relationship of gender inequality to other systems of unjust authority and the repression of individual freedom. Their failures result from what they did not explain, not from the errors of their inquiry. However, criticism notwithstanding, it is uncanny how truthful the Mills's ideas seem today. Apart from the particular eloquence of their style, their words could be those of a contemporary feminist. This discovery is, in fact, rather disheartening, for it indicates how little the status of women has changed since the Mills's time.

The Critique of Liberalism

The problems in the Mills's philosophy typify the limitations of the liberal perspective. Liberalism seeks changes in the way individuals are treated in social systems. In fact, the strengths of the liberal feminist position are its insistence on individual freedom, its toleration for diverse life-styles, and its support of economic, social, and political reform. These strengths reflect the bourgeois origins of liberal thought, which emphasizes the importance and autonomy of the individual. One reason liberalism is accepted as the norm for feminists is that its philosophy reflects Western cultural values of individualism and personal achievement (Eisenstein 1981). But its strengths are also its weaknesses, for each of these positions has serious limitations that the liberal framework does not address. Consider, for example, the issues of individual liberty and tolerance liberals accord to diverse life-styles. Many probably agree that it is important to tolerate the individual's rights to choose his or her life-style. Thus, the liberal perspective encourages us to say, for example, that lesbians are entitled to live as they please. What liberalism does not do is to recognize that heterosexuality is institutionalized in this society and, thus, is made compulsory for all except those who are deviant. From a liberal perspective, lesbianism is tolerated as a deviant choice, but it is not seen as a positive alternative to the patriarchal control of female sexuality.

Similarly, on race and class issues, the liberal perspective fails to explain the institutionalized basis for race and class oppression. By claiming that all persons, regardless of race, class, or sex, should have equal opportunities, liberals accept the existing system as valid often without analyzing the racist, sexist, and class system upon which it is based. From a liberal feminist perspective, black women's experience is one among many. But explaining how white women's and white men's experience is also conditioned by racism is not part of the liberal program. Liberal feminism sees race as a barrier to the individual freedom of blacks, but it does not see that the position of white women is structurally tied to that of women of color.

Liberal feminism's perspective on individual rights does remind us that social change must provide the basis for individual well-being. Therefore, it is premised on humanistic ethics for social change. Some feminists also argue that liberal feminism recognizes that women form a sexual class (Eisenstein 1981). Because liberal feminism is based on the premise that individuals are autonomous beings, it does recognize that women are independent of men. Early feminists (such as Wollstonecraft and the Mills) viewed women as having an independent and collective existence apart from men. They are not merely different as individuals. But liberal feminist programs for change leave this point underdeveloped by offering solutions that would simply grant individual rights. Therefore, liberal feminism to some extent denies the connections between individuals and leaves its political goal as one of equality. But in saying that women should be equal to men, liberal feminism does not specify which men women want to be equal to; thus, it glosses over the class and race structure of societal relations (Eisenstein 1981).

As a result, liberal feminism leaves much unanswered. It does not explain the emergence of gender inequality, nor can it account, other than by analogy, for effects of race and class stratification on the conditions of women's lives. Its analysis for change tends to be limited to issues of equal opportunity and individual choice. As a political ethic, it insists upon individual liberty and challenges any social, political, and economic practice that discriminates against persons on the basis of group or individual characteristics. The major change advocated by liberal feminists is that more women should be admitted to the existing political and economic systems. Consequently, discrimination is a key concept within the liberal framework, as is the conceptualization of women's oppression as the result of learned sex roles. Moreover, the liberal perspective emphasizes gradual reform and assumes that progress can be accomplished within the structure of existing political, social, and economic institutions. It remains for more radical perspectives to analyze the ways in which these institutions are the very basis for women's oppression.

Summary

The history of the nineteenth-century women's movement in the United States is inseparable from the anti-slavery movement. Abolitionist men and women saw strong similarities in the oppression of slaves and the oppression of women. In its beginning, the nineteenth-century women's movement was not a single-issue movement, though, as it developed, suffrage became its primary cause. Between the time of the granting of women's suffrage in 1920 and the contemporary women's movement, many women's organizations provided continuity between the two feminist movements.

The contemporary women's movement emerged through the political activities of professional women and the role of women in the Civil Rights and New Left movements of the 1960s. Black women's feminist activities in this period also emerged from their political activism in anti-racist struggle.

Sociological theory explains the relationship between observed social facts and the social structure of society and culture. Feminist theory purports to understand the conditions women and men face in society and to seek ways to liberate women and men from oppressive societal conditions. Feminist theory emerges from both liberal and radical traditions. Three theoretical perspectives have emerged in feminist theory: liberal feminism, socialist feminism, and radical feminism. Liberal feminists emphasize social and legal reform through policies designed to create equal opportunities for all.

The origins of contemporary liberal feminism are in the Age of Enlightenment, which valued critical inquiry and the ability of men's rationality to achieve social justice. Feminists have criticized the Enlightenment thinkers for excluding women from their philosophies and have depicted the Enlightenment as a period celebrating man's rational power. Mary Wollstonecraft was one of the earliest European feminists. Wollstonecraft argued that sex roles were the basis for women's experience and thinking. She rejected arguments asserting natural differences between the sexes. Harriet Martineau is a founding mother of sociology whose work established some of the early principles of sociological thought. John Stuart Mill and Harriet Taylor Mill's liberal philosophy is a basis for modern liberal feminism. Their work provides the basis for arguments promoting equal opportunity for women and the removal of barriers standing in the way of women's achievements.

The strength of liberal feminism is its emphasis on individual liberty, but it is weak in its analysis of the intersections of race, gender, and class in social structure. The emphasis on individual rights in liberal theory encourages changes that would admit more women to the existing political and economic system, but liberalism does not challenge the fundamental structure of existing institutions.

CHAPTER 11

Radical Alternatives: Socialist and Radical Feminism

Introduction

Radical perspectives in feminist theory arise from the critique of liberalism and also from a dialogue with Marxist perspectives on women's position in society. Two radical alternatives to liberal feminism are socialist feminism and radical feminism. Socialist feminists see women's oppression as primarily based in capitalism and its interrelationship with patriarchal gender relations. Radical feminists see patriarchal social relations as the primary cause of women's oppression.

Whereas the liberal framework emphasizes learned sex roles and the denial of opportunities as the primary causes of women's oppression, both of these more radical perspectives attempt to explain how gender develops and persists as a social, economic, and political category. The radical analysis goes beyond the goal of including women in existing societal institutions by arguing that dominant institutions are organized through gender, race, and class oppression. The specific process by which this oppression occurs forms points of divergence between socialist and radical feminist perspectives.

Radical feminists criticize liberal feminists for assuming that sexism is largely a remnant of traditional beliefs and practices. Because of their indignation over the continuation of past practices, liberal feminists have widely documented the effects of discrimination and have tried to locate the institutional practices and policies that foster continuing discrimination. As shown in the previous chapter, the liberal feminist perspective takes women's equality with men as its major political goal. In distinct contrast to this perspective, socialist and radical feminism challenge the social, political, and economic analysis of the liberal perspective. Equality, these alternatives suggest, would only put some women on a par with men, without transforming the conditions of oppression that produce gender as well as class and race relations. This chapter reviews socialist and radical feminism and shows how each emerges from an ongoing debate with Marxist theory and its analysis of gender, class, and race relations.

The focus of this presentation is on the contemporary issues posed by these perspectives, although their intellectual origins are rooted in the nineteenth century and in an ongoing dialogue with Marx since that time. As feminist analysis has shifted from liberal concerns with equality and sex roles, new questions have arisen regarding gender as a social, political, and economic category. In relation to Marxist theory, feminist theory asks how gender is socially produced and reproduced and how it is related to class analysis. Further, it asks whether women's oppression is a consequence of class oppression and how patriarchy — simply defined as rule by men — is linked to class relations. Each of these analytical questions is developed in this chapter, but first, some additional background to the emergence of radical feminism and a review of classical Marxist analysis are presented.

The Radical Feminist Movement

The second wave of feminism beginning in the 1960s included different strands of thought and action. While one dimension of the movement, as we have seen, was based in liberal politics and philosophy, more radical activities and orientations were an equally important part of the movement. Although both liberal and radical wings of the women's movement developed as part of other critical social movements during the 1960s and 1970s, the liberal and radical wings also attracted different constituencies and developed different strategies for change. The liberal wing tended to attract professional working women who were somewhat older than the participants in the more radical wing. Also, the organizational structure of liberal feminist groups tended to reflect the more traditional style of their politics. These organizations, as they have evolved, are typically more formal, with leadership and authority hierarchically ordered, and with formal procedures and membership rules (Freeman 1973).

The style and organization of more radical feminist groups reflected their more radical ideological base. In the beginning, participants in the radical branches of the feminist movement tended to be younger than their liberal counterparts, and the organization of their groups was nonhierar-chical, mass-based, and with informal procedures and networks (Freeman 1973). The looser, more flexible style of discussion in radical groups en-couraged analyses that were not only more critical of establishment sys-tems but also more person-oriented and more likely to engage individuals in examining their own experience and its relationship to institutionalized sexism. Thus, the radical branches of feminism recognized that personal life was tied to the structure of public institutions and would only be altered as these institutions changed.

The more radical feminist groups often emerged from the New Left and drew their participants from women who were critical of the often sexist and patronizing behavior of radical men (Evans 1979). Their early political analysis was forged from the appeals to justice that the civil rights and leftist movements had articulated and that women felt were being denied to them. Women in the anti-war and student movements of the 1960s were radicalized not only by the philosophies of these movements, but also by the sexist behavior of men within the movements. And black women whose leadership had been central in the Civil Rights Movement were often relegated to secondary status in the black power movement, as the move-ment was more influenced by black nationalism. Women's participation in all of these movements had the effect of further radicalizing black and white women's feminist perspectives.

Still, black women could not fully embrace the feminist position of white women; white women were more likely to see all men as oppressors and were less sensitive to the class and race differences among men that gave them differential access to power. The feminist alliance between radical black and white women feminists is still imperfect, in part, because of this issue and also because of racism among white women.

The radical branch of the women's movement has included diverse phi-losophies and strategies of protest and there is no single position that can be described as radical feminism. But radical feminists do see sexual rela-tions and men's dominance over women as the central cause of women's oppression. Different from socialist feminists who see women's relation-ship to the economy as the origin of women's oppression, radical feminists see women's relationships to men as the central problem. Furthermore, radical feminists see men's dominance over women as maintained through sexual violence and coercion. Patriarchy is established, supported, and maintained, radical feminists argue, through sexual violence, including rape, compulsory heterosexuality, sexual harassment, and misogynist practices in other cultures such as footbinding, female circumcision, and purdah. In Western culture, radical feminists in fact see all male-domi-nated institutions as part of the patriarchal system of oppression. Medi-cine and psychiatry, for example, are systems for the patriarchal social control of women. From a radical feminist perspective, they are extensions of organized violence directed against women by men. The elimination of male violence is the primary goal of radical feminist politics.

Because, from a radical feminist perspective, patriarchy is organized through men's relationships with other men, unity among women is the only effective means for women's liberation. The abolition of patriarchal systems from a radical feminist perspective requires the development of women's culture and women's relationships with other women. Some radical feminists argue that hierarchical forms of social organization are the consequence of masculine culture; therefore, eliminating hierarchy requires the creation of new cultural forms based on the nonhierarchical, other-oriented, and supportive values of women-centered culture. And, because they see women-centered culture as a means to women's liberation, some radical feminists see lesbians as the forefront of the women's movement since it is they who are most identified with other women.

Socialist and radical feminists together constitute the more radical wing of the women's movement. Though each has a different analysis of women's oppression and emphasizes different means for social change, they stand as a critique of the liberal position. But like liberal feminism, they also have intellectual roots in earlier historical periods and political philosophies. Socialist feminism, in particular, is based in an ongoing dialogue with Marxist analysis and, though radical feminism is less centrally based in Marxism, because it has evolved in tandem with socialist feminism, they share some intellectual roots. A review of the intellectual origins of radical theory follows.

The Political Context of Radical Feminist Perspectives ⎯⎯⎯⎯⎯⎯⎯⎯⎯⎯⎯⎯⎯⎯⎯

Just as liberal feminism has its roots in the historical frameworks of liberal thought, so do radical feminist perspectives have earlier intellectual and political roots. In the nineteenth century, the same political and economic changes that fostered the development of liberal political philosophy also stimulated the emergence of more radical perspectives, most notably the work of Karl Marx (1818–1883) and his collaborator, Friedrich Engels (1820–1895). Marx and Engels's major essay, *The Communist Manifesto,* was published in Paris in 1848, the same year and city as John Stuart Mill's primary work, *On Liberty.* The differences between the radical perspective of Marx and Engels and the liberal perspective of Mill point to the profound controversies over the analysis of social structure and social change that historical changes in the structure of Western society were generating at this time.

The middle and second half of the nineteenth century in western Europe and America was marked by the vast growth of capitalism and the rapid expansion of industrialization, along with widespread social and political changes inspired by the French Revolution and, in the United States, by the elimination of slavery, the expansion of western territories, and urbanization. The climate of social reform that began in this period set the stage for the British suffrage movement and the American feminist movement of the late nineteenth and early twentieth centuries. The political discourse that this period fostered created a diversity of political and social thought that fostered the growth of sociological theory (Bramson 1961; Zeitlin 1968).

Nineteenth-century feminism is typically characterized as a reform movement whose ideas are rooted in the liberal thought of persons such as John Stuart Mill and Harriet Taylor Mill. But the politics of this movement also emerged through debate and action between radical and reform leaders. Some groups in the nineteenth- and early-twentieth-century feminist movement were as much influenced by class and union politics as they were by the spirit of moral reform characterizing the women's rights approach of nineteenth-century feminism. Case studies of both the suffrage movement (DuBois 1978) and the women's trade union movement (Dye 1975) in the United States reveal the complexities of the movements' attempt to grapple with the complexities of class, race, and gender politics. In the end, however, most of the nineteenth-century feminists were unable to transcend the class biases of their middle-class majority leadership. Some feminist leaders, such as Susan B. Anthony, also used prevailing racist and anti-immigrant sentiments to attract members and to articulate movement ideologies (DuBois 1978; Dye 1975). These failures to unite women across classes and races limited the effectiveness of nineteenth-century feminism, but a radical tradition for alliances with working-class women and the beginnings of an analysis linking gender, race, and class oppression can be found in the work of some feminists in this period.

Many of the feminists of this period were also socialists and worked for radical causes in addition to their feminist politics. Charlotte Perkins Gilman (1860–1935) developed a socialist feminist analysis in *Women and Economics* (published in 1898). She proposed that housework should be communally organized, particularly for working mothers, who were entering the paid labor force at this time. She suggested that apartment houses have one common kitchen where all families could be served and that cleaning, child care, nursing, and teaching should be paid professional work. The responsibility for this work should not fall on individual families, but instead on apartment house managers (Rossi 1973). Other radical thinkers of the time, such as Emma Goldman (1869–1940) and Agnes Smedley (1892–1950), did not define feminism as their primary cause, but they clearly linked the oppression of women to other forms of economic and political oppression.

Although not all contemporary radical feminists have a Marxist analysis of women's oppression, the framework of Marxist thinking is extremely important in the evolution of feminist thinking, particularly, as we will see, for socialist feminism. As feminist theory has developed, it has become engaged with an ongoing dialogue with Marxist analysis. Reviewing Marxist thought thus provides a starting point for understanding later analytical frameworks in feminist thought.

The Marxist Perspective _____

Karl Marx (1818–1883)

Marxist thought is one of the most influential and insightful analyses in modern intellectual history. Some argue that most sociological theory even developed as a dialogue with the ideas that Marx inspired (Zeitlin 1968). Certainly, for modern feminism, Marx's ideas are pivotal.

Marx himself began writing as a student, first at the University of Bonn (1835–1836) and then at the University of Berlin (1836–1841), where he was involved in some of the most politically and intellectually controversial movements of his time. He was active in a group known as the Young Hegelians, who based their studies and activities on the work of the German philosopher Hegel (1770–1832). Hegel's philosophy is based on the idea that persons create their world through reason; thus, rational ideas form the objective reality through which human beings construct their world. Hegel's philosophy, furthermore, sees the "real" as emanating from the "divine" (Giddens 1971:3), and Christian theology is an important foundation for his work. The Young Hegelians followed Hegel's concern with theology and adopted his philosophical perspective, until their outlook was radically transformed by the appearance of Ludwig Feuerbach's work, *The Essence of Christianity*, in 1841. Feuerbach (1804–1872) reversed the philosophy of ideas in Hegel's work by arguing that ideas follow the existence of human action. Feuerbach wrote, "Thought proceeds from being, not being from thought" (Giddens 1971:3). From Feuerbach's thesis, the divine was a construction of human thought; human activity, not ideas, provides the basis for social reality.

This philosophy led Marx's teacher and sponsor, Bruno Bauer (1809–1882), to assert that the Bible was a historical document and that Christian theology was a social and historical myth. Bauer was consequently dismissed from the university, as he was declared to be dangerous to the state. For Marx, in a university system where one's future was dependent on academic sponsorship, Bauer's dismissal meant the end of his academic career. Although Marx received his doctorate of philosophy from the University of Jena in 1841, he, who had once been predicted to be the most outstanding professor of his time, was never to hold a university post. The remainder of his life was spent in political exile and in poverty. He continued to write, working occasionally as a journalist, but he was forced to move from Germany to Paris and later to London as he was expelled by various governments.

In 1849 Marx moved to London, where he was to spend the last thirty-four years of his life. His family was extremely poor; several of his children died of malnutrition and disease. When his sixth child was born, he saw the birth as a catastrophe, since two of his children had already died and a third was gravely ill. He was scarcely consoled when the child was born a girl, Jenny Julia Eleanor, as he announced to his friend and collaborator Friedrich Engels that the child was "unfortunately of the sexe par excellence" and "had it been a male the matter would be more acceptable" (Kapp 1972:21). Loans from Engels supported the family, along with Marx's occasional journalism jobs. Throughout this difficult time, Marx continued writing and studying, and he produced several works that would change the course of world history and the history of social thought.

Historical Materialism

The ideas Marx developed always reflected the early influence of Hegel and Feuerbach and resulted in a theoretical perspective often called *historical materialism* (also referred to as *dialectical materialism*). The central thesis of historical materialism is that persons live in interaction with their social and physical environments. Thus, human consciousness and behavior are formed by the interplay between persons as subjects and as objects in the world in which they live. Because human beings have the capacity to reflect upon their actions, their ideas (and ideals) are reflections of their material world. Persons' relationship to their environment and what they think of it is mediated by the particular historical and social mileau of which they are a part. The possibilities for human existence are shaped by the choices and constraints imposed by material organization. Specifically, for Marx, the materialist thesis saw human production — what men and women actually do — as the basis for social structure. Thus, the cause of social change, for Marx, lay not in ideas and values that are abstracted from human experience. Instead, he saw societal change as emerging from the social relations and activities that themselves emerge through human labor and systems of production (Giddens 1971).

The method of dialectical materialism, unlike that of many other sociological theories, is not deterministic. In other words, Marx did not see human history and experience as determined by particular features of social structure; rather, social structure and social change are always emerging and reemerging according to the choices human beings make. In addition, Marx said that this means there will always be contradictions within society and in the experience of human beings in society. That is to say, because social life is not simply determined, it will always involve inconsistencies and the tendency for conflict. Social change, according to Marx, arises from these contradictions and the action of human groups in trying to solve them. The dialectical method is "an approach to problems that visualizes the world as an interconnected totality undergoing a variety of changes due to internal conflicts of opposing forces with opposing interests" (Sokoloff 1980:71).

Marx also assumed that human beings are distinguished from animals because they produce their means of survival. Through their productive work, humans also create new needs. He concluded that if human work is oppressive, then all social life is distorted. Human beings do more than merely exist; they reach their full human potential for creative living through social consciousness and their struggle against oppression. According to Marx, systems of production that distort human potential and, consequently, deny the realization of the species must be transformed by changing social relations and, consequently, through revolution.

Marx explicitly rejected a biologically determinist view of human nature, because he saw human production and reproduction as interacting with social and physical environments. Different forms of social organization produce different social relations, because, in Marxist theory, the systems of human production and reproduction create the conditions for everyday life. Marx and Engels defined *production* as the labor humans perform to satisfy their immediate needs and *reproduction* as the physical re-creation of both the species and the social systems in which human beings reproduce. In Engels's words, production and reproduction are the central features of human society:

> According to the materialistic conception, the determining factor in history is, in the final instance, the production and reproduction of immediate life. This, again, is of a two-fold character: on the one side, the production of the means of existence, of food, clothing and shelter and the tools necessary for that production; on the other side, the production of human beings themselves, the propagation of the species. The social organization under which the people of a particular historical epoch and a particular country live is determined by both kinds of production; by the stage of development of labor on the one hand and of the family on the other. (Engels 1972:71–72)

Feminists have argued that Marx and Engels never fulfilled their promise of developing a materialist perspective to account for productive *and* reproductive activity (Eisenstein 1979; Flax 1976). Marx and Engels also clearly place reproduction solely within the family. But they devote most of their analysis to class relations and systems of production, the alienation of human labor, and the struggle of the working classes against capitalism.

So, in spite of their recognition of the dual importance of production and reproduction, their analysis subordinates reproduction and the family to economic systems of production. They consider production to be primary because it is necessary for maintaining the material basis for satisfying the most immediate requirements for survival. As we will see, classical Marxism sees women's oppression as a reflection of the more fundamental form of oppression by class. Thus, sexism is a secondary phenomenon and, assumedly, will disappear with a revolution in class relations. It is on this point that socialist and radical feminists depart from classical Marxist feminists, because they would argue that the oppression of women itself is fundamental (Jaggar and Struhl 1984).

Class and Capitalism

The materialist perspective of Marx and Engels sees human activity (as it is engaged in productive relations) as the mainspring of social change and as the determining feature of social organization. In Marx's analysis, the economic mode of production forms the *infrastructure* of social organization; other institutions from the *superstructure,* meaning that they reflect the essential character of the economic system.

In the Western capitalist societies that Marx observed, the economic infrastructure was marked primarily by class struggle — the division of society into groups characterized by their relationship to the means of production. Under capitalism, two new major classes emerge: capitalists, who own the means of production, and the proletariat (or working class), who sell their labor for wages to capitalist owners. Two minor classes also exist — the bourgeoisie (merchants, managers, and artisans, for example), who become functionally dependent on capitalism, although they do not own the means of production; and the lumpenproletariat, who have no stable social location because they are individuals from a variety of classes and social locations. In Marx and Engels's words, they form "the 'dangerous class,' the social scum, that passive rotting mass thrown off by the lowest layers of old society" (Tucker 1972:25).

The Marxist concept of class differs significantly from that of non-Marxist social scientists, who use it to refer to stratified status or income hierarchies (see Chapter 5). *Class,* in the Marxist sense, refers specifically to the relationship of a group to the societal means of production; thus, it indicates a system of relationships, not a unit of like persons. Similarly, the concept of *ownership* refers not primarily to the accumulation of goods (which in Marxist theory may occur in any class), but to the actual ownership of a society's productive enterprises.

Society emerges, according to Marxist thought, through class struggle; according to Marx and Engels, "the history of all hitherto society is the history of class struggles" (1970:16). Classes emerge as a society produces a surplus; as a division of labor emerges, thereby allowing for surplus production, the accumulation of a surplus can be appropriated by one group. As a result, this group stands in an exploitative relationship to the mass of producers, and class conflict is established (Giddens 1971). Marx and Engels point out that the first division of labor is the division of labor by sex for the purpose of propagating children, and controlling women's labor in the household; gender thus provides the first class antagonism. However, they (and most subsequent Marxist thinkers) leave this point without further development.

As capitalism develops, the capitalist class appropriates the wealth produced by the subordinate classes because the capitalists have the power to control the conditions under which other classes work. The working class owns only its labor, which it must sell for wages; the capitalists, in turn, exercise the power to determine what wages they will pay and the conditions under which people work. As capitalists try to increase their profit, they do so at the increasing expense of laborers. Profit comes from the fact that workers produce more value than the wages they receive. The craft of distinctive workers becomes less important than the value of mass-produced commodities. Material objects, then, take on greater value than the workers who produce them. In effect, in Marxist analysis, the value of individual human activity decreases as the material value of the products created increases.

Therefore, human beings become alienated in the sense that they do not control or own the products of their labor; they choose neither the form nor the use of the products they make. Additionally, workers are alienated from each other, and they become alienated from themselves because they do not exercise the human ability to transform nature to their own design.

Politically, according to Marx, workers must end the tyranny of private ownership of the means of production by reorganizing the means of production (and, feminists would add, reproduction); the accumulation of profit in the hands of a few must be eliminated. Marxists see that social changes that do not strike at the material basis of social life — capital accumulation by the owning class — will be insufficient because they will not change the underlying causes of social organization.

Ideology and Consciousness

The materialist thesis of Marx is also central to the perspective on consciousness and ideas that is developed throughout Marxist theory. Systems of knowledge take their historical form in response to the mode of production. Marx argued that the ideas of a period are a reflection of the interests of the ruling class (see Chapter 2).

Marx wrote:

> The production of ideas, of conceptions, of consciousness, is at first directly interwoven with the material activity and the material intercourse of men, the language of real life. . . . We do not set out from what men say, imagine, conceive nor from men as narrated, thought of, imagined, conceived, in order to arrive at men in the flesh. We set out from real, active men, and on the basis of their real life-process we demonstrate the development of the ideological reflexes and echoes of this life process. (Marx, *The German Ideology*, in Tucker 1972:118–119)

Basic to this perspective on the sociology of knowledge is the proposition that "it is not the consciousness of men that determines their being, but, on the contrary, their social being that determines their consciousness" (Marx, preface to *A Contribution to the Critique of Political Economy*, in Tucker 1972:4). Those who own the means of production also determine the ruling ideas of the period.

Consciousness is determined by class relations, for even though persons will normally try to identify what is their best interest, under capitalism sections of the ruling class control the production of ideas. Also, even though humans create practical ideas from experience, most of our experience is determined by capitalist relations of production. Thus, the ideas that are disseminated through communications systems, including language, serve to authorize a reality that the ruling class creates. In this sense, ideas become *ideology* — understood to mean a system of beliefs that legitimate and maintain the status quo.

For feminists, Marx's work on ideology is fundamental to their understanding of sexism. Sexism, as an ideology that justifies the power of men over women, emerges not in the best interest of women but as a defense of male domination. Like other ideologies, sexist ideology is a means by which one class rules a society and sanctions the society's social relations. The extent to which women believe in the precepts of sexist ideology is only a reflection of sexist social relations that include the powers of coercion (whether subtle or overt) and social control.

False consciousness emerges as the subordinate group accepts the world view of the dominant class. Because consciousness changes with historical change, at the time that workers see the nature of their exploitation, false consciousness would be transformed into class consciousness and workers would take the revolutionary struggle into their own hands.

Marx's theory is more than an academic analysis because the idea that theory must be connected to social and political practice (*praxis,* in his words) is central to his work. And revolutionary theory is to be created by intellectuals who emerge from and are associated with the working class. Social criticism has no value unless coupled with material change. In *The German Ideology,* he wrote:

> All forms and products of consciousness cannot be dissolved by mental criticism, by resolution into "self-consciousness" or transformation into "apparitions," "spectres," "fancies," etc., but only by the practical overthrow of the actual social relations which gave rise to this idealistic humbug; that not criticism, but revolution is the driving force of history. (Tucker 1972:128)

Thus, Marx saw human beings as potentially revolutionary because their capabilities for creative work and social consciousness far exceed those allowed them under capitalist organization (Eisenstein 1979). This fact provides the basis for optimism in Marx's work, for it lays the foundation for radical change and the transformation from human oppression to human liberation.

The Question of Women

Marx and Engels's analysis of women's oppression is drawn mostly from their writing on the family, especially Engels's essay, *The Origins of the Family, State and Property,* published in 1884 after Marx's death. Feminists who, in the beginning of the contemporary women's movement, were looking for alternative analyses to the liberal perspective began with this classical Marxist perspective. Their later criticisms of Marx and Engels are based primarily on the discussion of the family proposed by Marx and Engels.

Although Engels stated in the preface to *The Origins of the Family, State and Property* that production and reproduction together are the determining factors of history, he saw family relations as derived from the economic mode of production. From a Marxist perspective, in capitalist societies, forms of the family change as class relations change, thus making family relations secondary to economic and class relations. In keeping with their perspective on the social origins of ideas, Marx and Engels would say, however, that the social image of the family is an idealized one that disguises the real economic structure of family relations.

They described the family under capitalism as a microcosm of the society's larger class relations; so, particularly in bourgeois families, the wife is the proletariat. Engles wrote:

> In the great majority of cases today, at least in the possessing classes, the husband is obliged to earn a living and support his family and that in itself gives him a position of supremacy, without any need for special legal ties and privileges. Within the family he is the bourgeois and the wife represents the proletariat. (Engels 1972:137)

Monogamous marriage, Marx and Engels argued, develops as part of the formation of private property. Particularly in the bourgeois family, the development of private property creates the need to determine lineage for the purpose of inheritance. Engels wrote:

> Monogamy arose from the concentration of considerable wealth in the hands of a single individual — a man — and from the need to bequeath this wealth to the children of that man and of no other. For this purpose, the monogamy of the woman was required, not that of the man, so this monogamy of the woman did not in any way interfere with open or concealed polygamy on the part of the man. (Engels 1972:138)

Engels did not explain how men and not women came to control property. Therefore, feminists have criticized the Marxist perspective for not explaining the origins of patriarchy.

Marx and Engels discussed marriage as being, for women, a form of prostitution. Engels wrote:

> Marriage is conditioned by the class position of the parties and is to that extent always a marriage of convenience. . . . This marriage of convenience turns often enough into crassest prostitution — sometimes of both partners, but far more commonly of the woman, who only differs from the ordinary courtesan in that she does not let out her body on piece-work as a wage-worker, but sells it once and for all into slavery. (1972:134)

Marx and Engels defined marriage as based on economic relations, although they made it clear that they would have prefered to see it based on individual sex-love. In marriage and the family, Marx and Engels recognized the woman's role is to be responsible for household management and child care. They argued that household work becomes a private service under advanced capitalism, because it loses the public character it has in earlier forms of economic life. In advanced capitalism, the work of the housewife is both a private service to the male head of the household and an unpaid economic service to the society as a whole. Marx and Engels concluded that "the modern individual family is founded on the open or concealed domestic slavery of the wife, and modern society is a mass composed of these individual families as its molecules" (Engels 1972:137).

Based on their analysis of the family, Marx and Engels saw emancipatory social change in family relations as occurring only with the abolition of private property. Although they maintained a wish for monogamous relationships, they wanted monogamy to be the expression of a sexual commitment based on love, not property. Furthermore, although they did not use the modern language of double standards, what they hoped for was monogamy for *both* men and women, not masked polygamy for men and monogamy for women.

Because Marx and Engels saw male supremacy in the family as originating with the accumulation of property and the development of class relations, they suggested that the liberation of women will occur as the result of class struggle. Women's status is derived from the economic organization of society; therefore, the liberation of women will follow with the revolution of the workers and the abolition of private property. Thus, although Marx and Engels noted that the gender division of labor is the first class oppression, their analysis assumes that women's oppression is secondary to oppression by class and that women will be liberated when class oppression is ended.

It is on this point that socialist and radical feminists begin their critique of Marx. These feminists agree with much of Marx and Engels's analysis, but they disagree that the oppression of women is secondary to class oppression. Socialist feminists essentially agree with Marx's theory of class relations, although they believe that gender relations are equally important in the determination of historical social relations.

Radical feminists, on the other hand, identify patriarchy as an autonomous historical fact and consider gender relations to be the fundamental form of oppression. Class and race oppression, radical feminists argue, are extensions of patriarchal inequality. Accordingly, radical feminists see the abolition of male supremacy as their primary political goal. Although radical feminists differ in the extent to which they use Marxist theory, both socialist and radical feminists would agree that Marx and Engels ignored their own observations on gender oppression. The Marxist assumption that gender oppression would disappear with the abolition of private property too easily assumes that gender is of secondary importance in the determination of social, political, and economic relations.

Socialist Feminism

The Critique of Marx

The emergence of socialist feminism in the 1970s stems largely from feminists' dissatisfaction with classical Marxist perspectives on women and the family. Marx and Engels, socialist feminists would argue, did not seriously consider their own point that sexual division of labor is the first form of class antagonism. Consequently, they too easily assumed that economic class relations are the most critical relations defining women's place in society. Too many questions — cross-cultural, historical, and contemporary — stand in the way of such a theoretical assumption. Are women subordinated to men in preclass societies? Why does women's oppression continue even in socialist societies? Where, in advanced capitalist societies, do women fit in the Marxist definition of class?

Questions such as these lead socialist feminists to conclude that women's oppression cannot be reduced to capitalism alone, although capitalism remains as a highly significant source of women's oppression. The socialist feminist perspective begins with the point that, although economic class relations are important in determining women's status, gender relations may be equally important. Socialist feminists see that class and gender relations intersect in advanced capitalist societies (Hartmann 1976) and that class relations alone do not account for the location of women and men in social life (Jaggar and Struhl 1984). Moreover, according to this perspective, eradicating social class inequality alone will not necessarily eliminate sexism as well.

As feminists have asked these new questions, they have begun a dialogue with Marxist theory and an independent theoretical tradition in feminist studies. Feminist theory questions how biological and social reproduction are tied to the mode of production, how patriarchal relations are tied to the development and maintenance of class relations, whether women's oppression is primarily a question of gender or class, and how systems of race, class, and gender oppression interact with each other.

On the first point, feminists argue that Marx and Engels ignored their statement that forms of production and reproduction constitute the basis for social organization. Marxist theory defines *reproduction* as the social (as well as physical) production of workers. The family is the place, in advanced capitalism, where workers are restored (through food and shelter) so as to be able to reenter the labor force on a daily basis. Also, reproduction in the family includes the socialization of workers to capitalist values and personalities. Implicit in the classical Marxist argument is the idea that the family is a separate force in history, although one subordinate to the forces of production. Although Marx and Engels noted historical changes in the family as a productive unit, they did not develop an analysis of women's place in the family, nor did they explain the sexual politics of male-female relations in the family in any terms other than property relations.

The Dialectic of Sex

One of the first feminist theories attempting to fill this void was that of Shulamith Firestone in *The Dialectic of Sex* (1970), which uses the method of dialectical materialism to analyze the status of women. She compliments Marx and Engels for their dialectical perspective — one that sees history as an emerging process of social action and reaction — and she accepts their materialist proposition as the correct analysis of economic development. But she argues that Marx and Engels are mistaken in giving a strictly economic interpretation to the oppression of women. In her own analysis, she argues that just as the underclasses must seize the means of production as a way to eliminate economic classes, so must women control the means of reproduction if they are to eliminate the inequality of sexual classes. Firestone's controversial conclusion includes the advocacy of technological innovation through artificial reproduction and the consequent elimination of sexist institutions of childbirth and child rearing. She writes:

> The reproduction of the species by one sex for the benefit of both would be replaced by (at least the option of) artificial reproduction: children would be born to both sexes equally, or independently of either, however one chooses to look at it; the dependence of the child on the mother (and vice versa) would give way to a greatly shortened dependence on a small group of others in general, and any remaining inferiority to adults in physical strength would be compensated for culturally. The division of labor would be ended by the elimination of labor altogether (cybernation). The tyranny of the biological family would be broken. (1970:11)

Although her biological determinism is neither consistent with Marxist solutions nor agreeable to all feminists, her argument was the first to underscore the importance of considering reproduction, along with production, as necessary in explaining the status of women.

Family and Economy in Capitalist Society: Juliet Mitchell

Firestone's analysis was followed by Juliet Mitchell's classic work, *Woman's Estate* (1971), which at the time it was published provided the most comprehensive theory of women's position in advanced capitalist societies. Although both socialist and radical feminism have developed further since Mitchell discussed them, her work provides the foundation for understanding current feminist theory.

Mitchell begins with the classical Marxist premise that the economic mode of production is the defining factor of social organization, but she argues that, in Marx and Engels's theory, the liberation of women remains an abstract ideal, not a problem to be explained. Marx and Engels assumed that the liberation of women would occur with the transition from capitalism to socialism, but Mitchell contends that a specific theory of women's oppression is needed if the liberation of women is to occur with the transition from capitalism to socialism. Although women's role in production is central to their oppression, Mitchell argues that the subordination of women involves the interplay of women's role in reproduction, sexuality, and the socialization of children with the economic mode of production. The structure of production embraces the structure of the family, which, in turn, includes the structures of sexuality, reproduction, and socialization. Mitchell writes:

> The contemporary family can be seen as a triptych of sexual, reproductive, and socializatory functions (the women's world) embraced by production (the man's world) — precisely a structure which in the final instance is determined by the economy. The exclusion of women from production — social human activity — and their confinement to a monolithic condensation of functions within a unity — the family . . . is the root cause of the contemporary social definition of women as *natural* beings. (1971:148)

To some extent, Mitchell agrees with Firestone that technological development must be a precondition for the liberation of women. This conclusion is also consistent with Marx's perception that technological advances, if under the political and economic control of *all* humans, can liberate persons, allowing them to fulfill their creative potential. Mitchell argues that women were excluded from production in the past because of their presumed physical weakness and the involuntary character of childbearing. Technological developments and automation have now lessened the necessity for physical strength in labor, and the development of contraception makes childbearing a voluntary act. Because contraception makes it possible to separate sexual and reproductive activity, Mitchell argues that the ideological basis of family life as the unit of sexual and reproductive activity is destroyed. And because biological and social parentage need not be performed by the same person, she concludes that the development of technology and industrialization now makes the liberation of women a possibility. She concludes that "probably it is only in the highly developed societies of the West that an authentic liberation of women can be envisaged today" (1971:121).

Based on her theory, Mitchell assumes that "the entry of women fully into public industry and the right to earn a living wage" (1971:148–149) must be a fundamental goal of women's emancipation movements. The exclusion of women from public industry, their restriction to the private world of the family (where socialization, reproduction, and sexuality are located), and their lack of control over women's work form the basis for their subordination. The ideological assumption of women's dominance in the family obscures their inferior role in production, she argues. Women's full entry into the system of production, coupled with policies to transform the character of family relations, forms the practical implications of the argument she develops.

Mitchell raises a number of issues that remain central to feminist theory. For one, she opens the feminist discussion of the relationship of the family to the economy. In Mitchell's analysis, the family has both an economic and an ideological role in capitalist systems. As industrial capitalism of the nineteenth and twentieth centuries developed, the family changed from a unit of production to a unit of consumption. Because of the way the family contains women's work in reproduction, sexuality, and socialization, several specific consequences of the family's economic-ideological functions occur for women. The process of consumption obviously supports economic life, but in more subtle ways, it affects the status of women. Sexuality, for example, becomes intermixed with a consumption ethic; under modern capitalism, sexuality becomes marketable. Although this fact supposedly means more sexual freedom for women, it clearly increases their use as sexual objects (1971:142). The economic function of the modern family is also reflected in socialization and reproductive practices because it is in the family that workers are created and sustained for their labor force participation. A capitalist work force supports capitalist enterprises by leaving women with the responsibility for creating the personalities that are appropriate to a capitalist labor force.

In addition, Mitchell argues that the family's ideological role supports the rationale and the inherent contradictions of advanced capitalist societies. The ideology of the family supports values of individualism and personal freedom at the same time that it favors individual accumulation of property. The family becomes typified as a "haven in a heartless world" (Lasch 1977) where persons are free to be themselves and to consume goods at their pleasure. An essential contradiction of capitalism lies in the fact that, as capitalism develops, private property, as well as the real choices necessary for personal freedom, is taken away from the masses. So the individualism and freedom that the ideology of the family promises stand in opposition to the fact that capitalism makes these social and economic ideals impossible to realize.

For Mitchell, the result is a self-contradictory system in which, ideologically, women are asked to hold together a system that cannot operate as it is supposed to. Although many feminists would now disagree with Mitchell's analysis, this task constitutes women's oppression. She writes, "The family is a stronghold of what capitalism needs to preserve but actually destroys: private property and individualism. The housewife-mother is the guardian and representative of these. She is a backward, conservative force — and this is what her oppression means. . . . The 'freedom' of the housewife is her isolation" (1971:161). According to Mitchell, the one area of women's power — the socialization of children — becomes a mystique for their own oppression. In Mitchell's second book, *Psychoanalysis and Feminism* (1974), she points out that the process of socialization only projects the mother's anxieties and frustrations onto her children. Mitchell concludes that the overemphasis in the contemporary family on emotional development and individual growth is a rationale for denying women full social and economic participation.

Mitchell's book attributes the cause of women's oppression directly to the development of capitalism and the exclusion of women from equal participation in the labor force. Her solution to women's oppression is to eliminate the division of labor by gender and, ultimately, to support the transition from capitalism to socialism. Although she is critical of classical Marxist theory, she still relies on economic production as the primary cause of women's position. Since the publication of her book, socialist feminist theory has developed around several of the issues that Mitchell first suggested.

The Question of Separate Spheres

Women have traditionally been associated with the private sphere (the domestic world of home, children, reproduction, and sexuality) and men have been associated with the public sphere (paid work, institutionalized religion, and political authority). Also, women's work and activity in the private world have been invisible. One of the accomplishments of feminist theory has been to make the activities of both men and women in the private sphere more visible. Feminist theory has criticized traditional sociological and political theory for focusing primarily on the public world and assuming the public world to be the only place where history, social life, and culture are made. Because the private sphere has been identified with women, it has been perceived as inferior; the public sphere, superior. This conceptualization of the public and private spheres reaches deep into our consciousness, as reflected, for example, in the attitude that women's relationships with each other in the private sphere are insignificant or trivial in the making of history, society, and culture.

Based in the idea that the "personal is political," the feminist practice of consciousness raising is a method of seeing the connections between the public and private worlds. Consciousness raising attempts to bridge the gap between the public and private spheres by showing their interconnectedness and showing how they have been ideologically defined as separate (Eisenstein 1983). For example, feminist theorists point out that work in the private sphere (as, for example, in the care and feeding of paid laborers) is what makes work in the public world possible. And in identifying sexuality as a fundamental dimension of social experience, feminist theory shows how sexuality, even though believed to be contained in the private world, shapes public power relationships, clearly shown in the example of sexual harassment.

The relationship of the public and private spheres is an important theme in the development of feminist theory. Mitchell's work first called attention to the division between public and private spheres of social and economic life. Rosaldo and Lamphere (1974), for instance, pick up Mitchell's point and argue that women's relegation to the private, domestic sphere excludes them from public life and, thus, from equal access to social and economic resources. Recently, the increasing entry of middle-aged, married women and mothers into the labor force, makes it less true that women are confined to the home. Still, women's work in public labor is often said to mirror and extend the private services they provide in the home. Others have argued, more fundamentally, with Rosaldo and Lamphere and Mitchell by demonstrating that women's confinement to the private sphere is largely a white, middle-class phenomenon (Lewis 1977) and, thus, is a race- and class-bound analysis. But without arguing that women's exclusion from the public sphere is the primary basis for their subordination, feminists continue to point out that a theory of women's position must account for the relationship of the private, domestic realm to the public realm of social and economic life (Sacks 1975).

Zaretsky (1976), for example, argues that the supposed split in the public and private spheres obscures the economic role of the family. The production of food, shelter, and emotional nurturance, along with sexuality and reproduction, is a basic material necessity; consequently, even if it is unpaid, housework constitutes socially necessary labor. The idea that the private labor of women is separate from publicly productive labor is, in his analysis, specific to the historical development of capitalism. He argues that the idea of the family as separate from the productive world *and* as the sphere of women originated in the nineteenth century with the rise of industrial capitalism. At that time, women's work was ideologically defined as taking place in the home (Cott 1977) even though most working-class, poor, and minority women continued to work in factories, domestic service, agriculture, and other forms of public labor. Whereas others trace the division of the public and private spheres to earlier historical periods, Zaretsky's work points to the specific dynamics of this split under advanced capitalism.

What is innovative in his work is his equation of the public-private split with a second division — that between the newly emerging concept of personal life and the collective life as found in the social division of labor. Zaretsky writes, "This 'split' between the socialized labour of the capitalist enterprise and the private labour of women in the home is closely related to a second 'split' — between our 'personal' lives and our place within the social division of labour" (1976:29). Personal life, emerging under capitalism, appears to be an autonomous process — as if persons' private lives were governed by their own internal laws. Accordingly, Zaretsky argues that human relations become seen as an end in themselves, detached from the material world of economic fact. Individuals appear unique, and the subjective sphere of self and life-style takes preeminence over the economic relations that, for Zaretsky, define social organization.

Zaretsky's analysis shows how, in the advanced capitalist family, women's primary responsibility is for an emotional world that is ideological in character. Like Mitchell, he sees that advanced capitalism eliminates the production of goods as the basis of the family. But he adds to her analysis that the seeming independence of personal life is a falsehood. Consequently, socialist feminist theory and practice must include the elimination of capitalism *and* the transformation of the family and personal life.

Although Mitchell and Zaretsky point to the dynamics of family life as it is related to economic life, they still maintain the material perspective of Marxism by arguing that the economic mode of production provides the essential basis for social organization. Their socialist feminist position makes the important point that change in women's status will come only through the transformation of capitalist relations, along with independent efforts to transform family relations as well. Socialist feminism shares with classical Marxism the idea that the oppression of women is primarily an economic fact, although it is buttressed by ideological delusions about the family. Socialist feminism makes the additional point that women's oppression must be related to their position in the private world of reproduction and the family. In sum, socialist feminism makes the first suggestion that women's oppression extends beyond the area of economic production. As we will see, socialist feminists have recently incorporated an analysis of patriarchy into their theoretical analysis. But the inclusion of patriarchy follows from the analysis developed by radical feminists, so it is to their ideas that we now turn.

Radical Feminism

Patriarchy and the Domination of Women

At the same time that socialist feminism was developing, other feminists were arguing that male domination per se was the basis for women's oppression. Radical feminists define *patriarchy* as a "sexual system of power in which the male possesses superior power and economic privilege" (Eisenstein 1979:17), and they view patriarchy as an autonomous social, historical, and political force. Whereas socialist feminism emphasizes the economic basis of gender relations, radical feminism emphasizes male power, privilege, and psychological development as the bases of social relations. Radical feminism sees patriarchal relations as more fundamental than class relations in determining women's lives.

Since its inception, the radical feminist position has taken several different directions, some of them more explicitly tied to Marxism than others. Some current radical feminist thought is totally apart from the materialist thesis in Marxist work, locating the causes of oppression solely within patriarchal culture and its control of women (Daly 1978). But much of radical feminism has developed specifically because of Marxist perspectives to explain adequately the emergence and persistence of patriarchy. Thus, some early radical feminists attempted to explain the origins of patriarchy by claiming that women controlled many of the early hunting and gathering societies, but men organized themselves to conquer women by force, thereby also gaining control of originally woman-centered forms of social organization. This position is spelled out by Charlotte Bunch:

> The first division of labor, in pre-history, was based on sex: men hunted, women built the villages, took care of children, and farmed. Women collectively controlled the land, language, culture, and the communities. Men were able to conquer women with the weapons that they developed for hunting when it became clear that women were leading a more stable, peaceful, and desirable existence. We do not know exactly how this conquest took place, but it is clear that the original imperialism was male over female: the male claiming the female body and her service as his territory (or property). (1975:37)

The claim that matriarchal society predates the emergence of patriarchy is a debatable point. Popular feminist accounts often claim a universal matriarchal history in human social organization (Davis 1971), but anthropological evidence gives a more cautious interpretation. Research on the transition from primate to human society indicates a high level of cooperation between males and females in early human societies (Zihlman 1978), but studies of early hunting and gathering societies show that, although many groups were matrilineal, they tended to be egalitarian, not matriarchal (Leacock 1978). Anthropologists conclude that more careful conceptual definitions of power, authority, influence, and status are needed before we can accurately describe women's role in the evolution of human society (Webster 1975) and before we can make claims about the existence of matriarchal societies. It is the case that women's social position has not always been, in every society or in every way, subordinate to that of men (Sacks 1975). The arrangements between women and men vary widely from society to society and across history, and it has taken a great amount of new anthropological research to untangle the early history of male-female relations (Reiter 1975). Moreover, in traditional anthropological accounts, scholars have often projected contemporary assumptions of male supremacy and female social roles into the pasts they have studied (Hubbard 1979). Only now are scholars beginning to find answers to the questions that arise from considering the origins of women's oppression.

So, the question posed is: How did men gain control of the systems of production and reproduction, and how is women's oppression tied to the development of class systems? Radical feminists concentrate on the first half of the question. They argue that male control of women cannot be simply explained as based on class oppression and, as the feminist anthropologist Gayle Rubin has written, "no analysis of the reproduction of labor can explain foot-binding, chastity belts, or any of the incredible array of Byzantine, fetishized indignities, let alone the more ordinary ones, which have been inflicted upon women in various times and places" (1975:163). In part, the strength of the radical feminist position is that it is better able to explain male violence against women and the many cultural practices designed to control female sexuality and reproduction. Radical feminists see patriarchy as emerging from male control of female sexuality.

The Sex/Gender System

Rubin's own work on the genesis of women's oppression centers on the concept of *sex/gender system* as the "set of arrangements by which a society transforms biological sexuality into products of human activity, and in which these transformed sexual needs are satisfied" (1975:159). For Rubin, the oppression of women lies in social systems that create male solidarity, not simply in systems of economic production. Kinship systems, as the observable form of sex/gender systems, relate persons through social categories that may or may not have their basis in biological relations. Beginning with Levi-Strauss's theory in which the essence of kinship systems is the exchange of women (usually through marriage), Rubin goes on to say that "the subordination of women can be seen as a product of the relationships by which sex and gender are organized and produced" (1975:177). The solidarity expressed through the exchange of women represents solidarity between men. According to Rubin, "the 'exchange' of women is a . . . powerful concept. It . . . places the oppression of women within social systems, rather than in biology. Moreover, it suggests that we look for the ultimate locus of women's oppression within the traffic in women, rather than within the traffic in merchandise" (1975:175).

Rubin also develops the idea that gender is a socially imposed division of the sexes that is reproduced through the production of gender identities. As socialization theory has argued, persons are not created in a gender-neutral process. Their personalities represent the gendered categories around which kinship systems are organized. Thus, in the radical feminist analysis, the production of gender sets the preconditions for other forms of domination (Harding 1981). Men first learn to dominate women, setting a pattern for the domination of others. Economic systems may determine who these others are, but sex and gender systems establish the preconditions for domination to emerge. In the end, radical feminism sees systems of domination based on class, race, or tribe as extensions of the underlying politics of male supremacy (Bunch 1975).

Radical feminists see patriarchal institutions as creating myths and forms of social organization that constrain women to exist in male-centered worlds (Daly 1978). One radical feminist solution to women's subordination is the establishment of women-centered beliefs and systems. For some, this movement has produced the separatist philosophy of radical lesbian feminism (Bunch 1975; Daly 1978), whereby a woman-identified world is created through the attachments women have to each other, not to men.

Sexuality, the State, and Radical Feminism

Catherine MacKinnon proposes a radical feminist analysis that takes men's control of women's sexuality as the central fact of the domination of women. As she puts it, "sexuality is to feminism what work is to Marxism" (1982:515). MacKinnon describes sexuality as a social process that creates, organizes, and directs desire; the process of directing the expression of desire creates the social beings we know as women and men, and their relations create society. She reminds us that through gender socialization women and men come to identify themselves not just as social beings, but as sexual beings.

Sexuality is the primary sphere of male power in MacKinnon's radical feminist analysis. Through rape, sexual harassment, incest, and violence against lesbians, men exercise their sexual power over women. Heterosexuality is the institution through which male power is expressed; gender relations and the family are the specific forms of compulsory heterosexuality. Because this analysis sees heterosexuality as institutionalizing male dominance, male control of female sexuality is the linchpin of gender inequality.

In addition, MacKinnon departs from both liberal and left thinking about the state in analyzing state authority as masculine authority (MacKinnon 1983). She argues that liberals see the state as disembodied reason, while leftists see the state primarily as a reflection of material interests. As a result, liberal analyses of the state see women as simply another interest group and treat women as abstract persons with rights, but they do not see women as a specifically gendered group. In left analyses, the state is a tool of dominance and a force that legitimates ideology; women in this analysis are relegated to just another subordinated group.

MacKinnon argues that the law sees and treats women the way men see and treat women; that is, the state is coercive and ensures male control over women's sexuality. Thus, although the state assumes objectivity as its norm, in practice, women are raped by the state just as they are raped by men. The implication of MacKinnon's analysis is that as long as the "state is male," meaning that its meaning systems, its mode of operations, and its underlying assumptions are based in masculine power, women will be unable to overcome their subordination through actions of the state.

MacKinnon's analysis helps us understand some of the complexities of feminist positions on state intervention. While many feminists have demanded state intervention in areas such as sexual abuse, discrimination, and family policy, radical feminist analysis suggests that women cannot entrust their liberation to the state. This analysis also demonstrates how thoroughgoing feminist criticism of social structure and social theory is. By challenging the limited and male-centered frameworks of previous theoretical analyses, feminists — including liberals, socialists, and radicals — have forged new questions and new directions for sociological theory and political action.

In sum, whereas socialist feminism sees women's oppression as stemming from their work in the family and the economy, radical feminism sees the oppression of women as the result of male control of female sexuality and the patriarchal institutions that structure sex/gender systems. The radical feminist therefore takes male domination as the primary fact of women's oppression, whereas socialist feminists see capitalist social structure as the starting point for feminist analysis. Though there are important differences between these two frameworks of feminist thinking, as we can see in the following section, contemporary feminist theory often involves a synthesis of the two perspectives.

Intersections of Capitalism and Patriarchy _____

The assumption in radical feminist analyses that gender relations are more fundamental than class relations has posed important questions for feminist theory. The dialogue between radical feminists and socialist feminists has formulated new insights that reject the ahistorical and universalist claims in some radical feminist accounts, but that reckon with the empirical observation that patriarchal relations do precede and exist independently of class relations. Although women in general are not equal to men in class societies, recent anthropological works show that male property ownership is not the sole basis for male supremacy (Sacks 1975). Within this new synthesis, socialist feminists who might earlier have rejected the radical feminist perspective as a causal theory do take radical feminist perspectives on patriarchy seriously. Although socialist feminists still reject the universalist and ahistorical assumptions sometimes found in radical feminist accounts (Rosaldo 1980), they are grappling with the fact that the oppression of women predates the development of class society and, therefore, are trying to relate gender domination more carefully to patriarchal relations and other forms of oppression.

Heidi Hartmann's analysis of the interaction of patriarchal structures and the development of capitalism is one such work to make this synthesis. Hartmann, a socialist feminist theorist, argues that feminists must identify patriarchy as a social and historical structure if we are to understand Western capitalist societies. She says that Marxist analyses take the relationship of women to the economic system as their central question, but that feminist analyses must take their central question as the relationship of women to men. Understanding capitalism alone will not illuminate women's situation unless we recognize that capitalism is also a patriarchal system of social organization. Thus, Hartmann sees the partnership of patriarchy and capitalism as the critical starting point for feminist theory (Hartmann 1981b).

She argues that in precapitalist societies men controlled the labor of women and children in the family and "that in so doing men learned the techniques of hierarchical organization and control" (Hartmann 1976:138). As larger systems of exchange formed beyond local communities, men were faced with the problem of maintaining their control over women. Through the long-standing institution of patriarchy, men learned techniques of social control that, when capitalism emerged in Western societies, were transformed from direct and personal systems of control to indirect and impersonal systems of social control. Hartmann's analysis sees capitalism as emerging in interaction with and reinforcing patriarchy, but patriarchy is not the sole cause of gender inequality. Many have pointed out, in fact, that the categories of capitalist systems are potentially sex-blind. Gender stratification developed as a particular hierarchy under capitalism because the precondition of the sexual division of labor was extended to newly emerging systems of wage labor.

Hartmann's argument continues by arguing that "job segregation by sex . . . is the primary mechanism in capitalist society that maintains the superiority of men over women" (1976:139). She documents her argument through historical review of the change from cottage and farm production to industrial factory systems and the transformation of household industry, pointing out that the development of capitalism had a more severe impact on women than it did on men. Not only was women's productive role in the family altered, but they became more economically dependent on men. Thus, the gender division of labor is transformed from one of interdependence to one of the dependence of women on men. The crux of Hartmann's research lies in her analysis of men's control of the wage-labor market, where she says the reason men excluded, rather than organized, women workers "is explained, not by capitalism, but by patriarchal relations between men and women: men wanted to assure that women would continue to perform the appropriate tasks at home" (1976:155). Men benefit both from the higher wages they receive *and* from the household division of labor in which they receive women's services.

Although Hartmann's analysis explains much about job segregation by sex and about the interplay of capitalism and patriarchy, it still does not explain the origins of gender stratification. In fact, her work concludes, as earlier suggested by radical feminists, that we will not be able to eliminate the sexual division of labor until we have understood and transformed the process of the social production of gender.

The synthesis of radical and socialist feminism shows how women's role in the *division of labor* (simply defined as the work that different groups of people do) explains much about their position in the society as a whole. Current research in anthropology demonstrates that the gender division of labor in preclass hunting and gathering societies is not as rigidly divided along "man the hunter" and "female the gatherer" lines as has been assumed in traditional anthropological research (Lamphere 1977; Slocum 1975). Where a gender division of labor exists, women's roles are often seen as "complementary and equal" to those of men (Lamphere 1977; Matthiasson 1974), leading many to conclude that women's power in society is directly related to their contribution to production and the extent to which they control the resources they produce (Friedl 1975; Leacock 1978; Sanday 1973). These revisions of earlier assumptions show that our visions of societal development and gender stratification have been clouded by the cultural bias entailed in Western male-defined social research; also, they show that women's contributions to social organization and development have been highly underrated (Zihlman 1978). But more profoundly, they indicate that the emergence of gender inequality is more complex than Marxist accounts of the preeminence of capitalism can explain (Flax 1976).

The Status of Women in Socialist Societies

Questions about the relationship of women's oppression to capitalism and patriarchy beg the question of whether women's status improves under socialism. Socialist feminists have had a vision of societies in which women would have full equality before the law, in which they would enter economic production on a par with men, in which private household work would be transformed to a public enterprise through the collectivization of housework and child care, and in which the subjection of women to men would end. Many socialist societies, including Cuba, the People's Republic of China, the Soviet Union, the eastern European nations, and newly emerging African socialist societies such as Zimbabwe, have declared these to be their goals. Most, however, have fallen short of reaching them (Nazzari 1983). Why? Some scholars say this is because of an inevitable time lag between structural and attitudinal change, but feminists have pointed to other factors in the experience of different socialist countries that negate the potential for equality between men and women.

In Cuba, for example, prior to the revolution, most Cuban women were housewives, not laborers. Castro early spoke of the need to free women from domestic slavery so that they could participate equally in the revolution and share its benefits. Cuba provided increased educational opportunities for women, encouraged their labor force participation, and provided more public services to reduce women's domestic chores in the household. And, in 1975, Cuba passed the Cuban Family Code, making husband and wife equally responsible for housework and child care. But individual men resented this change and studies of housework in Cuba indicate that men continue to spend far less time on housework than either employed women or housewives.

But men's recalcitrance does not fully explain the difficulties encountered in creating equality between men and women in Cuba. Cuban law does require that men and women must be paid equal wages for equal work, but there are differences in wages for employees in different job classifications. The fact that women tend to be concentrated in the service sector means that, at least for minimum-wage workers, women earn less than men. Thus, many women still rely on men's financial support to be able to support their children. Cuban law also requires that men work; women are more likely to be part of a labor reserve. This exacerbates women's economic dependence on men for the support of their families. Moreover, by 1977 the government no longer provided free day care and working mothers had to bear the cost of providing child care. And, in addition, rules that require businesses to provide paid maternity leave to women may discourage businesses from hiring women when it would be cheaper to hire men. Finally, absenteeism among women workers indicates that many Cuban women still find it difficult to work for wages while they carry out household duties. In sum, despite the far-reaching changes that the Cuban revolution created for women, establishing equality between women and men is still incomplete and requires further social and legislative changes (Nazzari 1983).

The situation in the People's Republic of China is somewhat different. When the Chinese Communist Party came to power in 1949, China was primarily a patriarchal peasant society. Land reform was the cornerstone of the Communist Party's political platform, and peasants were encouraged to be disobedient to traditional landlords. But in order to win the peasants over to the revolutionary cause, the Communist Party embraced the ideals of the traditional patriarchal family and families were allowed to maintain their traditional patriarchal structure. The communist revolution had the effect of making the patriarchal family available to almost all men, instead of a privileged few, but it did little to liberate women from the domination of this familial form (Stacey 1983).

In the People's Republic of China, women have been given higher legal status and much has been said about the need to liberate women in this new society. During the period of land reform, land was distributed to heads of families, based on the number of dependents in the family. Individual members of a family unit were given work points that were credited to the family unit, but women were given fewer work points than men for a day's work. Fathers retained control over the family economy and family members.

The People's Republic of China has made efforts to socialize domestic work by providing social services such as public dining rooms, day-care centers, and food processing facilities. But services to relieve the pressures of women's work were the first services cut back when other tensions appeared. As a result, women continue to bear the main burden of domestic chores (O'Kelly and Carney 1986).

In the Soviet Union, observers are often struck by the number of women in wage labor and their central position in industrial, professional, and agricultural work. When the new government was established in 1917, programs were introduced to give women control over their fertility; to provide economic support for wives, widows, and divorcees; and to provide many public services that would enable women to work outside the home. The state established nurseries and boarding schools, as well as canteens and laundries intended to reduce the domestic work of women. However, despite the effort to reduce household labor, these services are inadequate to meet the current needs of working women. Families in the Soviet Union continue to produce most of their own food and must provide their own child care. This creates serious conflict in women's productive and reproductive roles. Furthermore, this conflict has been compounded by efforts in the Soviet Union and other eastern European socialist societies to make women bear more children as a way of halting the declining birth rate (Croll 1981).

A final example of women's status in socialist societies is Zimbabwe. During the colonial period, British rulers in Zimbabwe (then Rhodesia) used a system of passes and permits (similar to that used under apartheid in South Africa) to keep women and children on tribal trust lands, while men were used as laborers on white-owned mines and farms. Women on the tribal trust lands were responsible for feeding their own families. During the movement for independence during the 1970s, women worked in the guerrilla forces as support staff, food producers, cooks, and supply carriers. But by the end of the war, women and men in the guerrilla movement shared all tasks in common, including military fighting. Women's participation in the movement for independence challenged traditional attitudes toward women. Also, many women, influenced by the Western feminist movement, began to articulate explicit feminist ideals. When the Zimbabwe African National Union came to power in 1980, many party leaders believed that only socialism would provide the material basis for equality between women and men.

Yet, today it is not clear to what extent feminist ideas are actually represented in the government. Most women (82 percent) continue to live in rural areas, where they are responsible for meeting most of their families' needs. The government has seemed unwilling to change the existing family structure and its control over women's sexuality and reproduction. And though the government established a Ministry of Community Development and Women's Affairs, it is a weak unit. As a result, women in

Zimbabwe are caught in a contradictory position in which feminist ideals were a part of the revolutionary struggle, but in which the government has done little to make actual structural changes in traditional gender arrangements. Moreover, little has been done to give women greater control over reproduction (Seidman 1984).

Analysis of the different societies in which socialism has been established indicates that women's status does improve under socialism. But other factors have placed limits on the progress of women in socialist countries. Feminists argue that the attainment of equality for women has not always been a primary goal in socialist revolutions and, when it has been, revolutionary change has been incomplete because women's roles in reproduction have not been considered as equally important for transformation as their roles in production. Analysis of women's roles in socialist societies underscores the point made by feminists that women's roles are situated in both production and reproduction and that women's roles in reproduction have consequences for their involvement in all other spheres of life (Beneria and Sen 1982). Neglect of women's roles in reproduction makes any socialist revolution incomplete. Furthermore, transitions to socialism without the elimination of patriarchal forms of organization and rule mean that women are still subjected to oppressive social forces. Only with transformations in women's roles in production and reproduction, and the elimination of patriarchal social control, can women be fully liberated and will we find the possibility for true equality between women and men.

Women's Status in Egalitarian Societies

Anthropological work on women's roles in egalitarian societies begins to shed light on the necessary conditions for egalitarianism between women and women. Can groups maintain a sex division of labor and still have economic, political, and social freedom for women and men? Can women remain different but equal, or must differences between the sexes be eliminated altogether? Moreover, can changes in the gender division of labor eliminate women's subordination, or must we also consider transformations in the social production of gender? How, in effect, is the social production of gender tied to the modes of economic life that have emerged in modern Western societies?

In studying the social organization of hunting and gathering societies with relatively egalitarian gender relations, Leacock identifies three social structural conditions that seem necessary to produce egalitarianism: (1) the ties of collective economic dependency link *all* individuals directly to the well-being of the group as a whole; (2) the public and private spheres are not dichotomized; and (3) decisions are made by those who will also carry them out (1978:247).

On the first point, Leacock emphasizes that all members of an egalitarian society would be necessary to the system of production. They need not, it would seem, all contribute in the same way, but they would all be seen as equally valuable — quite a contrast to the socially and economically devalued labor of women under capitalism. Second, Leacock shows how the separation of the public and the private invites the restriction of women to the family. Other anthropologists, too, argue that the restriction of women to domestic work is an important precondition for the subordination of women. Domestic labor is production for the use of society's members, whereas public production creates goods for exchange. Because production for exchange takes on greater value than production for use, any group that is restricted to production for use is likely to be devalued (Sacks 1975). Moreover, in modern societies, the separation of the public and the private also invites ideological oppression of women that claims they are more fit for domestic life and, therefore, more likely to be restricted to it.

Finally, Leacock's analysis suggests that no group should have authority over the experience of others. Were women to be involved in the decision-making processes that affect them, they would exercise control over their own lives. Again, this arrangement would be the reverse of the contemporary situation, in which men rule even on matters, such as female reproduction, that greatly influence the course of women's experience. The development of modern patriarchy puts men in positions of authority in public and private institutions. The historical shift placing more authority in industry and government has meant that men control (through public patriarchy) areas that deeply affect women's lives — family law, welfare practices, reproductive issues, work policies, and the prosecution of male violence (Brown 1981). Leacock's analysis raises the question of how different gender relations might be in a society where women and men controlled decisions pertinent to their lives, where persons engaged in equally valuable labor, and where all members of the society were equally responsible for household work. Chodorow's (1978) work on the production of gender (see Chapter 6) suggests that such a society would produce men and women with less stereotypical personalities and, consequently, more flexibility in creating new social arrangements.

Integrating Feminist Theory and Politics: Race, Class, and Gender

Theoretical issues in feminist analysis are not simply academic exercises. Feminists from each of the perspectives we have reviewed — liberal, socialist, and radical feminism — agree that theoretical analyses are intended to sharpen political analyses and inform strategies for social change. Liberal, socialist, and radical feminism each makes unique contributions to our understanding of the situation of women. And, though for purposes of analysis the three are distinct from one another, in practice feminist politics are often informed by all three. Moreover, these theoretical viewpoints are not always as easily distinguished from each other as the preceding analytical discussion may indicate. Each of the feminist frameworks illuminates different dimensions of political and analytical issues and no single perspective provides a complete understanding of the many issues feminists have raised.

This review of feminist theory suggests that we ground discussion of women's position in the dynamics of the gender division of labor, the emergence of class systems, the formation of patriarchal relations, and the social organization of the family. In all, a complete theory of women's oppression must explain not only women's role in production but also the patriarchal control of female reproduction and sexuality. And feminist theory, from a radical perspective, directs us to look at the material conditions of women's lives and in so doing, to explain the basis for their oppression not only by gender but also by race and by class.

Early feminist work suggests that sex oppression is analogous to race oppression, by arguing that sexism has effects on its victims similar to those of racism (Hacker 1951) and that discriminatory policies based on sex are comparable to those based on race (Stimpson 1971). This reasoning by analogy, however, was more often an attempt to prove the existence of sexism than to analyze the conditions of minority women's experience. The first attempts to describe minority women's conditions were usually described as "double jeopardy," suggesting the cumulative effect of race and gender exploitation. Although these arguments are descriptively valuable, they are analytically limited. The idea that race and gender oppression are cumulative, although suggestive of the burdens these women face, does not explain the complex dynamics of race, gender, and class inequality. Race, class, and gender are systems of oppression experienced simultaneously by women of color (Combahee River Collective, 1979; Smith, B. 1979). Theory that begins with the conditions women of color experience in their lives must speak to the actuality of this experience in all its complexities if we are to move away from feminist analyses and politics that stem only from the experience of dominant groups (Eichelberger 1977).

The different feminist perspectives reviewed here each entails a different understanding of race and class. The liberal feminist analysis shares many assumptions with an assimilationist or civil rights perspective on race relations. The civil rights perspective identifies the cause of socioeconomic disparities as lying in discrimination and advocates that remedies for such disparities be sought through courts and administrative agencies as provided under law (Loury 1986). This perspective (and the reason it is also labeled assimilationist) assumes that, as barriers of race and sex discrimination are removed, minorities will move into the system and become assimilated into the dominant culture and institutions. The goal of such a liberal political philosophy is to establish sex- and color-blind categories of social, economic, and political relations. This vision of society is a popular one and, although its emphasis on civil rights is shared by all feminists, it offers little analysis of the persistence of racial and sexual equality. It also assumes that to become liberated, one must deny the particular conditions of one's experience (Rich 1979).

Socialist feminism provides a better starting point for an analysis of race, but only when its concern with the political economy of class and gender is extended to include race issues. The experience of all women is inextricably tied to the development of class relations; moreover, the development of productive and reproductive relations under capitalism provides much of the basis for the exploitation of racial groups in this country. The economic perspective of socialist feminism should also remind us that the liberation of white women from domestic labor has rested upon the availability of black and other minority domestic workers (Dill 1980), although this fact is frequently forgotten in feminist analyses. Moreover, the history of contraceptive technologies that helped liberate women followed experimentation on Third World women (Barker-Benfield 1976; Reid 1975). The socialist feminist perspective used in developing an economic framework for women's oppression tells us much about the interplay of gender and class, but it "does not entail a corresponding awareness of cultural differences" (Simons 1979:389). Without such a full-blown analysis, the assumptions of socialist feminism remain blind to the experience of women most oppressed by class, race, and gender domination.

The radical feminist perspective assumes that gender is the primary form of oppression and that class and race are extensions of patriarchal domination (Daly 1978). This perspective is perhaps the most problematic in providing a theory of race oppression. In assuming that patriarchy is the cause of women's oppression, it divides minority women and men and takes the experience of white American women as the universal social experience. In locating the causes of oppression in the domination of men, radical feminism provides little explanation of the powerlessness that minority men and women experience together. Its insistence that eliminating sexism is the key to eliminating racism has a hollow ring to women of color, who face oppression on both counts and who have experienced racism as a more fundamental (or at least equally fundamental) fact of their lives. Radical women of color clearly recognize that sexism exists in their communities. But attributing the primary cause of their experience to patriarchy ignores the racism they encounter not only from men but from white feminists as well (Moraga and Anzaldúa 1981).

The analysis of class is also underdeveloped in feminist theory, though it is becoming increasingly evident as economic changes in women's lives make poverty and class inequality an even more obvious reality. The movement of some women into traditionally higher-paying, higher-status occupations, coupled with the deterioration of women's economic situation in other segments of the labor force, are creating a class schism among women that has numerous consequences for feminist political action and theoretical analyses. Some frameworks of feminist theory (especially socialist and radical feminism) tend to be more attuned to class issues among women. Feminist theory must recognize that women are affected in different ways by the policies and programs that stem from feminist analyses. So, while budget cuts for social programs may benefit women in the corporate sector, they seriously disadvantage poor women (Power 1984). Such an example indicates the complexity of creating a feminist movement, united across class and race, at a time when class and race divisions are becoming exacerbated by political, economic, and social change.

In sum, while each of the feminist perspectives we have reviewed entails an implicit or explicit analysis of race and class, no one of them has been fully adequate for understanding the complexities of these interlocking systems of oppression. We have yet to develop feminist theory that is truly inclusive of women's experience, though different theoretical analyses provide different insights to this topic.

In Chapter 1 we noted phases of transformation in thinking about women, moving from studies where women are excluded altogether to those that recognize a notable few women, studies that document women's oppression, studies that study women on their own terms, and new ways of thinking that see women and men in relational terms. Integrating race, class, and gender into our thinking requires a similar pattern of transformation. Too often, feminist analyses themselves exclude women of color altogether, as, for example, studies discussing the supposed learned helplessness of women or the dependency of women on men. Other feminists have responded by adding notable women of color into their teaching and work and there is a long tradition, especially in sociology, of documenting the oppression of women by race and by class.

There is now more research available that studies women of color on their own terms, including collections of historical documents (Sterling 1984), oral histories (Wilson and Mullaly 1983), and the renaissance in literature by women of color (Hull 1984). But sociological analyses that see race, class, and gender in relational terms — in other words, those that understand that race, class, and gender relations fundamentally structure all of our lives — are still rare. The challenge for feminist theory in the coming years is to develop such work. This is the most important task lying ahead for feminist theory because, without it, research that describes and explains the experience of all women will not be established. Without such an analysis, feminists cannot hope to generate programs for social change designed for the liberation of all women and men.

Toward a Sociology for Women ———————————

At the heart of all feminist theory lies the idea that prior knowledge about women, society, and culture has been distorted by the exclusion of women from academic thought. In the beginning chapters of this book, we discussed ways that the male-centered perspectives of knowledge have been challenged by feminist concepts and research. Our review of feminist theory further shows that research and theory in the academic disciplines need fundamental reconstruction if it is to work on behalf of women.

In sociology, this is best represented by Dorothy Smith, whose work in the sociology of knowledge challenges some fundamental conceptions of objectivity, social research, and the construction of sociological theory. Smith (1979) begins with a fundamental sociological point — that social experience and consciousness are conditioned by the social location of our existence. As Smith shows, men and women have quite different life situations. To the extent that their situations differ, their consciousness, culture, conceptions, and ideas are also different. Smith's work begins with the premise, taken from Marx, that the real activity of women — their roles in production and reproduction — form the basis for their ideas. Because sex/gender systems organize our social relations and because intellectual thought is shaped by social relations, the sex/gender system also shapes our perspectives as social thinkers and social researchers.

This contradicts the image of sociology as a value-free science. Although feminists do not typically reject the use of scientific method in sociological study, they do see science as only one method of knowing and as a method that is situated in particular social and cultural assumptions. Feminists raise two important questions here — the first, what is the connection between theory and politics, and the second, what is the relationship of objectivity to the social production of knowledge?

If one assumes that social and scientific theory must be free of political commitments, then the very phrase *feminist theory* seems to be a contradiction in terms. Theory is allegedly void of social purpose, and its legitimacy, in the scientific framework, depends on its ability to explain events in the empirical world. What, then, does feminist theory mean, and how do we account for the connection it makes between theoretical construction and political commitment?

The history of modern science demonstrates that science has often been tied to the cause of social reform (Mendelsohn 1977). In the seventeenth century, as modern science began, scientific inquiry was justified for its specific social value. Moreover, the legitimacy of scientific inquiry rested on the same principles of reform that today sound like feminist social practices — anti-authoritarianism, progressiveness, anti-elitism, educational reform, humanitarianism, and the unity of experience and knowing (Van Den Daele 1977). Contemporary debates about the social and political application of scientific knowledge (such as the examples of nuclear energy and the atomic bomb) also indicate that even in scientific circles the question of scientific purpose is not separate from the practice of scientific inquiry.

Historically, the scientific movement also emerged in specific opposition to the canons of traditional belief, especially as a challenge to the state and the political authority of the church. As one historian of science writes, "The breakdown of older patterns of authority and traditionally-held dogmas or consensus positions allows much broader boundaries for exploration and the staking out of positions previously proscribed — either tacitly or implicitly" (Mendelsohn 1977:10). By removing the blinders of earlier commitments, scientists have argued that more objective inquiry would provide the new facts and new perspectives needed to meet the needs of emerging social institutions.

Feminists argue that the neutral claims of traditional scholarship mask nonobjective interpretations of women's lives that have been produced. According to feminist inquiry, new perspectives on women's lives, and specifically, ones that challenge sexist assumptions, will result in more accurate explanations of women's experiences. Feminists still use scientific methods in their studies, but they claim that their work is more objective because it is more inclusive of all persons' experiences.

A central question in feminist scholarship is the issue of objectivity and its relationship to the process of knowing (Harding 1986). According to standard arguments about sociological research, rigorous observation and the use of the scientific method eliminate observer bias. But feminists argue that the observer is not a neutral party. Because knowledge is socially produced, the particular experiences and attitudes that observers bring to their work influence what they study, how they study it, and what they conclude about it. Untangling the relationship between the knower and the known is essential, according to feminist scientists.

Dorothy Smith (1979) and Nancy Hartsock (1983) note that all research is done from a particular standpoint or location in the social system. The world is known from the perspective of the researcher. In any given research project, we must know both the subjects' and the researcher's point of entry to the project. Most often, sociologists enter research projects through official institutions (such as the schools, the police, or social welfare agencies). Consequently, the work they do may support the status quo and be distorted by the view of official agencies. Instead, Smith suggests that most objective inquiries can be produced only by those with the least interest in preserving the status quo.

She explains this idea by using an example from the German philosopher Hegel. Suppose we want to comprehend the world of a master and a slave. Both of them live in the same world, but their experience within that world is quite different. The master takes the slave's labor (in fact, his or her very existence) for granted; thus, the master's needs are immediately satisfied. The slave, on the other hand, conforms to the master's will; his or her labor is an object of the master's consciousness. The organization of this relationship is invisible to the master. If the master were describing the world they both inhabit, his account would be less objective because the structures of that world are invisible to him. But the slave's description of the world would include the master, plus the fact of his or her labor and its transformation to the status of an object. Consequently, the slave is more objective because his or her account is both more complete and more directly related to the empirical events within the relationship and the world in which it is located.

When we begin describing the world by examining women's experience, the knowledge we create does not merely add to the already established constructs of sociological thought. The experience of women, like that of the slave, has been invisible. Women inhabit the same world as men; in fact, women's labor shapes men's experience in the world (through housework and the maintenance of social and bodily relations). Women's labor makes the male mode of operation — detached and rational — possible; yet it remains invisible to men as the dominant class. An objective sociological account of reality must make sense of both women's and men's experiences and, therefore, must be constructed from the vantage point of both.

Smith (1981) also argues that sociological research and theory must situate social actors within their everyday worlds. In other words, unless research begins with the ordinary facts of lives, then the knowledge that sociologists construct will be both alienating and apart from the actual experiences of human actors. Sociological analysis begins with the immediate experience of social actors but goes beyond it by discovering the social-institutional context of their lives. Although the institutional context of everyday experience is not immediately visible to those who experience it, the sociological perspective makes this context available and, thus, is a powerful agent of social change. Like the perspective of C. Wright Mills, Smith is working to establish the relationship between social structure and everyday life. This relationship is especially important in comprehending women's experience, because the affairs of everyday life are the specific area of women's expertise. Given the gender division of labor, women are charged with maintaining everyday life. To overlook it or to treat it as insignificant is to deny women's reality as an important part of social existence. (Reinharz 1983).

In sum, feminists have both introduced women's experience into sociological knowledge and shown how traditional knowledge has been generated from specific gender relations. Informed by the empirical facts of women's experience and recognizing the influence of gender relations in the development of knowledge, the feminist perspective has created new analyses of the social order and established new goals for social change. Although feminist scholarship does not discard all the insights and understandings from past sociological thought, it does revise the assumptions, content, and purpose of sociological inquiry (Westkott 1979). Feminist scholarship emerges specifically from the feminist consciousness and has followed a clear path of development.

The origins of feminist scholarship are found within women's experience — first, as the simple recognition that a collective wrong has been suffered. The feminist movement emerged when women organized to correct these wrongs; the social movement itself then generated new forms of women's culture. Second, feminist consciousness is producing autonomously defined modes of thinking and theory (DuBois et al., 1980). With this transformation lies the historical possibility of creating knowledge that will provide the basis for the construction of societies that are enabling of us all.

Summary

Socialist and radical feminism emerge from a critique of the limitations of liberal feminist theory. The more radical wings of the women's movement in the 1960s and 1970s were less hierarchical and more informally structured than liberal feminist groups. Radical feminist groups of the 1960s emerged from the civil rights, black power, and anti-war student movements of the 1960s. Socialist feminists see women's relationship to economic production as the central cause of women's oppression. Radical feminists see women's relationship to men and male control of female sexuality as the primary cause of women's oppression.

Nineteenth-century feminists developed radical programs for feminist change that linked the oppression of women to other economic and political oppression. The work of Karl Marx and Friedrich Engels is central to socialist feminism. Marx is a historical materialist and sees human social organization as emerging from the choices and constraints posed by historical conditions. Social change emerges from the contradictions inherent in social structures. Marx defines capitalist society as marked by class struggle. The ideas of a period and the consciousness of people within that period are controlled by those who own the means of production. Marx and Engels see family relations as derived from the economic mode of production. They describe women's place in the family as a microcosm of society's class relations.

Feminists criticize Marx and Engels for seeing women's oppression as secondary to class oppression. Socialist feminism sees women's oppression as stemming from their dual oppression in the family and economy. Radical feminists define male domination as the source of women's oppression. They identify patriarchy as a social arrangement that systematically disadvantages women as a sexual class. The intersection of capitalism and patriarchy is the basis for women's oppression in this society.

The status of women improves under socialism, but the persistence of patriarchy means most socialist societies have fallen short of full equality between men and women. Also, socialist policies that neglect women's roles in reproduction make women's equality with men incomplete. Studies of egalitarian societies reveal the structural conditions under which equality between men and women is made possible. Feminist analyses inclusive of class, race, and gender are necessary to develop feminist programs and theories that work to liberate all women and men.

Conclusion

The theoretical perspectives reviewed here make the point that social change is informed by different premises about the social organization of society. The different feminist perspectives examined here each suggest different kinds of social change. Therefore, for feminists to realize their goals for an egalitarian society requires careful examination of the underlying assumptions of given theoretical and political perspectives. As Karl Mannheim suggests, "A theory is wrong if in a given practical situation, it uses concepts and categories which, if taken seriously, would prevent man from adjusting himself at that historical stage" (1936:95).

Liberal feminism emphasizes that social change should establish individual civil rights so that no one is denied access to the existing social-economic system based on sex, race, or class. Liberal feminism also tells us that sexism is the result of past traditions and learned psychology; consequently, it suggests reform in sex role socialization practices and puts much of its faith in the raised consciousness of future generations. The political tactics of liberal feminism are primarily those of interest group politics in which liberal feminists attempt to increase the political influence and power of women. Their political strategy involves building coalitions that align the issues of feminism with other political causes, thereby increasing the strength of the women's movement. This strategy also has its costs, however, because political compromises mean that only the most moderate feminist demands can gain the support necessary for a solid coalition.

Socialist and radical feminism, on the other hand, locate the cause of

359

sexism in the fundamental character of political and economic institutions. These perspectives pose a challenge to the very basis of our social existence by suggesting that revolutionary changes need to be made in the systems of capitalism and patriarchy.

Socialist feminists make the issue of social class central to their theoretical analysis and argue that classical Marxist theory has obscured the economic and social roles of women. In their dialogue with Marx and Engels, socialists feminists go beyond seeing women as just another victim of capitalism by making women's liberation central to all struggles for revolutionary change. They suggest that the issue of class alone cannot account for the complex relationship between the family, reproduction, and productive relations in the society. Nonetheless, the class analysis that socialist feminists include does necessitate understanding the experience of women of all classes and races. Both socialists and radical feminists take a material perspective on social life — that is, they see things (including those with subjective value, such as ideas, personalities, and social values) as taking on objective value through the relations of human production and reproduction. In the materialist perspective, the actual work and activity of men and women constitutes the social world; therefore, to change that world requires a change in the actual labor and reproductive relations among human beings.

Because of their Marxist perspective, socialist feminists often align themselves with other oppressed groups in their programs for social change. Their politics remain Marxist in tone, but with the added issue of ending women's oppression in ways that traditional Marxists overlook. Their strategies, then, are analytical and practical — seeking to find the common grounds of oppression and trying to establish collective ways to solve the problems that communities and individuals experience.

Distinct from socialist feminism, radical feminism locates the development of sexism in the independent existence of patriarchy and the social relations that it generates. Thus, the radical feminist perspective asks us to look at the structure of consciousness — not just as it is reproduced through sex roles but specifically as it reflects the patriarchal organization of society. Radical feminism suggests that only the elimination of patriarchy will result in the liberation of women in society. Much of the strategy of radical feminist programs for change has been to redefine social relations by creating a woman-centered culture. Radical feminists emphasize the positive capacities of women by focusing on the creative dimensions of women's experience. Radical feminists celebrate the creative dimension of women's lives, specifically because women's culture and experience are seen as resisting patriarchal social relations.

The distinctions drawn here among these three feminist perspectives are in no way a perfect description of any. In theory and in practice, there are as many shared ideas and politics among feminists as there are differences. But discussion of the different feminist perspectives demonstrates that the questions that feminists raise have different answers and that they are as complex as the systems they seek to change. Also, the substantive observations of empirical research on gender and women's lives that have been made by social research can be understood in the context of the larger theoretical issues that surround them. This research literature documents the experience of women in society, whereas the theoretical issues describe the possibilities for creating change in women's position. Thus, in sociology at least, the thrust of the feminist movement has been to observe and interpret women's experience with the larger purpose of creating a nonsexist society.

If we take direction from all three feminist perspectives, it seems that a nonsexist society would be a society with no race, gender, and class distinctions in the production and distribution of economic resources. It would also be a society where power is not distributed by virtue of one's class, race, or gender and where individual civil rights are respected and maintained. And finally, such a society would have to respect and encourage traditional female values, but not restrict them to only one-half of the population, who, by virtue of their gender, are categorized as subordinate to the other. Although that society seems a long way off, feminist research and theory provide the guidelines for creating it.

Bibliography

"Abortion: Women Speak Out." *Life* **4**(1981):45–50.

Adams, S. L. "Blackening in the Media: The State of Blacks in the Press." In J. D. Williams (ed.), *The State of Black America 1985*. New York: The National Urban League, 1985, 65–104.

Adler, C. "An Exploration of Self-Reported Sexually Aggressive Behavior." *Crime and Delinquency,* **31**(April 1985):306–331.

Adler, F. *Sisters in Crime.* New York: McGraw-Hill, 1975.

Ageton, S. "The Dynamics of Female Delinquency, 1976–1980." *Criminology,* **4**(November 1983):555–584.

Albin, R. "Review Essay: Psychological Studies of Rape." *Signs,* **3**(Winter 1977):423–435.

Aldrich, M. L. "Women in Science." *Signs,* **4**(Autumn 1978):126–135.

Almquist, E. "Women in the Labor Force." *Signs,* **21**(Summer 1977):843–855.

———. *Minorities, Gender, and Work.* Lexington, Mass.: D. C. Heath, 1979.

———. "Gender Inequality Within Minority Groups in the Labor Market: Issues of Gender, Race, and Class." Paper presented at the Annual Meetings of the American Sociological Association, New York, August 1986.

Almquist, E., and Wehrle-Einhorn, J. L. "The Double Disadvantaged: Minority Women in the Labor Force." In A. Stromberg and S. Harkess (eds.), *Women Working.* Palo Alto, Calif.: Mayfield, 1978, 63–88.

Amir, M. *Patterns of Forcible Rape.* Chicago: University of Chicago Press, 1971.

Andersen, M. "Corporate Wives: Longing for Liberation or Satisfied with the Status Quo?" *Urban Life* **10**(1981):311–327.

Andersen, M., and Renzetti, C. "Rape Crisis Counseling and the Culture of Individualism." *Contemporary Crises,* **4**(1980):323–339.

362

Anderson, A., and Gordon, R. "Witchcraft and the Status of Women — The Case of England." *British Journal of Sociology,* **29**(June 1978):171–184.

Andrews, W., and Andrews, D. C. "Technology and the Housewife in Nineteenth Century America." *Women's Studies,* **2**(1974):309–328.

Arditti, R., Duelli-Klein, R., and Minden, S. *Test-Tube Women: What Future for Motherhood?* Boston: Pandora Press, 1984.

Aries, P. *Centuries of Childhood.* New York: Vintage, 1962.

Armstrong, P., and Begus, S. "Daddy's Right: Incestuous Assault." In Irene Diamond (ed.), *The Family, Politics and the State.* New York: Longman's Press, 1982.

Axelson, D. E., "Women as Victims of Medical Experimentation: J. Marion Sims' Surgery on Slave Women, 1845–1850," *Sage* **2**(Fall 1985):10–13.

Axtell, J. *The Indian Peoples of Eastern America: A Documentary History of the Sexes.* New York: Oxford University Press, 1981.

Babco, E. *Salaries of Scientists, Engineers, and Technicians: A Summary of Salary Surveys.* Washington, D.C.: Scientific Manpower Commission, 1981.

Baca-Zinn, M. "Chicanas: Power and Control in the Domestic Sphere." *De Colores,* **2**(Fall 1976):19–31.

———. "Chicano Men and Masculinity." *Journal of Ethnic Studies,* **10**(Summer 1982a):29–44.

———. "Mexican-American Women in the Social Sciences." *Signs,* **8**(Winter 1982b):259–272.

Baker, S. H. "Women in Blue-Collar and Service Occupations." In A. Stromberg and S. Harkess (eds.), *Women Working.* Palo Alto, Calif.: Mayfield, 1978, 339–376.

Baldridge, J. V. *Sociology.* New York: Wiley, 1980.

Bandura, A., and Walters, R. H. *Social Learning and Personality Development.* New York: Holt, Rinehart & Winston, 1963.

Barfoot, C. H., and Sheppard, G. T. "Prophetic vs. Priestly Religion: The Changing Role of Women Clergy in Classical Pentecostal Churches." *Review of Religious Research,* **22**(September 1980):2–17.

Barker-Benfield, G. J. *Horrors of the Half-Known Life.* New York: Harper & Row, 1976.

Barrett, M., and Roberts, H. "Doctors and Their Patients." In C. Smart and B. Smart (eds.), *Women, Sexuality, and Social Control.* London: Routledge & Kegan Paul, 1978, 41–52.

Barry, K. *Female Sexual Slavery.* Englewood Cliffs, N.J.: Prentice-Hall, 1979.

Bart, P. "The Loneliness of the Long-Distance Mother." In J. Freeman (ed.), *Women: A Feminist Perspective.* Palo Alto, Calif.: Mayfield, 1979, 245–261.

Bart, P., and O'Brien, P. *Stopping Rape: Successful Survival Strategies.* New York: Pergamon Press, 1985.

Bates, B. "Doctor and Nurse: Changing Roles and Relations." *New England Journal of Medicine,* **283**(1970):129–134.

Baumgaertner, W. (ed.). *Fact Book on Theological Education for the Academic Year 1985–86.* Vandalia, Ohio: Association of Theological Schools, 1986.

Baxandall, R. F. "Who Shall Care for Our Children? The History and Development of Day Care in the United States." In J. Freeman (ed.), *Women: A Feminist Perspective.* Palo Alto, Calif.: Mayfield, 1979, 134–149.

Beck, E. M., Horan, P. M., and Tolbert, C. M. II. "Stratification in a Dual Economy: A Sectoral Model of Earnings Determination." *American Sociological Review,* **43**(1978):704–720.

Becker, B. J., and Hedges, L. V. "Meta-analysis of Cognitive Gender Differences: A Comment on an Analysis by Rosenthal and Rubin." *Journal of Educational Psychology,* **76**(August 1984):583–587.

Becker, H. *The Outsiders.* New York: Free Press, 1963.

Bell, C. "Implementing Safety and Health Regulations for Women in the Workplace." *Feminist Studies,* **5**(Summer 1979):286–301.

Bell, I. P. "The Double Standard: Age." In J. Freeman (ed.), *Women: A Feminist Perspective.* Palo Alto, Calif.: Mayfield, 1979, 233–244.

Bem, S. "Psychology Looks at Sex Roles: Where Have All the Androgynous People Gone?" Paper presented at the UCLA Symposium on Women, May 1972.

Bem, S., and Bem, D. J. "Training the Woman to Know Her Place: The Power of a Non-conscious Ideology." In M. Garskof (ed.), *Roles Women Play: Readings Toward Women's Liberation.* Belmont, Calif.: Brooks/Cole, 1971.

Benbow, C., and Stanley, J. "Sex Differences in Mathematical Ability: Fact or Artifact?" *Science,* **210**(1980):1262–1264.

Benet, M. K. *The Secretarial Ghetto.* New York: McGraw-Hill, 1972.

Benokraitis, N., and Feagin, J. *Modern Sexism.* Englewood Cliffs, N.J.: Prentice-Hall, 1986.

Benson, S. P. "'The Clerking Sisterhood': Rationalization and the Work Culture of Saleswomen in American Department Stores, 1890–1960," *Radical America* **12**(March-April 1978):41–55.

Bernard, J. "Marriage: His and Hers." *Ms.,* **1**(1972):46ff.

———. *The Future of Marriage.* New York: Bantam Books, 1973.

———. *Women, Wives, Mothers: Values and Options.* Chicago: Aldine, 1975.

———. *The Female World.* New York: Free Press, 1981.

Berry, J. W. "Ecological and Cultural Factors in Spatial Perceptual Development." *Canadian Journal of Behavioral Science,* **3**(1971):324–336.

Best, R. *We've All Got Scars.* Bloomington: Indiana University Press, 1983.

Bienen, L. "Rape II." *Women's Rights Law Reporter,* **13**(Spring/Summer 1977):90–137.

Billingsley, A. *Black Families in White America.* Englewood Cliffs, N.J.: Prentice-Hall, 1966.

Blackwell, J. *The Black Community: Diversity and Unity.* New York: Harper & Row, 1985.

Blau, F., and Jusenius, C. L. "Economists' Approaches to Sex Segregation in the Labor Market: An Appraisal." *Signs,* **1**(Spring 1976):181–199.

Blau, P., and Duncan, O. D. *The American Occupational Structure.* New York: Wiley, 1967.

Bleier, R. *Science and Gender.* New York: Pergamon Press, 1984.

Blood, R. D., and Wolfe, D. M. *Husbands and Wives.* New York: Free Press, 1960.

Blum, L. "Women and Advancement: Possibilities and Limits of the Comparable Worth Movement." Paper presented at the Annual Meetings of the American Sociological Association, New York City, September 1986.

Blumberg, R. L. *Stratification: Socioeconomic and Sex Equality.* Dubuque, Iowa: William C. Brown, 1978.

Boals, K. "Political Science." *Signs,* **1**(Autumn 1975):161–174.

Bock, E. W. "The Female Clergy: A Case of Professional Marginality." *American Journal of Sociology,* **72**(March 1967):531–539.

Bock, E. W., and Webber, I. "Suicide Among the Elderly: Isolating Widowhood and Mitigating Alternatives." *Journal of Marriage and the Family,* **34**(1972): 24–31.

Bogdan, J. "Care or Cure? Childbirth Practices in Nineteenth-Century America." *Feminist Studies,* **4**(1978):92–99.

Boskind-White, M. "Bulimarexia: A Sociocultural Perspective." In Steven Emmet (ed.), *Theory and Treatment of Anorexia Nervosa and Bulimia.* New York: Brunner/Mazel Publishers, 1985, 113–126.

Boskind-White, M., and White, W. C. Jr. *Bulimarexia: The Binge-Purge Cycle.* New York: W. W. Norton, 1983.

Boston Women's Health Book Collective. *The New Our Bodies, Ourselves.* New York: Simon & Schuster, 1984.

Bowie, N. "Blacks and Mass Media: Where Do We Stand?" *Crisis,* **92**(June/July 1985):27ff.

Bowker, L. H. "Gender Differences in Prisoner Subcultures." In L. Bowker (ed.), *Women and Crime in America.* New York: Macmillan, 1981a, 409–419.

———. "Women as Victims: An Examination of the Results of L.E.A.A.'s National Crime Survey Program." In L. Bowker (ed.), *Women and Crime in America.* New York: Macmillan, 1981b, 158–179.

Bramson, L. *The Political Context of Sociology.* Princeton, N.J.: Princeton University Press, 1961.

Broverman, I. K., Broverman, D. M., Clarkson, F., Rosenkrantz, P., and Vogel, S. "Sex Role Stereotypes and Clinical Judgment of Mental Health." *Journal of Consulting and Clinical Psychology,* **34**(1970):1–7.

Brown, C. "Mothers, Fathers, and Children: From Private to Public Patriarchy." In L. Sargent (ed.), *Women and Revolution.* New York: South End Press, 1981, 239–267.

Brown, M. "Radiation and the Unborn Child." *Data Processing,* **27**(March 1985):37–38.

Brown, S. E. "Love Unites Them and Hunger Separates Them." In R. Reiter (ed.), *Toward an Anthropology of Women.* New York: Monthly Review Press, 1975, 322–332.

Brownmiller, S. *Against Our Will.* New York: Simon & Schuster, 1975.

Bruch, H. *The Golden Cage: The Enigma of Anorexia Nervosa.* London: Open Books, 1978.

Bryan, J. H. "Apprenticeships in Prostitution." *Social Problems,* **12**(Winter 1965):287–297.

Bryson, J., and Bryson, R. "Salary and Job Performance Differences in Dual-Career Couples." In Pepitone-Rockwell, F. (ed.), *Dual-Career Couples.* Beverly Hills, Calif.: Sage, 1980, 241–259.

Bunch, C. "Lesbians in Revolt." In N. Myron and C. Bunch (ed.), *Lesbianism and the Women's Movement.* Oakland, Calif.: Diana Press, 1975, 29–38.

Burgess, L. L., and Holmstrom, A. W. *The Victim of Rape: Institutional Reactions.* New York: Wiley, 1978.

Burkhardt, J. E. *Crime and the Elderly—Their Perceptions and Their Reactions.*

Rockville, Md.: National Criminal Justice Reference Service, Microfiche Program, 1977.

Burlage, D. "Judaeo-Christian Influences on Female Sexuality." In A. L. Hageman (ed.), *Sexist Religion and Women in the Church.* New York: Association Press, 1974, 93–116.

Burt, M. R. "Cultural Myths and Support for Rape." *Journal of Personality and Social Psychology,* **38**(February 1980):217–230.

Busby, L. J. "Sex-role Research on the Mass Media." *Journal of Communication,* **25**(1975):107–131.

Cameron, M. O. *The Booster and the Snitch.* Glencoe, Ill.: Free Press, 1964.

Cant, G. "Valiumania." *New York Times Magazine,* **6**(February 1, 1976):34ff.

Canter, R. J. "Sex Differences in Self-Reported Delinquency." *Criminology,* **20**(November 1982):373–393.

Carothers, S. C., and Crull, P. "Contrasting Sexual Harassment in Female- and Male-Dominated Occupations." In K. B. Sacks and D. Remy (eds.), *My Troubles Are Going to Have Trouble with Me.* New Brunswick, N.J.: Rutgers University Press, 1984, 209–228.

Carrigan, T., Connell, B., and Lee, J. "Toward a New Sociology of Masculinity." *Theory and Society,* **14**(September 1985):551–604.

Carrington, C. H. "Depression in Black Women: A Theoretical Appraisal." In L. F. Rodgers-Rose (ed.), *The Black Woman.* Beverly Hills, Calif.: Sage, 1980, 265–272.

✓ Carroll, J. W., Hargrove, B., and Lummis, A. T. *Women of the Cloth.* San Francisco: Harper & Row, 1981.

Cathey-Calvert, C. "Sexism on Sesame Street." Know, P.O. Box 86031, Pittsburgh, Pa. 15221.

Caulfield, M. D. "Imperialism, the Family, and Cultures of Resistance." *Socialist Revolution,* **20**(1974):67–85.

———. "Sexuality in Human Evolution: What Is 'Natural' in Sex?" *Feminist Studies,* **11**(Summer 1985):343–364.

Chafetz, J. *Sex and Advantage: A Comparative Macro-Structural Theory of Sex Stratification.* Totowa, New Jersey: Rowman and Allenheld, 1984.

Chambliss, W., and Seidman, R. *Law, Order and Power,* 2/e. Reading, Mass.: Addison-Wesley, 1982.

Chavkin, W. "Occupational Hazards to Reproduction: A Review Essay and Annotated Bibliography." *Feminist Studies,* **5**(Summer 1979):310–325.

Chernin, K. *The Obsession.* New York: Harper Colophon, 1981.

———. *The Hungry Self: Women, Eating, and Identity.* New York: New York Times Books, 1985.

Chesler, P. *Women and Madness.* Garden City, N.Y.: Doubleday, 1972.

Chesney-Lind, M. "Judicial Paternalism and the Female Status Offender." In L. Bowker (ed.), *Women and Crime in America.* New York: Macmillan, 1981, 354–366.

Chester, R., and Streather, J., "Cruelty in English Divorce: Some Empirical Findings." *Journal of Marriage and the Family,* **34**(1972):706–710.

Child, I., Potter, E., and Levine, E. "Children's Textbooks and Personality Development: An Exploration in the Social Psychology of Education." In M. L. Haimonitz and N. R. Haimonitz (eds.), *Human Development: Selected Readings.* New York: Crowell, 1960, 292–305.

Chodorow, N. *The Reproduction of Mothering.* Berkeley: University of California Press, 1978.

Chow, E. "Acculturation Experience of Asian American Women." In A. G. Sargent (ed.). *Beyond Sex Roles,* 2nd ed. St. Paul, Minn.: West Publishing Co., 1985, 238–251.

––––––. "The Development of Feminist Consciousness Among Asian American Women." *Gender and Society,* 1 (forthcoming, 1987).

Christ, C. "Why Women Need the Goddess: Phenomenological, Psychological and Political Reflections." In C. P. Christ and J. Plaskow (eds.), *Womanspirit Rising.* New York: Harper & Row, 1979, 273–287.

Christ, C. P., and Plaskow, J. (eds.). *Womanspirit Rising.* New York: Harper & Row, 1979.

Cicone, M. V., and Ruble, D. N. "Beliefs About Males." *The Journal of Social Issues,* **34**(Winter 1978):5–16.

Clark, L., and Lewis, D. *Rape: The Price of Coercive Sexuality.* Toronto: Women's Press, 1977.

Clarke, E. *Sex in Education; Or, A Fair Chance for the Girls.* Boston: Osgood and Company, 1873.

Clay, V. S. *Women: Menopause and Middle Age.* Pittsburgh: Know, Inc., 1977.

Coates, B., Anderson, E. P., and Hartup, W. W. "Interrelations in the Attachment Behavior of Human Infants." *Development Psychology,* **6**(1972):218–230.

Cohen, L., and Stark, R. "Discriminatory Labeling and the Five-Finger Discount —An Empirical Analysis of Differential Shoplifting Dispositions." *Journal of Research in Crime and Delinquency,* **11**(1974):25–39.

Collins, M. "Ageism in the Medical Profession." Paper presented at the Women's Caucus, Annual Meeting of the American Public Health Association, Miami, 1976.

Colman, A. and Colman, L. *Earth Father/Sky Father: The Changing Concepts of Fathering.* Englewood Cliffs, New Jersey: Prentice-Hall, 1981.

Colten, M. E., and Marsh, J. C. "A Sex Roles Perspective on Drug and Alcohol Use by Women." In C. S. Widom (ed.), *Sex Roles and Psychopathology.* New York: Plenum Press, 1984, 219–248.

Combahee River Collective. "A Black Feminist Statement." In Z. R. Einstein (ed.), *Capitalist Patriarchy and the Case for Socialist Feminism.* New York: Monthly Review Press, 1979.

Comfort, A. "Likelihood of Human Pheromones." *Nature,* **230**(1971):432–433.

Congressional Research Service and Congressional Budget Office. *Children in Poverty.* Reported in *Washington Post* (May 23, 1985):1ff.

Connell, R. W. "Theorizing Gender." *Sociology,* **19**(May 1985):260–272.

Conover, P. J., and Gray, V. *Feminism and the New Right.* New York: Praeger, 1983.

Cooper, V. W. "Women in Popular Music: A Quantitative Analysis of Feminine Images Over Time." *Sex Roles,* **13**(November 1985):499–506.

Cooperstock, R. "Sex Differences in the Use of Mood-Modifying Drugs: An Explanatory Model." *Journal of Health and Social Behavior,* **12**(1971):238–244.

Cope, N. R., and Hall, H. R. "The Health Status of Black Women in the U.S.: Implications for Health Psychology and Behavioral Medicine." *Sage,* **2**(Fall 1985):20–24.

Corea, G. *The Hidden Malpractice.* New York: William Morrow, 1977.

————. "The Caesarian Epidemic." *Mother Jones,* **5**(1980):28ff.

————. *The Mother Machine: Reproductive Technologies from Artificial Insemination to Artificial Wombs.* New York: Harper & Row, 1985.

Costello, C. B. "'WEA're Worth It!' Work Culture and Conflict at the Wisconsin Education Association Insurance Trust." *Feminist Studies,* **11**(Fall 1985):497–518.

Cott, N. *The Bonds of Womanhood.* New Haven, Conn.: Yale University Press, 1977.

Coverman, S. "Gender, Domestic Labor Time, and Wage Inequality." *American Sociological Review,* **48**(October 1983):623–637.

Cowan, R. S. "Two Washes in the Morning and a Bridge Party at Night: The American Housewife Between the Wars." *Women's Studies,* **3**(1976):147–171.

Cowie, J., Cowie, V., and Slater, E. *Delinquency in Girls.* London: Heinemann, 1968.

Croll, E. J. "Women in Rural Production and Reproduction in the Soviet Union, China, Cuba, and Tanzania: Case Studies." *Signs,* **7**(Winter 1981):375–399.

Cromwell, V., and Cromwell, R. "Perceived Dominance in Decision-Making and Conflict Resolution Among Black and Chicano Couples." *Journal of Marriage and the Family,* **40**(1978):748–759.

Curran, D. A. "Judicial Discretion and Defendant's Sex." *Criminology,* **21**(February 1983):41–58.

Curran, D. J. "The Myth of the 'New' Female Delinquency." *Crime and Delinquency,* **30**(July 1984):386–399.

Currie, E., Dunn, R., and Fogarty, D. "The New Immiseration: Stagflation, Inequality and the Working Class." *Socialist Review,* **10**(1980):7–31.

Daly, M. *Beyond God the Father.* Boston: Beacon Press, 1973.

————. *Gyn/Ecology: The Meta-Ethics of Radical Feminism.* Boston: Beacon Press, 1978.

————. "After the Death of God the Father: Women's Liberation and the Transformation of Christian Consciousness." In C. P. Christ and J. Plaskow (eds.), *Womanspirit Rising.* New York: Harper & Row, 1979, 53–62.

————. *The Church and the Second Sex.* New York: Harper & Row, 1975.

Daniels, A. K. *Invisible Careers: Women Civic Leaders From the Volunteer World.* Chicago: University of Chicago Press, forthcoming, 1988.

Daniels, P., and Weingarten, K. "A New Look at the Medical Risks in Late Childbearing." *Women and Health,* **4**(Spring 1979):5–36.

Datesman, S., and Scarpitti, F. (eds.), *Women, Crime, and Justice.* New York: Oxford University Press, 1980.

Davis, A. "Reflections on Black Women's Role in the Community of Slaves." *The Black Scholar,* **3**(1971):2–15.

————. *Women, Race and Class.* New York: Random House, 1981.

Davis, A. J. "Sex-Differentiated Behaviors in Nonsexist Picture Books." *Sex Roles,* **11**(July 1984):1–16.

Deaux, K., White, L., and Farris, E. "Skill Versus Luck: Field and Laboratory Studies of Male and Female Preferences." *Journal of Personality and Social Psychology,* **32**(1975):629–636.

deBeauvoir, S. *The Second Sex.* New York: Knopf, 1952.

DeFleur, M. L., D'Antonio, W. V., and DeFleur, L. N. *Sociology: Human Society.* Glenview, Ill.: Scott, Foresman, 1977.

Deitz, S. R., Blackwell, K. T., Daley, P. C., and Bentley, B. J. "Measurement of Empathy Toward Rape Victims and Rapists." *Journal of Personality and Social Psychology,* **43**(August 1982):372–384.

Delaney, J., Lupton, M. J., and Toth, E. *The Curse: A Cultural History of Menstruation.* New York: New American Library, 1976.

deTocqueville, A. *Democracy in America.* New York: Knopf, 1945.

Deutscher, I. *What We Say/What We Do.* Glenview, Ill.: Scott, Foresman, 1973.

De Vault, M. "Housework: Keeping in Mind What's Out of Sight." Paper presented at the Annual Meetings of the American Sociological Association, Washington, D.C., August 1985.

Dill, B. T. "The Dialectics of Black Womanhood." *Signs,* **4**(Spring 1979):543–555.

———. "'The Means to Put My Children Through': Childrearing Goals and Strategies Among Black Female Domestic Servants." In L. F. Rodgers-Rose (ed.), *The Black Woman.* Beverly Hills, Calif.: Sage, 1980, 107–123.

———. "Race, Class, and Gender: Prospects for an All-Inclusive Sisterhood." *Feminist Studies,* **9**(Spring 1983):131–150.

Dinnerstein, D. *The Mermaid and the Minotaur.* New York: Harper-Colophon, 1976.

DiPrete, T. "Unemployment Over the Life Cycle: Racial Differences and the Effect of Changing Economic Conditions." *American Journal of Sociology,* **87**(September 1981):286–307.

Dobash, R. E., and Dobash, R. "Love, Honor, and Obey: Institutional Ideologies and the Struggle for Battered Women." *Contemporary Crises,* **1**(1977):403–415.

———. *Violence Against Wives.* New York: Free Press, 1979.

Dodson, J. E., and Gilkes, C. T. "Something Within: Social Change and Collective Endurance in the Sacred World of Black Christian Women." In R. Reuther and R. Keller (eds.), *Women and Religion in American, Volume 3: 1900–1968.* New York: Harper & Row, 1986, 80–130.

Doeringer, P. B., and Piore, M. J. *Internal Labor Markets and Manpower Analysis.* Lexington, Mass.: D. C. Heath, 1971.

Dominick, J., and Rauch, G. "The Image of Women in Network TV Commercials." *Journal of Broadcasting,* **16**(1972):259–265.

Donegan, J. Women and Men Midwives: *Medicine, Morality and Misogyny in Early America.* Westport, Conn.: Greenwood Press, 1978.

Donovan, P. "Parental Notification: Is It Settled?" *Family Planning Perspectives,* **13**(1981):243–246.

Donzelot, J. *The Policing of Families.* New York: Pantheon, 1979.

Douglas, A. *The Feminization of American Culture.* New York: Knopf, 1977.

Douglas, P. "Minority Groups Push Olympic ABC-TV Hirings." *The National Leader,* (December 29, 1984):5.

Downey, A. M. "The Relationship of Sex-Role Orientation to Self-Perceived Health Status in Middle-Aged Males." *Sex Roles,* **11**(August 1984):211–223.

Draper, R. "The History of Advertising in America." *New York Review of Books* **33**(June 26, 1986):14–18.

DuBois, E. C. *Feminism and Suffrage.* Ithaca, N.Y.: Cornell University Press, 1978.

DuBois, E. C., Buhle, M. J., Kaplan, T., Lerner, G., and Smith-Rosenberg, C. "Politics and Culture in Women's History: A Symposium." *Feminist Studies,* **6**(Summer 1980):26–64.

Dworkin, A. *Woman Hating.* New York: E. P. Dutton, 1974.

Dye, N. S. "Creating a Feminist Alliance: Sisterhood and Class Conflict in the New York Women's Trade Union League, 1903–1914." *Feminist Studies,* **2**(1975):24–38.

———. "History of Childbirth in America." *Signs,* **6**(1980):97–108.

Eagly, A., and Carli, L. "Sex of Researchers and Sex-Typed Communications as Determinants of Sex Differences in Influenceability: A Meta-analysis of Social Influence Studies." *Psychological Bulletin,* **90**(1981):1–20.

Eccles, J. J., Adler, T., and Meece, J. L. "Sex Differences in Achievement: A Test of Alternate Theories." *Journal of Personality and Social Psychology,* **46**(January 1984):26–43.

Ehrenreich, B. "Combat in the Media Zone." *Seven Days,* **2**(1978):13–14.

———. *Hearts of Men.* Garden City, N.Y.: Anchor, 1983.

Ehrenreich, B., and English, D. *Complaints and Disorders.* Old Westbury, Conn.: Feminist Press, 1973.

———. *Witches, Midwives, and Nurses: A History of Women Healers.* Old Westbury, Conn.: Feminist Press, 1973.

———. *For Her Own Good.* Garden City, N.Y.: Anchor-Doubleday, 1978.

Eichelberger, B. "Voices on Black Feminism." *Quest,* **3**(Spring 1977):16–27.

Eisenstein, H. *Contemporary Feminist Thought.* Boston: G. K. Hall, 1983.

Eisenstein, Z. *The Radical Future of Liberal Feminism.* New York: Longmans, 1981.

——— (ed.). *Socialist Feminism and the Case for Capitalist Patriarchy.* New York: Monthly Review Press, 1979.

Emmet, T. *Principles and Practices of Gynecology.* Philadelphia: Lea, 1879.

Engels, F. *The Origin of the Family, Private Property, and the State.* Ed. with an introduction by E. Leacock. New York: International, 1972.

English D. "The Politics of Porn." *Mother Jones,* **5**(1980):20ff.

Epstein, C. *Woman's Place: Options and Limits in Professional Careers.* Berkeley: University of California Press, 1970.

———. "Positive Effects of the Multiple Negative: Explaining the Success of Black Professional Women." *American Journal of Sociology,* **78**(1973):912–935.

Ernest, J. "Mathematics and Sex." *American Mathematical Monthly,* **83**(1976):595–614.

Evans, S. *Personal Politics: The Roots of Women's Liberation in the Civil Rights Movement and the New Left.* New York: Knopf, 1979.

Falk, N. "Introduction." In Y. Y. Haddad and E. B. Findly (eds.), *Women, Religion and Social Change.* Albany: State University of New York Press, 1985, xv–xxi.

Fauls, L. B., and Smith, W. D. "Sex-Role Learning of Five-Year Olds." *Journal of Genetic Psychology,* **89**(1956):105–117.

Fausto-Sterling, A. *Myths of Gender.* New York: Basic Books, 1985.

Featherman, D. L., and Hauser, R. M. "Sexual Inequalities and Socioeconomic Achievement in the U.S., 1962–1973." *American Sociological Review,* **41**(1976):462–483.

Fein, R. A. "Men and Young Children." in J. Pleck and J. Sawyer (eds.), *Men and Masculinity.* Englewood Cliffs, New Jersey: Spectrum Books, 1974, 54–61.

Fee, E. "Woman's Nature and Scientific Objectivity." In M. Lowe and R. Hubbard (eds.), *Woman's Nature.* New York: Pergamon Press, 1983.

———. "Good Science=Feminist Science." *Women's Review of Books,* **3**(September 1986):9–10.

Feldberg, R. L., and Glenn, E. N. "Job vs. Gender Models in the Sociology of Work." *Social Problems,* **26**(June 1979):524–538.

Fennema, E., and Sherman, J. A. "Sex-Related Differences in Mathematics Achievement, Spatial Visualization, and Affective Factors." *American Educational Research Journal,* **14**(Winter 1977):51–71.

Ferguson, A., et al. "Forum: 'The Feminist Sexuality Debates.'" *Signs,* **10**(Autumn 1984):106–135.

Ferrara, K., and Johnson, J. "How Women Experience Battering: The Process of Victimization." *Social Problems,* **3**(February 1983):325–339.

Ferree, M. M. "Class, Housework, and Happiness: Women's Work and Life Satisfaction." *Sex Roles,* **11**(December 1984):1057–1074.

———. "Sacrifice, Satisfaction, and Social Change: Employment and the Family." In K. B. Sacks and D. R. (eds.), *My Troubles Are Going to Have Trouble with Me.* New Brunswick, N.J.: Rutgers University Press, 1984, 61–79.

Ferree, M. M., and Hess, B. *Controversy and Coalition: The New Feminist Movement.* Boston: Twayne Publishers, 1985.

Fidell, L. S. "Put Her Down on Drugs: Prescribes Drug Usage in Women." Paper presented at the Western Psychological Association Meeting, Anaheim, Calif., 1973.

Figes, E. *Patriarchal Attitudes.* New York: Stein and Day, 1970.

Finkelhor, D. *Sexually Victimized Children.* New York: Free Press, 1979.

——— (ed.). *The Dark Side of Families: Current Family Violence Research.* Beverly Hills, Calif.: Sage Publications, 1983.

Finkelhor, D., and Yllo, K. *License to Rape: Sexual Abuse of Wives.* New York: Holt, Rinehart, and Winston, 1985.

Firestone, S. *The Dialectic of Sex: The Case for Feminist Revolution.* New York: William Morrow, 1970.

Flacks, R., and Turkel, G. "Radical Sociology: The Emergence of Neo-Marxian Perspectives in U.S. Sociology." *Annual Review of Sociology,* **4**(1978):193–238.

Flax, J. "Do Feminists Need Marxism?" *Quest,* **3**(Summer 1976):46–58.

Flexner, E. *Mary Wollstonecraft: A Biography.* New York: Coward, McCann, and Geoghegan, 1972.

———. *Century of Struggle: The Woman's Rights Movement in the United States,* Rev. Ed. Cambridge: Harvard University Press, 1975.

Fling, S., and Manosevitz, M. "Sex Typing in Nursery School Children's Play Interests." *Developmental Psychology,* **7**(1972):146–152.

Flora, C. B. "The Passive Female: Her Comparative Image by Class and Culture in Women's Magazine Fiction." *Journal of Marriage and the Family,* **33**(1971):435–444.

———. "Changes in Women's Status in Women's Magazine Fiction: Differences by Social Class." *Social Problems,* **26**(1979):558–569.

Flowers, R. B. *Religion in Strange Times: The 1960s and 1970s.* Macon, Ga.: Mercer University Press, 1984.

Foucault, M. *Madness and Civilization: A History of Insanity in the Age of Reason.* London: Social Science, 1967.

Fox, L. H., Fennema, E., and Sherman, J. (eds.). *Women and Mathematics: Research Perspectives for Change.* Washington, D.C.: National Institute of Education, November 1977.

Fox, L. H., Tobin, D., and Brody, L. "Sex Role Socialization and Achievement in

Mathematics." In M. A. Wittig and A. C. Peterson (eds.), *Sex-Related Differences in Cognitive Functioning*. New York: Academic Press, 1979.

Frankfurter, F. "Hours of Labor and Realism in Constitutional Law." *Harvard Law Review,* **29**(1916):353–373.

Franklin, A. "Criminology in the Workplace: A Comparison of Male and Female Offenders." In F. Adler and R. J. Simon (eds.), *The Criminology of Deviant Women*. Boston: Houghton-Mifflin, 1979, 167–179.

Frazier, E. F. *The Negro Family in the United States*. New York: Citadel Press, 1948.

――. *The Negro Church in America*. New York: Schocken, 1964.

Freedman, E., and Thorne, B. "Introduction to 'The Feminist Sexuality Debates.'" *Signs,* **10**(Autumn 1984):102–105.

Freeman, J. "The Origins of the Women's Liberation Movement." *American Journal of Sociology,* **78**(1973):792–811.

Frey, K. "Middle-Aged Women's Experience and Perceptions of Menopause." *Women and Health,* **6**(1981):31–36.

Friedan, B. *The Feminine Mystique*. New York: Norton, 1963.

Friedl, E. *Women and Men*. New York: Holt, Rinehart & Winston, 1975.

Friedman, M., and Rosenman, R. H. *Type A Behavior and Your Heart*. New York: Knopf, 1974.

Frieze, I. H. "Investigating the Causes and Consequences of Marital Rape." *Signs,* **8**(Spring 1983):532–553.

Frieze, I., Parsons, J., Johnson, P., Ruble, D. N., and Zellman, G. (eds.). *Women and Sex Roles*. New York: Norton, 1978.

Frieze, I., and Ramsey, S. J. "Nonverbal Maintenance of Traditional Sex Roles." *Journal of Social Issues,* **32**(1976):133–141.

Frieze, I. H., Whitley, B. E., Hanusa, B. H., and McHugh, M. H. (eds.). "Sex Differences in Casual Attributions for Success and Failure: A Current Assessment." *Sex Roles,* **8**(April 1982):333–343.

Frueh, T., and McGhee, P. E. "Traditional Sex Role Development and Amount of Time Spent Watching Television." *Development Psychology,* **11**(1975):109.

Fulbright, K. "The Myth of the Double Advantage: Black Female Managers." In M. Simms and J. M. Malveaux (eds.), *Slipping Through the Cracks: The Status of Black Women*. New Brunswick, N.J. Transaction Books, 1986, 33–46.

Fullerton, H. N., Jr. "The 1995 Labor Force; BLS' Latest Projections." *Monthly Labor Review,* **108**(November 1985):17–25.

Furstenberg, F., Jr., and Nord, C. W. "Parenting Apart: Patterns of Childrearing After Marital Disruption." *Journal of Marriage and the Family,* **47**(November 1985):893–904.

Gallup Report, *Religion in American 50 Years: 1935–1985*. Princeton, New Jersey: Gallup Poll, May 1985.

Garfinkel, P. *In a Man's World*. New York: New American Library, 1985.

Garrett, G. R., and Bahr, H. M. "The Family Backgrounds of Skid Row Women." *Signs,* **2**(Winter 1976):369–381.

Genovese, E. *Roll, Jordan, Roll*. New York: Pantheon, 1972.

Gerbner, G. "The Dynamics of Cultural Resistance." In G. Tuchman, A. K. Daniels, and J. Benét (eds.), *Hearth and Home: Images of Women in the Media*. New York: Oxford University Press, 1978, 46–50.

Gershenson, H. "Redefining Fatherhood in Families with White Adolescent Mothers." *Journal of Marriage and the Family,* **45**(August 1983):591–599.

Gerson, J. "Women Returning to School: The Consequences of Multiple Roles." *Sex Roles,* **13**(July 1985):77–91.

Gerstel, N. R., and Gross, H. *Commuter Marriage.* New York: Guilford, 1984.

Gerth, H. H., and Mills, C. W. (eds). *From Max Weber: Essays in Sociology.* New York: Oxford University Press, 1958.

Ghent, W. *Our Benevolent Feudalism.* New York: Macmillan, 1902.

Giallombardo, R. *Society of Women: A Study of A Women's Prison.* New York: Wiley, 1966.

Giddens, A. *Capitalism and Modern Social Theory: An Analysis of the Writings of Marx, Durkheim, and Max Weber.* Cambridge: Cambridge University Press, 1971.

Gilder, G. *Wealth and Poverty.* New York: Basic Books, 1981.

Gilkes, C. T. "'Holding Back the Ocean with a Broom': Black Women and Community Work." In L. F. Rodgers-Rose (ed.), *The Black Woman.* Beverly Hills, Calif.: Sage Publications, 1980.

———. "Together and in Harness: Women's Traditions in the Sanctified Church." *Signs,* **10**(Summer 1985):678–699.

Gilligan, C. *In a Different Voice.* Cambridge: Harvard University Press, 1982.

Glaser, R. D., and Thorpe, J. S. "Unethical Intimacy." *American Psychologist,* **41**(January 1986):43–51.

Glenn, E. N. "The Dialectics of Wage Work: Japanese American Women and Domestic Service, 1905–1940." *Feminist Studies,* **6**(Fall 1980):432–471.

———. "Split Household, Small Producer, and Dual Wage Earner: An Analysis of Chinese-American Family Strategies." *Journal of Marriage and the Family,* **45**(February 1983):35–46.

———. *Issei, Nisei, War Bride: Three Generations of Japanese-American Women in Domestic Service.* Philadelphia: Temple University Press, 1986.

Glenn, E. N., and Feldberg, R. "Degraded and Deskilled: The Proletarianization of Clerical Work." In R. Kahn-Hut, A. K. Daniels, and R. Colvard (eds.), *Women and Work: Problems and Perspectives.* New York: Oxford University Press, 1982, 202–217.

Glick, P. C., and Norton, A. J. "Marrying, Divorcing, and Living Together in the U.S. Today." *Population Bulletin,* **32**(1977):2–38.

Glick, R. M., and Neto, V. V. *National Study of Women's Correctional Programs.* Washington, D.C.: U.S. Government Printing Office, 1977.

Godfrey, M. A. "Nurses' Salaries Around the Country." *Nursing '74,* **4**(1974):54–55.

Goldberg, S. *The Inevitability of Patriarchy.* New York: William Morrow, 1974.

Goldberg, S., and Lewis, M. "Play Behavior in the Year-old Infant: Early Sex Differences." *Child Development,* **40**(1969):21–31.

Goldsmith, S. *Prison Health: Travesty of Justice.* New York: Prodist, 1975.

———. *The Constitutional Rights of Women.* Madison: University of Wisconsin Press, 1988.

Golub, S. (ed.). "Lifting the Curse of Menstruation." *Women and Health,* **8**(Summer/Fall 1983):1–156.

Goode, W. J. "Community Within a Community: The Professions." *American Sociological Review,* **22**(1957):195–200.

Goodman, M. "Toward a Biology of Menopause." *Signs,* **5**(1980):739–753.

Gordon, L. *Woman's Body/Woman's Right.* New York: Penguin Books, 1977.

Gordon, M. T., Riger, S., LeBailly, R. K., and Health, L. "Crime, Women, and the Quality of Urban Life." *Signs,* **5**:3 supplement(Spring 1980):5144–5160.

Gornick, V. "Woman as Outsider." In V. Gornick and B. Moran (eds.), *Woman in Sexist Society.* New York: Basic Books, 1971, 126:144.

Gough, K. "The Origin of the Family." In R. Reiter (ed.), *Toward an Anthropology of Women.* New York: Monthly Review Press, 1975.

Gould, C. C., and Wartosky, M. W. *Women and Philosophy.* New York: Putnam, 1976.

Grandberg, D. G., and Grandberg, B. W. "Abortion Attitudes, 1965–1980: Trends and Determinants." *Family Planning Perspectives,* **12**(1980):250–261.

Graney, M. J. "An Exploration of the Social Factors Influencing the Sex Differential in Mortality." Paper presented at the Thirtieth Annual Meeting of the Gerontological Society, San Francisco, 1977.

Grant, J. "Black Women and the Church." In G. Hull, P. B. Scott, and B. Smith (eds.), *All the Women Are White, All the Blacks Are Men, But Some of Us Are Brave.* Old Westbury, N.Y.: The Feminist Press, 1982, 141–152.

Greenburg, B. "Children's Reactions to TV Blacks." *Journalism Quarterly,* **49**(1972):5–14.

Griffin, S. "Rape: The All-American Crime." *Ramparts,* **10**(1971):26–35.

Grimm, J. W. "Women in Female-Dominated Professions." In A. Stromberg and S. Harkess (eds.), *Women Working.* Palo Alto, Calif.: Mayfield, 1978, 293–315.

Grimm, J. W., and Stern, R. N. "Sex Roles and Internal Labor Market Structures: the 'Female' Semi-professions." *Social Problems,* **21**(1974):690–705.

Gross, H. "Couples Who Live Apart: Two Types." *Journal of Marriage and the Family,* **42**(1980):567–576.

Gross, L., and Jeffries-Fox, S. N. "What Do You Want To Be When You Grow Up, Little Girl?" In G. Tuchman, A. K. Daniels, and J. Benét (eds.), *Hearth and Home: Images of Women in the Mass Media.* New York: Oxford University Press, 1978, 240–265.

Grossman, A. S. "Women in Domestic Work: Yesterday and Today." *Monthly Labor Review,* **103**(1980):17–21.

Gump, J. "Reality and Myth: Employment and Sex Role Ideology in Black Women." In F. Denmark and J. Sherman (eds.), *The Psychology of Women.* New York: Psychological Dimentions, 1980.

Alan Gutmacher Institute. "Sterilization Rates Rose Most for Women 15–24 Before 1976 and 1978." *Family Planning Perspectives,* **13**(1981):236–237.

Gutman, H. *The Black Family in Slavery and Freedom.* New York: Vintage, 1976.

Hacker, H. "Women as a Minority Group." *Social Forces,* **30**(1951):60–69.

Hacker, S. L. "Sex Stratification, Technology, and Organizational Change: A Longitudinal Case Study of AT&T." *Social Problems,* **26**(1979):539–569.

———. "Farming Out the Home: Women and Agribusiness." In J. R. Kaplan (ed.), *A Woman's Conflict: The Special Relationship Between Women and Food.* Englewood Cliffs, N.J.: Prentice-Hall, 1980, 233–263.

Haft, M. "Women in Prison: Discriminatory Practices and Some Legal Solutions."

In S. Datesman and F. Scarpitti (eds.), *Women, Crime and Society.* New York: Oxford University Press, 1980, 320–338.

Hall, E. J., and Ferree, M. M. "Race Differences in Abortion Attitudes." *Public Opinion Quarterly,* **50**(1986):193–207.

Hall, R. M. "The Classroom Climate: A Chilly One for Women?" Washington, D.C.: Project on the Education and Status of Women, Association of American Colleges, 1982.

Hans, V. P., and Vidmar, N. *Judging the Jury.* New York: Plenum Press, 1986.

Harding, S. "Is the Equality of Opportunity Principle Democratic?" *Philosophical Forum,* **10**(1979):206–223.

———. "What Is the Real Material Base of Patriarchy and Capital?" In L. Sargent (ed.), *Women and Revolution.* Boston: South End Press, 1981, 135–163.

———. *The Science Question in Feminism.* Ithaca, N.Y.: Cornell University Press, 1986.

Hargrove, B., Schmidt, J. M., and Davaney, S. G. "Religion and the Changing Role of Women." *Annals of the American Academy of Political and Social Science,* **480**(July 1985):117–131.

Harland, M. *House and Home: The Complete Housewives' Guide:* Philadelphia: Clawson, 1889.

The Harris Survey. Orlando, Florida, Tribune Media Services, Inc., August 1985.

Harrison, J. "Men's Roles and Men's Lives." *Signs,* **4**(Winter 1978):324–336.

Hartley, R. E. "Sex Role Pressures and the Socialization of the Male Child." *Psychological Reports,* **5**(1959):457–468.

Hartmann, H. "Capitalism, Patriarchy, and Job Segregation by Sex." *Signs,* **1**:3, Part 2(Spring 1976):137–169.

———. "The Family as the Locus of Gender, Class, and Political Struggle: The Example of Housework." *Signs,* **6**(Spring 1981a):366–394.

———. "The Unhappy Marriage of Marxism and Feminism: Towards a More Progressive Union." In L. Sargent (ed.), *Women and Revolution.* New York: South End Press, 1981b, 1–41.

Hartsock, N. "The Feminist Standpoint: Developing the Ground for a Specifically Feminist Historical Materialism." In N. Hartsock (ed.), *Money, Sex, and Power.* New York: Longman's, 1983, 231–251.

Hawkes G., and Taylor, M. "Power Structure in Mexican and Mexican-American Farm Labor Families." *Journal of Marriage and the Family,* **37**(1975):807–811.

Hawkins, R. A., and Oakey, R. E. "Estimation of Oestrone Sulphate, Oestradiol-17B and Oestrone in Peripheral Plasma: Concentrations During the Menstrual Cycle and in Men." *Journal of Endocrinology,* **60**(1974):3–17.

Headen, A. E., and Headen, S. W. "General Health Conditions and Medical Insurance Issues Concerning Black Women." In M. Simms and J. M. Malveaux (eds.), *Slipping Through the Cracks: The Status of Black Women.* New Brunswick, N.J.: Transaction Books, 1986, 183–197.

Hemmons, W. M. "The Women's Liberation Movement: Understanding Black Women's Attitudes." In L. F. Rodgers-Rose (ed.), *The Black Woman.* Beverly Hills, Calif.: Sage, 1980, 285–299.

Hendershot, G. E. "Pregnant Workers in the U.S." *Advancedata.* National Center for Health Statistics, U.S. Department of Health, Education, and Welfare, No. 11, September 15, 1977.

Herman, J. *Father-Daughter Incest.* Cambridge: Harvard University Press, 1981.

Herman, J., and Hirschman, L. "Father-Daughter Incest." *Signs,* **2**(Summer 1977):735–756.

Herskovits, M. *The Myth of the Negro Past.* Boston: Beacon Press, 1958.

Hess, B. B. "Sex Roles, Life Course, and Friendship." Paper presented at Miami University, Ohio, 1977.

Hess, B. B., and Markson, E. W. *Aging and Old Age.* New York: Macmillan, 1980.

Hess, B., Markson, E., and Stein, P. *Sociology.* New York: Macmillan, 1982.

Higginbotham, E. "Is Marriage a Priority? Class Differences in Marital Options of Educated Black Women." In Peter J. Stein (ed.), *Single Life: Unmarried Adults in Social Context.* New York: St. Martin's Press, 1981, 259–267.

Higham, J. *Strangers in the Land.* New York: Atheneum, 1965.

Hill, A. C. "Protection of Women Workers and the Courts: A Legal Case History." *Feminist Studies,* **5**(Summer 1979):247–273.

Hiller, D., and Philliber, W. H. "The Division of Labor in Contemporary Marriage: Expectations, Perceptions, and Performance." *Social Problems,* **33**(February 1986):191–201.

Hilton, T. L., and Berglund, G. W. "Sex Differences in Mathematical Achievement: A Longitudinal Study." *Journal of Educational Research,* **67**(1974):231–237.

Himmelstein, J. L. "The Basis of Antifeminism: Religious Networks and Culture." *Journal for the Scientific Study of Religion,* **25**(1986):1–15.

Hindelang, M. "Race and Involvement in Crime." *American Sociological Review,* **43**(1978):93–109.

Hochschild, A. "The Sociology of Feeling and Emotion." In M. Millman and R. M. Kanter (eds.), *Another Voice.* Garden City, N.Y.: Doubleday-Anchor, 1975, 280–307.

———. *The Managed Heart: Commercialization of Human Feeling.* Berkeley: University of California Press, 1983.

Hoffman-Bustamante, D. "The Nature of Female Delinquency." *Issues in Criminology,* **8**(Fall 1973):117–36.

Hofstadter, R. *Social Darwinism in American Thought.* New York: Braziller, 1959.

Hole, J., and Levine, E. (eds.). *Rebirth of Feminism.* New York: Quadrangle Books, 1971.

Hoover, T. "Black Women and the Churches: Triple Jeopardy." In A. L. Hageman (ed.), *Sexist Religion and Women in the Church.* New York: Association Press, 1974, 63–76.

Horan, P. M. "Is Status Attainment Research Atheoretical?" *American Sociological Review,* **4**(1978):534–540.

Hornig, L. S. "Untenured and Tenuous: The Status of Women Faculty." *Annals of the American Academy of Political and Social Science,* **448**(1980):115–125.

Horwitz, C. "Factors Influencing Shoplifting Activity Among Adult Women." Ph.D. Dissertation, University of Delaware, Department of Sociology, June 1986.

Hosken, F. P. *The Hosken Report: Genital and Sexual Mutilation of Females.* Lexington, Mass.: Women's International Network News, 1979.

Howe, L. K. *Pink Collar Workers.* New York: Putnam, 1977.

Hoyenga, K. B., and Hoyenga, K. *The Question of Sex Differences: Psychological, Cultural, and Biological Issues.* Boston: Little, Brown, 1979.

Hubbard, R. "Have Only Men Evolved?" In R. Hubbard, M. S. Henifin, and B. Fried (eds.), *Women Look at Biology Looking at Women.* Cambridge, Mass.: Schenckman, 1979, 7–36.

————. "Feminist Science: A Meaningful Concept?" Paper presented at the Annual Meetings of the National Women's Studies Association. New Brunswick, New Jersey, 1984.

Hughes, H. S. *Consciousness and Society.* New York: Knopf, 1958.

Hull, G. T. "Reading Literature by U.S. Third World Women." *Working Papers Series.* Wellesley, Mass.: Wellesley College Center for Research on Women, 1984.

Hunt, V. R. "A Brief History of Women Workers and Hazards in the Workplace." *Feminist Studies,* **5**(Summer 1979):274–285.

Hurst, M., and Zambrana, R. E. "The Health Careers of Urban Women: A Study in East Harlem." *Signs,* **5**:3 Supplement(Spring 1980):S112–S126.

Hyde, J. "How Large Are Cognitive Gender Differences? An Analysis Using w and d." *American Psychologist,* **36**(August 1981):892–901.

Illich, I. *Disabling Professions.* Salem, N.H.: Boyars, 1977.

Infante, P. "Genetic Risks of Vinyl Chloride." *Lancet,* **3**(1975):734–735.

Ireson, C. "Adolescent Pregnancy and Sex Roles." *Sex Roles,* **11**(August 1984):189–201.

Jacklin, C. N., MacCoby, E. E., and Dick, A. E. "Barrier Behavior and Toy Preference: Sex Differences (and Their Absence) in the Year-old Child." *Child Development,* **44**(1973):196–200.

Jackson, J. J. "Aged Black Americans: Double Jeopardy Re-examined." In James D. Williams (ed.), *The State of Black America 1985.* New York: National Urban League, 1985, 143–184.

Jacobs, J. "The Economy of Love in Religious Commitment: The Deconversion of Women from Nontraditional Religious Movements." *Journal for the Scientific Study of Religion,* **23**(June 1984):155–171.

Jacobs, R. *Life After Youth: Female, Forty, What Next?* Boston: Beacon Press, 1979.

Jacobson, D. "The Women of North and Central India: Goddesses and Wives." In C. Matthiasson (ed.), *Many Sisters.* New York: Free Press, 1974, 99–175.

Jacquet, C. H., Jr. *Women Ministers in 1977.* New York: National Council of Churches, 1978.

Jaget, C. (ed.). *Prostitutes: Our Life.* Bristol, England: Falling Wall Press, 1980.

Jaggar, A., and Struhl, P. R. *Feminist Frameworks: Alternative Theoretical Accounts of the Relations Between Women and Men,* 2/e. New York: McGraw-Hill, 1984.

James, J. W. *Women in American Religion.* Philadelphia: University of Pennsylvania Press, 1980.

Jencks, C. *Who Gets Ahead? The Determinants of Economic Success in America.* New York: Basic Books, 1979.

Jensen, G. J., and Eve, R. "Sex Differences in Delinquency." *Criminology,* **13**(1976):427–448.

Joffe, C. "Sex Role Socialization and the Nursery School: As the Twig Is Bent." *Journal of Marriage and the Family,* **33**(1971):467–475.

Johnson, W. R. *Human Sexual Behavior and Sex Education.* Philadelphia: Lea and Febiger, 1968.

Johnston, L. C., Bachman, G. G., and O'Malley, P. M. *Student Drug Use in America: 1975–1981.* Rockville, Md.: National Institute on Drug Abuse, 1982.

Jones, A. *Women Who Kill.* New York: Holt, Rinehart & Winston, 1980.

Jones, B.A.P. "Black Women and Labor Force Participation: An Analysis of Sluggish Growth Rates." In M. Simms and J. M. Malveaux (eds.), *Slipping Through the Cracks: The Status of Black Women.* New Brunswick, N.J.: Transaction Books, 1986, 11–32.

Jones, J. "My Mother Was Much of a Woman: Black Women, Work, and the Family Under Slavery." *Feminist Studies,* **8**(Summer 1982):235–270.

———. *Labor of Love, Labor of Sorrow: Black Women, Work, and the Family from Slavery to the Present.* New York: Basic Books, 1985.

Jordan, W. *White Over Black.* Baltimore: Penguin Books, 1968.

Joseph G. "Mothers and Daughters: Traditional and New Perspectives." *Sage,* **1**(Fall 1984):17–21.

Jourard, S. M. "Some Lethal Aspects of the Male Role." In J. Pleck and J. Sawyer (eds.), *Men and Masculinity.* Englewood Cliffs, N.J.: Spectrum Books, 1974, 21–29.

Julty, S. "A Case of 'Sexual Dysfunction.'" In J. Pleck and J. Sawyer (eds.), *Men and Masculinity.* Englewood Cliffs, N.J.: Spectrum Books, 1974, 35–40.

Jusenius, C. L. "Review Essay: Economics." *Signs,* **2**(Autumn 1976):177–189.

Kagan, J., and Lewis, M. "Studies of Attention in the Human Infant." *Merrill-Palmer Quarterly,* **11**(1965):95–137.

Kamin, L. J. "Is Crime in the Genes?" *Scientific American,* **254**(February 1986):22–27.

Kanter, R. M., *Men and Women of the Corporation.* New York: Basic Books, 1977.

Kapp, Y. *Eleanor Marx, Volume One.* New York: Pantheon, 1972.

Katzman, D. *Seven Days A Week: Women and Domestic Service in Industrializing America.* New York: Oxford University Press, 1978.

Kaufman, S., and Wylie, M. L. "One Session Workshop on Sexual Harassment." *Journal of the National Association for Women Deans, Administrators, and Counselors,* **46**(Winter 1983):39–42.

Kehrer, B. H. "Factors Affecting the Incomes of Men and Women Physicians: An Exploratory Analysis." *Journal of Human Resources,* **11**(Fall 1976):526–545.

Keller, E. F. *Reflections on Gender and Science.* New Haven, Conn.: Yale University Press, 1985.

Kelly-Gadol, J. "The Social Relations of the Sexes: Methodological Implications of Women's History." *Signs,* **1**(Summer 1976):809–824.

Kessler-Harris, A. "Women, Work, and the Social Order." In B. A. Carroll (ed.), *Liberating Women's History.* Urbana: University of Illinois Press, 1976, 330–343.

———. *Out to Work: A History of Wage-Earning Women in the U.S.* New York: Oxford University Press, 1982.

Kilbourne, J. "Killing Us Softly." Film. Cambridge, Mass.: Cambridge Documentary Films, 1979.

Kinsey, A. C., et al. *Sexual Behavior in the Human Female.* New York: Pocket Books, 1953.

Klass, A. *There's Gold in Them Thar Pills.* London: Penguin Books, 1975.

Klein, D. "The Etiology of Female Crime: A Review of the Literature." In S. K.

Datesman and F. R. Scarpitti (eds.), *Women, Crime, and Justice*. New York: Oxford University Press, 1980, 70–105.

Kleinbaum, A. R. "Women in the Age of Light." In R. Bridenthal and C. Koonz (eds.), *Becoming Visible: Women in European History*. Boston: Houghton-Mifflin, 1977, 217–235.

Kluckhohn, C. *Culture and Behavior*. New York: Free Press, 1962.

Kohlberg, L. "A Cognitive-Developmental Analysis of Children's Sex Role Concepts and Attitudes." In E. Maccoby (ed.), *The Development of Sex Differences*. Stanford, Calif.: Stanford University Press, 1966, 82–166.

Kohn, M., and Schooler, C. "Job Conditions and Personality: A Longitudinal Assessment of Their Reciprocal Effects." *American Journal of Sociology*, **87**(May 1982):1257–1283.

Komarovsky, M. *Women in the Modern World*. Boston: Little, Brown, 1953.

———. "Cultural Contradictions and Sex Roles: The Masculine Case." *American Journal of Sociology*, **78**(1973):873–884.

Konopka, G. *The Adolescent Girl in Conflict*. Englewood Cliffs, N.J.: Prentice-Hall, 1966.

Kraditor, E. *Up from the Pedestal: Selected Writings in the History of American Feminism*. Chicago: Quadrangle Books, 1968.

Kruttschnitt, C. "Sex and Criminal Court Dispositions: The Unresolved Controversy." *Research in Crime and Delinquency*, **21**(August 1984):213–232.

Kruttschnitt, C. and McCarthy, D. "Familial Social Control and Pretrial Sanctions: Does Sex Really Matter?" *The Journal of Criminal Law and Criminology*, **76**(Spring 1985):151–175.

Ladner, J. *Tomorrow's Tomorrow*. Garden City, N.Y.: Doubleday-Anchor, 1971.

———. "Teenage Pregnancy: The Implications for Black Americans." In J. D. Williams (ed.), *The State of Black America 1986*. New York: National Urban League, 1986, 65–84.

Ladner, J. A., and Gourdine, R. M. "Intergenerational Teenager Motherhood: Some Preliminary Findings." *Sage*, **1**(Fall 1984):22–24.

LaFree, G. "The Effect of Sexual Stratification by Race on Official Reactions to Rape." *American Sociological Review*, **45**(October 1980):842–854.

Lambert, H. H. "Biology and Equality: A Perspective on Sex Differences." *Signs*, **4**(Autumn 1978):97–117.

Lamphere, L. "Anthropology." *Signs*, **2**(Spring 1977):612–627.

———. "On the Shop Floor: Multi-ethnic Unity Against the Conglomerate." In K. B. Sacks and D. Remy (eds.), *My Troubles Are Going to Have Trouble with Me*. New Brunswick, N.J.: Rutgers University Press, 1984, 247–262.

Lamphere, L. "Bringing the Family to Work: Women's Culture on The Shop Floor." *Feminist Studies* **11**(Fall 1985):519–540.

Langlois, K. "Interview with Sonia Johnson." *Feminist Studies*, **8**(Spring 1982):7–18.

La Rossa, R., and La Rossa, M. *Transition to Parenthood*. Beverly Hills: Sage Publications, 1981.

Lasch, C. *Haven in a Heartless World: The Family Besieged*. New York: Basic Books, 1977.

Laub, J. H., and McDermott, M. J. "An Analysis of Serious Crime by Young Black Women." *Criminology*, **23**(February 1985):81–98.

Lawrence, M. *The Anorexic Experience.* London: The Women's Press, 1984.

Leacock, E. "Women's Status in Egalitarian Society." Contemporary Anthropology, **19**(1978):247–275.

Leghorn, L., and Parker, K. *Woman's Worth: Sexual Economics and the World of Women.* Boston: Routledge & Kegan Paul, 1981.

Lehman, E. C., Jr. "Organizational Resistance to Women in Ministry." *Sociological Analysis,* **41**(Winter 1980):317–338.

Lemert, E. *Human Deviance, Social Problems, and Social Control.* Englewood Cliffs, N.J.: Prentice-Hall, 1972.

Lemon, J. "Dominant or Dominated? Women on Prime-Time Television." In G. Tuchman, A. K. Daniels, and J. Benét (eds.), *Hearth and Home: Images of Women in the Mass Media.* New York: Oxford University Press, 1978, 51–68.

Leonard, E. B. "Judicial Decisions and Prison Reform: The Impact of Litigation on Women Prisoners." *Social Problems,* **31**(October 1983):45–58.

Lerner, G. *Black Women in White America: A Documentary History.* New York: Vintage, 1973.

――――. "Placing Women in History: A 1975 Perspective." In B. Carroll (ed.), *Liberating Women's History.* Urbana: University of Illinois Press, 1976, 357–367.

Lever, J. "Sex Differences in the Complexity of Children's Play and Games." *American Sociological Review,* **43**(1978):471–483.

Levine, J. *Who Will Raise the Children? New Options for Fathers and Mothers.* New York: Lippincott, 1976.

Levinger, G. "Sources of Marital Dissatisfaction Among Applicants for Divorce." *American Journal of Orthopsychiatry,* **36**(1966):803–807.

Levitan, S. A., and Belous, R. "Working Wives and Mothers: What Happens to Family Life?" *Monthly Labor Review,* **104**(1981):26–30.

Lewis, D. K. "A Response to Inequality: Black Women, Racism, and Sexism." *Signs,* **3**(Winter 1977):339–361.

――――. "Black Women Offenders and Criminal Justice." In M. Q. Warren (ed.), *Comparing Female and Male Offenders.* Beverly Hills, Calif.: Sage, 1981, 89–105.

Lewis, K. G. "Children of Lesbians: Their Point of View." *Social Work,* **25**(May 1980):198–203.

Lewis, R. A. "Emotional Intimacy Among Men." *The Journal of Social Issues,* **34**(Winter 1978):108–121.

Lewis, S. G. *Sunday's Women: A Report on Lesbian Life Today.* Boston: Beacon Press, 1979.

Liebert, R. M., Neale, J. N., and Davidson, E. S. *The Early Window: Effects of Television on Children and Youth.* New York: Pergamon, 1973.

Linn, M. C., and Petersen, A. C. "Emergence and Characterization of Sex Differences in Spatial Ability: A Meta-analysis." *Child Development,* **56**(December 1985):1479–1498.

Lipset, S. M. (ed). *Harriet Martineau: Society in America.* New York: Doubleday, 1962.

Liss-Levinson, W. "Men Without Playfulness." In R. A. Lewis (ed.), *Men in Difficult Times: Masculinity Today and Tomorrow.* Englewood Cliffs, New Jersey: Prentice-Hall, 1981.

Litoff, J. B. *American Midwives, 1860 to the Present.* Westport, Conn.: Greenwood Press, 1978.

Livson, F. B. "Cultural Faces of Eve." Paper presented at the Annual Meeting of the American Psychological Association, San Francisco, 1977.

Lizotte, A. "The Uniqueness of Rape: Reporting Assaultive Violence to the Police." *Crime and Delinquency,* **31**(April 1985):169–190.

Locksley, A. "On the Effects of Wives' Employment on Marital Adjustment and Companionship." *Journal of Marriage and the Family,* **42**(1980):337–346.

Lombroso, N. *The Female Offender.* New York: Appleton, 1920.

Longino, H., and Doell, R. "Body, Bias, and Behavior: Comparative Analysis of Reasoning in Two Areas of Biological Science." *Signs,* **9**(Winter 1983):206–227.

Lopata, H. Z. *Occupation: Housewife.* New York: Oxford University Press, 1971.

———. *Widowhood in an American City.* Cambridge, Mass.: Schenckman, 1973.

Lopata, H. Z., and Thorne, B. "On the Term 'Sex Roles.'" *Signs,* **3**(Spring 1978):718–721.

Lorber, J. "Women and Medical Sociology: Invisible Professionals and Ubiquitous Patients." In M. Millman and R. M. Kanter (eds.), *Another Voice.* Garden City, N.Y.: Doubleday-Anchor, 1975, 75–105.

Lorber, J., Coser, R. L., Rossi, A. S., and Chodorow, N. "On 'The Reproduction of Mothering': A Methodological Debate." *Signs,* **6**(1981):482–514.

Loury, G. "Beyond Civil Rights." In J. Williams (ed.), *The State of Black America 1986.* New York: National Urban League, 1986, 163–174.

Lowe, M. "The Dialectic of Biology and Culture." In M. Lowe and R. Hubbard (eds.), *Woman's Nature.* New York: Pergamon Press, 1983, 39–62.

Lowe, M., and Hubbard, R. (eds.). *Woman's Nature.* New York: Pergamon Press, 1983.

Lozoff, M. "Changing Life Style and Role Perceptions of Men and Women Students." Paper presented at Radcliffe College, Cambridge, Mass., 1972.

Luker, K. *Taking Chances.* Berkeley: University of California Press, 1975.

———. *Abortion and the Politics of Motherhood.* Berkeley: University of California Press, 1984.

Lundberg, F., and Farnham, M. *Modern Woman: The Lost Sex.* New York: Harper, 1947.

Lynn, N. B., Vaden, A. G., and Vaden, R. E. "The Challenge of Men in a Woman's World." *Public Personnel Management,* **4**(1975):4–17.

Maccoby, E. E., and Jacklin, C. N. *The Psychology of Sex Differences.* Stanford, Calif.: Stanford University Press, 1974.

MacCorquodale, P. L. "Gender Roles and Premarital Contraception." *Journal of Marriage and the Family,* **46**(February 1984):57–62.

MacDonald, J. F. *Black and White TV: Afro-Americans in Television Since 1948.* New York: Nelson Hall Publishers, 1983.

Machung, A. "Word Processing: Forward for Business, Backward for Women." In K. B. Sacks and D. Remy (eds.), *My Troubles Are Going to Have Trouble with Me.* New Brunswick, N.J.: Rutgers University Press, 1984, 124–139.

MacFarlane, K. "Sexual Abuse of Children." J. R. Chapman and M. Gates (eds.), *The Victimization of Women.* Beverly Hills: Sage Publications, 1978, 81–109.

———. "Feminism, Marxism, Method, and the State: An Agenda for Theory." *Signs,* **7**(Spring 1982):515–544.

MacKinnon, C. "Feminism, Marxism, Method, and the State: Toward Feminist Jurisprudence." *Signs,* **8**(Summer 1983):635–658.

Macklin, E. D. "Nonmarital Heterosexual Cohabitation." *Marriage and Family Review,* **1**(1978):1–12.

Malbin-Glazer, N. "Housework." *Signs,* **1**(Summer 1976):905–922.

Mandelbaum, D. R. "Women in Medicine." *Signs,* **4**(Autumn 1978):136–145.

Mann, J. "Infant Death Toll." *Washington Post,* **B**(January 24, 1986):3.

Mannheim, K. *Ideology and Utopia.* New York: Harcourt, Brace, and World, 1936.

Markson, E. W., and Hess, B. B. "Older Women in the City." *Signs,* **5**(Spring 1980):S127–S141.

Martin, D. *Battered Wives.* San Francisco: Glide, 1976.

Martineau, H. *Society in America.* Paris: Baudry's European Library, 1837.

———. *How to Observe Manners and Morals.* London: C. Knight, 1838.

Marx, G. "Religion: Opiate or Inspiration of Civil Rights Militancy Among Negroes." *American Sociological Review,* **32**(February 1967):64–72.

Marx, K., and Engels, F. *The Communist Manifesto.* New York: Pathfinder Press, 1970.

Mason, K. O., and Bumpass L. "U.S. Women's Sex Role Ideology, 1970." *American Journal of Sociology,* **80**(March 1975):1212–1219.

Malson, M. R. "Black Women's Sex Roles: The Social Context of a New Ideology." *Journal of Social Issues,* **39**(1983):101–113.

Masters, W. H., and Johnson, V. E. *Human Sexual Response.* Boston: Little, Brown, 1966.

Matthiasson, C. *Many Sisters.* New York: Free Press, 1974.

Matza, D. *Becoming Deviant.* Englewood Cliffs, N.J.: Prentice-Hall, 1969.

Maxwell, B. D. *Employment of Minority Ph.D.'s: Changes Over Time.* Washington, D.C.: National Academy Press, 1981.

McBride, T. *The Domestic Revolution.* London: Croom Helms, 1976.

McClintock M. "Menstrual Synchrony and Suppression." *Nature,* **229**(1971):244–245.

McConnell-Ginet, S. "Intonation in a Man's World." *Signs,* **3**(Spring 1978):541–559.

McCormack, A., Janus, M. D., and Burgess, A. W. "Runaway Youths and Sexual Victimization: Gender Differences in an Adolescent Runaway Population." *Child Abuse and Neglect,* **10**(1986):387–395.

McCray, C. A. "The Black Woman and Family Roles." In L. F. Rodgers-Rose (ed.), *The Black Woman.* Beverly Hills, Calif.: Sage, 1980, 67–78.

McGhee, J. D. "Profile of the Black Single Female–Headed Household." In J. D. Williams (ed.), *The State of Black America 1984.* New York: National Urban League, 1984.

McGuire, M. B. *Religion: The Social Context.* Belmont, Calif.: Wadsworth Publishing, 1981.

McIntosh, M. "Who Needs Prostitutes?" In C. Smart and B. Smart (eds.), *Women, Sexuality, and Social Control.* London: Routledge & Kegan Paul, 1978, 63–64.

McIntosh, P. "Interactive Phases of Curricular Re-vision: A Feminist Perspective." *Working Papers Series.* Wellesley, Mass.: Wellesley Center for Research on Women, 1983.

McKinley, J. "The Drug Pusher in the Grey Flannel Suit." *Playboy,* **25**(1978):165ff.

McKinney, F. "Employment Implications of a Changing Health-Care System." In

M. Simms and J. M. Malveaux (eds.), Slipping Through the Cracks: The Status of Black Women. New Brunswick, N.J.: Transaction Books, 1986, 199–215.

McNulty, D. J. "Differences in Pay Between Men and Women Workers." *Labor Review,* **90**(1967):40–43.

McNulty, J. "The VDT Controversy." *Mothering,* **39**(Spring 1986):69–77.

Mead Johnson and Company. "Names for Boys and Girls." Evansville, Ind., 1978.

Mead, M. *Sex and Temperament in Three Primitive Societies.* New York: Dell, 1949.

Mehrabian, A. "Verbal and Nonverbal Interaction of Strangers in a Waiting Situation." *Journal of Experimental Research in Personality,* **5**(1971):127–138.

Meier, A., and Rudwick, E. *From Plantation to Ghetto.* New York: Hill & Wang, 1966.

Meigs, C. D. *Lecture on Some of the Distinctive Characteristics of the Female. Delivered Before the Class of the Jefferson Medical College. January 5, 1847.* Philadelphia: Collins, 1847.

Meissner, M., et al. "No Exit for Wives: Sexual Division of Labour and the Cumulation of Household Demands." *Canadian Review of Sociology and Anthropology,* **12**(1975):424–439.

Melosh, B. *"The Physician's Hand": Work Culture and Conflict in American Nursing.* Philadelphia: Temple University Press, 1982.

Mendelsohn, E. "The Social Construction of Scientific Knowledge." In E. Mendelsohn, P. Weingart, and R. Whitley (eds.), *The Social Production of Scientific Knowledge.* Dordrecht: Riedel, 1977, 3–26.

Meriwether, L. "Teenage Pregnancy." *Essence,* **14**(April 1984):94ff.

Merritt, S., and Gross, H. "Women's Page/Life Style Editors: Does Sex Make a Difference?" *Journalism Quarterly,* **55**(1978):508–519.

Messing, K. "The Scientific Mystique: Can a White Lab Coat Guarantee Purity in the Search for Knowledge About the Nature of Women?" In M. Lowe and R. Hubbard (eds.), *Woman's Nature.* New York: Pergamon Press, 1983, 75–88.

Meyer, W. J., and Thompson, G. G. "Sex Differences in the Distribution of Teacher Approval and Disapproval Among Sixth-grade Children." *Journal of Educational Psychology,* **47**(1956):385–397.

Milkman, R. "Women's History and the Sears Case." *Feminist Studies,* **12**(Summer 1986):375–400.

Mill, J. S. *The Subjection of Women.* New York: Source Book Press, 1970.

Miller, D. *American Indian Socialization to Urban Life.* San Francisco: Institute for Scientific Analysis, 1975.

Miller, E. *Street Woman.* Philadelphia: Temple University Press, 1986.

Miller, J. B. *Toward a New Psychology of Women.* Boston: Beacon Press, 1977.

———. "Psychological Recovery in Low-Income Single Parents." *American Journal of Orthopsychiatry,* **52**(April 1982):346–352.

Millman, M. "She Did It All for Love." In M. Millman and R. M. Kanter (eds.), *Another Voice.* Garden City, N.Y.: Doubleday-Anchor, 1975, 251–279.

———. *Such a Pretty Face: Being Fat in America.* New York: W. W. Norton, 1980.

Millman, M., and Kanter, R. M. (eds.). *Another Voice.* Garden City, N.Y.: Doubleday-Anchor, 1975.

Mills, C. W. *The Sociological Imagination.* New York: Oxford University Press, 1959.

Milton, G. A. "Five Studies of the Relation Between Sex Role Identification and Achievement in Problem Solving." Department of Industrial Administration, Department of Psychology, Yale University, December 1958.

Mincer, J., and Polacheck, S. "Family Investments in Human Capital: Earnings of Women." *Journal of Political Economy,* **82**(1974):76–111.

Mirandé, A. "Machismo: A Reinterpretation of Male Dominance in the Chicano Family." *The Family Coordinator,* **28**(1979):447–479.

———. "Machismo, Rucas, Chingasos, y Chingaderas." *De Colores,* **6**(1982): 17–31.

Mischel, W. "Sex-typing and Socialization." In P. H. Mussen (ed.), *Carmichael's Manual of Child Psychology,* 3rd ed., Vol 2. New York: Wiley, 1970.

Mitchell, J. *Woman's Estate.* New York: Pantheon Books, 1971.

———. *Psychoanalysis and Feminism.* New York: Pantheon Books, 1974.

Modleski, T. "The Disappearing Act: A Study of Harlequin Romances." *Signs,* **5**(Spring 1980):435–448.

Mohr, J. *Abortion in America.* New York: Oxford University Press, 1978.

Money, J., and Ehrhardt, A. A. *Man, Woman, Boy and Girl: The Differentiation and Dimorphism of Gender Identity from Conception to Maturity.* Baltimore: Johns Hopkins University Press, 1972.

Mongeau, B., Smith, H. L., and Maney, A. C. "The 'Granny' Midwife: Changing Roles and Functions of a Folk Practitioner." *American Journal of Sociology,* **66**(1961):497–505.

Moore, J., and Pachon, H. *Hispanics in the U.S.* Englewood Cliffs, N.J.: Prentice-Hall, 1985.

Moraga, C., and Anzaldúa, G. *This Bridge Called My Back: Radical Writings by Women of Color.* Watertown, Mass.: Perspehone Press, 1981.

Morgan, J. N. "A Potpourri of New Data Gathered from Interviews with Husbands and Wives." In G. J. Duncan and J. N. Morgan (eds.), *Five Thousand American Families: Patterns of Economic Progress.* Ann Arbor: University of Michigan Press, 1978, 367–401.

Morin, S. F., and Garfinkle, E. M. "Male Homophobia." *The Journal of Social Issues,* **34**(Winter 1978):29–47.

Morton, W., and Ungs, T. "Cancer Mortality in the Major Cottage Industry." *Women and Health,* **4**(Winter 1979):305–354.

Moulds, E. F. "Chivalry and Paternalism: Disparities of Treatment in the Criminal Justice System." In S. Datesman and F. Scarpitti (eds.), *Women, Crime, and Justice.* New York: Oxford University Press, 1980, 277–299.

Moynihan, D. P. *The Negro Family: The Case for National Action.* Washington, D.C.: U.S. Government Printing Office, 1965.

Murillo, N. "The Mexican American Family." In N. Wagner and M. Hang (eds.), *Chicanos: Social and Psychological Perspectives.* St. Louis: Mosby, 1971, 97–108.

Myers, L. W. "Black Women and Self Esteem." In M. Millman and R. M. Kanter (eds.), *Another Voice.* Garden City, N.Y.: Doubleday-Anchor, 1975, 240–250.

Nadelson, C., and Nadelson, T. "Dual-Career Marriages: Benefits and Costs." In F. Pepitone-Rockwell (ed.), *Dual-Career Couples.* Beverly Hills, Calif.: Sage, 1980, 91–109.

Nathanson, C. "Illness and the Feminine Role: A Theoretical Review." *Social Science and Medicine,* **9**(1975):57–62.

————. "Social Roles and Health Status Among Women: The Significance of Employment." *Social Science and Medicine,* **14A**(1980):463–471.

National Center for Health Statistics, U.S. Department of Health and Human Services. *Health, United States 1985.* Washington, D.C.: U.S. Government Printing Office, December 1985.

National Research Council Committee on the Education and Employment of Women in Science and Engineering. *Career Outcomes in a Matched Sample of Men and Women Ph.D.s.* Washington, D.C.: National Academy Press, 1981.

Nazzari, M. "The 'Woman Question' in Cuba: An Analysis of Material Constraints on the Solution." *Signs,* **9**(Winter 1983):246–263.

Nelson, H. M., Cheek, N. H., and Au, P. "Gender Differences in Images of God." *Journal for the Scientific Study of Religion,* **24**(December 1985):396–402.

Neugarten, B. L. (ed.). *Middle Age and Aging.* Chicago: University of Chicago Press, 1975.

Niemi, B., and Lloyd, C. "Sex Differentials in Earnings and Unemployment Rates." *Feminist Studies,* **2**(1975):195–200.

Nisbet, R. A. *The Social Bond: An Introduction to the Study of Society.* New York: Knopf, 1970.

Nochlin, L. "Why Are There No Great Women Artists?" In V. Gornick and B. Moran (eds.), *Women in Sexist Society.* New York: Basic Books, 1971, 480–510.

Novick, L., Della Penna, R., Schwertz, M., Remmlingert, E., and Lowenstein, R. "Health Status of the New York City Prison Population." *Medical Care,* **205**(1977):205–216.

Nowak, T., and Snyder, K. "Sex Differences in the Long Term Consequences of Job Loss." Paper presented at the Annual Meeting of the American Sociological Association, New York City, September 1986.

Oakley, A. *The Sociology of Housework.* London: Mertin Robertson, 1974.

————. *Woman's Work: The Housewife, Past and Present.* New York: Pantheon Books, 1975.

————. "A Case of Maternity: Paradigms of Women as Maternity Cases." *Signs,* **4**(Summer 1979):607–631.

O'Kelly, C. G., and Carney, L. S. *Women and Men in Society,* 2nd ed. Belmont, Calif.: Wadsworth, 1986.

Olesen, V. L., and Katsuranis, F. "Urban Nomads: Women in Temporary Clerical Services." In A. Stromberg and S. Harkess (eds.), *Women Working.* Palo Alto, Calif.: Mayfield, 1978, 316–338.

Ortmeyer, L. E. "Female's Natural Advantage? Or, The Unhealthy Environment of Males?" *Women and Health,* **4**(Summer 1979):121–133.

Orwant, J. E., and Cantor, M. "How Sex Stereotyping Affects Perceptions of News Preferences." *Journalism Quarterly,* **54**(Spring 1977):99ff.

Osmond, M. W., and Yancey, P. M. "Sex and Sexism: A Comparison of Male and Female Sex Role Attitudes." *Journal of Marriage and the Family,* **37**(1975):744–752.

Owen, B. A. "Race and Gender Relations Among Prison Workers." *Crime and Delinquency,* **31**(January 1985):147–159.

Padavic, I., and Reskin, B. "Supervisors as Gatekeepers: Supervisor's Role in the Sex Segregation of Jobs." Paper presented at the Annual Meeting of the American Sociological Association, New York City, September 1986.

Pagelow, M. D. "Double Victimization of Battered Women." Paper presented at the Annual Meeting of the American Society of Criminology, San Francisco, November 1980.

Parelius, A. "Change and Stability in College Women's Orientations Toward Education, Family and Work." *Social Problems,* **22**(1975):420–432.

Parker, D., Parker, E., Wolz, M., and Harford, T. "Sex Differences and Alcohol Consumption: A Research Note." *Journal of Health and Social Behavior,* **21**(1980):43–48.

Parlee, M. B. "The Premenstrual Syndrome." *Psychological Bulletin,* **80**(1973):454–465.

Payer, M. "Is Traditional Scholarship Value Free? Toward a Critical Theory." Paper presented at the Scholar and the Feminist IV, Barnard College, New York, 1977.

Pederson, D. M., Shinedling, M. M., and Johnson, D. L. "Effects of Sex of Examiner and Subject on Children's Quantitative Test Performance." *Journal of Personality and Social Psychology,* **10**(1968):251–254.

Pearce, D. and McAdoo, H. *Women and Children: Alone and in Poverty.* Washington, D.C.: National Advisory Council on Economic Opportunity, September 1981.

Pekkanen, N. "Controlling Librium and Valium: The Tranquilizer War." *New Republic,* **173**(1975):17–19.

Petchesky, R. "Women, Reproductive Hazards and the Politics of Protection." *Feminist Studies,* **5**(Summer 1979):233–246.

———. "Reproductive Freedom: Beyond a Woman's Right to Choose." *Signs,* **5**(Summer 1980):661–685.

———. "Antiabortion, Antifeminism and the Rise of the New Right." *Feminist Studies,* **7**(Summer 1981):206–246.

Phillips, E. B. "The Artists of Everyday Life: Journalists, Their Craft, and Their Consciousness." Ph.D. dissertation, Syracuse University, 1975.

Piaget, J. *The Moral Judgment of the Child.* New York: Free Press, 1965.

Pleck, J. H. "The Work-Family Role System." *Social Problems,* **24**(1977):417–427.

———. "Men's Family Work: Three Perspectives and Some New Data." Unpublished paper, Wellesley College Center for Research on Women, Wellesley, Mass., 1979.

Pleck, J. H., and Brannon, R. (eds.). "Male Roles and the Male Experience." *Journal of Social Issues,* **34**(1978):1–195.

Pleck, J. H., and Sawyer, J. (eds.). *Men and Masculinity.* Englewood Cliffs, N.J.: Prentice-Hall, 1974.

Pohli, C. V. "Church Closets and Back Doors: A Feminist View of Moral Majority Women." *Feminist Studies,* **9**(Fall 1983):529–558.

Polachek, S. W. "Discontinuous Labor Force Participation and Its Effect on Women's Market Earnings." In C. Lloyd (ed.), *Sex, Discrimination, and the Division of Labor.* New York: Columbia University Press, 1975, 90–122.

Pollak, O. *The Criminology of Women.* Philadelphia: University of Pennsylvania Press, 1950.

Poloma, M. M., and Garland, T. N. "The Married Professional Woman: A Study in the Tolerance of Domestication." *Journal of Marriage and the Family,* **33**(1971):531–540.

Poston, C. (ed.). *A Vindication on the Rights of Woman.* New York: Norton, 1975.

Pottieger, A. Personal correspondence, March 1981.

Power, M. "'Falling Through the Safety Net': Women, Economic Crisis and Reagonomics." *Feminist Studies,* **10**(Spring 1984):31–58.

Powers, E., and Bultena, G. "Sex Differences in Intimate Friendships of Old Age." *Journal of Marriage and the Family,* **38**(1976):739–747.

Powers, M. "Menstruation and Reproduction: An Oglala Case." *Signs,* **6**(Autumn 1980):54–65.

Prather, J., and Fidell, L. S. "Sex Differences in the Content and Style of Medical Advertisements." *Social Science and Medicine,* **9**(1975):23–26.

Project on the Education and Status of Women. *Sexual Harassment: A Hidden Issue.* Washington, D.C.: American Association of Colleges, June 1978.

Propper, A. "Importation and Depriviation Perspectives on Homosexuality in Correctional Institutions: An Empirical Test of Their Relative Efficacy." Ph.D. dissertation, University of Michigan, 1976.

Prus, R. C., and Vassilakopoulos, S. "Desk Clerks and Hookers: Hustling in a Shady Hotel." *Urban Life,* **8**(1979):52–72.

Purifoy, F., and Koopmans, L. "Androstenedione, Testosterone, and Free Testoterone Concentration in Women of Various Occupations." *Social Biology,* **26**(1980:179–188.

Quinney, R. *The Social Reality of Crime.* Boston: Little, Brown, 1970.

Ramey, J. "Experimental Family Forms — The Family of the Future." *Marriage and Family Review,* **1**(1978):1–9.

Randall, S. C., and Rose, V. M. "Barriers to Becoming a 'Successful' Rape Victim." In L. Bowker (ed.), *Women and Crime in America.* New York: Macmillan, 1981, 336–353.

Rapp, R., Ross, E., and Bridenthal, R. "Examining Family History." *Feminist Studies,* **5**(Spring 1979):174–200.

Reagon, B. J. "My Black Mothers and Sisters, Or, On Beginning a Cultural Autobiography." *Feminist Studies,* **8**(Spring 1982):81–96.

Redhorse, J. G., Lewis, R., Feit, M., and Decker, J. "American Indian Elders: Needs and Aspirations in Institutional and Home Health Care." Manuscript, Arizona State University, 1979.

Rees, A., and Schultz, G. P. *Workers and Wages in an Urban Labor Market.* Chicago: University of Chicago Press, 1970.

Reid, I. S. "Science, Politics, and Race." *Signs,* **1**(Winter 1975):397–422.

Reinharz, S. "Experiential Analysis: A Contribution to Feminist Research." In G. and R. Duelli-Klein (eds.), *Theories of Women's Studies.* Boston: Routledge & Kegan Paul, 1983, 162–191.

———. "The Social Psychology of a Miscarriage: An Application of Symbolic Interaction Theory and Method." In M. J. Deegan and M. Hill (eds.), *Women and Symbolic Interaction.* New York: Allen and Unwin, 1986, 229–250.

———. "What's Missing in Miscarriage?" *Journal of Community Psychology* 16, forthcoming, January 1988.

Reiter, R. R. (ed.). *Toward an Anthropology of Women.* New York: Monthly Review Press, 1975.

Reitz, R. *Menopause: A Positive Approach.* Radnor, Pa.: Chilton, 1977.

Resnik, J., and Shaw, N. "Prisoners of Their Sex: Health Problems of Incarcerated Women." *Prison Law Monitor,* **3**(Winter 1981):55ff.

Reuther, R. "Motherearth and the Megamachine: A Theology of Liberation in a Feminine, Somatic, and Ecological Perspective." In C. P. Christ and J. Plaskow (eds.), *Womanspirit Rising*. New York: Harper & Row, 1979, 43–51.

Reuther, R. R., and Keller, R. S. (eds.). *Women and Religion in America, Volume 3: 1900–1968*. New York: Harper & Row, 1986.

Rheingold, H. L., and Cook, K. V. "The Contents of Boys' and Girls' Rooms as an Index of Parents' Behavior." *Child Development*, **46**(1975):459–463.

Rhodes, A. L. "Effects of Religious Denomination of Sex Differences in Occupational Expectations." *Sex Roles*, **9**(January 1983):93–108.

Rich, A. *Of Woman Born: Motherhood as Experience and Institution*. New York: Norton, 1976.

———. "Disloyal to Civilization: Feminism, Racism, and Gynephobia." *Chrysalis*, **7**(Summer-Fall 1979):9–28.

———. "Compulsory Heterosexuality and Lesbian Existence." *Signs*, **5**(Summer 1980):631–660.

Richardson, L. W. *The Dynamics of Sex and Gender*. Boston: Houghton-Mifflin, 1981.

Robertson, I. *Sociology*. New York: Worth, 1977.

Robinson, B. E., and Barret, R. L. *The Developing Father*. New York: The Guilford Press, 1986.

Rodgers-Rose, L. F. (eds.). *The Black Woman*. Beverly Hills, Calif.: Sage, 1980.

Rollins, J. *Between Women: Domestics and Their Employers*. Philadelphia: Temple University Press, 1985.

Roof, W. C., and Roof, J. L. "Review of the Polls: Images of God Among Americans." *Journal for the Scientific Study of Religion*, **23**(June 1984):201–205.

Rooks, E., and King, R. "A Study of the Marriage Role Expectations of Black Adolescents." *Adolescence*, **8**(1973):317–324.

Roper Organization. *The 1980 Virginia Slims American Women's Opinion Poll*. Storrs, Conn.: The Roper Center, 1985.

Rorvik, D. M. *Brave New Baby: Promise and Peril of the Biological Revolution*. Garden City, N.Y.: Doubleday, 1971.

Rosaldo, M. Z. "Use and Abuse of Anthropology: Reflections on Feminism and Cross-cultural Understanding." *Signs*, **5**(Spring 1980):389–417.

Rosaldo, M. Z., and Lamphere, L. (eds.). *Women, Culture, and Society*. Stanford, Calif.: Stanford University Press, 1974.

Rosenbaum, M. *Women on Heroin*. New Brunswick, N.J.: Rutgers University Press, 1981.

Rosenberg, M., and Simmons, R. *Black and White Self-Esteem: The Urban School Child*. Washington, D.C.: American Sociological Association, 1971.

Rosenberg, R. *Beyond Separate Spheres: Intellectual Roots of Modern Feminism*. New Haven, Conn.: Yale University Press, 1982.

Rosenblum, K. E. "Female Deviance and the Female Sex Role: A Preliminary Investigation." *British Journal of Sociology*, **26**(1975):169–185.

Rosenfeld, S. "Sex Differences in Depression: Do Women Always Have Higher Rates?" *Journal of Health and Social Behavior*, **21**(1980):33–42.

Rosenthal, R., and Rubin, D. B. "Further Meta-analytical Procedures for Assessing Cognitive Gender Differences." *Journal of Educational Psychology*, **74**(October 1982):708–712.

Rosow, I. "And Then We Were Old." *Trans-Action/Society*, **2**(1965):20–26.

Ross, D. M., and Ross, S. A. "Resistance by Preschool Boys to Sex-Inappropriate Behavior." *Journal of Educational Psychology,* **63**(1972):342–346.

Ross, H. L., and Sawhill, V. *Time of Transition: The Growth of Families Headed by Women.* Washington, D.C.: Urban Institute, 1975.

Rossi. A. "A Biosocial Perspective on Parenting." *Daedulus,* **106**(Spring 1977):1–31.

Rossi, A. (ed.). *Essays on Sex Equality.* Chicago: University of Chicago Press, 1970.
———. *The Feminist Papers.* New York: Columbia University Press, 1973.

Rossi, A. S., and Rossi, P. E. "Body Time and Social Time: Mood Patterns by Menstrual Cycle Phase and Days of the Week." *Social Science Research,* **6**(1977):273–308.

Rossiter, M. *Women Scientists in America.* Baltimore: Johns Hopkins University Press, 1982.

Rothman, B. K. *In Labor: Women and Power in the Birthplace.* New York: W. W. Norton and Company, 1982.

Rothschild, M. A. "White Women Volunteers in the Freedom Summers." *Feminist Studies,* **5**(Fall 1979):466–495.

Rubin, G. "The Traffic in Women." In R. Reiter (ed.), *Toward an Anthropology of Women.* New York: Monthly Review Press, 1975, 157–211.

Rubin, J. Z., Provenzano, F. J., and Luria, Z. "The Eye of the Beholder: Parents' Views on Sex of Newborns." *American Journal of Orthopsychiatry,* **44**(1974):512–519.

Rubin, Z., Peplau, L. A., and Hull, C. T. "Loving and Leaving: Sex Differences in Romantic Attachments." *Sex Roles,* **7**(August 1981):821–835.

Rupp, L. "The Women's Community in the National Woman's Party, 1945 to the 1960's." *Signs,* **10**(Summer 1985):715–740.

Russell, D.E.H. *Rape in Marriage.* New York: Macmillan, 1982.

Ruzek, S. *The Women's Health Movement: Feminist Alternatives to Medical Control.* New York: Praeger, 1978.

Ryan, W. *Blaming the Victim.* New York: Random House, 1971.

Sacks, K. "Engels Revisited: Women, the Organization of Production, and Private Property." In R. Reiter (ed.), *Toward an Anthropology of Women.* New York: Monthly Review Press, 1975, 211–234.

Sacks, K. B. "Generations of Working Class Families." In K. B. Sacks and D. Remy (eds.), *My Troubles Are Going to Have Trouble with Me.* New Brunswick, N.J.: Rutgers University Press, 1984, 15–38.

Safran, C. "What Men Do to Women on the Job." *Redbook,* **148**(November 1976):149ff.

Sahlins, M. *The Use and Abuse of Biology: An Anthropological Critique of Sociobiology.* London: Tavistock, 1977.

Saiving, V. "The Human Situation: A Feminine View." In C. P. Christ and J. Plaskow (eds.), *Womanspirit Rising.* New York: Harper & Row, 1979, 25–42.

Sanday, P. "Toward a Theory of the Status of Women." *American Anthropology,* **75**(1973):1682–1700.

Sandmaier, M. *The Invisible Alcoholic: Women and Alcohol Abuse in America.* New York: McGraw-Hill, 1980.

Sario, T., Jacklin, C. N., and Tittle, C. K. "Sex Role Stereotyping in the Public Schools." *Harvard Educational Review,* **43**(1973):386–404.

Schlozman, K. L. "Women and Unemployment." In J. Freeman (ed.), *Women: A Feminist Perspective.* Palo Alto, Calif.: Mayfield, 1979, 290–312.

Scholten, C. M. "On the Importance of the Obstetric Art: Changing Customs of Childbirth in America." *The William and Mary Quarterly,* **34**(1977):426–445.

Schuster, M., and Van Dyne, S. "Stages of Curriculum Transformation." In M. Schuster and S. Van Dyne (eds.), *Women's Place in the Academy: Transforming the Liberal Arts Curriculum.* Totowa, N.J.: Rowman and Allenheld, 1985, 13–29.

Schwendinger, H., and Schwendinger, J. R. *Sociologists of the Chair: A Radical Analysis of the Formative Years of North American Sociology.* New York: Basic Books, 1974.

Scully, D., and Bart, P. "A Funny Thing Happened on the Way to the Orifice: Women in Gynecology Textbooks." *American Journal of Sociology,* **78**(1973):1045–1050.

Scully, D., and Marolla, J. "Convicted Rapists' Vocabularies of Motive: Excuses and Justifications." *Social Problems,* **31**(June 1984):530–543.

————. "Riding the Bull at Gilley's: Convicted Rapists Describe the Rewards of Rape." *Social Problems,* **32**(February 1985):251–263.

Sears, R. R., Maccoby, E., and Levin, H. *Patterns of Child Rearing.* Evanston, Ill.: Row, Peterson, 1959.

Seidman, G. "Women in Zimbabwe: Postindependence Struggles." *Feminist Studies,* **10**(Fall 1984):419–440.

Seifert, K. "Some Problems of Men in Child Care Center Work." In J. Pleck and J. Sawyer (eds.), *Men and Masculinity.* Englewood Cliffs, N.J.: Prentice-Hall, 1974, 69–73.

Senna, J., and Siegel, L. *Introduction to Criminal Justice.* St. Paul, Minn.: West, 1981.

Senour, M. N., and Warren, L. "Sex and Ethnic Differences in Masculinity, Femininity and Anthropology." Paper presented at the meeting of the Western Psychological Association, Los Angeles, 1976.

Serbin, L. A., and O'Leary, K. D. "How Nursery Schools Teach Girls to Shut Up." *Psychology Today,* **9**(1975):56ff.

Serbin, L. A., O'Leary, K. D., Kent, R., and Tolnick, I. J. "A Comparison of Teacher Response to the Preacademic and Problem Behavior of Boys and Girls." *Child Development,* **44**(1973):776–804.

Shakur, A., and Chesimard, J. "Women in Prison: How We Are." *The Black Scholar,* **9**(1978):8–15.

Shange, N. *For Colored Girls Who Have Considered Suicide/When the Rainbow Is Enuf.* New York: Macmillan, 1975.

Sherman, J. "Problems of Sex Differences in Space Perception and Aspects of Intellectual Functioning." *Psychological Review,* **74**(1967):290–299.

Sherman, J., and Beck, E. T. (eds.). *The Prism of Sex: Essays in the Sociology of Knowledge.* Madison: University of Wisconsin Press, 1979.

Simmel, G. "The Stranger." In K. Wolff (ed.), *The Sociology of Georg Simmel.* New York: Free Press, 1950, 402–408.

Simon, R. *Women and Crime.* Lexington, Mass.: Lexington Books, 1975.

————. "American Women and Crime." In L. Bowker (eds.), *Women and Crime in America.* New York: Macmillan, 1981, 18–39.

Simons, M. "Racism and Feminism: A Schism in the Sisterhood." *Feminist Studies,* **5**(Summer 1979):384–401.

Skolnick, A. *The Intimate Environment.* Boston: Little, Brown, 1978.

Slater, A. A., and Feinman, S. "Gender and the Phonology of North American First Names." *Sex Roles,* **13**(October 1985):429–440.

Slocum, S. "Woman the Gatherer: Male Bias in Anthropology." In R. Reiter (ed.), *Toward an Anthropology of Women.* New York: Monthly Review Press, 1975, 36–50.

Smart, C. *Women, Crime and Criminology: A Feminist Critique.* London: Routledge & Kegan Paul, 1977.

Smedley, A. "Women of Uder: Survival in a Harsh Land." In C. Matthiasson (ed.), *Many Sisters.* New York: Free Press, 1974, 205–228.

Smith, B. "Notes for Yet Another Paper on Black Feminism, Or Will the Real Enemy Please Stand Up." *Conditions: Five,* **2**(Autumn 1979):123–127.

Smith, D. E. "Women's Perspective as a Radical Critique of Sociology." *Sociological Inquiry,* **44**(1974):7–13.

———. "An Analysis of Ideological Structures and How Women Are Excluded: Considerations for Academic Women." *Canadian Review of Sociology and Anthropology,* **12**(1975):353–369.

———. "A Sociology for Women." In J. A. Sherman and E. T. Beck (eds.), *The Prism of Sex.* Madison: University of Wisconsin Press, 1979, 135–187.

———. "A Method for a Sociology for Women." Paper presented at the meeting of the American Sociology Association, Toronto, 1981.

Smith, L. S. "Sexist Assumptions and Female Delinquency." In C. Smart and B. Smart (eds.), *Women, Sexuality, and Social Control.* London: Routledge & Kegan Paul, 1978, 74–86.

Smith, M. D., and Bennett, N. "Poverty, Inequality and Theories of Forcible Rape." *Crime and Delinquency,* **31**(April 1985):295–305.

Smith-Rosenberg, C. "The Female World of Love and Ritual: Relations Between Women in Nineteenth Century America." *Signs,* **1**(Fall 1975):1–29.

Smuts, R. W. *Women and Work in America.* New York: Columbia University Press, 1959.

Sokoloff, N. *Between Money and Love: The Dialectics of Women's Home and Market Work.* New York: Praeger, 1980.

Sorenson, P. *Adolescent Sexuality in Contemporary America.* New York: World, 1973.

Spanier, G. "Married and Unmarried Cohabitation in the U.S.: 1980." *Journal of Marriage and the Family,* **45**(May 1983):277–288.

Speigel, D. "Mothering, Fathering, and Mental Illness." In B. Thorne (ed.), *Rethinking the Family: Some Feminist Questions.* New York: Longman's, 1983.

Spence, J. T., Helmreich, R. L., and Stampp, J. "Ratings of Self and Peers on Sex-Role Attributes and Their Relation to Self-Esteem and Conceptions of Masculinity and Femininity." *Journal of Personality and Social Psychology,* **32**(July 1975):29–39.

Sprafkin, J., and Liebert, R. "Sex-Typing and Children's Television Preferences." In G. Tuchman, A. K. Daniels, and J. Benét (eds.), *Hearth and Home: Images of Women in the Mass Media.* New York: Oxford University Press, 1978, 228–239.

Spretnak, C. (ed.). *The Politics of Women's Spirituality: Essays on the Rise of Spiritual Power Within the Feminist Movement.* Garden City, N.Y.: Anchor Books, 1982.

St. George, A., and McNamara, P. H. "Religion, Race, and Psychological Well-Being." *Journal for the Scientific Study of Religion,* **2**(December 1984):351–363.

Stacey, J. *Patriarchy and Socialist Revolution in China.* Berkeley: University of California Press, 1983.

Stacey, J., and Thorne, B. "The Missing Feminist Revolution in Sociology." *Social Problems,* **32**(April 1985):301–316.

Stack, C. *All Our Kin: Strategies for Survival in a Black Community.* New York: Harper Colophon, 1974.

Stafford, R., Backman, E., and Dibona, P. "The Division of Labor Among Cohabiting and Married Couples." *Journal of Marriage and the Family,* **39**(1977):43–57.

Staines, G. L., Pleck, J., Shepard, L. J., and O'Connor, P. "Wives' Employment Status and Marital Adjustment: Yet Another Look." In J. Bryson and R. Bryson (eds.), *Dual-Career Couples.* New York: Human Sciences Press, 1978, 90–120.

Stanton, E. C. *The Woman's Bible.* New York: European Publishing, 1895. Introduction by Barbara Welter, *The Original Feminist Attack on the Bible (The Woman's Bible).* New York: Arno Press, 1974.

Staples, R. *The Black Family.* Belmont, Calif.: Wadsworth, 1971.

———. "Masculinity and Race: The Dual Dilemma of Black Men." *The Journal of Social Issues,* **34**(Winter 1978):169–183.

Staples, R., and Jones, T. "Culture, Ideology, and Black Television Images." *Black Scholar,* **16**(May-June 1985):10–20.

Staples, R., and Mirandé, A. "Racial and Cultural Variations Among American Families." *Journal of Marriage and the Family,* **42**(1980):887–903.

Steffensmeier, D. "Crime and the Contemporary Woman: An Analysis of Changing Levels of Female Property Crime, 1960–1975." In L. Bowker (ed.), *Women and Crime in America.* New York: Macmillan, 1981a, 39–59.

———. "Patterns of Female Property Crime, 1960–1978: A Postscript." In L. Bowker (ed.), *Women and Crime in America.* New York: Macmillan, 1981b, 59–65.

Stein, D. K. "Women to Burn: Suttee as a Normative Institution." *Signs,* **4**(Winter 1978):253–268.

Stellman, J. M. *Women's Work, Women's Health: Myths and Realities.* New York: Pantheon, 1977.

Stellman, J. M., and Henifin, M. S. *Office Work Can Be Dangerous to Your Health.* New York: Pantheon, 1983.

Sterling, A. *We Are Your Sisters: Black Women in the Nineteenth Century.* New York: W. W. Norton, 1984.

Stevenson, M. H. "Relative Wages and Sex Segregation by Occupation." In C. Lloyd (ed.), *Sex, Discrimination, and the Division of Labor.* New York: Columbia University Press, 1975, 175–200.

———. "Wage Differentials Between Men and Women: Economic Theories." In A. Stromberg and S. Harkess (eds.), *Women Working.* Palo Alto, Calif.: Mayfield, 1978, 89–107.

Stimpson, C. "They Neighbor's Wife, They Neighbor's Servants: Women's Liberation and Black Civil Rights." In V. Gornick and B. Moran (eds.), *Woman in Sexist Society.* New York: Basic Books, 1971, 622–657.

Strauss, M. A., Gelles, R., and Steinmetz, S. *Behind Closed Doors.* Garden City, N.Y.: Doubleday-Anchor, 1980.

Stromberg, A. H., and Harkess, S. (eds.). *Women Working.* Palo Alto, Calif.: Mayfield, 1978.

Strouse, J. "To Be Minor and Female: The Legal Rights of Women Under 21." *Ms.,* **1**(1972):70ff.

Stump, R. W. "Women Clergy in the United States: A Geographical Analysis of Religious Change." *Social Science Quarterly,* **67**(June 1986):337–352.

Suter, L., and Miller, H. "Income Differences Between Men and Career Women." *American Journal of Sociology,* **78**(1973):962–974.

Swerdlow, A., Bridenthal, R., Kelly, J., and Vine, P. *Household and Kin.* Old Westbury, N.Y.: Feminist Press, 1980.

Szasz, T. *Manufacture of Madness.* New York: Dell, 1970.

Taffel, S., Placek, P., and Moien, M. "One Fifth of 1983 Births by Caesarean Section." *American Journal of Public Health,* **75**(February 1985):90.

Tanner, D. M. *The Lesbian Couple.* Lexington, Mass.: Lexington Books, 1978.

Tanner, N., and Zihlman, A. "Women in Evolution, Part I: Innovation and Selection in Human Origins." *Signs,* **1**:3, Part 1(Spring 1976):585–608.

Tarr-Whelan, L. "Women Workers and Organized Labor." *Social Policy,* **9**(1978):73–77.

Tavris, C., and Offir, C. *The Longest War.* New York: Harcourt Brace Jovanovich, 1977.

Taylor, V. "Review Essays of Four Books on Lesbianism." *Journal of Marriage and the Family,* **42**(1980):224–228.

Tea, N. T., Castanier, M., Roger, M., and Scholler, R. "Simultaneous Radio-immunoassay of Plasma Progesterone and 17-Hydroxyprogesterone in Men and Women Throughout the Menstrual Cycle and in Early Pregnancy." *Journal of Steroid Biochemistry,* **6**(1975):1509–1516.

Tedin, K. L. "If the Equal Rights Amendment Becomes Law: Perceptions of Consequences Among Female Activists and Masses." Paper presented at the Annual Meeting of the Midwest Political Science Association, Chicago, April 1980.

Tetreault, M.K.T. "Feminist Phase Theory." *Journal of Higher Education,* **56**(July/August 1985):363–384.

The Gallup Poll, Public Opinion, 1980. Wilmington Delaware: Scholarly Resources Inc., 1981.

The Gallup Poll, Public Opinion 1985. Wilmington Delaware: Scholarly Resources Inc., 1986.

Thoits, P. A., "Multiple Identities." *American Sociological Review,* **51**(April 1986):259–272.

Thomas, W. I. *The Unadjusted Girl.* Boston: Little, Brown, 1923.

Thompson, E. H., Grisanti, C., and Pleck, J. "Attitudes Toward the Male Role and Their Correlates." *Sex Roles,* **13**(October 1985):413–427.

Thompson, E. P. "Time, Work-Discipline and Industrial Capitalism." *Past and Present,* **38**(1967):56–90.

Thorne, B., and Luria, Z. "Sexuality and Gender in Children's Daily Worlds." *Social Problems,* **33**(February 1986):176–190.

Thorne, B. with Yalom, M. (eds.). *Rethinking the Family: Some Feminist Questions.* New York: Longman's, 1982.

Thornton, A., Alwin, D. E., and Camburn, D. "Causes and Consequences of Sex

Role Attitudes and Attitude Change." *American Sociological Review,* **48**(April 1983):211–227.

Tillich, P. *The Dynamics of Faith.* New York: Harper & Row, 1957.

Tilly, L. A., and Scott, J. W. *Women, Work, and Family.* New York: Holt, Rinehart & Winston, 1978.

Tinsley, E. G., Sullivan-Guest, S., and McGuire, J. "Feminine Sex Role and Depression in Middle-Aged Women." *Sex Roles,* **11**(July 1984):25–32.

Tobias, S. *Overcoming Math Anxiety.* New York: Norton, 1978.

Tolson, A. *The Limits of Masculinity.* New York: Harper Colophon, 1977.

Treiman, D. J., and Terrell, K. "Sex and the Process of Status Attainment: A Comparison of Working Men and Women." *American Sociological Review,* **40**(1975):174–200.

Tuchman, G., Daniels, A. K., and Benét, J. *Hearth and Home: Images of Women in the Mass Media.* New York: Oxford University Press, 1978.

Tucker, R. (ed.). *The Marx-Engels Reader.* New York: Norton, 1972.

Turner, R., and Killian, L. *Collective Behavior.* Englewood Cliffs, N.J.: Prentice-Hall, 1972.

U.S. Bureau of the Census, 1980 Census of Population: Detailed Population Characteristics. Washington, D.C.: U.S. Government Printing Office, 1984.

U.S. Bureau of Labor Statistics, *Employment and Earnings,* Vol. 32. Washington, D.C.: U.S. Government Printing Office, January 1987.

U.S. Bureau of Labor Statistics, *Employment and Earnings,* Vol. 33. Washington, D.C.: U.S. Government Printing Office, January 1986.

U.S. Bureau of Labor Statistics, *Employment and Earnings,* Vol. 34. Washington, D.C.: U.S. Government Printing Office, January 1985.

U.S. Bureau of the Census, Current Population Reports, Series P-20, No. 366. *Household and Family Characteristics: March 1980.* Washington, D.C.: U.S. Government Printing Office, September 1981.

U.S. Bureau of the Census, Current Population Reports, Series P-20, No. 398. *Household and Family Characteristics: March 1984.* Washington, D.C.: U.S. Government Printing Office, April 1985.

U.S. Bureau of the Census, Current Population Reports, Series P-20, No. 402, *Households, Families, Marital Status and Living Arrangements: March 1985.* Washington, D.C.: U.S. Government Printing Office, October 1985.

U.S. Bureau of the Census, Current Population Reports, Series P-20, No. 412, *Households, Families, Marital Status and Living Arrangements: March 1986 (Advanced Report).* Washington, D.C.: U.S. Government Printing Office, November 1986.

U.S. Bureau of the Census, Current Population Reports, Series P-20, No. 410, *Marital Status and Living Arrangements: March 1985.* Washington, D.C.: U.S. Government Printing Office, November 1986. .

U.S. Bureau of the Census, Current Population Reports, Series P-60, No. 151, *Money Income and Poverty Status of Families and Persons in the U.S.: 1984.* Washington, D.C. U.S. Government Printing Office, April 1986.

U.S. Bureau of the Census, Current Population Reports, Series P-60, No. 154. *Money Income and Poverty Status of Families and Persons in the U.S., 1985.* Washington, D.C.: U.S. Government Printing Office, August 1986.

U.S. Bureau of the Census. *Statistical Abstracts of the U.S. 1986.* Washington, D.C.: U.S. Government Printing Office, 1986.

U.S. Department of Justice, Bureau of Justice Statistics. *Crime Victimization in the U.S., 1984.* Washington, D.C. U.S. Government Printing Office, May 1986.

U.S. Department of Justice, Federal Bureau of Investigation. *Uniform Crime Reports, 1985.* Washington, D.C.: U.S. Government Printing Office, 1986.

U.S. Department of Labor. *Handbook of Labor Statistics.* Washington, D.C.: U.S. Government Printing Office, June 1985.

U.S. Senate Committee on Labor and Human Resources. *Adolescent Family Life.* 97th Congress, 1st Session, Report No. 97-161, 1981.

Vance, C. "Pleasure and Danger: Toward a Politics of Sexuality." In C. Vance (ed.), *Pleasure and Danger.* Boston: Routledge & Kegan Paul, 1984.

Van Den Daele, W. "The Social Construction of Science: Institutionalization and Definition of Positive Science in the Latter Half of the Seventeenth Century." In E. Mendelsohn, P. Weingart, and R. Whitley (eds.), *The Social Production of Scientific Knowledge.* Dordrecht: Riedel, 1977, 27–54.

Vanek, J. A. "Housewives as Workers." In A. H. Stromberg and S. Harkess (eds.), *Women Working.* Palo Alto, Calif.: Mayfield, 1978, 392–414.

Verdesi, E. H. *In But Still Out: Women in the Church.* Philadelphia: Westminster, 1976.

Vetter, B. M. "Women Scientists and Engineers: Trends in Participation." *Science,* **214**(1981):1313–1321.

Vetter, B. M., and Babco, E. L. *Professional Women and Minorities.* Washington, D.C.: Commission on Professional in Science and Technology, February 1986.

Vida, G. Our Right to Love: A Lesbian Resource Book. Englewood Cliffs, N.J.: Prentice-Hall, 1978.

Visher, C. A. "Gender, Police Arrest Decisions and Notions of Chivalry." *Criminology,* **21**(February 1983):5–28.

Waite, L. J., Goldscheider, F. K., and Witsberger, C. "Nonfamily Living and the Erosion of Traditional Family Orientations Among Young Adults." *American Sociological Review,* **51**(August 1986):541–554.

Waldron, I., and Johnston, S. "Why Do Women Live Longer Than Men?" *Journal of Human Stress,* **2**, Part II(1976):19–30.

Walker, K. E. "Time-Use Patterns for Household Work Related to Homemakers' Employment." Paper presented at the National Agricultural Outlook Conference, Washington, D.C., 1970.

Wallen, J. "Physician Stereotypes About Female Health and Illness." *Women and Health,* **4**(Summer 1979):135–146.

Wallerstein, I. *The Modern World System.* New York: Academic Press, 1976.

Walsh, M. R. *Doctors Wanted: No Women Need Apply.* New Haven, Conn.: Yale University Press, 1977.

Ware, M. C., and Stuck, M. F. "Sex Role Messages vis-a-vis Microcomputer Use: A Look at the Pictures." *Sex Roles,* **13**(August 1985):205–214.

Warr, M. "Fear of Rape Among Urban Women." *Social Problems,* **32**(February 1985):238–250.

Weber, M. *The Theory of Social and Economic Organization.* New York: Free Press, 1947.

Webster, P. "Matriarchy: A Vision of Power." In R. Reiter (ed.), *Toward an Anthropology of Women.* New York: Monthly Review Press, 1975, 141–157.

Weinstein, F., and Platt, G. M. *The Wish to Be Free; Society, Psyche, and Value Change.* Berkeley: University of California Press, 1969.

Weissman, M. M., and Paykel, E. S. *The Depressed Woman: A Study of Social Relationships.* Chicago: University of Chicago Press, 1974.

Weisstein, N. "Psychology Constructs the Female, Or, The Fantasy Life of the Male Psychologist." In M. H. Garskof (ed.), *Roles Women Play: Readings Toward Women's Liberation.* Belmont, Calif.: Brooks/Cole, 1971, 68–83.

Weitz, R., and Sullivan, D. A. "The Politics of Childbirth: The Re-emergence of Midwifery in Arizona." *Social Problems,* **33**(February 1986):163–175.

✓ Weitzman, L. *Sex Role Socialization: A Focus on Women.* Palo Alto, Calif.: Mayfield, 1979.

——. *The Divorce Revolution: The Unexpected Consequences for Women and Children in America.* New York: Free Press, 1985.

Weitzman, L., Eifler, D., Hokada, E., and Ross, C. "Sex Role Socialization in Picture Books for Preschool Children." *American Journal of Sociology,* **77**(1972):1125–1150.

Welch, S., and Booth, A. "Employment and Health Among Married Women." *Sex Roles,* **3**(1977):385–397.

Welter, B. "The Feminization of American Religion, 1800–1860," In B. Welter (ed.), *Dimity Convictions.* Athens: Ohio University Press, 1976.

Wermuth, L. "Book Review: *The Policing of Families* by Jacques Donzelot." *Contemporary Sociology,* **10**(1981):414–415.

Wertheimer, B., and Nelson, A. H. *Trade Union Women.* New York: Praeger, 1975.

Wertz, R. W., and Wertz, D. C. *Lying In: A History of Childbirth in America.* New York: Free Press, 1977.

West, C. and Zimmerman, D. "Small Insults: A Study of Interruptions in Cross-Sex Conversations Between Unacquainted Persons." In B. Thorne, C. Kramarae, and N. Henley (eds.), *Language, Gender and Society.* Rowley, Mass.: Newbury House, 1983, 102–117.

Westkott, M. "Feminist Criticism of the Social Sciences." *Harvard Educational Review,* **49**(1979):422–430.

Wilkinson, D. "Minority Women: Social-Cultural Issues." In Annette Brodsky and Rachel Haremustin (eds.), *Women and Psychotherapy.* New York: The Guilford Press, 1980, 285–304.

——. "Afro-American Women and Their Families." *Marriage and Family Review* **7**(Fall 1984):125–142.

Williams, D. A., and King, P. "Do Males Have a Math Gene?" *Newsweek,* **15**(December 5, 1980):73.

Williams, L. "The Classic Rape: When Do Victims Report?" *Social Problems,* **31**(April 1984):459–467.

Willie, C. V. *Black and White Families: A Study in Complementarity.* Bayside, N.Y.: General Hall, 1985.

Wilson, D. "Sexual Codes and Conduct." In C. Smart and B. Smart (eds.), *Women, Sexuality, and Social Control.* London: Routledge & Kegan Paul, 1978, 65–73.

Wilson, E. H., and Mullaly, S. *Hope and Dignity: Older Black Women of the South.* Philadelphia: Temple University Press, 1983.

Wilson, G. L. "The Self/Group Actualization of Black Women." In L. F. Rodgers-Rose (ed.), *The Black Woman.* Beverly Hills, Calif.: Sage, 1980, 301–314.

Wilson, J. Q., and Herrnstein, R. J. *Crime and Human Nature.* New York: Simon and Schuster, 1985.

Wilson, W. J. *The Declining Significance of Race.* Chicago: University of Chicago Press, 1978.

Winokur, G., and Cadoret, R. "The Irrelevance of the Menopause to Depressive Disease." In E. J. Sachar (ed.), *Topics in Psychoendocrinology.* New York: Grune and Stratton, 1975.

Wiseman, J., and Aron, M. *Field Projects for Sociology Students.* Cambridge, Mass.: Schenkman, 1970.

Wittig, M. A. "Genetic Influence on Sex-Related Differences in Intellectual Performance: Theoretical and Methodological Issues." In M. A. Wittig and A. C. Petersen (eds.), *Sex-Related Differences in Cognitive Functioning.* New York: Academic Press, 1979, 21–66.

Wolcott, I. "Women and Psychoactive Drug Use." *Women and Health,* **4**(Summer 1979):199–202.

Wolf, W. C., and Fligstein, N. D. "Sex and Authority in the Workplace: The Causes of Sexual Inequality." *American Sociological Review,* **44**(1979):235–252.

Wolfgang, M. *Patterns in Criminal Homicide.* New York: Wiley, 1958.

Wolfgang, M., and Feracuti, F. *The Subculture of Violence: Toward an Integrated Theory in Criminology.* London: Tavistock, 1967.

Wolfson, A. "Caution: Health Care May Be Hazardous to Your Health." *Up from Under,* **1**(1970):7–10.

Wollstonecraft, M. *A Vindication of the Rights of Woman.* Ed. by C. Poston. New York: Norton, 1975.

Women on Words and Images. "Dick and Jane as Victims: Sex Stereotyping in Children's Readers." Princeton, N.J., 1972.

Wong, A. K. "Women in China: Past and Present." In C. Matthiasson (ed.), *Many Sisters.* New York: Free Press, 1974, 220–260.

Wood, P. L. "The Victim in a Forcible Rape Case: A Feminist View." In L. Bowker (ed.), *Women and Crime in America.* New York, Macmillan, 1981, 190–211.

Woodruff, J. T. "Premarital Sexual Behavior and Religious Adolescents." *Journal for the Scientific Study of Religion,* **25**(December 1985):343–386.

Wright, M. J. "Reproductive Hazards and 'Protective' Discrimination." *Feminist Studies,* **5**(Summer 1979):302–309.

Wrong, D. "The Oversocialized Conception of Man in Modern Sociology." *American Sociological Review,* **26**(1961):183–193.

Yagamuchi, K. "The Structure of Intergenerational Occupational Mobility-Generality and Specificity in Resources, Channels, and Barriers." *American Journal of Sociology,* **88**(January 1983):718–745.

Yamauchi, J. S. "Asian American Communications: The Women's Self-Concept and Cultural Accommodations." Paper Presented at the Conference on the Minority Woman in America, San Francisco, 1979.

Yates, G. G. "Spirituality and the American Feminist Experience." *Signs,* **9**(Autumn 1983):59–72.

Ybarra, L. "Conjugal Race Relationships in the Chicano Family." Doctoral dissertation, University of California, Berkeley, 1977.

Zabin, L. S., and Clark, S., Jr. "Why They Delay: A Study of Teenage Family Planning Clinic Patients," *Family Planning Perspectives,* **13**(1981): 205–217.

Zabin, L. S., Kantner, J. F., and Zelnik, M. "The Risk of Adolescent Pregnancy in the First Months of Intercourse." *Family Planning Perspectives,* **11**(1979):215–226.

Zaretsky, E. *Capitalism, the Family, and Personal Life.* New York: Harper & Row, 1976.

———. "Female Sexuality and the Catholic Confessional." *Signs,* **6**(Autumn 1980):176–184.

Zavella, P. "'Abnormal Intimacy': The Varying Work Networks of Chicana Cannery Workers." *Feminist Studies,* **11**(Fall 1985):541–558.

Zeitlin, I. *Ideology and the Development of Sociological Theory.* Englewood Cliffs, N.J.: Prentice-Hall, 1968.

Zelnick, M., and Kantner, J. F. "Contraceptive Patterns and Premarital Pregnancy Among Women Aged 15–19 in 1976." *Family Planning Perspectives,* **10**(1978):135–143.

Zelnick, M., Kim, Y. J., and Kantner, J. F. "Probabilities of Intercourse and Conception Among U.S. Teenage Women, 1971–1976." *Family Planning Perspectives,* **11**(1979):177–183.

Zihlman, A. L. "Women and Evolution, Part II: Subsistence and Social Organization Among Early Hominids." *Signs,* **4**(Autumn 1978):4–20.

Index